GENEALOGICAL ABSTRACTS

DUPLIN COUNTY WILLS

1730-1860

WILLIAM L. (BILL) MURPHY

I0091165

Southern Historical Press, Inc.
Greenville, South Carolina

Please direct all correspondence and orders to:

www.southernhistoricalpress.com
or
SOUTHERN HISTORICAL PRESS, Inc.
PO BOX 1267
Greenville, SC   29601
southernhistoricalpress@gmail.com

ISBN #0-89308-597-9

Printed in the United States of America

CONTENTS

PUBLISHER'S NOTE

In presenting this volume to the public the Duplin County Historical Society, as publisher, wishes to record its gratitude to the two
young men who made it possible: first, to Mr. Wm. L. (Bill) Murphy, of
Wendell, N. C., who read all of the Duplin wills and carefully abstracted
the data recorded here and prepared the appendix and three indices; and,
second, to Mr. Horace Fussell, Jr., of Rose Hill, N. C., who faithfully
typed every word and proofread the volume before publication.

The result is a work of inestimable value to everyone whose heritage
includes the individuals whose names are recorded in it and to all who
are interested in the social and economic history of these times in this
place. The painstaking care with which the manuscript was prepared and
the typed copy was made ready for publication merits our highest respect.

The Research Committee
DUPLIN COUNTY HISTORICAL SOCIETY
P. O. Box 130, Rose Hill, N. C.
28458

15 March 1982

FOREWORD

Duplin County wills which were written during the years 1730 - 1860 have been chosen for this work. Although Duplin County was not established until 1750, several earlier wills from New Hanover Precinct have been included because it was known that the devisors lived in Duplin. The year 1860 was selected as the cut off date because it was the year before the beginning of the Civil War, which changed much of the area's lifestyle. It will be noted that the probate dates for some of the wills written in 1860 or earlier are as late as the early twentieth century.

A number has been assigned to each will and precedes the divisor's name. Following the name is a set of call numbers which give the location of the will. They are:

> CR.035.801.1 - 12: This is the county record number for the original wills which are filed in twelve fiberdex boxes in the N. C. State Archives in Raleigh.

> A or 1 - 4: These are the letter and numbers denoting the will books on file in the Clerk of Court's office in Kenansville. The number after each of the book designations is the page on which the will is located. Microfilm copies of these volumes are also on file at the State Archives.

> S. S.: These wills are filed in the Secretary of State's Papers. They were originally bound in volumes but have since been filed in fiberdex boxes which at this time have not been assigned call numbers.

> DRB 2: Deed Record Book 2 is located in the Clerk of Court's office in Clinton. This book contains a number of early wills from Duplin which were also recorded in Sampson County after it was formed from Duplin in 1784.

> CRX Box 243: This is a box of miscellaneous Duplin County papers on file in the State Archives in Raleigh.

The date on which the will was written is given on the second line of each abstract. This is followed by the probate date.

The original wills were used whenever possible in preparing these abstracts because the clerks often made mistakes in transcribing the originals into the will books. The original

spellings and as much of the original phrasing as deemed
practical have been used in an effort to retain the flavor
of the wills. Every effort has been made to duplicate exactly
all "marks" used by persons signing the wills.

The appendix lists the wills which were written in Duplin
from 1861 to 1900 and should prove helpful to those who wish
to conduct further research. The code numbers indicating the
location of each will are the same as noted previously.

In each index, the number following a name denotes the
number assigned to the will and not the page number. Under-
lined numbers indicate devisors.

In the slave index, the slaves are listed not only under
the surname of the devisor but also under the surnames of the
devisees to whom they were willed. It was a common practice
for the slave to assume the surname of each new master. Those
who use the slave index should be aware that descriptive terms
such as "young", "old", "yellow", "black", "stuttering", etc.
were often used in the names of some slaves and should be
checked when looking for a certain name.

GENEALOGICAL ABSTRACTS

OF

DUPLIN COUNTY WILLS

1730 - 1860

1. ADKINSON, JOHN (CR.035.801.1/A-6)
26 Aug 1771 - no probate
wife SARAH plantation whearon I now live with all lands & aportainces
thareunto, all stock of every kind, houshold furnitor; son TIMOTHY
land at wife's death or remarriage But He the sd. TIMOTHY Being infirm
& Decriped in Case He should Die in His Nonage then to my Son THOMAS;
eldest son JOHN 1 Shilling Sterlin He Being Allrody provided for; heirs
of my dau. MARY 1 Shilling Sterlin Her portion Being allready paid;
dau. SARAH 1 Shilling Sterlin Her portion Being allreddy paid; dau.
RACHEL 1 Black Heifer of three years old Next Spring; dau. ANN
RIVEINGBERG 1 Shilling Sterling She Being allreddy provided for;
dau. MARY the youngest Child 1 Black Heifer Calf of one year old Next
Spring
extr: wife SARAH
wit: HENRY HOLLINGSWORTH, RACHEL ♌ ADKINSON
signed: John Adkinson

2. ALBERTSON, SAMUEL (CR.035.801.1/A-8)
24 Nov 1819 - Jan Term 1824
son WILLIAM 1 Shilling; dau. ELIZABETH 1 shilling; son EDWARD 1 shilling;
dau. NANCY 200 acres between Miry branch & the North East; grdau. ELIZA-
BETH KEATON 1 bed & furniture; grdaus. CATHRINE & POLLEY 1 fether bed &
furniture & 2 cows & calves each; grdau. SALLEY 1 bed & furniture;
residue of property divided equally between POLLEY KEATON, NANCY WINDORS,
DAVID ALBERTSON, SARAH SMITH; grdau. NANCY WINDORS 1 fether bed & furnitur
extrs: DAVID ALBERTSON, EDWARD WINDORS
wit: EDWD. OUTLAW, LEWIS OUTLAW
signed: Saml. Albertson

3. ALDERMAN, DANIEL (CR.035.801.1/A-7)
11 Apr 1818 - Oct Term 1824
wife SARAH 1 featherbed & stead & furniture; dau. MARY CRUMPTON $12;
dau. ELISABETH $12; to the rest of my children that are married and
settled the following sums and no more, except my blessings, viz. to
DAVID, SARAH NEWTON, ISAAC, the heirs of JEMIMA BLAND Decd., the heirs
of RACHEL BUXTON Dcd. not exceeding twenty five cents each; son ELISHA
residue of my estate in consideration of his faithful care and decent maintenance of his aged and indulgent Mother
extrs: sons DAVID & ELISHA
wit: JONATHAN WILLIS, DANIEL ALDERMAN JNR., DAVID WILLIAMS JUNR.
signed: Daniel Alderman

4. ALDERMAN, JOHN (CR.035.801.1/A-3)
21 Sep 1824 - Oct Term 1824
extrs. to sell 1 horse, one yoke of oxen, 60 acres on reedy branch adj.
BRITIAN POWEL, 2 cows & calves, five killable hogs, and 5 sows & pigs;
son ENOCH 20 acres more of the land adj. the out end of that I have already
deeded him reserving the use of the uper field on the south side of the
creek for him for a term of six years; sons JAMES & ISAAC N. 200 acres adj.
son ENOCH, the marsh, the uper edge of the place opened for a ford across
the creek also the land inclosed by fence round the house and the use of the
house for a term of 5 years; wife ANN residue of lands during widowhood,
my gray horse & colt, 3 cows & calves, 2 heffers, 6 uwes, 4 weathers, 4 sows,
20 dry hogs 16 years olds, all the crop, two beds, bedstids & furniture,
household and kiching furniture, 2 peer of cart wheals, one riding chear,
all tools except the smith tools; negro Joshua to wife ANN during widowhood
then sold and money to be delivered to my dauther [not named] and child in
esse if it is a dau. and if child is a son the money to him and my four
youngest sons JOHN B., DANIEL, AMARIAH B. & HOSEA; lands and mill to those
of my children living at the time of my wife's death; son ISAAC N. blacksmiths tools, 1 heifer, 1 steer & 4 sheep; son JAMES one mor heifer & a
peer of cart wheals; dau. MARY BLAND 1 cow & calf, 5 sheep and $15 to buy
fethers; wife to sell what stock necessary to pay debts & to support &
school children
extrs: wife ANN & son ENOCH
wit: JAMES NEWTON, ISAAC N. BLAND, ISAAC N. ALDERMAN
signed: John Alderman

5. ALDERMAN, DANIEL SENER (CR.035.801.1/A-2)
19 Dec 1782 - Oct Court 1785
wife ABIGAL 1/3 of cleared ground & 1/3 of the orchard during her life
& half of all my house furniture and other movibles such as Cattle horses
hogs and sheep; son DAVID plantation whereon I now live and the other half
of house furniture & movibles; all my sons & daus. [not named] 5 shillings
a pease
extrs: sons DANIEL & DAVID
wit: ROBART ROLINGS, JOSHUA LEE
signed: Daniel Aldermun

6. ALLAN, HENARY (CR.035.801.1/A-5)
16 Jul 1791 - Jul Term 1795
son HENARY fourth part of young cattle out of my olde stock of Cattle;
sons HENARY & LEVEN equal shares of all hogs, cattle, hausen furnatud &
working twols; son WILLIAM 20 shillings; son EZEKEL 20 shillings; dau.
SABROUGH KING 20 shillings; dau. RUTH JONES 20 shillings; dau. SARAH 20
shillings; dau. ELISABETH THALLY 20 shillings; dau. RODY TEACHEY 20
shillings
extrs: sons HENARY & LEAVAN
wit: DANELL TEACHY, TIMOY TEACHY
                              signed: Henary ⚹ Allan

7. ANDREWS, ABRAHAM (CR.035.801.1/A-1)
29 Mar 1804 - Jan Term 1806
wife DELILAH use & benefit of plantation of 450 acres during her natural
life, work & labour of negro Nell, necessary plantation tools & household

& kitchen furniture, one cow & calf; dau. ELIZABETH MANNING 1 feather
bed & furniture, negro Lyddy, one cow & one calf; dau. WENEYFORD negro
Amy, one bed & furniture, 1 cow & calf; dau. SUSANAH negro Jack, 1 bed &
furniture, 1 cow & calf; sons ABRAHAM & WHITMELL HILL land whereon I live
containing 450 acres & 3 negroes when they arrive at 21, 1 bed & furniture,
1 cow & calf each; dau. MARY negro Hardy, 1 bed & furniture, 1 cow & calf;
between 5 & 6 hundred dollars on hand to be used to support & bring up
children
extrs: friends JOSEPH T. RHODES, JOHN FARRIOR
wit: JOSEPH T. RHODES, POLLY HALL
                        signed: Abraham ⟍⟋ Andrews

8. BACHELDOR/BATCHELOR, JOHN SR. "on Cypress Creek" (CR.035.801.1/2-63)
23 Mar 1851 - Apr Term 1851
son JOHN one horse & cart in his possession; daus. BARBARA JAMES, RACHAEL
SCOTT, SUSAN $48 to be divided equally; residue sold and $1 apeace to go
to THOMAS HORNS first wife's children & rest divided equally between my son
and three daus.
extrs: son JOHN & son-in-law ISAAC JAMES
wit: JOHN ✗ BROW JR, AMOS ROCHELLE
                        signed: John ✝ Bachelder

9. BARBRE/BARBERY, PETER (CR.035.801.1/A-35)
29 May 1781 - Oct Court 1783
wife PEGE horse, bridle & Saddle; son ALAN J. plantation where on I Live the
North Side of the Rode with wife to have use of the house & half the field;
son JOHN J. remainner of my land on the South Side of the Rode and ALLAN to
be at the Expence of helping JOHN to Building a peate Log house 20 and Sixteen and a out Side Chimny plank floor civered with Short Shingles; dau.
SALLY J. cow & calf & their in Crece to son JOHN; son ALLAN to have privilege
to cut timber from Halls Mill; residue to wife and children after first one
comes to Eage 21
extrs: wife PEGE & friend JESSE BARBERY
wit: WM. ODOM, JOHN BECK, MARTHA ✝ BARBERY
signed: Peter Barbre

10. BARDIN, JOHN (CR.035.801.1/2-102)
26 Apr 1856 - Oct Term 1856
wife ZILPHA negros Ceasar, Tenner, & Dolly, 2 horses, 4 cows & calves, one
yoke of oxen & cart, Riding Carriage & what household & Kitchen furniture
she may need; son GEORGE B. C. negroes Tom & Amelia when he reaches 21
years; children DICEY ANN, MARY JANE & GEORGE BUCKNER negroes Lydia & Dave
when GEORGE BUCKNER reaches 21 years; dau. MARY JANE COOPER $1175 and negroes
Mariah, Caroline, Eliza, Charlotte & Johnston; dau. DICEY ANN MURRAY $1175
and negroes Eliza, July, Joseph, Dick & Sarah; son GEORGE BUCKNER C. negroes
Edward, Dick, Silas, Rachel & her child Jenny Ann, my bay colt, 1 double
barreled Shot Gun, plantation whereon I live with dwelling house my wife
having use of same during her life or widowhood; wife ZILPHA a years provisions, 1 hundred Barrels Corn, 2000 pds. bacon or its equivalent, $100
extrs: wife ZILPHA, son-in-law BENJAMIN R. COOPER
wit: JAMES DICKSON, WILEY ⟋⟍ COBB
signed: John Bardin

11. BARFIELD, RICHARD (S. S. Wills/DRB2)
1 May 1754 - Jun 1755
sun HENRY plantation I now live on, negor wench Cat, one Bed, to Small
Dishes, 1 learge Dish, one hors; sun JESSE neger Boy Called Bob, all the
Land Be Loe the Branc Being on gum Running to the Bay line, to Cow and
Caves, toe Basen, toe dish, tow Chear, to Soues and piges, tow Bed and
furtud; darter MARY Bed and furtute, toe Dish, toe Chear, to Cow and
Caves; grandater LEBETH TALER 1 yeo; doter LEBETH one Bed and furn-
etuted to to year old hefirs, toe Dish and to plate, to six spunes;
dater AN GRADY 1 Soue and peges; darter CATHREN TALER Sven shilings;
wife [not named] to potes, to chiest, 1 Box, one horse, one taBle and
all the housul goods that ant givn, all my Cattel, toe Bed and furnetud,
all the Shep, all the Hogs; son SOLOMON 1 to year old hefer
extrs: sons JESSE & SOLOMON
wit: JAMES BARFIELD, JOHN MORRIS, SOLOMON BARFIELD
                          signed: Richard   Barfield

12. BARNS, WILLIAM (CR.035.801.1/A-55)
12 Dec 1769 - no probate
son LEWIS maner plantation of 140 acres, water mill & still, negroes
Bosen, Jude & Rechall, gray Horse Caled Maijor with his bridle & Sadle
when he comes of age 20 years; dau. MARY plantation on white Oake Branch
wheir JAMES DOB lives and 135 acres on Panther Swamp, negroes Peter, Genny,
Isaac, Lucy & Pheby, roan Mair Caled Trim with her Sadle & Bridle; dau's
negroes to be kept at my Mills and they to have 6 Cows & calves and 10 sows
& pigs; residue of estate sold & plantation rented & money arising devided
between my two children
extrs: Frends FELIX KENAN, WILLIAM GODDEN, GEORGE SMITH
wit: JAMES ͞f BARNET
signed: William Barnes

13. BASDEN, JOHN (CR.035.801.1/A-19)
11 May 1811 - Jul Term 1811
brother JOSEPH 1 shilling Sterling; sister SARAH 1 shilling Sterling;
sister RITTE 1 shilling Sterling; sister ZILPHIA 1 shilling Sterling;
sister MOLSEY 1 shilling Sterling; brother JESSE 1 shilling Sterling;
brother WILLIAMS 1 shilling Sterling; wife REBECCA residue of estate
extr: My New and Trusty friend NATHAN WALLER
wit: W. SOUTHERLAND, ROBERT SOUTHERLAND, ALEXR. SOUTHERLAND
                          signed: Jo   Basden

14. BASS, RICHARD SENR (CR.035.801.1/A-31)
9 May 1780 - Jan Court 1781
son WILLIAM 4 pds; son RICHARD 4 pds; dau. MARY 4 pds.; son ANDREW 4 pds.;
son WILLIS 4 pds.; son BURREL 300 acres; son LUES land whereon I now live;
wife ELISABETH 1 negro wench, house & firnatude, all stock for natural life
or widowhood & at death to be divided between my children FARIBY, BURREL,
LUESS, ANN & ELIZABETH
extr: Doct. ANDREW BASS, WILLIAM BASS, ANDREW BASS JUNR
wit: JAMES HEART LEE, WILLIAM ᛞ LAIGHTEN
                          signed: Richard   Bass Senr.

15. BATTS, JESSEE (CR.035.801.1/3-127)
29 Jun 1850 - Jan Term 1868
eldest son NATHAN land on west side of the North East River whereon he now
lives, the Sholer & Pearce tracts South of Cypress Creek, the tract near
the new Bridge across Said Cypress Creek Known as the STEPHEN LENAIR track,
the tract known as the Holy Meadow and one half of the Ceder pond tract;
dau. MOLSEY, wife of JAMES LANIER all the tract whereon they now live & the
other half of the Ceder pond tract; son WILLIAM H. all the plantation
whereon I now live and all My lands adj. except 150 acres of the DENNIS
PICKETT tract; to JESSE THOMAS COLE 150 acres of the DENNIS PICKETT tract
adj. the Melus tract belonging to the heiars of COURTNEY COLE ded.; oldest
son NATHAN negros Lon, Ellick, Right, Nurcy, Sarah, Isaac, Henry & Seine;
grson. _____, son of NATHAN negro Jim; dau. MOLSEY LANIER negros Rias &
Jane & her children; son WM H. negroes Abe, Hannah & her children; JESSE
THOMAS, CIVIL LOUISA & JAS RICHARD, children of COURTNEY COLE negroes Ned,
Cato, Hester, George, Mary & Monda to be hired out until they become of age;
residue sold & dived amongst children NATHAN, WM. H. & MOLSEY LANIER
extrs: not named
wit: WILLIAM FARRIOR, JOSHUA COLE
signed: Jesse Butts

16. BECK, JOHN (CR.035.801.1/A-20)
2 Sep 1790 - Oct Term 1790
dau. ANNE negroes Tom & Myley, 1 Feather Bed & furniture, 2 cows & calves;
grsons BENJAMIN & GIBSON ESOM 2 tracts of land bought of my son JOHN, one
on the Persimon Branch containing 200 acres and the other on the north side
of Bear Pond Perquoson containing 50 acres; dau. CHARITY WRIGHT negro boy
Frank, 1 Bed & Furniture, 2 cows & calves which she has in possession;
dau. SARAH JERNIGAN negroe Girl Cate, 2 cows & calves which she has in
possession; dau. MARY WHITFIELD negroes Sam & Sabrina, 2 cows & calves
which she has in possession, 1 Feather Bed & Furniture; dau. MARY ANN
SLOCOMB negro girl Jenney, 1 Feather Bed & Furniture, 2 cows & calves she
now has in possession; son WILLIAM 3 acres of land purchased of Docter
GEORGE FRAIZER on Goshen Swamp at the Boat Landing Joyning his own land;
wife ELIZABETH remainder of whole estate during her Natural Life or Widowhood; son STEPHEN land whereon I live at wife's death; CHARITY WRIGHT &
SARAH JIRNIGAN $125 each; MARY ANN SLOCOMBE $43 2/3
extrs: JOS. SANDIFUR, JOHN FORD, J. LINTON
signed: John Beck

17. BECK, WILLIAM SENIOR (CR.035.801.1/A-37)
26 Dec 1813 - Jan Term 1814
wife SARAH land whereon I live on South side of the Camp branch including
my Dwelling House, the unimproved land to the south and west of the home
plantation, negroes Lewis, Moses, Abby, Joanna, Frad, Ezabela & her child
Edna, 2 horses, the young bay mare & young Sorrel Mare, 4 cows & calves,
10 sheep, 4 sows & pigs, 1 yoke of Oxen & cart, Riding Chair & Harness,
2 feather beds & furniture, what household & kitchen furniture and plantation
tools necessary to carry on necessary business of plantation; son ALFRED
all land in Duplin & Sampson except for life estate of wife, 2 lots in Town
of Lisbon in Sampson, my Desk & Book Case; dau. ELIZABETH WRIGHT negro girl
Louisana in addition to that already given her; dau. CHARLOTTE BORDEN negro
boy Hampton in addition to that already given her; extrs. to divide slaves

into 5 lots & daus. ELIZABETH WRIGHT, CHARLOTTE BORDEN & RACHEL SHAW to
have 1 lot each; son JOHN & son-in-law COLIN SMITH 1 lot of slaves in
trust for my dau. SARAH HILL; grson WILLIAM & children 1 lot of slaves at
age 21
extrs: son ALFRED, son-in-law THOMAS WRIGHT
wit: WM. WHITFIELD, JAMES WRIGHT, SOLOMON   ROUSE
signed: Wm. Beck

18. BECK, WILLIAM   (CR.035.801.1/A-41)
7 Feb 1814 - Apr Term 1814
wife SARAH MARAH negros Andy, Peter, & Venus & her child Clary, 1 young
Bay Mare called Cate, 3 cows & calves, 3 sows & pigs, 3 Ewes & lambs, 2
feather Beds & furniture; children ANNY JANE & WILLIAM JOHN residue of
property when ANNY JANE is 21 or marries; 900 acres in Robeson bought of
JOHER & ARCHIBALD McFAIL to be sold & money divided between wife & two
children
extr: wife SARAH M. & brother JOHN BECK
wit: LEVI BORDEN, ALFRED BECK, JO. KORNEGY
signed: Wm. Beck

19. BEESLEY, AUSTIN   (CR.035.801.1/A-9)
30 Sep 1822 - Jan Term 1823
wife MARY land on the west Side of the alligator pond on the line which
I bought of JACOB MATTHIS adj. the old field pond, Millers Creek below my
mill, the south side of the Wildcat pond for her natural life, 1 bed &
furniture, 4 cows & calves, 1 gray horse & riding chair, negro boys Jim &
Willis for ten years; son AUSTIN land at his mother's death; son BASS land
on west Side of the Allegator pond adj. wife's part, Millers Creek, my 200
acre survey, the millpond, my 100 acre survey & HENRY PORTER; son AUSTIN
land on north Side of Millers Creek & a survey of 50 acres bought of DENIS
CANNON adj. PETER CARLTON; dau. ALLY GAVIN 100 acres at head of clear Run;
land bought of JAMES KENAN'S heirs sold and money divided between children
JOHN, LEMUEL KELLY [?] & BRYAN $10 each; dau. ELIZABETH negro girl Hannah;
dau. NANCY negro girl Dinah; dau. MARY negro girl Clary; dau. KITTYANN
negro boy Ervin; dau. SARAH GORE negro fellow Samo; dau. EDAWENNA negro
woman Mary; 30 acres whereon EDA CARROLL now lives sold reserving for said
EDA CARROLL the use of same during her lifetime
extrs: good friends GIBSON SLOAN, LEWIS CARLTON, wife MARY
wit: JOHN LINTON, HENRY PORTER, NICHOLAS ᛏᛜ ROGERS
signed: Austin Beesley

20. BELL, ARCHBILL   (CR.035.801.1/A-59)
23 Sep 1779 - Oct Court 1779
wife MARY whole of estate for natural life or widowhood; son GEORGE five
Shillings; son ORSON five Shillings; son BENJAMIN five Shillings; dau.
NEOMY JERNIGAN negro wench Rose, 2 cows & calves; dau. DORAS CLARK negro
fellow Darley; dau. SARAH FRAZAR 2 cows & calves; dau. MARY negro boy
Delph, 1/2 of cattle on the Plantation where I Now live except 26 which are
to be divided Equally unto SARAH FRAZAR, NEOMY JERNIGAN & NANCY NOBLES, also
2 feather beds and Furniture, 1/2 of my pewter, 1 bay Mare & fair ewes &
lambs; dau. NEOMY JERNIGAN 4 ewes & lambs; son JOSEPH 1400 acres whereon
I Now live, negro boy Andrew, part of the cattle & sheep on the Plantation
whereon I now live, one whole Stock of Cattle on South river in the Poss-
ission of DAVID MAGINNIS, all tools, my still, handmill grindstones, 1 bay

mare which he is to sell to buy as much Callico as will make a Gownd for
my dau. NEOMY, pair of oxen, two rifle guns, 1 shot gun, my stock of hogs;
if JOSEPH dies without heirs JESSE JERNIGAN's children are to have all the
land on the South Side of the Beverdam and GEORGE CLARK's Children to have
that on the North side of said Beverdam
extr: wife MARY, son JOSEPH
wit: GEORGE BELL, GEORGE CLARKE, DAVID DODD
signed: Archbil Bell

21. BELL, JOHN   (CR.035.801.1/A-18)
5 May 1783 - Jul Court 1783
son THOMAS lower part of the Land I live on Black Branch; son ARCHBALD
upper part of the Land at the Mouth of Priests Branch; son JOHN remainder of
the said Land with the plantation & improvements; rest of land divided
equally amongst my three sons; dau. ELIZABETH 3 Cows & Calves to be paid
her at Age or Day of Marriage; wife [not named] younge Horse Called Prince
and rest of estate during her Widowhood and afterwards to children
extr: THOMAS COGAN, HEZEKIA BELL, GEORGE BELL
wit: WM. ROBERSON, ROBT. BELL, JESSE BELL
signed: John Bell

22. BENNETT, THOMAS   (CR.035.801.1/A-45)
12 Jun 1816 - Jul Term 1816
son THOMAS 50 acres adj. said THOMAS & bought at JOSEPH WADE sale; son
JOHN & KINNARD residue of lands including the Plantotion whereon I now live;
son JESSE $100 to be raised out of my Estate; dau. CATHARINE $100 & 1
feather bed & furniture; dau. HANNER 1 feather bed & furniture, 1 cow &
calf; son KINNARD 1 feather bed & furniture; residue of estate sold &
money equally divided between the Hole of my children WILLIAM dc. children,
ROWEANA [?] SHEAR, SAMUEL, heirs of SARAH MELLARD Ded, MARY WILEY, REBEKKAH
HINES, THOMAS, JAMES, JERRY, JESSE, GEORGE, J., KINNARD, SARAH ROGERS, HANNER,
CATHARINE
extrs: sons THOMAS & JOHN
wit: ELIJAH BIZZELL, SAMUEL BIZZELL, ISAAC WOODARD
                              signed: Thomas   Bennett

23. BENNETT, WILLIAM   (CR.035.801.1/A-49)
3 Aug 1804 - Oct Term 1804
wife MARY all lands until son THOMAS Becomes of age and no longer; sons
THOMAS & JOHN lands when THOMAS Becomes of age and should either die, his
half to be divided between the surviving one and his sister LETHA; son
THOMAS my young Grey mare; son JOHN my young yallow mare; residue of
property to wife MARY & dau. LITHA
extr: worthy friends SAMUEL DUNN & DAVID WRIGHT
wit: OWEN CONERLY, MARY ⅄ BENNETT
                    signed: Wm ⅁Ⅎ Bennett

24. BEST, CATHARINE   (CR.035.801.1/A-63)
9 May 1813 - Jul Term 1818
daus. MARY & ELIZABETH my interest in Negroe woman Slave Cloe & her two
children Jacob & Travis, cattle, hogs, tools, household & kitchen furniture;
neice CATHARINE FREDERICK 1 three year old heifer; grson JOHN WILLIAM BEST
$10
extr: ANDREW McINTIRE
wit: STEPHEN GRAHAM, GEORGE McGOWEN ALEXANDER McGOWEN
                    signed: Catharine   Best

25. BEST, GEORGE (CR.035.801.1/3-62)
14 Apr 1859 - Jan Term 1863
wife ELIZABETH negroes Pleasant, Harry, Toney, Hannah, Little Toney for her
natural life; oldest dau. PATSEY ELIZA FREDERICK negro Harry after wife's
death; son GEORGE S. negroes Toney, Hannah & Little Toney after wife's
death; oldest dau. PATSEY ELIZA FREDERICK negroes Harriet & her children
Amanda & Mary Magdaline, also 45 acres of land on Buckskin Branch known as
the Buckskin land which she has by deed, $400, 1 Buggy & Harness; wife
ELIZABETH 2 horses, 4 cows & calves, 2 Sows & Pigs, all my Poultry, all my
household & Kitchen furniture, 2 plows & gear, 1500 pds of Pork, 100 pds of
lard, 50 barrells of corn, 50 pds of Coffee, 50 pds of sugar, 1 barrel of
flour; son GEORGE S. tract of land whereon I live which he has deed for
after my wife's death, negroes Primus, Diloway, Daniel, Milly, Sam, Jack &
Sallie Eliza; son GEORGE S. & dau TABITHA C., wife of STARKEY COX jointly
negroes Calvin the Blacksmith & Mary Ann; the children of my dau. PLEASANT
ROSA, wife of JACOB BEST negroes Eliza & Riley; dau. ELIZABETH B., wife of
JESSE B. QUINN $410 which she already has & negro Marenda; dau. MILLY C.,
wife of WILLIAM ERVIN negroes Dick & Charles; dau. MARINDA G. STOKES negroes
Spicy Jane, Little Calvin, Hannah & Peter; dau. TEMESEY PRUDENCE, wife of
HENRY BEST negroes William & Elizabeth; dau. TABITHA C. COX negroes Henry
Pleasant & Roland; son GEORGE S. ballance of estate
extr: son GEORGE S.
wit: JOHN J. WHITEHEAD, C. W. GRAHAM
signed: George Best

26. BEST, HENRY (CR.035.801.1/2-62)
5 Mar 1850 - Apr Term 1851
dau. REBECKAH negroes Bobbin, Lizure & her two children Susan & Thomas &
Rose; grdau. HANNER JANE FREDERICK negroes now in her posession Ann Jane
& her 6 children Lucie, David, Ben, Arabelow, Mary & Rose & Sarah & her 5
children Cate, George, Henry, Elizer & David; grdau. ELIZABETH negroes
Florow and four of her children Martha, Jim, Elizuri & Orrey, Caroline &
her child Cissero, Patience, Rachel & Jane; grson HENRY land whereon I now
live & also 466 acres, negroes Reddin, Lewis, Alexander, Kit, Nancy and her
child Elizabeth, my old negro Woman Patience, Tony, Rachel & her five children Mary, Milley, Beckah, Rose & John & Sam, all stock & residue of estate
extr: grson HENRY & friend NORIS FREDERICK
wit: WILLIS WILSON, WILLIAM BOYETT
                                signed: Henry   Best

27. BEST, HOWEL (CR.035.801.1)
22 Jul 1833 - Jul Term 1839
son JACOB young Sorrel mare; son REDDIN year old horse Colt; wife PRUDENCE
land & property during her natural life or widowhood; 4 grandchildren, the
children of JAMES & PATIENCE DOBSON $5 each & their parents to have $2.50
each; at wife's death, estate to be divided amongst children JOHN, REDDEN,
HALSEY, WILLIAM, PRISCILLA, ELISABETH, BARBARA & REBECCA
extr: friend JEREMIAH PEARSALL & son JACOB
wit: J. OLIVER, JRE. PEARSALL
                        signed: Howel X Best

28. BEST, JOHN (CR.035.801.1/A-13)
10 May 1798 - Jul Term 1799
wife HANNAH all of my estate & at her death my Executors to rais out of my
Estate before it is divided so much as will pay my seven oldest Children
who have married and left the sum of ten shillings - that is to say PATTY,
BENJAMIN, JOHN, REBECCA, ELISABETH, ABSOLUM & HOWEL; residue to be divided
between my three youngest sons HENRY, ETHELDRED & REDDIN; son HENRY to
have lower part of land where it Joins ROBERT WILLIAMS; son ETHELDRED
upper part where it Joins CHARLES WARD; son REDDEN the middle or Centar
part of my Land which Contains my buildings & other improvements
extrs: sons BENJAMIN & ABSOLEM
wit: EDWD PEARSALL, HENRY BEST
                    signed: John ⚒ Best

29. BEST, PRUDENCE (CR.035.801.1/3-120)
2 Mar 1859 - Jul Term 1867
dau. ELISABETH who has continued to live with & take care of me my Loom
and all its fixteres, 1 Cow & Calf, 1 Sow & Pigs and all Household &
Kitchen firniture; residue divided amongst my children JACOB, BARBARA
GRADY, REBEKAH GRADY & ELISABETH
extr: dau. ELISABETH
wit: JERE. PEARSALL, JEMIMA H. PEARSALL
                    signed: Prudence ✝ Best

30. BEST, REDDEN (CR.035.801.1/2-115)
15 Jul 1851 - Apr Term 1857
son BENJAMIN 150 acres adj. land whereon I live, ABSALEM BEST, HARPER
WILLIAMS & the main run of Nahonja Swamp; son WILLIAM H. 150 acres adj.
land given to son BENJAMIN, one grindstone & one sorrel colt which he now
claims; daus. MARTHA & ELLEN K. 34 acres whereon I now live including my
dwelling House, all out houses and other improvements, negro named Statira
& her child Mary, all fowls & poultry, 2 mares or horses, 1 cart, all tools,
saddle, bridle, Household & kitchen furniture, all crops and provisions at
hand; daus. now married BETSEY, the wife of JAMES BROWN, HANNAH wife of
MORRIS GUY, POLLY wife of THOMAS PHILLIP & SUSAN wife of ALEXR. CHAMBERS
$50 each; sons ABSALOM & HOWEL 50¢ each which seems together with the
advancements they have had from me will make theirs a fair and equitable
portion
extr: son WILLIAM H.
wit: JOHN J. KELLY, ROBERT STOKES
                    signed: Redden ✗ Best

31. BEST, WILLIAM (CR.035.801.1/A-44)
20 Oct 1790- Jan Term 1791
wife CATHIRINE use of all my estate until son JOHN is of age or marries
and she to raise & school my children [not named] at the Descretion of my
Executors and when each child comes of age or marries shall recieve a part
of my estate
extrs: wife CATHERINE, JAMES KENAN, WILLIAM FREDERICK
wit: G. MORREY [?], CHA. WARD, FELIX FREDERICK
signed: Wm Best

32. BIRD, ROBERT (CR.035.801.2/A-32)
1 May 1802 - Oct Term 1802
wife SARAH the plantation whereon I now live, negro Tony & his wife Phillis,
mare called Spinnet, all my Stock of Hogs & Cattle, Farming Utensils &
Household furniture; son NATHAN CLARK 5 shillings & negro Jane which is
divide between his two oldest children JOHN & MARY; THOMAS POWEL negro
Phebe; MICAJAH BIRD negro Jenny; son SHADRACH 5 shillings he having
Received his Share Already; son JOHN 5 shillings he having Received his
Share Already; son DANIEL 5 shillings he having Received his Share Already;
son ROBERT horse Called Tarleton he having Received his Share Already; son
JOSHUA BEARD 100 acres including the plantation whereon I now live reserving
a life right for wife SARAH, horse named Sweeper, 2 Cows & Calves; son
MICAJAH 100 acres adj. above mentioned plantation
extrs: son ROBERT & THOMAS WRIGHT
wit: ALEXR. McMILLAN, DANIEL PARKER, PETE PARKER
                                signed: Robert X Bird

33. BIZZEL, WILLIAM (CR.035.801.1/A-14)
6 Aug 1800 - Oct Term 1800
wife HANNER all my lands on the Eastside of white oak branch, all stock
and household fernture for her natural life; son ISAAC lands & plantation
whereon I now live adj. the mouth of the branch above my house which Runs
in to white oake branch, the main Road, a pond at or near the Corner of the
fence nearest to my house of the upper field on the East side of the Road,
JAMES BIZZELS upper line and white oake; son HARDAY all lands on the East
side of white oak branch above the uper boundary line of ISAAC BIZZELS,
2 Cows & Calves & one fether bed; son ARTHUR 5 shillings and no mour;
son JAMES 5 shillings and no mour; dau. NANCY lands I hold lying on the
west side of white oake joining Cherys lines; 300 acres bought of Pipkin
lying on a branch of goshon in samson County to be sold and 1/3 of money
to dau. RACHAL WOODARD and 2/3 to dau. NANCAY; at wife's death stock &
household firniture to be sold & money divided amongst my daus. & one of
my grdaus. MARY WORREL, SARAH CHERRY, NANCY, ELIZABETH GOODMAN, PATTE
WORREL, RACHEL WOODDARD & NANSEY ROGERS; executors to keep money in trust
for NANSEY ROGERS untill She Com of age
extrs: HARDAY BEZZEL, ISAAC BEZZEL
wit: WM DUNKAN, NANCY BEZZEL, JAMES DUNMARK
                                signed: William WX Bezzel

34. BIZZELL, JAMES (CR.035.801.1/A-50)
22 May 1822 - Jul Term 1822
wife [not named] land and Improvements on the west side of the Main Road
Which my Father gave to me In addition the land on the East Side of said
Road From the Negro Woman Filis House straight a Cross the plantation to
hoop pole Run with the priviledge of Gitting Timber from the Rest of my
lands, Household & Kitchen Furniture, plantation tools, Mare Called Blaze,
stock of Cattle, Sheep & Gees, negroes Tom & Ester; 3 youngest daus.
BETSEY, MOLSEY & ALESEY cattle, sheep & geese, negroes Tom & Ester at wife's
death, also Negro Fillis & her Three Children; son SAMUEL land on East side
of the Main Road from the mouth of the lane branch adj. the South Side of
a pond, Bourdens lines & the land I Bought of NICHOLAS BOURDEN, negros Jake
& Abraham on the condition he pay son ELIJAH $450 on or before May 20, 1826

& if he fails to do so I give negro Abraham to son ELIJAH; son JAMES all
the rest of my land Except the lands I bought of JAMES JOHNSTON, negroes
Calop, Lucy & George provided he pays my son WILLIAM $450 on or before
May 20, 1826 But Should he fail I give negro George to my son WILLIAM,
negro Martin provided he pay my dau. NANCY GULLY $300 on or Before May 20,
1826 But should he fail I give negro Martin to my dau. NANCY GULLY, also
Deformed Negro boy Joe with the Injunction That he Maintain and Support him
During his life; dau. SALLY SWINSON lands I Bought of JAMES JOHNSON sold
and a negro girl bought for her; dau. CATY SANDERS $5; stock to son JAMES
for the Support of the Family
extrs: son-in-law LEVI SWINSON & sons SAMUEL & JAMES
wit: D. WRIGHT, JOHN BENNETT
signed: James Bezzel

35. BIZZELL, MARY (CR.035.801.1/A-12)
25 Jan 1829 - Nov Term 1829
dau. ELIZABETH my Bay Archy horse; dau. MOLCY my sorrel colt; balance of
property to daus. ELIZABETH & MOLCY
extr: son JAMES
wit: SAMUEL BIZZELL, JAMES BIZZELL
                    signed: Mary + Bizzell

36. BLACKBORN, WILLIAM "Planter" (CR.035.801.1/A-21)
15 Apr 1762 - May Court 1762
JESSEY HORRICK my Sisters Sun Both my plantations on the west Side of
Cohary the one that i now Live on Containing four hundred Acres and the
other Containing fifty, I also make Said JESSEY HORRICK my Soule and only
excutor & he to pay the quit rents on the said land; my Honnoured Mother
MARTHA BLACKBORN to have the use of the improvements of the Plantation I
now Live upon during her Life, also 1 bed with furniture, 1 Box iron, 2 pots,
1 fryingpan, 1 bason, 1 dish, 2 plates, 1 Duzen of Spoons, 2 Jugs & Great
Wheal, 1 pair of Cotten Cards, 2 pails, 1 tub, 1 pigin, 1 Sifter, all the
Spun Cotten, 2 bottels, 1 half pint bottel, 1 mug, 3 Cups & the Stilyards,
1 Candelstick, 1 Chist, 2 howes, 1 ax, 1 Grubing how, 1 plow how & plow,
1 Fistament, the book intitled the whol duty of man and the book Called the
Seven Serm[ons], 6 Cows & Calves, 4 two hirowld Steres, 2 year owld heffers,
my Sorril hors, Saddil & bridle for her lifetime & then to JESSEY HORICK;
JESSEY HORROCK 2 Cows & Calves, 2 Cows & 1 yerling, 1 yearowld heffer, 1
mair & Colt, 1 Great pot, 1 dish, 1 bason, 1 Littel Chist, 1 bed with one
rug, 2 Sheats, 2 Jugs, 2 bottels, 3 Cups, 1 Broadax, 1 Chizel, 2 augers,
1 hand saw, 1 frow, 1 round Shave, 1 Cross, 1 joynter, 1 pair of iron weges,
1 taper bit, 1 gimblil, 1 Gun, 1 pair of Sturrup irons, 1 pair of Bridel bits
wit: ADONIROM TREADWELL, BENJAMIN ⅓ COCKBORN
[Will Book shows witnesses as FROWERMAN TREADWELL & BENJAMIN ⅓ BLACKBONE]
Signed: William ⅄⍝ Blackborn

37. BLACKMAN, JOSEPH "Planter" (CR.035.801.1/A-48)
2 Feb 1768 - no probate [original badly damaged]
well beloved wife ELIZABETH all my stock & household Furniture & the Plantation where on I dwell during her natural life; son JOAB 400 acres on the
Beaver dam Swamp, negro George, 1 good feather bed; dau. EDY negro Tony,
1 feather bed; son JOSIAH plantation whereon I dwell after his mother's

decease with 100 acres Joining above & 100 acres Joing below bought of
COLONEL SMITH, 1 feather bed; dau. MARY negro Bob 1 good feather bed
extrs: wife ELIZABETH & STEPHEN BLACKMAN
wit: JOSEPH RHOADS, THOS. THORNTON, TH. THORNTON
signed: J. Blakman

38. BLACKMORE, HARROLL SR. "of Spring Hall at the Welch Tract in the
        County of New Hanover" (CR.035.801.1/A-22)
10 Apr 1781 - Jul Ct. 1781 [Original will missing]
son EDWARD the plantation where on I now live, a lot of ground in the
town of Wilmington in Dock Street formally purchased of JOSEPH WATERS,
one moiety of three Acres of land on the island opposite to the town of
Wilmington formally purchased of ROBERT & JOHN HOGG, 200 acres of land in
New Hanover County adj. the plantation where on GEORGE McGOWAN now lives;
dau. MARY all the land I formally purchased of McLloyd, the moiety of
three acres of land on the Island opposite to the town of Wilmington
formally purchased of ROBERT and JOHN HOGG, 200 acres on the north side
of the house where on THOMAS ARMSTRONG now lives and 150 acres where on
THOMAS ARMSTRONG now lives after his decease or removing from the same;
son EDWARD & dau. MARY all negroes cattle Horses sheep Hogs money Bonds
Notes Book accounts and other of my personal estate to be divided between
them share & share alike division to be made when my said dau. shall be
of age or on the day of her marriage; Father-in-law FELIX KENAN 1 silver
watch now in his possession & a gold ring with a stone the following devise
Viz. to hearts linked together; Mother-in-law CATHERINE KENAN a plain
gold ring with the following motto Viz (Virtue be your guide) she to have
the care of my Children; WILLIAM KENAN a silver hilt of a sword now in
his possession, my silver shoe and Knee buckles, all my wearing apparel;
FELIX HILL 2 cows & calves, tin ewes; JOHN HILL a mourning ring with the
names of HARRALL and NANCY BLACKMORE in the same the said ring to be purchased; Mistress JANE HILL 2 dining tables & a desk with eagle claws feet;
CATHARINE HILL a pair of plain gold earrings; ROSE KENAN now in England
negro boy named Hector, 50 pds. sterling, 2 good suits of broadcloth cloaks
together with shirts, shoes and other clothing in proportion the clothes
to be purchased and the whole to be paid him on his arrival (if living) and
all debts & demands contracted by ROSE KENAN for Education, board and
clothing while in England be discharged & paid
extrs: FELIX KENAN Esq, WM. KENAN, JOHN HILL all of Duplin Co.
wit: W. SHARPLES, DAVID EVANS
signed: Herrall Blackmore

39. BLAKE, JOSHUA (CR.035.801.1/1-59)
11 Nov 1832 - Oct Term 1834
dau. NANCY COGGIN all my land, Household & Kitchen furnitur & stock of every
kind; friend EZEKIEL MATHIS 50 acres adj. a small branch running an East
course into Burrel Hill Branch, 1 feather bed & furniture, 1 Chest, 1 cow
& calf
extr: GEORGE W. HUFHAM
wit: GEORGE W. HUFHAM, CALVIN J. DICKSON
                                signed: Joshua ⪦ Blake

40. BLANCHARD, REUBEN (CR.035.801.1)
26 Apr 1844 - Jul Term 1844
wife SARAH part of the plantation on which I now reside including my dwelling
house, out houses and all the lands on the north and west side of Buck Hall
and bounded on the south side by Raccoon branch containing 240 acres, negroes
Mary, Moses, Jim, Owen, Sam, Rosena & Doll, 2 horses, 1 mule viz. Jack,
Pleasure & Jenny, 10 cattle, all my sheep, all the bunch of house hogs, all
household & kitchen furniture & plantation tools, 1 yoke of Oxen, Cart &
waggon; son JOHN lands after wife's death & all the negroes except Rosena,
also negro George, 1 mare called Poll; dau. ALICE TORRANS negro Dick, 4
cattle; dau. MOLSY BASS negro Calvin, 4 cattle & 1 colt going on 2 years
old; wife to have $15 after debts are paid and remainder of money to be
equally divided between daus. ALICE TORRANS & MOLSY BASS; grdau. ELIZABETH
TORRENS negro Rosena
extrs: son JOHN & THOMAS TORRENS
wit: JAS G. DICKSON, EDWD. C. GAVIN
signed: Rbn. Blanchard

41. .BLAND, WILLIAM "Planter" (CR.035.801.1/A-25)
19 Mar 1775 - Jul Court 1775
son WILLIAM 300 acres lying in Virginia on the head of powels Branch, a
Soril mare & Colt; granson JAMES, son of WILLIAM and RACHEL his Wife 2 Cows
& 1 Calf, 3 Earlings, 2 feather beds & furniture, 20 pds. prochlimation
money, my Riding horse, Saddle & bridle; son THOMAS 5 Shilings; son
CHARLES 5 Shilings; dau. MARY PARKER 1 Side Saddle and all my hogs; son
JAMES all the goods of mine that he has in possession; son JOHN 5 Shilings;
son JOSEPH 5 Shilings
extrs: sons WILLIAM & JAMES
wit: THOMAS LEE, HARDY ⊢ POWEL, RACHEL / POWEL
signed: William Bland

42. BLAND, WILLIAM (CR.035.801.1/2-88)
1 Sep 1854 - Oct Term 1854
son JAMES to sell negroes Hannah, Joseph, David, Timothy, John & Jock to pay
debts & burial expenses; dau. RACHEL POWEL negro Mariah which she has
received about twenty five years ago, $200; dau. NANCY, wife of BRYAN LEE
negro Edmund & $200; dau. LUCRETIA, wife of WILLIAM NEWTON negro Prince
which they received about 25 years ago, $200; to JACOB HIGHSMITH who mar-
ried my dau. ELIZABETH negro Daniel, $200; dau. SUSANNAH who married a man
by the name of EPHRAIM JOHNSON who is now dead and who I heard has since
married a man by the name of Stephens and are living some where in the
South or western states negro John which they received about 20 years ago,
$200; son JAMES ballance of estate
extr: GEORGE W. HUFHAM
wit: JOHN HUFHAM
          signed: William ⨪ Bland

43. BLANSHARD, MARY (CR.035.801.1/2-26)
18 Feb 1847 - Jan Term 1848
my attendant nurse FANNY HERRING 12 head of hogs, all my corn & bacon, 1 Safe,
1 Loom, 2 Tables, all my Kitchen Furniture, 2 chest, all my Siting cheers,
1 Bedstead, all money, notes & papers calling for money; dau. NANCY EZELL
1 bed, bedsead & furniture
extr: THOMAS M. HERRING
wit: DAVID F. RIVENBARK, JOHN WEST
          signed: M y ✕ Blanshard

44. BLANTON, RICHARD (CR.035.801.1/A-12)
12 Jun 1821 - Jul Term 1821
wife MARGRET 1 horse, 8 head of cattle, all hogs, sheep & gees, all houshold
& Kitchen furniture and tools during her natural life; son BENJAMIN property
given to my wife after her death; dau. MARGRET 1 Cow & a two year old hefer;
son ABRAHAM 1 horse; dau. NANCY 1 cow & calf, 1 two year old hefer
extrs: BENJAMIN FUSSEL, DAVID WILLIAMS
wit: Dd. WILLIAMS, BENJAMIN FUSSEL
                         signed: Richard X Blanton

45. BLOUNT, ELEANOR (CR.035.801.1/3-53)
13 Oct 1860 - Apr Term 1862
eldest son DANIEL B. NEWTON negro Phillis; eldest dau. ELIZA, wife of
SAMUEL R. IRELAND negro Nelly & her son Jack only if SAMUEL R. IRELAND
relinquishes all rights to the rents for his wife's distribution share of
the land of which I have held dower since the death of my first husband
and on which I have lived since that event till very recently; grdau.
MARY E. HUGGINS, only surviving child of my dau. MARY E. HENRY decd. $600;
dau. ELEANOR, wife of CLAIBORNE J. OATES 2 tracts of land on Town-Creek
in Brunswick County purchased of ANDREW J. POTTER & a small tract adj.
both bought of JANE & WILLIAM CUMBO and at her death to her children;
if son-in-law SAMUEL R. IRELAND claims rents from dau. ELIZA's share the
negroes Nelly & Jack to be sold and money paid over to ELIZA; residue of
estate sold and youngest dau. JULIA A. BLOUNT & youngest son JAMES W. BLOUNT
are to receive $1375 each and the remainder equally divided between daus.
ELEANOR OATES & JULIA A. BLOUNT & son JAMES W. BLOUNT
extr: JAMES W. BLOUNT
wit: JOSEPH T. RHODES, W. C. HIGHTOWER
signed: Eellonor Blount

46. BLOUNT, WARREN (CR.035.801.1/A-47)
27 Feb 1823 - Apr Term 1823
wife's eldest son DANIEL B. NEWTON $5; her next son JULIOUS NEWTON $5; her
dau. MARY ELIRZAR NEWTON $5; dau. MARY BLOUNT $5; dau. ELINOR BLOUNT $5;
dau. JULIAUR ANN BLOUNT $5; wife ELENOR residue of estate to support
family & school children until JULIAUR ANN is 18 years old; negroes Rose
& Sam sold to pay debts
extr: wife ELENOR
wit: MAJR NEWTON, FELIX FREDERICK
signed: Warren Blount

47. BONEY, DANIEL (CR.035.801.2/3-33)
3 Aug 1844 - Oct Term 1860
son TIMOTHY certain part of my land adj. Streets Branch on the north edge
of the ford, DANIEL GEORGE, WIMBERK BONEY and a little pond; dau. BARBARA
10 acres between my house and my son WILLIAM's; son WILLIAM D. Balance of
my land, my Black Horse, Hand Mill; son WIMBERK $25; dau. ELIZABETH NORRIS
$1; dau. MARY STREETS $1; dau. NANCY FUSSELL $1, 1 bed & furniture which
she already claims; dau. BARBARA all the furniture in the house that she
made or Bought within herself; balance of Property divided between children
except TIMOTHY & WILLIAM D.
extrs: son WILLIAM D. & friend CORNELIUS McMILLAN
wit: JAMES W. BONEY, C. McMILLAN
signed: Daniel Boney

48. BONEY, JOHN (CR.035.801.2/1-18)
10 Sep 1831 - Nov Term 1831
wife MARY all lands east of the mill including the grist mill during her
natural life, negroes Bill, Jack, Phebe & Maria; son WILLIAM land at wife's
death; wife 6 cows, my stock of hogs & sheep, 2 Horses, plantation & farming
tools, Household & kitchen furniture, 1 cart & a yoke of oxen; sons WELLS
& WILLIAM perishable property given wife except for negro Maria; son WRIGHT
negroes Dave, Jim & Chloe's children; dau. SUSAN SLOAN negroes Sarah, Eliza
& Sam; dau. MARY negro Rachel & her children; son WELLS all my lands west
of my mills including the Saw Mill except a piece of land under fence known
as the Newground Field, also 116 acres on Rock Fish Creek adj. WILLIAM BONEY
& HENRY HILL, negroes Henry & Jupiter, Bet & her children; son WILLIAM the
New Ground Field with the woodland included, negroes Windsor, Jacob, Caroline,
Alice, a young Horse & mare and lands east of the Mills at wife's demise
including the Grist Mill, $200, a small cart; dt. CATHARINE A. TEACHEY negroes
Cassia, Wright & Maria at wife's demise; crop of turpentine now pending be
sold in market and money used to support family; turpentine lands to be shared
by wife & sons WELLS & WILLIAM; blacksmiths tools to sons WELLS & WILLIAM
extrs: WRIGHT BONEY, DAVID SLOAN
wit: G. H. McMILLEN, DEMPSEY HASSELL
signed: John Boney

49. BONEY, WILLIAM SENR. (CR.035.801.2/2-46)
10 Aug 1841 - Apr Term 1849
wife DOROTHY all my land adj. the place whereon I now live for her natural
life and afterwards to be divided equally among all my children [not named],
household & Kitchen furniture, plantation tools, 1 horse & Chair, 1 Yoke of
Oxen & Cart, 4 Cows & Calves, 4 Sows & 20 Pigs or Shoats, negroes Dilly, Flora,
Jinny & Furrismon & she to take care of the old negro Dinah; remainder of my
negroes divided among all my children; daus. SUSAN L. & ELIZA a bed & furniture & 1 cow & calf each; the board of Foreign Missions to have $30
extrs: sons JOHN WILLIAM & GABRIEL & son-in-law JOHN CARR
wit: W. J. LOVE JR., JOHN W. CARR
signed: Wm. Boney Sr.

50. BONEY, WILLIAM (CR.035.801.2/2-82)
28 Nov 1853 - Apr Term 1854
brother WELLS plantation on which I reside including my dwelling house, all
out houses, grist mill & improvements, all household & Kitchen furniture &
all right in a tract of Turpentine land bequeathed by my father JNO BONEY to
my Mother MARY BONEY brother WELLS and myself in Common, negroes Jacob, Pat,
Carroline & her children Annie, Dempsey & Sarah Eliza; brother WRIGHT negroes
Enoch, Francenia, Julia & her youngest children Margarit & Ellen; sister
SUSAN SLOAN negroes Juda & Emily; sister MARY negroes Linda & Chloe; sister
CATHARINE A. STOAKES negroes Patsey, Aly & her children Tom & Pene
extrs: brother WELLS & brother-in-law JAMES C. SOAKES [sic]
wit: HANSON F. MURPHY, JOHN W. CARR
signed: William Boney

51. BONEY, WRIGHT (CR.035.801.2/2-108)
18 Apr 1854 - Jan Term 1857
having conveyed to my three sons DANIEL T., JAMES W. & TIMOTHY W. by deed
dated March 24, 1854 what I regard as a fair & equitable portion I make no

further provision for my said sons; wife LINDA all my property effects
and estate of every nature kind and description for her natural life;
$500 to each dau. [not named] who attains the age of 21; children to
release all right to the land my son JOHN WRIGHT died siezed of unto my
son DANIEL T., JAMES W. & TIMOTHY W.; residue of property to my children
share & share alike
extrs: friends JAMES DICKSON & DAVID J. MIDDLETON
wit: W. D. PEARSALL, N. W. HERRING
signed: Wright Boney

52. BONNEY, JACOB (CR.035.801.2/A-6)
15 Aug 1761 - no probate
wife [unnamed] 1/3 of whole estate; son JACOB twentey pound Procklamation
To Be paid in Cattle Besides two Childs part of my whole Estate; rest of
estate to be valued by two free hoalders and divided amongst my Children
[not named] with youngest Child JOHN a part over & above to be used for
Cloathing and Scooling; eldest son [not named] plantation at wife's death
extrs: JOHN BROCK, DAVID JEANES
wit: JOHN **C** COOCK, WILLIAM CANNE [?]
signed: Jacubb Boney

53. BOSTIC, JOHN SR. (CR.035.801.2/2-30)
7 Mar 1846 - Apr Term 1848
wife EMILY all the lands I possess including the plantation whereon I now
live, Mansion House, all out house and other improvements, all household
& Kitchen furniture, all stock & crops, negro Simon and at her death he to
be hired out until youngest child comes of age; children [not named]
property at wife's death; son JOHN MILLER 1 bed, bedstead & furniture,
1 sorrel Mare; negro Frank Kave sold & money divided between daus. MOLSEY,
wife of DREW THIGPEN & CELEA, wife of HOSEA HUNTER; money remaining after
payment of debts to be divided between my oldest Children MOLSEY THIGPEN,
CELEA HUNTER & JOHN MILLER BOSTIC & grandson JOHN EDWARD HUNTER
extr: WILLIAM FARRIOR
wit: JOHN FARIOR, N. J. FARRIOR
          signed: John ☙ Bostic

54. BOWZER, EMANUEL (CR.035.801.2/A-29)
21 Jun 1798 - Apr Term 1801
wife MARY all stock of cattle & hogs, 1 horse saddle & Bridle, household
firniture & 1 note of hand for 30 pds; son-in-law HARDY PARKER 100 acres
on Indian branch a Branch of Iland Creek, 67 acres adj. on the so. sid⁻
whaire the house now stands and my wife to have Quiet possision During hir
life; son-in-law HENRY ALLIN 145 acres a survey Bot of JOHN COOK SNR on
the north side of indian Branch Including the plantation the sd. HENRY
ALLIN Cleerd; son-in-law JACOB WELLS 105 acres being the lower part of the
above survey & 50 acres on both sides of Iland Creek Bot of FRIDRICK WELLS:
sons-in-law to have 1 horse, Two saddles & all my Plantation tools; MARY
FUTCH 1 loome & 1 slay
extrs: wife MARY & TIMOTHY TEACHEY
wit: TIMOTHY TEACHEY, LEWIS GILSTRAP
          signed: Emanuel 𝒩𝒥 Bowzer

55. BOWZER, MARY (CR.035.801.2/A-46)
3 Aug 1807 - Oct Term 1810
daus. ANN ALLIN & MARY WELLS to divide 1 Bason, 7 plates, 1 pegion, 1 frien
pan, 1 flesh fork, 1 Chirne, 1 Looking Glass, 1 Cotton wheale, 1 Chest,
1 four hundred slay & 2 three years old Steers; dau. SUSANAH all Cattle,
Hogs, house hold firniture & plantation tools, 1 woman's saddle, $20 note
from AMOS HARRIS
extr: son-in-law HARDY PARKER
wit: JOSHUA PLATT, TIMOY. TEACHEY
                           signed: Mary   Bowzer

56. BOYET, MOSES (CR.035.801.2/A-61)
26 Sep 1780 - Oct Court 1780
wife ANNE 1 Horse, bridle & saddel, 1 fether bed & furnitued, 1 Cow and
Calf, 1 mare, land & plantation for her life; son ARTHER land & plantation,
1 year old Colt, 1 Cow & Calf, 1 Two year old heffer, 1 feather bed &
furnitued; dau. MILLAE HOLLAND 1 Shilling Starling
extr: unnamed
wit: THOMAS JERNIGAN, JONATHAN GORE, CHRISTOPHER MARTIN
                                    signed: Moses   Boyett

57. BOYETT, MARTHA (CR.035.801.2)
25 Jul 1839 - Jul Term 1840
dau. BEYSEY JANE JONES 233 1/3 acres whereon I live, negroes Toney, Rachel,
Dolly, Alice, Caroline, Abram & Caezar, all stock, household & Kitchen
furniture
extr: JAMES K. HILL
wit: JAMES K. HILL, GRIFFIN   JONES
                            signed: Martha   Boyett

58. BOYKIN, JOSEPH (CR.035.801.2/A-58)
8 Nov 1766 - 12 Dec 1766 "at Wilmington"
dau. SARAH 6 Cows & Calves; son WILLIAM 6 Cows & Calves; son SMEDDICK
6 Cows & Calves; dau. EDEY 6 Cows & Calves; son JON 20 Neat Steers; dau.
MARY 6 Cows & Calves; DAVID DOD that married my Daughter ELIZABETH one
Certain Black Horse that Runs in ye Woods; wife MARY rest of my estate
extrs: wife MARY & friends WILLIAM POPE & WILLIAM MAGEE
wit: JOHN PIERCE, JAMES   MYHAND
                         signed: Joseph Boykin

59. BOYT, SAMUEL (CR.035.801.2/A-30)
14 May 1791 - Jul Term 1791
wife PHEREBY maner plantation, mare Saddle & Bridl, all house hold furniture,
1 Cow & Calf & heifer for her natural life or widowhood and then to my two
sons; son JOHN BOYET maner plantation at wife's death, 1 mare, 1 cow &
yearling, 1 two year old Stear, 7 Silver Dollars; son HARDY BOYT Track of
Land Down Ash Branch Below & Joining the maner plantation, 1 Cow & yearling,
young Sorrel Mare, 7 Silver Dollars
extrs: brothers WILLIAM B. BOYET & ARTHER BOYET
wit: THOMAS PHILLIPS, EAPHRIAM   BOT
                            signed: Samuel   Boyet

60. BRANCH, ARCHEBIL (CR.035.801.2/A-28)
19 May 1819 - Oct Term 1819
wife HEPSEBETH all my lands lying below the main path adj. the main road,
JAMES GUFFORDs field, the woolf field & the new ground, negroes Toney,
Silve, Sall, Dick, & Lewis; youngest son BRYANT land near the Crossing of
the woolf branch adj., negroes Toney, Silve & Lewis at wife's death; son
ARCHEBIL negro Sam; dau. POLEY KETHLEY negroes Sall & Rows; son ARTHUR
$100; son REUBEN one negro or the value ther of; son BENJAMON land lying
above Woolf branch, negro Dick, bay horse, 1/2 of stock & working tools;
sons BENJAMON & BRYANT household & Kitchen firnature
extrs: REUBEN BRANCH & ARCHEBIL BRANCH
wit: JAMES GUFFORD, NANCY   WILLIAMS
                                  signed: Archebil   Branch

61. BRANCH, ARCHILOUS (CR.035.801.2/3-97)
19 May 1842 - Jul Term 1865
extrs to sell land on Guffords branch known as the Sullivan Lands, negro
woman Ceily & her child Sarah, all stock, furniture & tools to pay debts
and funeral expenses; dau. CLARY A. DANIEL $5 together with what I have
heretofore given her; son JAMES G. negro man 1som & 1/2 of lands not
mentioned before; son ARCHILAUS BRIGHT 1/2 of lands in trust to son
JAMES G. & friend DANIEL HERRING; remainder of negroes divided between
son JAMES G., my trustees aforesaid and dau. CLARKY [?] DANIEL
extrs: son JAMES G. & friend DANIEL HERRING
wit: JERE. PEARSALL, THOS HILL
signed: Archelius Branch

62. BRANCH, EDELPH (CR.035.801.2/A-26)
4 Dec 1808 - Jan Term 1815
grandchildren RICHARD EDMUNDSON, PATSY BLOW, WILLIAM EDMUNDSON, JAMES
EDMUNDSON, NANCY BLOW, EDELPH LAIN, POLLY EDMUNDSON, SALLY EDMUNDSON &
SMITHY EDMUNDSON all money, notes & accounts except one note on DAVID
WRIGHT; son WILLIAM note on DAVID WRIGHT, 1 Feather Bed & furniture;
grson MATTHEW all stock of cattle except 1 Cow & Calf; grson JESSE Cow &
Calf above excepted; other grandchildren WILLIAM BRANCH, ARTHUR BRANCH &
SALLY RIVENBARK having already recieved their full Share of my Estate I have
not left thim any part of it at this time
extrs: son WILLIAM & Trusty friend DAVID WRIGHT
wit: D. WRIGHT, ALXR. HERRING
                          signed: Edeph   Branch
Codicil: 21 Feb 1814 cow & yearling purchased of grson MATTHEW is to go to
my son WILLIAM
wit: ELISHA HERRING, H. HODGES
                          signed: Edelph   Branch

63. BRICE, GEORGE (CR.035.801.2/1-11)
4 Mar 1831 - May Term 1831
dau. MARTHA ANN of Macon Co., Geo. $10; friend JOHN HUFHAM my part of the
distributive Share both real and personal in the estate of My Brother JOHN
and his dau. MARY BRICE both decd.
extr: GEORGE W. HUFHAM
wit: GEORGE W. HUFHAM, PENELOPE FENNELL
                          signed: George   Brice

64. BRICE, JOSEPH (CR.035.801.2/A-40)
20 Feb 1829 - May Term 1829
wife MARTHA Negroes Simon, Jean, Minerva for her natural life and then to
my Male Children; dau. MOLCY JANE HICKS Children $300 or a negro Girl to
be bought and Kept until the Children becomes of Age; daus. RACHEL A.,
ELIZA & AMANDA negro Mehala & should any of them dye the deceaseds part
to my sons JOHN & WILLIAM; son FRANCIS piece of land lately purchased from
Henry & priviledg of 30 acres on the east side of rockfish; son JOHN L.
all my land lying West of rockfish, 1 featherbed & furniture; son WILLIAM B.
all my land lying West of rockfish that is to say the place whereon I now
live, 1 bed & furniture; 500 acres on the northeast river sold to pay debts
extrs: MARTHA BRICE & WILLIAM STALLINGS
wit: HENREY BOON, RACHEL BRICE
signed: Jos. Brice

65. BRICE, MARTHA (CR.035.801.2/2-51)
13 Dec 1848 - Jul Term 1849
son WM. in trust for son JOHN 1/2 interest in negro Minerva; son WM. 1/2
interest in sd. Minerva, negro boy Dave, all stock of hogs, sheep, Cattle &
Poultry, all corn & fodder that was made on the plantation on which I now
live, all household & kitchen furniture & should he leave no children then
all the above to go to my youngest dau. AMANDA K. wife of JOHN WILSON; JOHN
& AMANDA K. WILSON negro man Ireland, 2 beds and their necessary firniture,
1 chest & contents, 1 trunk & contents, 1 large looking glass, my bay mare
and mule, my saddle, crop of corn and fodder which was made on my ten Acre
field; son WM. all the provisions that I may be possessed of at the time of
my death; grson JOSEPH FRANKLIN son of JOHN & AMANDA K. WILSON 2 heifer
yearlings two years old, one a black one and the other red and white, 1 small
bed and bedstead and furniture; the Account I have against FRANCIS BRICE's
heirs, which I have sued for through the agency of HENRY MURPHY of the County
of Thomas and State of Georgia, and the said FRANCIS BRICES heirs is of the
County of Thomas and State of Georgia, when collected be paid to my Executors,
to pay off a debt which I am bound to pay the children of MOLSEY J. HICKS of
the State of Georgia, which by will of JOSEPH BRICE I now stand indebted to
them for that I collected, viz. for RACHEL REASONS, MARTHA ELIZA SOUTHERLAND
and AMANDA K. WILSON
extrs: trusty friend TIMOTHY NEWKIRK & son WM.
wit: TIMOTHY NEWKIRK, WM. B. WELLS
signed: Martha Brice

66. BRIGHT, WILLIAM (CR.035.801.2/A-62)
2 Jul 1762 - no probate
son-in-law JOHN WINDERS 2 feather Beads; son in law STEPHEN HERRING 1
feather Bead; sons in law JOHN WINDERS & STEPHEN HERRING all my hole astate
extrs: sons in law JOHN WINDERS & STEPHEN HERRING
wit: WM. TAYLOR, DANIEL LANIER [?]
                        signed: William XY Bright

67. BRITTON, THOMAS (CR.035.801.2/A-54)
30 Jan 1779 - Oct Court 1779
son EDMOND plantation Wheron I now liv; wife [not named] negro boy Will,
4 cows and calves, 1 Mair and hors, 4 head of Sheep, 2 father beds, 1 doz.

Puter Basons, 1 Doz of plates, 4 Chears, 1 Chast, 1 Barr plow & a flook;
son EDMOND property at wife's Deceas; son JOHN 50 pds in money; dau.
CATERINE 1 father Bed, 1 Chast, 2 Dishes, 2 Basons, 1/2 doz. plates,
1 Iron pott, 1 wooling wheal; grdau. ELIZEBETH 50 pds in money; wife
negro Abrum for hir life & then sold & money divided between JOHN, CATERINE
and THOMAS QUIN; THOMAS QUIN 50 pds in money; residue to THOMAS QUIN &
dau. CATERINE
extrs: THOMAS QUIN, JOHN BRITTON & JOHN WILLIAMS
wit: ROBT. SOUTHERLAND, LOTT GREGORY
signed: TOS. BRITTON

68. BROCK, JOHN (CR.035.801.2/2-36)
11 May 1848 - Jul Term 1848
wife SELEY 2 Beds & fureneture, all house hold & kitchen furniture, all
stock of Hogs & sheep
extr: not named
wit: JOHN G. WESTON, WILLIAM ✝ ALPHIN
signed: John ✝ Brock

69. BROCK, LEWIS (CR.035.801.2)
29 Mar 1839 - Jul Term 1839
wife ELIZABETH dower on my lands and one years provisions according to law;
son JOHN A. 200 acres at the lower end of the land I purchased of HENRY GRADY,
2 Cows & Calves, 1 bed & furniture; ballance of land to 2 sons-in-law
WILLIAM MERSER & JAMES L. SMITH; wife ELIZABETH negro girl Esther; WILLIAM
MERCER negro Woman Evaline; JAMES L. SMITH negro girl Asa; ballance of
negroes divided between wife & 2 sons-in-law; other property sold & ballance
of money to wife & 2 sons-in-law
extrs: WILLIAM MERCER & JAMES L. SMITH
wit: ELIZABETH MERCER, A. O. GRADY
signed: Lewis Brock

70. BROWN, ALSA (CR.035.801.2/3-65)
3 Dec 1858 - Jan Term 1863
wife ELIZA 226 acres Known as the ASCION MORRIS tract that I now live on
including my mansion house all out houses and other improvements, slaves
Lewis, Sarah & Hannah, 2 beds Steads & furniture, 1 Set Chairs, Crockery,
Knives & forks Spoons, Coocking utensils, coopers ware & Loom, horse & buggy,
2 cows & calvs, 2 sows & pigs & poultry, years allowance of 25 barrels of corn,
1000 pds of pork or 700 pds of Bacon & $25 in money; dau. DOLLY slaves
Vilet & Dallas, 1 bed bedStead & furniture, 1 chest, 2 cows & calvs; dau.
CATHARINE SANDLIN slaves Thussey & Mary; son ROBERT H. slaves Ned, Caroline,
Moses, Sarah & Hannah after wife's death, 1 bed bed Stead & furniture,
ballance of stock & property
extr: son ROBERT H.
wit: WM FARRIOR, E. W. FARRIOR
signed: Alsa Brown

71. BROWN, BENJAMIN (CR.035.801.2)
3 Aug 1839 - Oct Term 1841
son ISAAC negro man Bob & negro boy Squier, Bay horse, Stock of hogs,
Sheape & Cattle; grandawter KILLEY 1 Cow & Calf, 1 Bead & furniture; son
ISAAC all farming utensils & plantation tools, household & Kitchen furneture

and all the Crop that is Growing on the Land whearon I Now live; son ALSA
Negro Girl Thursey; dau. ANNA WILLIAMS Negro Girl Hanah; son BRANTLEY
Negro woman Sarah & her child Ned, $100 in money; dau. SALLY BEST negro
woman Marey; wife CATHREN negro woman feby Durin her Natrel life & then to
dau. NELLEY CHASTON and if NELLEY should Die with out Ishue then Feby to go
to sons ALSA, ISAAC & BRANTLEY; son ISAAC to Seporte my wife CATHRAN
extr: not named
wit: DAVID SOUTHERLAND, DAVID BROWN
signed: Benjamin Brown

72. BROWN, EDWARD   (CR.035.801.2/A-16)
12 May 1784 - April Court 1784
son ARTHUR 225 acres on East side of Great Cohery part of a purchase I made
from JOHN SAMPSON and part of a purchase from JOHN TURNER in the Whole Six
hundred & twenty acres adj. my Land, JOHN TURNER, SIMON TURNER, JOHN SAMPSON,
a branch, a Larger branch, a larg marsh Branch, the head of Reedy Branch,
Great Cohery Swamp & mouth of the Dividing Branch; son SHERROD 225 acres on
the North Side of the Marah Branch Joining EDW. TOOLE's Land; wife PRUDENCE
land & Plantation on the South Side of marsh Branch & at her Discease to my
son SHERROD With my still; son SHERROD Stock of Cattle in the Care of JOHN
SIGGRIST, 1 Puter Dish, 1 Bason, 6 plates; dau. SUSANAH 1 Feather Bed &
Furniture, 6 Puter plates, 1 puter Dish, 1 puter Bason; dau. MOURNING 1
feather Bed & Furniture, 6 pewter plates, 1 puter Dish, 1 pewter Bason;
Stock of Cattle in the Care of WILLIAM SMITH & another In Care of AMOS RUNNELS
to be Divided between daus. SUSANAH & MOURNING; residue of estate to wife
During her Natural Life and then Devid between SHERROD, SUSANAH & MOURNING;
dau. JEMIMA STEPHENS 20 shillings
extrs: friend HARDY STEPHENS, sons ARTHUR & SHERROD
wit: FLEET COOPER, WILLIAM *oWꝗ* BUTLER, WRIGHT RYALL
signed: Edward Brown

73. BROWN, ELISEBETH "widow of WM BROWNS decest" (CR.035.801.2/2-18)
25 May 1846 - Apr Term 1847
son JAMES 1 Clock, 1 bofot & firnture, all my Seting chirs, Table, 1 Chest,
all Kitchen firnture & plantation tools, 1 mare & colt, 4 cows & calvs,
3 Stears, 3 Sows & 20 Shotes, all sheep, 2 charts, 1 loom, 1/2 of growin crop;
other half of growin crop sold with 1 Sulkey & harnis & money divided Between
my youngest children [not named]; son COUNCIL 1 fether bed & firture;
3 youngest sons [not named] 1 fether bed & firniture each; dau. SARAH $25 to
purchase a bed & firnture, 1 Looking glass, 1 Small tabl, 1 Chest, Spining
wheel; sons NEEDOM & WM. $1 each; negro man Dove to Remain on the Plantation
as he is until the 9th of Febry next at which time I want him hird out until
the youngest child comes of age
extr: son JAMES
wit: A. NEWKIRK, HENRY SANDLIN
                  signed: Elisabeth ◀ Brown

74. BROWN, JACOB SENR (CR.035.801.2/A-52)
28 Nov 1811 - Oct Term 1812
son JESSE negroe Jack, 1 Bed & Furniture, some Cattle; dau. POLLY MALLARD
negro Nance, 2 feather Beds, 2 Cows & Calves; dau. SARAH WILKINS decd. 1
feather Bed & furture, 3 Cows & calves given in her lifetime; son STEPHEN
negro Arthur, 1 Bed & furneture, some Cattle; son JACOB negro Bob, my Rifle

gun, 1 feather Bed & furniture, 1 Cow & Calf; son BENJAMIN negro Phebie,
a mair, a feather bed & furneture; dau. MARY COTTLE Decd 1 Featherbed,
2 Cows & Calves, a Horse given in her lifetime; dau. MARYANN CANADY negro
Hannah, 2 Cows & Calves, 1 Bed & furniture; son JOHN 159 acres whereon I
now live Reserving only 50 acres there of on the North End including my
buildings to my wife ABIGALE, negro Old Hannah; wife ABIGALE all my stock
of Cattle & Hogs, 2 feather Beds & furniture, all my Household & Kitchen
furniture & plantation tools; son DANIEL & HENRY negro Sam, Stock of Cattle
& Hogs, Beds & furniture, Household & Kitchen furniture & plantation tools
at death or marriage of my wife; negro Sam to stay on the plantation for
the Support of my wife and my children by her
extrs: sons JESSE & BENJAMIN
wit: DANL. SOUTHERLAND JUNR., JOSEPH T. RHODES
signed: Jacob Brown

75. BROWN, JOHN (CR.035.801.2/A-42)
4 Apr 1801 - Apr Term 1801
wife plantation whare on I now Live & the plantation tooles; dau. MARY
all the stock of Cattle & hogs marked in a mark for her; wife LIDEA all
Stocks of cattle & hogs and all the rest of my hole Estate; son HOWEL my
bay maire when he comes to mature age; if wife Shall marrey she shall
have one third part of my Land Dureing her life and residue of estate
divided between the rest of my Children [not named] Excepting MARY & HOWEL;
son HOWEL & dau. MARY 10 pds each at wife's marrag or Decas; sons HOWEL
& JOHN 300 acres adj. my plantation where on I now Live; at wife's marrage
or Death residue of estate sold & money Divided between dau. SARY & sons
FELEX & FREDRECK
extr: BENJAMIN LANIER JUN.
wit: JOAB FOUNTAIN, JESSE $\mathcal{F}$ LANIER JUNIR, ZULPHE $\mathbf{\xi}$ LANIER
                                        signed: John $\mathcal{O}$ Brown

76. BROWN, NANCY (CR.035.801.2)
4 Apr 1834 - Oct Term 1836
grandson AMOS B. WALLER whole estate
extrs: HOWEL BROWN & JOHN HALSO
wit: JOHN HALSO, HOSEA LANIER, ALLEN LANIER
                    signed: Nancy $\curlywedge$ Brown

77. BROWN, SALLY (CR.035.801.2/1-45)
20 Feb 1822 - Nov Term 1833
negro Grace taken care of out of estate; sister PATIENCE BROWN & her Heirs
balance of my estate
extr: JOHN FARRIER
wit: ISHAM ARMSTRONG, SOLOMAN SOUTHERLAND
signed: Sarah Brown

78. BRYAN, NEEDHAM (CR.035.801.2/3-40)
2 May 1840 - Oct Term 1861
wife MARGARETTE JANE negroes Isaac, Premis, Silar, Esther, Alexander, Evan,
Joseph, Clarisa, Jacob, Dilsa & Petar, stock of Horses hogs & Cattle, household & kitchen furniture, working tools, all my Crop, all my land
extrx: wife MARGARETTE
wit: WILEY STALLINGS, WILLIAM BYRD, WILLIAM MURPHY
[see CODICIL on next page]

codicil: 28 Feb 1858
to wife in addition to what is given to her in will negro Harriet & a lot of
land in the corporate limits of the Town of Magnolia I lately bought of
Messes Merriman & Newbury
wit: C. TATE MURPHY, JAS. W. WELLS
signed: Needham Bryan

79. BRYAN, RIGDON (CR.035.801.2/A-11)
23 Jan 1793 - Apr Term 1793
CATHERINE, dau. of ROBERT DICKSON deceased negro Juno & her youngest child;
brother KEDAR's 2 youngest children, sister CHARLOTTE WHITFIELD's 2 youngest
children & my Sister ESTHER CURTISS two youngest children the whole of my
remaining estate
extrs: brother KEDAR & LEWIS WHITFIELD
wit: WM. MCANNE, EDWARD ARMSTRONG, JOHN DICKSON
signed: Rigdon Bryan

80. BRYANT, JACOB (CR.035.801.2/A-34)
1 Sep 1828 - Nov Term 1828
wife MARY land on the south Side of Island creek & all on this Side of the
Creek, the Powel Place & JOHN ALLAN place adj. the creek for her natural
life, all stock, tools, house & Kitchen furniture except what is to be Sold
to defray expense for the Schooling & Raising my Small Children, 1 bed &
furniture, negro Tuff & her three children John, Isaac & baby & Chaney
at my mother's decease; son WILLIAM land at wife's decease along with the
LEVIN ALLIN place; son DAVID land on North Side of Island creek except my
LEVEN ALLIN place, negro Linda Meriah, 1 bed & furniture now in his possession
at his Grandmother's, all stock, huse whole & Kitchen furniture at his
grand Mother's decease; dau. MARY bed & furniture now in hir possession &
negro Molsey; dau. ELIZABETH negro Hepsey Jane at hir grandmother's deceas,
1 bed & furniture whin departs the family; dau. EASTER negro Charity, 1 bed
& furniture whin depart the family; dau. ANNE or NANCY negro Stephen Gilbert,
1 bed & furniture when she depart the family; dau. CATHRIN JANE negro Kitty
Ann, 1 bed & furniture when she departs the family; son WILLIAM S. SPARKS
aforementioned negro Jerry, one bed & furniture when he departs the family;
dau. SUSANNAH 1 bed & furniture when She departs the family & one negro if
any of the wenches now left in the life dower [of the widow] Should have any
child & if not she to have negro John
extr: friend DAVID SLOAN
wit: JOHN MCANN, MARGARET ᛞ BRIANT
signed: Jacob Bryan

81. BUCKMAN, GUY E. "of the District of Warsaw" (CR.035.801.2/2-90)
17 Jan 1854 - Oct Term 1854
wife BRUNETTE the Lot & House and appurtenances Situated thereon lying in
the District of Warsaw; son CHARLE G. $5; son GEORGE L. $5
extr: not named
wit: CURTIS C. OATES, NORRIS FREDERECK
signed: Guy E. Buckman

82. BURCH, JOSEPH "Planter" (CR.035.801.2/A-56)
25 Aug 1765 - no probate
executors to sell 200 acres on the head of Baremarsh to pay debts; wife
ANN all Others of my Lands, household Goods and Creatures of Every Sort
as I am Possest With or Do Own; and at her death Estate to be Equally
Devided amongst my Dear Beloved Children CHARLES, ARAMINTY, RICHARD,
JOSEPH, JOHN, CHRISTOPHER & BENJAMIN
extrs: URIAH BLANSHARD, JOHN GIBBS
wit: URH. BLANSHARD, JOHN GIBBS, KATHERINE TALER [?]
                    signed: Joseph JB Burch

83. BYRD, JOHN (CR.035.801.2/A-57)
5 Feb 1761 - 12 May 1761
son JOHN 100 acres with the Plantation whearon I now Live, negro Lue,
1 cow & yearlin, 1 horse colt Named Major; son MICHAEL negro Fillis,
1 cow & Yearling, 1 Rifle Gun, 1 mare cold Named Murih; dau. BETHTHIOH
1 meluter named Cloe, 2 cows & yearlins; dau. SELAH first child that my
negro Pat shall have to Live to be Two years, 2 cows & Calfs; wife
CATHRINE negro Pat and all the remaining part of my estate except Twelf
sows and pigs & my other Negroes that is not yet mentioned which are to be
Equily Devided between my fore Children
extrs: MICHAEL KING, EDWARD BYRD
wit: JOHN YARBROUGH, GEORGE BELLE
signed: John Byrd

84. CANADY, JOSEPH (CR.035.801.3)
nuncupative will
proved by JOSEPH BRAY & MARTHA JAMES Dec 31, 1793 before JOSEPH DICKSON,
Justice; stated that Canady died on Dec. 30 and that he wished his wife
JEAN to have the land & plantation whereon he then Dwelt for life and at
her death the land to be Eaqually the property of sons ARCHIBALD & DAVID

85. CANNADY, PATRICK (CR.035.801.3/A-87)
16 Mar 1761 - Aug Court 1761
eldest son PATRICK 100 acres with ye plantation whereon I now [dwell],
1 feather Bed and furniture, 3 puter plates, 2 gallon Basons & a Large
puter Dish, 1 Black Cow & Calf, 1 Red hide Yearling, ye Largest Iron pott,
a Ewe & Lamb, a sett of Iron Wedges; eldest dau. ELISABETH 200 acres the
remainder of the land I left son PATRICK, a Cow & Calf called his own &
white Cows Yearling heifer, 1 Yew & Lamb & young Ewe with her second Lamb,
a new Dutch flax wheal that is Call'd her's, 6 head of Geese, 3 puter
plates, 1 Dish, 1 Gallon Bason, Doz. of Spoons, 2 Sows & pigs, 10 pds
Proc. money to be paid her at ye day of Marrage; dau. SARRAH 100 acres
on ye north side of hose Swamp, a new Linnen Dutch wheal Call'd hers, white
Cow & Black side heifer yearling, 6 head of Gease, a young Ewe & Lamb, 3
plates, a Dish, a gallon Basan & Dozen of Spoons, a Box Iron that is now
new & heeter, 1 Gallon & half Iron pott, 2 sows & pigs, 10 pds proc. money
to be paid out ye Day of Marriage; son ALIXANDER 100 acres in ye fork of
Hoes Swamp and wolf branch, 4 Gallon pots, 3 puter plates & 2 Gallan Basons,
a Dish & feather Bed that is now Begun & is to be fill'd up to fourty weight
with furniture Sufficient, 2 Ewes & Lambs, [?] Cow & Calf & 10 pd. proc.
money; dau. ABIGAIL 100 acres adj. WILLM DRAKE, 1 Dutch flax wheal, 2
Bason & Dozen of Spoons, 6 head of Geese, Cow & Caft, & 20 pds proc. money;
if any dau. should die with out heirs her share to go to son ALIXANDER;
negro Tom & 2 horses, a mare & yearling colt to be sold; wife ABIA Riding

horse, Bridle & Saddle, 8 yds of fine silk, 3 yds. of Double holon, my
own silver Shoebuckells, 3 pds proc money
extrs: wife ABIA & brother JOSHUA
wit: WM. CLARKE, DEMZEY CANADAY, SAMUEL TINDALL
signed: Patrick Canady

86. CANNON, HENRY (CR.035.801.3/A-89)
12 Feb 1781 - Apr Court 1781
son DAVID all my Lands & Clames of Lands, 1 hors Known by the Name of Driver,
one two year old Leapord Mare; wife MARY all stock of horses, Cattle, hogs
& sheep, household goods & Slaves During her Life and then to be Equally
Devided among My Children [not named]
extrs: JOHN GIBS, son DAVID
wit: JOHN WRIGHT, WM. TAYLOR, DAVID CANNON
signed: Henry Cannon

87. CARLTON, PETER (CR.035.801.3/2-19)
13 May 1840 - no probate
wife ELIZABETH 607 acres my home plantation or house lot lying on both
sides of Stewards Creek, negroes Ben, Bildad, Julia, Silva & Susan, all
stock of horses, cattle, hogs & sheep, my saddles & bridles, all money,
notes & accounts except $300, all my crops & all my Books requesting her
to give my relation THOMAS CARLTON some of them; MARY, my nephew ISAAC
CARLTON's wife money from the sale of 150 acres lying on Murrays branch
near Beasley's mill pond; MARY E., dau. of ISAAC & MARY CARLTON $300;
nephew JESSE CARLTON negro Irvin or money from his sale; nephew HARDY
CARLTON JUNR. negro Sam; niece TEMPY, wife of MURPHEY LENYEAR negro Joe;
niece NANCY, wife of GEORGE ALDERMAN negro Nance; niece PHEBE, wife of
SHADRCH WELLS negro Jinney; JOHN CARLTON, THOMAS CARLTON, RACHEL ROGERS,
ANN GILSTRAP & LYDIA MATTHIS each a share of the land formerly belonging to
my Father in law THOMAS CARLTON and MARTHA his wife they being the sons and
Daughters of the aforesaid THOMAS and MARTHA; brothers DAVID, ISAAC, LEWIS
& HARDY money from the sale of 200 acres on the warters of the Persimmon
called the Mallard tract, 50 acres called the JOHN SELLERS tract & 263 acres
called the JACOB MATTHIS tract; wife ELIZABETH Household & kitchen Furniture,
Farming utentials, tools of all kinds, waggons and carte geer, grindstone;
750 acre Red house tract to be sold and money to be divided into 4 shares;
1/4 to JAMES PEARSAL, JEREMIAH PEARSAL, JAMES MIDDLETON, JOHN FURLOW &
JAMES LARKIN Trustees in trust to erect and build a Meeting hous or place of
worship for the use of the congregation of the Methodist Episcopal Church
on a lot of ground given me for that purpose; 1/4 to the Treasurer of the
missionary society of the methodist episcopal Church for the spread of the
gospel amongst the heathen; 1/4 to the N. C. annual conference of the
methodist episcopal Church for the support of the superanuated preachers &
the poor widows of said conference; 1/4 put out at Interest forever & the
Interest to be appropriated and applied annually for the purpose of educating
the poor children that appears to have no other way or means of being educated
within a circle of at least six miles every way around the meeting house lot
extrs: JAMES PEARSAL Esqr, JEREMIAH PEARSAL Esqr.
wit: EDWARD C. GAVIN, ANCRAM A. BOYETT
signed: Peter Carlton
codacil: 28 Jul 1841
as I have sold the JOHN SELLERS tract containing 50 acres I wish my Executors

not to meddle or interfere with the afore said land
wit: EDWARD C. GAVIN, ANCRAM A. BOYETT
signed: Peter Carlton
Codacel: 14 May 1845
as I have sold the land on Murrays branch near Beasley's Mill pond containing
150 acres and the Mallard tract on the warters of the Persimmon containing
200 acres I wish my Executors not to middle with that, only look to my wife
ELIZABETH for the principle of the money
wit: EDWARD C. GAVIN, ANCRAM A. BOYETT
signed: Peter Carlton

88. CARLTON, THOMAS "of the Parish of St. Gabriel" (CR.035.801.3/A-69)
7 Sep 1795 - Oct Term 1795
daus. RACHEL, ANNA, ELIZABETH & LYDDA 15 pds a piece; son JOHN 100 pds.;
wife MARTHA residue of estate for her life; at her death youngest sons
STEPHEN to have all the land on this side of Murrows branch & THOMAS all
the land on the other side; son THOMAS 20 pds.
extrs: MARTHA CARLTON, JOHN CARLTON
wit: AUSTIN BEESLEY, JOHN CARLTON, MARTHA CARLTON
signed: Thomas Carlton

89. CARR, JAMES (CR.035.801.3/A-64)
1 Aug 1796 - Oct Term 1796
wife SUSANNAH negroes Fortune, Namoa, Roze & Hagar, my Sorrel Mare, a
Rideing Chair that is Making at THOMAS FINDLYs, my Chair Harness, 1 Feather
Bed and furniture, the whole of the Land and Plantation Whereon I now live
During her Natural Life; at her death land to be Equally Divided Between
sons OSBURN & JOHN; sons OSBURN & JOHN & dau. NANCY all the Rest of my
Negroes; wife a child's part of my Hogs & Sheep; remainder of Sheep,
Gees & Hogs, Household furniture & plantation tools be sold if necessary
for the Immediate Benifit of Raising my Children; dau. NANCY or ANN to
have 60 pds when she reaches age 21 or when she marries; when any
appertunity admits of a School in the Neighborhood and my Children be
capable of Going from home that they be then Sent Such as are of an age
sufficient for to Recieve Instruction & at the age of twelve years my
executors Board them at School abroad and not Board them out from home
younger; executors to act as guardians to children until they reach the
age of fourteen years
extrs: Friends ROBERT SLOANE, & ANDREW McINTIRE
wit: JOSEPH DICKSON, JNO. HOLDON, JOHN CARR
signed: James Carr

90. CARR, JOHN (CR.035.801.3/A-90)
1 Sep 1823 - Oct Term 1823 [original badly damaged]
wife ELIZABETH the old plantation from the line between WILLIAM CARR & my
own unto a line Including part of a track Bought of WILLIAM CARR adj. the
avenue, the Swamp & the Island ditch Encluding part of the Bunting land
for her natural life and then to my youngest son OBED, use of all Cattle,
hogs, sheep, house hould and Kitchen furniture, Plantation tools, the cart
& one yoke of oxen, my old Riding chear & harness, negroes Tom, Sharp,
Lemon, Andrew, old Nanney, Cloe, Silva & Adey and at hir decease they to
be divided between my 3 daus. SUSANNA, LIVENA & ELIZABETH except for Adey;

son WILLIAM the remainging part of my island field bounded by JOHN & OBED, 100 acres patent taken out by myself so. side Maxfile swamp to the fork of the branch, below the bridge, one cow & calf, one bed and furniture, one sow & pigs; dau. LIVINA negro Dina, one cow & calf, one bed & furniture and her part of Adey; dau. ELIZABETH negro Moses, one cow & calf, one bed & furniture and her part of Adey; son OBED one cow & calf, one bed & furniture, one sow and pig; crop of turpentine with all the surplus and necessary stock or crop & negroe Old Isaac sold to pay debts; wife ELlZABETH young horses and bay mare and she to draw the expenses of schooling my young children out of my estate; remaining stock to be sold and money divided amongst my children except DAVID who has his share already; son DAVID negro Frank, one horse, two sows and pigs, six head of sheep, one bed & furniture, $200 cash; dau. BARBRA MALLARD negro Ming specially given already unto her, one mare, one cow & calf, 2 sows & pigs, two ewes & lambs, one bed and furniture all new in her possession; dau. MARY GREER negro Jack, one cow & calf, one barren cow, two sows & pigs, one bed & furniture, $210.18 cash; son BARNET land he now lives on, one horse, one cow & calf, one sow & pigs, one bed & furniture, all new in his possession; son JAMES 2 tracts of land bought from Teachey and Allin containing 344 acres, 1/2 of negro Young Isaac, one bed & furniture, one cow and calf when departs the family; son JACOB the peace of new ground in my island whare he has begun to clear from the slew between it & my island field bought at shff sale containing 100 acres, part of a tract bot from Thally adj. Thally and Williams south of Maxwell Swamp, RICHARD CHASTEN, over the Indian Graves branch, the pond at the head of urethego meadow or march, Teachey, 1/2 of negro Young Isaac, one cow and calf when departs the family, one bed and furniture, one sow and pigs, $50, two surveys patented by myself & HENRY ROUSE now occupied by sd. Rouse containing 250 acres as in & unto sd. HENRY ROUSE for to occupy and reserve & injoy for the space of seven years; sons JAMES & JACOB a sum out of my estate perportinable to them for the sums imposed on them for the suport of the family; son JOSEPH the remaining part of my Thally land east ward of the dividing line, negro Aaron, one filley mare, one bed and furniture, one sow and pigs, a patent peace on the south side Maxwell Swamp bounded by the big run of Maxwell Swamp & Harrel & Chastin lines at Harrel's Ford; dau. SUSANNA negro Nanny, dau. of old nanny, her part of Adey, one cow and calf when she departs the family; son JOHN the other portion of my island field
extrs: son JAMES & worthy friend JOHN McCANN
wit: WM. CARR JUNR, JOSEH CARR
signed: John Carr

91. CARR, JOSEPH (CR.035.801.3/A-73)
4 Feb 1777 - Jan Court 1781
wife BARBARY the Management of my whole Estate both Lands & Moveble during her Widowhood for the Good of my Children [not named] and at her Marriage all my Lands Houses & Plantation shall Immediately devolve to my 3 sons JAMES, WILLIAM & JOHN; PETER MORRIS 5 shillings
extrs: Friends ROBERT DICKSON & HUGH MCANNE
wit: THOS ROUTLEDGE, ANDW **A** WALLACE, MARY BONEY
signed: Josep **F** Carr

28

92. CARR, JOSEPH (CR.035.801.3/2-106)
14 Aug 1856 - Oct Term 1856
nephew JOSEPH H., son of OZBORN CARR 100 acres on the east side of Miry
Branch adj. JOHN CARR & HALSTED BOURDENS; sister-in-law LIVINA CARR negro
Eley; residue sold and $100 to be applied to the payment of a debt incurred
by the Grove Church (Presbytirian) in erecting the New Church at Kenansville;
remaining money divided into 8 parts; 1/8 part to WILLIAM & JAMES, sons of
my sister ANN CARRELL; 1/8 to sister ISABELLA, wife of OZBORN CARR; 1/8
to WILLIAM D. CARR & LUCY SOUTHERLAND, children of my deceased brother DAVID;
1/8 part to sister BETSEY, wife of JOHN HOWARD; 1/8 to WILLIAM, JOSEPH &
JOHN, sons of my dec'd brother WILLIAM; 1/8 to sister DORITHY, wife of
ELIJAH CROSBY of Ohio; 1/8 to MARGARET, wife of EDWD HALL & dau. of my
deseased Sister MARY McCANNE; 1/8 to LUCY ANN, wife of JOHN CARR MALLARD,
MARGARET, wife of ROBERT CARRELL and the surviving Children of MARY JANE
BONEY
extrs: nephews WILLIAM D. CARR & JOSEPH H. CARR
wit: JAMES DICKSON, G. S. CARR
signed: Joseph Carr

93. CARR, WM. (SS Wills/DRB2)
5 Dec 1753 - Oct Court 1754
wife HANNAH 1/3 part of all my Moveable Estate, the Houses & plantation
where I now live to Such times as my Son ARCHBALD CARR comes to ye Age of
Twenty one Years and then to be his for Ever; remaining 2/3 to children
ARCHBALD, JANE & ye one that is yet unborn
extr: not named
wit: JOHN DICKSON, WILLIAM MccREE, SUSANNA MccALEXDR.
signed: William Car

94. CARR, WILLIAM (CR.035.801.3/2-3)
21 Apr 1842 - Jan Term 1846
wife LINDA all my property of every discription that she may use it to hir
own support and to the support and Education of my Children [not named]
extrs: brothers JOSEPH & OZBORN
wit: not named
signed: W. Carr

95. CARRILL, JOHN SENOR (CR.035.801.3/A-84)
12 Jan 1761 - 23 Mar 1761
wife MARY my Whole Estate; son JOHN plantation Whearon I Now Live after
the Death or Entar Marage of His Mother; all my Moveable Estate to Be
Equaly Devided amongst my Children JOHN, JOSEPH, DARIOS & RACHEL; one Bay
Hors Known By the Name of Galant sould & the price Equaly Divided as the
Rest of my Estate
extrs: wife MARY & son JOHN
wit: DEMPSEY BENTON, JOHN ⨍ BARKER, HENRY HOLLINGSWORTH
signed: John Carrill

96. CARROLL, JAMES G. (CR.035.801.3/3-89)
16 Sep 1852 - Apr Term 1864
brother WILLIAM C all my interest in negroes Jo, Alec, Easther & Sophia
extr: cousen GIBSON CARR
wit: ROBT. B. CARR, JOSEPH H. CARR
signed: James G. Carroll

97. CARTER, EDWARD "of New Hanover Precinct" (SS Wills)
23 Mar 1735/6 - 10 May 1736
Plantation and Tract of Land I Now Live upon on East side of the No. East
branch of Cape faire River be sold by my Executor in Conjunction with my
Eldest Grandson WILLIAM who shall Emediately upon the Sale Receive his share
and the Other Two shares to be Lodged in the Hands of my Executor for the use
of my Grand Children EDWD & SOLOMON till they be of the age of 21; grandchildren WILLIAM, EDWD, and SOLOMON money from the sale of three fourths of
all my Cattle; grdau. THOMASIN the other fourth Part of all my Cattle my
[rid]ing mare the feather Bed She Now Lies on, what Pewter I have and One
Half of all the Hoggs, Likewise sum other things such as the Chairs, the
Table and a Pott and the Chest; negro man Peter be free for himself and I
Thereby Publish and Decleare him free from the moment of my Death unto the
space of sixty years and that none of my Heirs no my Executor shall have any
Power Over him and in Consideration of his faithfull Service he shall have
and Enjoy all the Catle and Hoggs Now Runing with Mine that have of Long
Crop in Each Ear as also a Cow unmarkt and if he Pleasent During the forsd
Term of Sixty years may Settle upon and Occupy the Part of my forsd. Tract
of Land Lying beyond the Branch to the East ward of the Plantation also all
my wearing apperrell together with and ax & hoe Delivered to him as Soon as
I Die
extr: Friend Mr. WILLIAM GRAY
wit: ARMOND DE ROSSET M. Drs., BERRIAH GRANT, PHILEMON MCINTOSH
                                         signed: Edward   Carter

98. CARTER, EDWD. JOHN JAS. AUGUST (CR.035.801.3/A-86)
25 Jun 1779 - Apr Court 1783 & Jul Court 1783
wife RACHEL 4 Cows & Calves, 1 Midle Sized pot, 1 Large Bason, 1 poringer;
son GEORGE GREEN all my Lands and Improvements, 9 Cows & Eight Calves, 2 pots,
2 small pewter Basons, 1/2 Dozen of pewter spoons; wife to Endeavour to
Exchange the old Cows for Young Breding Cattle and that she use Every Endeavour
to have her son Instructed in Reading, Writing and figures
extrs: wife RACHELL & JAMES GILLESPIE
wit: WILLIAM SOUTHERLAND, WEST SHUFFIELD
             signed: Edwd. Jno. Jams. Augt.   Carter

99. CARY, ELISABETH (CR.035.801.3/2-35)
19 Jan 1843 - Jul Term 1848
nephue JAMES, eldest son of DRUCY HALL 86 acres Including the house where I
now live on the east side of the North East River
extr: DRUCY HALL
wit: H. WILLIAMS, HIRAM STALLINGS
signed: Elizabeth Carey

100. CAVENAUGH, SILVESTER (CR.035.801.3/A-63)
23 Apr 1799 - Jul Term 1799
son WILLIAM 105 acres at the Newe field where I Now Live, 1 Mare, 5 Breding
Sows, 1 Black hefer & Calf, 1 Brinded hefer with Calf, 1 white backed hefer,
1 Black Cow and yearling, 3 ewes & lambs, 1 black Barren ewe, one bed and
bedsteed and firniture that I now Lie on, 1 Carplow, 1 Musket, fore plats,
one dish, 1 Bason, one big pot, one Skilit, 1 lumb, 1 good ax, 1 good grubing
how, 1 fluke, 1 Smuthing iron, 3 newe Cheears & the use of my Carte; son JAMES
100 acres at the old field, 1 horse Colt, 5 breeding Sows, 1 black white fast

hefer and calf, 1 white hefer with Calf, one pide hefer, 1 white Cow,
1 Red bool yearling, 3 ewes & Lambs, 1 black Barren ewe, one bed and bedsteed and firniture, 1 shotgun, foare plats, one Bason, 1 Small pot, one
Lining wheel, 1 wooling wheel, 1 new ax, 1 good grubing hoe, 1 fluke, two
Iron wedges, 3 newe Cheares, 1 parsel of new feathers and gees lent to fill
his bed; Indentured Servent FEDRICK BOWIN 2 Breeding Sows, a ewe and lamb .
extr: DANIEL MURRAY
wit: ISAAC ⚡ JAMES, DANIEL MURRAY
                    signed: Silvister ⤬ Cavenaugh

101. CHAMBERS, CHARLES (CR.035.801.3/3-44)
25 Aug 1858 - Jan Term 1862
son DAVID FRANCIS all my Lands on Goshen including the plantation whereon I
now live & a Small piece bought from JAMES PEARSALL, 1 Bed and furniture,
1 Horse, negro Joe; dau. ELIZA SHEPARD & her dau. MARY negroes Jinny &
Eveline, 1 Bed and furniture which they have heretofore received; dau.
MARGARET MURRAY & her Children [not named] negroes Mareah & Rachel, one Bed
& furniture which they have heretofore recieved; dau. MARY JANE WILLIAMS
& her children [not named] negro Sally & her children Edgar, Kate, John &
an infant name not Known, One Bed and furniture, $630 now in her possession;
daus. DOLLY & SUSAN a Share of my Negroes each equal in Value to the portion
given my daus. MARGARET & ELIZA; remainder of negroes to be divided into
4 lots and drawn by MARGARET MURRAY, DOLLY EDWARDS, SUSAN CHAMBERS and
son DAVID F. in trust for my dau. ELIZA & her dau. MARY
extrs: friend JAMES DICKSON & son DAVID F.
wit: JOSEPH PEARSALL, JERE PEARSALL
                    signed: Charles ⤞ Chambers

102. CHASON, RICHARD (CR.035.801.3/A-67)
14 Mar 1788 - Apr Term 1788
wife AGNESS all the land Below the little Branch above The plantation adj.
ROBERT DICKSON, the sd. Branch, the Swamp, the new footway to my Back line,
During her widowhood; son JOSEPH to live on land with his mother should he
marry, to have the young mare by the name of his, all the Cattle & hogs In
his mark, 1 feather bed & furniture, my Steeltrap & Rifle Gun; residue of
Cattle, hogs & Sheep & other property to wife & three young Children BENAJAH,
WILLIAM & MARY; son RICHARD all the Remaining part of my land above Sd.
Branch, all the Cattle & hogs in his mark, twoo mairs Now by the name of
his, my large Cittle & My Smouth bour Gun
extrs: wife AGNES & son JOSEPH
wit: WM. ⟊ HALL, JOHN ⤳ CRANFORD
not signed

103. CHERRY, WILLIS (CR.035.801.3/A-79)
12 Oct 1800 - Oct Term 1801
wife SARAH 1 Feather bead and furniture, 1 mare, negro Luse, 2 cows & calvs,
1/3 of my plantation whare I now live for her widdowhood; at her death or
marrag property except land to my daus. MARY BENNETT, ELIZABEH MILLARD,
REBECCA, NANCY, & SALLY PACEY; son GORGE all my nanuel plantaion whare I
now live Except a pece of land I devise to my son LAMUEL adj. LAMBS CHERREYS;
son WILLIAM plantation I Bought of JOHN BRADLEY liing on the southside of the
Ary Pond Branch; son GORGE at age 21 shall pay son WILLIAM 100 silver dollars

son WILLIAM Nigro Harry; son LAMBE Nigro Lewis; son GORE Nigro Bob; dau.
REBECCA 1 Feather Bed and furniture, 1 mare to about the price of $80, 2 cows
& calvs; dau. NANCY 1 Feather Bed and furniture, 1 mare to about the price
of $80, 2 cows & calvs; dau. SALLY 1 Feather Bed and furniture, 1 mare to
about the price of $80, 2 cows & calvs; dau. PATIENTS 1 Feather Bed and
furniture, 1 mare to about the price of $80, 2 cows & calvs; sons WILLIAM
& GORCE 1 horse creater a piece at the price of $80; sons LAMB, WILLIAM &
GORGE Each of them a feather Biad and Furniture
extrs: HARDY BIZZELL & LAMUEL CHERRY
wit: HARDY BIZZELL, WILLIAM CHERREY, REBICKA CHERREY
                                    signed: Willis 𝒲 Cherry

104. CHESTNUTT, GAVIN L. (CR.035.801.3/2-97)
12 Nov 1855 - Jan Term 1856
wife ANN 2 cows, 1 Horse Cart, my beds, bed-clothing, House-hold & kitchen
furniture, cooking utinsils, 17 1/2 acres with the House I now live in
Known as the Fussell Place and at her death to my children JOHN K., GRANTUM F.,
EDWARD G., MARY J., NANCY E. & SARAH W.; 2 lots in the town of Stricklandsville containing 1/2 acres each & 2 Horse Carts sold to pay debts & surplus
divided among my several children; Barden lot to be divided and sold
seperately
extr: friend THOMAS S. FAISON
wit: B. WHITEHEAD, THOS. E. SHEPARD
                    signed: Gavin L. ✕ Chestnutt

105. CLARK, ARCHIBALD (CR.035.801.3/A-76)
6 Mar 1770 - no probate
wife ALICE my Black Horse, 1 Feather Bed and Furniture, 1 Spining wheel;
residue of estate left after debts are paid to be divided by my Wife and all
my Brothers and Sisters [not named]
extr: Brother JOHN
wit: THO GRAY, GEORGE FRAZAR, MICHAEL KING JUNR.
signed: Archd. Clark

106. CLARK, DIANA (CR.035.801.3/A-90)
16 Sep 1821 - May Term 1828
grandson ALBERT HICKS 1 Feather Bed and Furniture; residue of estate
devided into three shares with one share to be given my daus. NANCY
FREDERICK & PATSEY FAISON and the children of my dau. FANNY SHAW
extrs: sons ISHAM FAISON & ELIAS FAISON
wit: MARY ELIOT, JOHN ELIOT JNR
signed: Diana Clak

107. CLARK, JOHN (A-82)
16 Apr 1767 - Aug Term 1767 & Jul Term 1796
negroes Maria & Phillis sold & money divided equally among my seven oldest
children WILLIAM, ARCHEBOLD, JOHN, LEWIS, ELIZABETH, DANIEL & NATHAN; negro
Violet to be kept for my four youngest children BENJAMIN, DAVID, PENELOPE &
JAMES until the youngest of the four comes of age and then she and her increase
to be equally divided among the four; son BENJAMIN one cow & calf; son JAMES
one cow & calf; all my children the cattle in a common way therein which
the oldest boys knows to be whether in a mark of their own or in my proper
mark; rest of my stock of cattle, horses & meares, hogs & sheep, all moveable
with all my house hold goods, Beds & furniture, putter, pots, still & worms

and everything that is mine about the plantation or elsewhere to be sold and
money equally divided among all my children; dau. ELIZABETH a linen wheel
& a woolen wheel; youngest boys DAVID & JAMES the plantation I now live one,
the lower portion to DAVID adj. the run in panther Swamp to where the little
branch goes through the field, up the east branch through the piney woods
& to JAMES the upper part with the houses, orchards and other conveniences
thereunto at the mouth of the little branch that divides the field on panther
swamp; brother JOHN care of my son JAMES; cousin DUNCAN care of my son
DAVID; cousin GILBERT to raise my youngest dau.; 3 youngest children to
have 2 to 10 pds a year; oldest dau. to have the care of my sons DANIEL &
ARCHEBOLD; son NATHAN to have the care of my son WILLIAM
extrs: sons JOHN & ARCHEBOLD & cousin GILBERT CLARK "living on Barbecue
        Creek south side of the Norwest"
wit: ROBERT BYRD, GILBERT ✝ McCALLOP, WILLIAM CLARK
signed: John Clark

108. COLE, ROBERT (CR.035.801.3/A-74)
28 Jan 1829 - Feb Term 1829
son ROBERT all my household & Kitchen furniture; son THOMAS 5 pds; grson.
JAMES 240 acres in the Back woods; grdau. SEBBRIENA LANDEN $10; grdau.
ELISABETH $10; son ROBERT the rest of my Estate
extrs: JOHN FARIOR, son ROBERT
wit: JOHN FARIOR, ABRAHAM ANDREWS
signed: Robert Cole Senr.

109. COLE, THOMAS (CR.035.801.3)
15 Oct 1840 - Jan Term 1841
wife [not named] 1 wooling wheel, 1 pare of cards, 1 Closetub; dau. SARY
150 acres including the plantation where I now live; LIEUZAR, CUTNEY, RACHEL
JOSEPH, SOLOMON, NIXON, PRICILAH & my dau. NANCEY's children [not named] &
my dau. CLERKEY's Eldest sone JAMES COLE the rest of my lands Except 3 acres
including the Mill House and dam as it now Stands; daus. SEBRINIA LANDIN &
ELIZABETH BRINSON $80 each; my mill, mill irons, Saw mill & Saw mill irons
and all the utentials belonging to both and the three acres of land where the
mill Set and all the rest of my estate sold to pay my just debts and the
remainder of the money divided amongst the hole of my heirs except POLEY
BONEY, NANCY MEREDY & CLERKY COLE their parts all Except fifty Cents Each
to be put to the use of Schooling their Children
extr: JOHN J. JAMES Esqr
wit: B. B. WHITE, F. PICKETT
signed: Thomas Cole

110. CONERLY, JOHN (CR.035.801.3)
13 Jun 1839 - Jul Term 1839
son JOHN all the land Whereon my mother now lives lying on the South Side
of Poly Bridge Branch
extr: not named
wit: L. F. WILLIAMS, RICHARD 🐺 WOLF
                        signed: John 🖋 Conarly

111. CONNERLY, CULLIN (CR.035.801.3/A-70)
11 Nov 1811 - Jan Term 1812
wife TELESHE the plantation and House Where I now live, all working tools,
3 Mares and 2 Colts, 6 Cows & Calves, Stock of Sheep, negroes Moses, Easter,
Jim, Charles, Cesar, Willis, Bob, Zenos & Clary; son JOHN all my Lands
lying on the North Side of Poly Bridge Branch with 1/2 of the Tract purchased of JOHN BLOUNT lying Above the fork of said Branch only Reserving
such part of said lands as Mill Overflows with the priviledge of Grinding
his own Grain in Said Mill Toll free as long as he helps to Keep Said Mill
in Repair, 1 Bed and furniture, 1 Cow and Calf, 1 Horse Bridle & Saddle,
2 head of Sheep; son OWEN the $450 I paid Towards the lands he Now lives
one, 1 Horse Bridle & Saddle, 1 Bed & furniture, 1 Cow and Calf, 2 head of
Sheep; son WILLIAM tract of Land I purchased of SAMUEL STANFORD, 1 Horse
Bridle and Saddle, 1 Bed and furniture, 1 Cow and Calf, 2 head of Sheep;
son LUKE all my Lands on the South Side of the Poly Bridge Branch Including
the Lands I Bought of ROBERT BYRD & 1/2 of the tract I purchased of JOHN
BLOUNT lying Above the fork of Poly Bridge Branch, 1 Horse Bridle & Saddle,
1 Bed and furniture, 1 Cow and Calf, the Blacksmith Tools, my Still, 2 head
of Sheep; dau. POLLY GUY negro Dinah, 1 Bed and furniture, 2 Cows and Calves,
one Womans Saddle, 2 head of Sheep; dau. TULITHA LAWS negro Rose, 1 Bed
and furniture, 2 Cows and Calves, one Womans Saddle, 2 head of Sheep; dau.
FRANCES DUNKIN negro Ginny, 1 Bed and furniture, 2 Cows and Calves, one
Womans Saddle, 2 head of Sheep; dau. SUSAN PAGE negro Lucy, 1 Bed and
furniture, 2 Cows and Calves, one Womans Saddle, 2 head of Sheep; dau. CHELLY
BLOUNT negro Rachel, 1 Bed and Furniture, 2 Cows and Calves, 2 head of Sheep,
$14 in Lieu of the Womans Saddle; dau. BETSY negroes Doll & Sinah, 1 Bed
and furniture, Two Cows & Calves, 1 Womans Saddle, 2 head of Sheep; after
wife's Decease JOHN to have negro Jim, OWEN to have negro Charles, WILLIAM
to have negro Cesar, LUKE to have negro Moses and they to pay my 6 daus.
$400; residue of negroes to be divided among daus. each getting 1/6 part,
only dau. POLLY GUY is to have 1/3 part of a 1/6 part, the other 2/3 to go
to her 2 children, JOHN & LITHA, by her first husband WM. BENNIT
extrs: sons JOHN & LUKE
wit: D. WRIGHT, ALFRED BECK, LEWIS DICKSON
signed: Culen Conerly

112. COOK, HENRY (CR.035.801.3)
27 Jan 1843 - Apr Term 1843
friend JAMES CARR SENIOR $100; Mrs. LAVINIA CARR 1 note on DAVID SLOAN;
my Relations (the heirs of MARY HULETTE) $1; JAMES OWEN CARR the ballance
of all my property
extr: friend JAMES CARR SENR.
wit: SUSAN JANE McCANNE, DAVID ⤳ ROUSE JR.
                          signed: Henry ⨉ Cook

113. COOK, JOHN SENAR (CR.035.801.3/A-77)
12 Feb 1788 - Apr Term 1788
sons HENRAY & LEWIS plantation and land on which I live with the upper portion
where I live belonging to LEWIS with my wife CATRIN to have peaceful possession
dureing hur natural life; son JOHN 150 acres on Iland Creek; wife CATHRIN
1 gray mare named fance; son HENREY to have the remainder of the horses when
he reache 21, also three 2 year olde heffers; dau. MARAY 2 Cows & Calvs,

1 Two year old heffer, 1 bed and furnature already Cauld hurs; sons JAM,
LEWIS & JOHN all my houshould furnature & plantation tools
extrs: wife CATRIN & ROBERT DICKSON Esquire
wit: ANDREW THALLY, JOHN COOK I. C. [Island Creek]
signed: John (w) Cook

114. COOK, JOHN (CR.035.801.3/A-85)
3 Mar 1799 - Jul Term 1799
son REUBEN one small feather bed & my gun; dau. FEREBY BLANTON all the
cattle & sheap that I lent to JAMES BLANTON, one pewter dish, two baisons,
two plates, one feather bed and furniture, one box iron and heaters, two
iron pots, one tea pot, one milk pot, half a dozen of tea spoons, one cutting
axe, one iron widge, one half of dozen tea cups and saucers, one pail, one
piggin, two chairs, one hackle, one chest; son JESSE one pewter dish, two
plaits, $2; son THOS. all my carpenters tools, one pewter bason, my mare
bridle and saddle and her first colt to be his son THOMAS; son NATHAN all
my coopers tools, two small hoes. one sifter, one cow & her heifer yarling
known by the name of the red cow; son JOHN 1 shilling sterling; dau. SARAH
MARTIN 1 shilling sterling; heirs of my son WILLIAM decd. 1 shilling sterling
dau. AMY PEPIN 1 shilling sterling; heirs of my dau. ELIZABETH NEWTON decd.
1 shilling sterling; dau. MARY MARTIN 1 shilling sterling
extrs: son THOS. & JAMES BLANTON
wit: FEDERICK COOK, LEWIS ૪ SMITH
signed: John Cook

115. COOKE, JOHN JUNIOR (CR.035.801.3)
9 Mar 1774 - no probate
wife MARY 1/3 of my Estate both Real and personal dureing her life time;
dau. MARGARET negro Bess she paying my dau. ANN 30 pds. proclamr money;
son JOHN negro Harry; if negro Bess Should Breed and have Children that
they Should be divided Equally amongst my Children WILLIAM, JEHU, DANIEL &
EVAN JONES & if she Should bring forth a daughter I bequeath it to my dau.
MIRAM; sons DANIEL & EVAN JONES my plantation on Bare Branch that I now do
live upon; son RICHARD 1 shilling sterling; residue of estate held untill
my youngest Son EVAN JONES arrives to the Age of 21 years and then to my
children
extrs: wife MARY & son JOHN
wit: THOMAS BLAKE, WILLIAM JAMES, DANIEL 𝒯 TEACHEY SENR.
signed: John Cooke

116. COOPER, BENJAMIN (CR.035.801.3/2-33)
30 Mar 1845 - Jul Term 1848
dau. SARAH WILLIAMS $500; dau. ELIZABETH LEE $175; dau. PATSEY BERDAUS only
$150 to be applied to the use of her children; dau. THURSDAY BERDANT $500;
grdau. MARY ANN FOSTER $300; grandchildren the Sons & Daughters of GEORGE
COOPER decd. $25 each making a sum of $125; dau. HANNAH HENRY's 4 sons $25
each; dau. REBECCER McCULLY negro Albert; son JOHN negroes John & James;
son WILLIAM negroes Dick, Solomon, Moses and Aaron, Eady & her child Mitilda,
Tract of land where on I Know live about 300 acres on the south side of the
mill & 73 acres on the north side and industry of the Mill, also my Blacksmith Shop and tools and the Cooper Shop and tools
extr: son WILLIAM
wit: H. SULLIVAN, LEBBEUS MIDDLETON
signed: Benjamin ✗ Cooper

117. COOPER, GEORGE SEN (CR.035.801.3)
nuncupative will 10 Nov 1792 - Jan Term 1793
[this will is very faded and hard to read]
died 8 Nov 1792 JOHN COOPER JNR & JOHN COOPER say they heard Deceased Say
that DAVID COOPER Should have all the Estate he was possessed With Horses,
Cattle and hogs, All Houshold Furnture, All the Crop, Money, bonds [?]
and Debts [?], all the plantation Tools, Negro Wench Ruth
sworn before CHA. WARD, J. P.

118. COTTLE, ROBERT (CR.035.801.3/A-68)
19 Feb 1817 - Jul Term 1817
wife BARBARY all the rest of my Estate only the Land that lies In Onslow
County
extr: JOHN FARIOR
wit: WM FARIOR, JOSEPH BROOKS
                    signed: Robert ✻ Cottle

119. COX, CHARLES (SS Wills)
24 Nov 1752 - 10 Apr 1759
wife FRANCESINEA my Land whereon I now Dwell & 1/2 of my goods and Chattels,
Righthand Credit be it More or Less, Nagroes, Live Stocke, Redey Money,
Household goods, Debts, Dues and working tools and Everything; dau. ANNE
other half of my property & 500 acres in the provence of pencelvany in the
County of Newcastle in Sante Georgs Necke
extrs: wife FRANCESINA & JOSEPH WILLSON
wit: AMBROSE DUDLEY, AARON HODGSEN
signed: Charles Cox

120. CRANFORD, JOHN (CR.035.801.3/A-78)
14 Apr 1818 - Apr Term 1818
wife REBECCA negro Esther & her children Dilly & Rilly for her natural life
& then to my children WILLIAM, JOHN, NETER, SALLY, ELIZABETH, REBECCA, LIDDY,
RACHEL & MARY, 1 Cow & yearlin; son JAMES all my lands including my house
and plantation; residue of stock to nine children
extrs: friend ARCHIBALD MAXWELL & son JAS.
wit: D. BROCK, MARY BROCK, A. MAXWELL
                    signed: John ✻ Cranford

121. CRUMPLER, JOHN (CR.035.801.3/A-81)
7 Feb 1782 - Apr Court 1782 (Sampson Co. CR.087.801.5)
son JACOB 100 acres whereon he now lives yt. I bought of PIERY BELL CLAY
Lying on bearskin Swamp, the Cattle he formerly was possessed of and one bed
now in the possession of ELIHU WIGGINS, 1 black mair & coalt; son JOHN 230
acres on both sides of the Road Joining BENJN WILLIAMS and Crumplers Marsh,
100 acres on Magason Branch, 320 acres being part of an Entry of 640 acres
Lying on both sides of Hauls branch whereof LAZARUS HAUL is to have 320
acres, stock of Cattle now in the Cear of WILLIAM LATON, use of the plantation & Negro whereon I now live for to Rais my Children [not named] thereon,
1 Feather bed; dau. RACHEL 5 cows & calves to be paid her at age 21 or when
Maried, 10 pds in Silver or Gold, 1 fether bed and Sheet; dau. SARAH 5 Cows
& Calves, 10 pds. in Silver or gold, 1 Feather Bead, Rug and Sheet; dau.
NANCY 5 Cows & Calves, 10 pds in Silver or gold, 35 pds of Feathers; dau.
ELIZABETH 5 cows & calves, negro Rose and the first child She Ever Brings,

1 Feather Bead, Rug and Sheet; son CAJAH 200 acres whereon I now live, 100 acres adj. the former and Maguson Swamp, 100 acres adj. THAT & WILLIAM BOYKIN, 100 acres on the East Side of Daniels Branch, negro Seacar, 5 Cows & Calves, Feather bead, Rug and Sheet; son JACOB 1/2 of sheep at EPHRAIM EMANUELS and the remainder to all my children [not named] except JACOB & GRACE
extrs: sons JACOB & JOHN & ELIHU WIGGINS
wit: ARTHUR COOR, DANIEL COOR, WILLIAM ✈ WIGGS
signed: John Crumpler

122. CRUMPTON, THOMAS (CR.035.801.3)
21 Feb 1806 - Jan Term 1808
wife RACHEL all the property I possess of Every Kind Dureing her natural life; dau. REBECAH WATSON 5 shillings She being other ways provided for; son JOHN all my property at my wifes Decease
extrs: wife RACHEL & son JOHN
wit: WM. STOAKES JUR, AUSTIN BEESLEY, WM. WILLS
signed: Thos Crumpton

123. CUMMINS/COMMANS, THOMAS (CR.035.801.3/A-75)
10 May 1796 - Jan Term 1798
sons THOMOUS, BENJEMAN & HUGH the plase whare I Now live With My beloved wife [not named] haveing hur thurds of the Same plase hur life time; sons GEORG & AARON 150 acors on the Et. Side of No. Et. Rivor; son JAMES 100 acors in the No. Side Island Creek; all my Goods and Chttels to Kept togather until Sum one of my Children Shall part off from the Rest
extrs: son THOMOUS & TIMMOTHY TECHEY
wit: ANDREW THALLY, JOHN THALLY
signed: Thomas Cummins

124. DAIL, ABEL [also listed as ALBERT] (CR.035.801.4/A-105)
4 May 1818 - Jul Term 1821
wife [not named] 1 Sorrel mear, 1 fether Bed and furniture, 2 pots, all my Household furniture and after She is Dun with it I Desire to Give it to my Sun ISAAC
extr: not named
wit: ELEZABETH DAIL, RICHARD KETHLEY
signed: Abel ✶ Dail

125. DAIL, ELEZABETH (CR.035.801.4/A-125)
4 Jun 1824 - Jul Term 1827
Cosin MORNENING, dau. of Sister POLLEY DAILS 3 head of Cattle, 1 fether bed and furniture, all my money and Notes and all the rest of the property Excepting my Weareing Clothes and them to be Equeally Devided between my mother and Cosin MORNNING DAIL and my Sisters SALLEY DAIL, SUSIEY GRADY & ANN DAIL
extrs: RICHARD KETHLEY, DANIEL DAIL
wit: RICHARD KETHLEY, DANIEL DAIL
signed: Elizabeth ✕ Dail

126. DARDEN, CHARLES "of New hanover and Duplin County on a Prong
          of Mores Creek" (CR.035.801.4/A-106)
30 Dec 1800 - Apr Term 1801
dau. ELIZEBETH PITMAN what Catle and Puter I have Possest hir with; the
Catle and Puter and other things I have al redy Persester SABRINA PARRADIS
During life then between hir Children; dau. CYRENE BURTON 3 Cows and Calves;
dau. PATIENCE 2 Cows and Calves; dau. MARY 2 Cows and Calves; wife MARIANN
use of this Plantation wheare I now live on During Hir natul life then to
dau. PATIANCE including the GEORGE MARADEN land, 50 akers STRATTEN BURTON
land & the Swan land; dau. MARY 150 akers on both sides of bull Joining
swns land; dau. PATIANCE 1 feather Bed and furniture; dau. MARY 1 feather
Bed and furniture; wife MARIANN negro Rose; dau. MARY Rose's first child;
dau. PATIENCE Rose's second child; dau. CERENA BURTON Rose's third child;
dau. ELIZEBETH PITMAN Rose's fourth child; dau. MARY Rose's fifth child;
dau. PATIANCE Rose's sixth child; dau. CERENA BURTON Rose's seventh child'
dau. ELIZEBETH PITMAN Rose's eight child; dau. SABRINA PARRADISE negro Rose
at her mothers death and then to her dau. NANCY; wife MARIANN one feather
Bed and furnetud, hole Stocks of horses, Cattle and hogs, goods and Chattels
during hir life and then to PATIENCE & MARY
extr: wife MARIANN
wit: MARK WOOD, FRANCES ✝ PICKET
signed: Charles Darden

127. DAVIS, DAVID (CR.035.801.4/A-126)
26 Apr 1824 - Jul Term 1824
wife ANN all my property Real and personal during her Natural life; three
eldest children ANN RIVENBARK, MARY ENGLISH, ELISEBETH BOEN $5 each; ballance
to my three youngest children REBECCAANN, SARY JANE & MEHALAY
extrs: good friends ALFRED WARD & JOHN HUFHAM
wit: ALFRED WARD, SARY GREEN
signed: David Davis

128. DAVIS, JOHN (CR.035.801.4/A-117)
19 Jan 1760 - 13 Aug 1760
friend JOHN COOKE JOUR the whole of my Estate
extr: JOHN COOKE
wit: DAVID JONES, JOHN COOK, VALINTINE BEST SENR.
signed: John Davis

129. DAVIS, RACHEL (CR.035.801.4/A-129)
27 Nov 1827 - no probate
brothers WINDOL DAVIS SENR & ZACHARIAH DAVIS, Sisters ELIZABETH DOBSON &
JANE DAVIS, Brother WINDOL DAVIS oldest son SAMUEL & the Grandchildren of
SUSANNAH STANLEY 1/6 part each of the money arising from the sale of all my
propperty, goods & chattels, Negroes, Household & Kitchen furniture; MARY
WILLIAMS 50¢; ANN CIRCY LEARY & hire Heires 50¢; Heires of CATHERINE TAYLOR
50¢; ALCY ALBERTSONs Heires 50¢; NANCY LAWSONs Heires 50¢; Heires of
MALCHIER DAVIS 50¢; SUSANNAH STANLEYs Adopted sons & Dawhters [not named]
extr: not named
wit: JAMES STANLEY, AMOS STANLEY, ELLY ✝ WAATERS/WAISTIN
signed: Rachel Davis

130. DAVIS, SAMUEL (CR.035.801.4)
21 May 1838 - Oct Term 1838
wife CATHARINE negro Chloe, 1 bed and furniture, Horse & Gig Harness, home
Plantation & land on the north Side of Mathews Branch being 900 acres, all
my lands 2400 acres, negroes, household & Kitchen furniture, tools of every
kind, stock of horses, Cattle and Hogs & Sheep for her life time or widowhood;
dau. ELIZABETH PIPKIN $10 with all the property I have given her before; son
CALVIN $10 with all the property I have given him before; son JAMES P. negro
Allen, 1 Bed & furniture with the Stock I have given him before; dau.
HEPHZIBAH ADELIA JERMAN negro Ama which she has in possession, negros Tenor
& Joe with all the property she has had before; sons SETH & IRA my Towerhill Plantation and lands on Burncoat and Suttons Branch being about 1000
acres, negroes Peter, Daniel, Laney & Eif, 2 Beds & furniture, $100 when
IRA shall come to the age of 21; son JOHN EDWARD T. all the land lent his
mother supposed to be about 900 acres, negros Bill, Robbin, & Martha, one Bed
& furniture, $50; 5 daus. NANCY, WINIFRED, EMMA, MARIA C. & SEPHRONIA E.
negroes Isaac, Aron, Bobb, Rose, Phillis, Lizza, Hannah, Lucinda, Richmon,
Edie, Jinny & Henry when each comes of age & each a Bed & furniture, if it
should happen that there are not Beds enough they must be purchased
extrs: son JAMES P. & JAMES H. JERMAN
wit: HEPHZIBAH TUTLE, J. E. SWINSON
signed: Sml. Davis

131. DAVIS, SIMON (CR.035.801.4/A-104)
8 Mar 1798 - Apr Term 1800
wife FRANCIS 1 Bead Beadstead & furneture, 2 Cows and Calves, 1 Iron Pot &
Large Chest for her Natural life or widowhood & then to my son LEWIS; legal
heirs of son LEWIS & dau. NANCY BAKER Cattle given to wife; dau. LUCRETIA
BASS 1 shilling Sterling; dau. SARAH GUY 1 shilling Sterling; dau. BARBARY
BASS 1 shilling Sterling; dau. NANCY BAKER 1 shilling Sterling; son LEWIS
all my Lands and Plantation whereon I now live
extr: son LEWIS
wit: SAMUEL SANLIN, JOSEPH T. RHODES
                     signed: Simon ✗ Davis

132. DICKSON, ALEXANDER (CR.035.801.4/A-95)
19 Jun 1813 - Jul Term 1814
300 acre Manor Plantation bought of JOSEPH DICKSON decd., 213 acres adj. the
Manor Plantation bought of JOSEPH DICKSON and WILLIAM RIGBEY, 113 acres adj.
the same bought of AUSTIN BEASLEY, 4 1/4 acres adj. that where the dead tree
is bought of THOMAS MAGEE and 86 acres his own & JOSEPH BRAY's lines bought
of said Bray containing in the whole 716 1/4 acres to be Sold all in one
lott to pay debts; 150 acres on the West side of Maxwell Swamp on the head
of Jimmies Branch bought of ABNOR HUDGINS, 50 acres on the South side of the
head of Green Branch bought of ROBERT DICKSON decd., 50 acres adj. the same
at the east end adj. JOHN McGOWIN's line Patented by myself, 300 acres below
the cross roads and on boath sides of the main road adj. and between GABRIEL
H. JAMES, ROBERT DICKSON and JOHN HUNTERs lines Patented by myself to be sold;
nephew JOHN, Son of my Brother ROBERT DICKSON of Cumberland County Blockers
Ferry negro Amy; nephew JOSEPH McGOWIN negro Nancy; nephew JONES DICKSON
$500 to be paid in Notes; negroes Old Lucy & her Daughter Lucy & her Son
Frank Sold in one lott, and not Seperated; Kitt and the three youngest

children that she may have at the time of my decease to be sold in one lott
& not Seperated; Old Tarisman to be well treated by my executors & not let
him wont for anything; residue of Negroes sold to the highest bidded; residue
of estate sold and moneys used to keep a Free-School or Schools for the Benefit
of the Poor of Duplin County
extrs: Nephew JOHN son of my Brother ROBERT DICKSON decd., livin at Blocker's
         Ferry, Cumberland County and nephew JOSEPH, son of WILLIAM McGAWIN
         decd of Duplin County
wit: STEPHEN GRAHAM, WILLIAM MALLARD
signed: Alexander Dickson

133. DICKSON, BENADICK (CR.035.801.4/A-97)
22 Jun 1833 - Apr Term 1838
son JOSEPH $1;   dau. SUSANNAH $1;   dau. ANNEY $1;   son BRYANT $1;   sons
WILLIAM, ALFRED & JAMES all my lands to be equally divided among them;   dau.
ELIZABETH JANE 4 head of Cattle, 1 cow and yearling, 1 heifer and one stere;
children BRYANT, WILLIAM, ALFRED, ELIZABETH JANE & JAMES money arising from
sale of my pereshable property
extrs: BRYANT MALLARD, DAVID SOUTHERLAND
wit: JESSE BOYET, LOUIE [?] MANER
                        signed: Benadick   Dickson

134. DICKSON, JAMES (CR.035.801.4/A-118)
4 May 1812 - Jul Term 1812
wife SUSANNAH negroes Rose, Finetta, Dorrithy, Milly & Fortain;   youngest
children MARY, DORRATHY, ANNE JANE, JAMES, SINDEY, JOSEPH and ROBERT negroes
Sam, Nancy, Virgil, Simion, Cate, Sarah, Grace, Rias, Sanders & Pharo each
to get his part at the time they arive at the age of twenty one years or
Should any Marry Sooner they are to recieve their part at the time of Marrage;
oldest children ELLINOR, MARGARET, WILLIAM, ALEXANDER, ELISABETH and ANNE
Keep hold and retain the property which I have given them both in land and
Negroes;   extr. to sell as much property as will bring $200 and to pay it to
dau. MARGARET to make up her deficiency in other property;   extr. to sell
land which I hold in the State of Tennessee and money applied to Such use
for the benefit of the Estate as he may think most advisable;   movable property
sold to pay debts, for the Schooling and rasing of my younger Children & to pay
THOMAS JOHNSTON of South Carolina $44
extr: son-in-law JOE MAXWELL
wit: EDWD. PEARSALL, ANDW. THALLY, JOHN CARR
signed: James Dickson

135. DICKSON, JAMES (CR.035.801.4/4-180)
28 Oct 1850 - 25 Mar 1882
brother ROBERT all of my real estate including my plantation where I farm
and my turpentine lands near Strickland depot on the Wilmington & Raleigh
Rail Road, negroes Sanders, Manuel, Nance, and her children Hugh, Gabriel,
Furney & Ned and Susan and her children Nelson & Jere;   extr. to sell negro
Eliza and her Children Henry, Martha, Sarah, Mike, Cassey Jane & Shade &
buy a plantation worth $1000 or $1200 for the seperate use and benefit of my
Sister DORITHA MAXWELL and after her death to her sons DAVID C. & JAMES D.,
residue of money from sale to be used to stock the farm;   sister LINDA CARR
negroes Bob, Spicey, Virgil, Lucy & Linda;   sister ANN JANE OLIVER negroes

Matilda & her children Tenir & Rachel and Clarrissey; niece BETSEY JANE
MAXWELL negro Peggy; niece SUSAN ANN POLLOCK negro Julia Ann; ROBERT
DICKSON in trust for sister DORITHY MAXWELL negroes Sam, Drinder and her
children Milley, Caroline and Owen for her life and then to her children
SUSAN ANN, DAVID C., JAMES D. & ELIZABETH JANE; daus. of CHARLES CHAMBERS
[not named] negro Jenny; sister ANN ROBINSON's children [not named] proceeds
from the sale of negros Austin & Andrew; JAMES P. CARR & JAMES B. CARR negro
Howard; JAMES D. MAXWELL negro john; brother ROBERT residue of my property;
JOSEPH, son of JAMES PEARSALL $250; sister LINDA CARR all my Interest in
my brother JOSEPH's estate which I have by purchase from OZBORN CARR, JOHN
CARR, my Own and of BENJN OLIVER and the heirs of ALEXR. DICKSON
extr: brother ROBERT
wit: not named
signed: James Dickson

136. DICKSON, LEWIS (CR.035.801.4/A-130)
11 Feb 1815 - Apr Term 1815
wife CATHARINE all the land & Plantation whereon I now live dureing her own
life, negroes Sam, Priss and her Child Venus, Sina & Isaac and at her death
to Children PATSEY and ELIZA, one Horse, my Riding Chair and Harness, Houshold
and Kitchen furniture; daus. PATSEY & ELIZA negroes Sambo, Querry, Dinah and
her two Children Celatha and Clarrissa, & Dilsey and her Child Mary, 2 Beds
Bedstids and furniture, slaves to be hired out until one of my Daughters
Shall Marry or arrive at the age of 21 years; extr. to sell land lying on
the Poley Bridge branch by the Meeting house to pay debts and residue of money
to daus. PATSEY & ELIZA; wife CATHERINE to act as Guardian of my Daughters
and She to School and Educate and Cloath them at her own discretion
extrs: wife CATHERINE, friends DAVID HOOKS, ELIAS FAISON
wit: LEVI BORDEN, DICKSON HOOKS
signed: Lewis Dickson

137. DICKSON, MORRIS (CR.035.801.4/A-120)
12 Nov 1802 - Apr Term 1803
GEORGE DREW and his Children that he had by My Daughter LUCEY his Wife and
the Children She bare to WILLIAM JONES her former Husband 5 shillings to be
divided Equally amongst them and nomore; dau. SARAH one Cow and Calf; dau.
HANNAH PHILLIPS 5 shillings; son JOHN 5 shillings & his son SAMUEL the Cow
and yearling that I Directed him to mark for his Son; dau. FANNEY WARD 5
shillings; son BENEDICK all the Resedue of My property
extr: son BENEDICK
wit: JOHN SOUTHERLAND, GORG SOUTHERLAND, JAMES REARDON
                                      signed: Morris   Dickson

138. DICKSON, ROBERT (CR.035.801.4/A-98)
18 Mar 1790 - Apr Term 1790
if the Child my Wife BARBARA is Now Great with be a Male Child he is to share
all my Lands with my sons EDWARD and ROBERT; if the Child my wife BARBARA
is Now Great with be a Female Child my son JOHN is to share the Lands with
my sons EDWARD and ROBERT; wife BARBARA to have 1/3 of my Mannor plantation
and Buildings During her Widowhood; moveable property sold and the money
Eaqually Divided Between my Wife and all my Children Except dau. ANN BRYAN
& son JOHN who are to have 1/2 share each; should any of my sons die without

heirs their part is to go to my son EDWARD; Should my Wife upon her Marreage
Refuse to Resign up to my heirs her Right of Dower She then forfeits her Share
of the Moveable Estate which is to be Equally Divided among all my Children
JOHN DICKSON & ANNE BRYAN Excepted; negro Celah in the possession of DOROTHY
DICKSON to remain in her Possession and service for the Term of Seven years;
step children LINCOLN & MARY SHUFFIELD 200 acres on the River adj. JAMES
WALLACE and ISOM SHUFFIELDs old plantation; stepdau. MARY SHUFFIELD one
Cow and Calf out of the Stock Called the River Stock; for the Bennefit of
my children Extr. is Empowered to sell land on Maxwell adj. JOHN BONEY and
Chasons Land, 150 acres on Alder adj. the Land Swinson Bought of PETER MORRISS
and Such other Part of my Estate they Shall Judge Best and buy a Tract of 100
acres on Elder below the Bridge Now the property of JOHN CHAMBERS which will
be Considered as part of the Lands hereby Willed to be Divided among my Sons
extr: son JOHN, brothers WILLIAM & JOSEPH
wit: JAMES DICKSON, DORATHY DICKSON, JANE DICKSON
signed: Robert Dickson

139. DICKSON, ROBERT (CR.035.801.4)
11 Jan 1815 - Jan Term 1815
mother BARBARY WILKINSON my estate both real and personal during her natural
life; brother WILLIAMS $200; DICKSON, son of CHARLES HOOKS $200; nephew
ROBERT DICKSON, son of DAVID HOOKS residue of estate
extr: Brother in Law DAVID HOOKS
wit: STEPHEN GRAHAM, WILLIAM L. HILLS
signed: Robt. Dickson

140. DICKSON, SUSAN (CR.035.801.4/2-72)
23 Feb 1844 - Oct Term 1852
BENJAMIN OLIVER negroes Nettis, Bill & Hagan in trust for dau. DORETHY
MAXWELL and at her death to the Children that may Survive her; my children
ANN PEARSALL, OZBORN CARR, JOHN CARR, ANN JANE OLIVER & LINDA CARR negroes
Milly, Hamlit, Daniel, Austin, Doll, Frank & Fortune; son ROBERT DICKSON
my mare or young horse Timoleon, 2 Beds and furniture; grdau. BETSEY JANE
MAXWELL 1 bed and furniture; son JAMES DICKSON 2 beds and furniture; residue
of my property sold and equally divided in Seven parts with 1/7 to BENJAMIN
OLIVER in trust for my dau. DORITHY MAXWELL, 1/7 to ANN PEARSALL, 1/7 to
OZBORN CARR, 1/7 to JOHN CARR, 1/7 to ANN JANE OLIVER, 1/7 to LINDA CARR, 1/7
to ROBERT DICKSON
extr: son JAMES DICKSON
wit: DAVID SLOAN, JOHN SWINSON
        signed: Susan   Dickson

141. DICKSON, COL. WILLIAM (CR.035.801.4/A-109)
20 Sep 1816 - Jul Term 1820 "being arrived to an advanced Age"
As my Children are all grown up and Setled for themselves and have received
Portions of my Property from me, tho not all of Eaqual value, it is my Sincere
wish and hope that Each and every of them will be contented and Satisfied with
such Portions as they have heretofore received from me, together with such
additions as I shall now make to them; And as Sundry of my Children have
Recently departed this life, and have left Issue, by them legally begotten,
I now hereby give and bequeath to the Children of my Sons who have departed
this life, such Portion of my Estate, as I had heretofore devised and bequeathed

to my Sons in their life times; grdau. CORNELIA ANN, dau. of my son WILLIAM late of the State of Tenessee deceased negro Swann and should she die before She shall Marry, or attain to the Age of twenty one years then to her next Sister INDIANA And in Case She Shall die unmarried and under the age of twenty one then to her younger Sister FLORIDA; son JAMES by a former will 400 acres of Piney land on Persimmon Swamp, Negro Spencer and the said JAMES being since deceased and having left three Infant daus. MARIA, ELIZA & PATSEY I desire the 400 acres & negro Spencer Sold for the sum of $400 and the Sum to be laid out on Interest for the use of the sd. JAMES's three daus. And may at any time at the discretion of my Executor with Consent of ELENOR the Mother of said MARIA, ELIZA & PATSEY be appropriated to Purchase young Slaves for the Use of the sd. daus. and Slaves or monies Eaqually divided between them as they attain the Age of twenty one or Marry which may first happen; son LEWIS by a former will my Manor Plantation whereon I now live lying on the south side and in Goshen Swamp including all my lands adjoining thereto lying between and bounded by the lands of DAVID WRIGHT, JOSEPH DICKSON, ELISHA HERRING, ELIAS FAISON, LEWIS DICKSON & DAVID HOOKS Containing Seven hundred and thirty acres and Negro Slaves Cato, old Ned & Old Cesar and sd. LEWIS being since deceased have left two Infant daus. PATSEY & ELIZA I now Will and bequeath to PATSEY and ELIZA my said Manor Plantation and all my lands to be Eaqually divided under the direction of the County Court between them when either of them shall attain the Age of twenty one or Marry which ever my first happen And extrs. to Rent out the Plantation for the Use of the sd. PATSEY and ELIZA, the sd. Plantation Kept in Repair and Prohibit those who Farm the same from Cuting or wasting any Timber more than what may be necessary for Repairing Houses, fences, firewood & c. And that none of the Cleared land shall be Cultivated more than one year in two unless they Manure it; negro Slaves Cato, Old Ned and Old Cesar sold and monies arising kept on Interest until the division of the lands shall take place; should both PATSEY and ELIZA die before they attain the age of twenty one years or Marry the lands and Monies to be given to my grson. WILLIAM Son of JOSEPH DICKSON by LUCY his wife; Whereas my dau. ELIZABETH wife of EDWARD WARD Esq. of Onslow County died, and left no Issue of her own Body all the property which I gave and delivered to the sd. EDWARD and ELIZABETH shall Continue to the said EDWARD WARD; son JOSEPH Negroes Harry, Charles, old Feba, Toby & Toney; Negroes Doll and Silvia sold and Monies appropriated to purchase a Young Slave for my grson. WILLIAM Son of JOSEPH and SUSANNA GILLESPIE; grdau. FRANCES ANN CRABB, dau. of WILLIAM and ANN LANIER Negro Sidney and her little Son She Calls Jackson; grson WILLIAM DICKSON, son of ISAAC and MARY LANIER Negro Hamlet; grdau. CLARRISSA, dau. of ISAAC and MARY LANIER Negro Derry; grson WILLIAM DICKSON, Son of WILLIAM R. PICKETT and FRANCES his wife Negro Martin; Rest and Residue of Estate not willed Consisting of my Stock of Horses, Cattle, Sheep, Hogs, Household and Kitchen furniture, Plantation Tools and Implements of Husbandry, and every other Species of Property whatsoever, with my Crop of every kind, whether Gathered in and Housed, or Standing out on the Plantation be Sold to pay just debts and funeral Charges and residue of Monies to be Eaqually divided amongst my Daus. ANN LANIER, MARY LANIER, FRANCES PICKETT and SUSANNA GILLESPIE
extrs: son JOSEPH, Worthy and loving friends DAVID WRIGHT and DAVID HOOKS
wit: JOHN DICKSON, D. L. KENAN, ANN DICKSON
signed: Wm. Dickson
codicil: 4 Feb 1817
Whereas I did give my grdau. FRANCES ANN CRABB, the dau. of WILLIAM and ANN

LANIER Negro Sidney and her little son Jackson And whereas I have since been
informed by letters that my sd. grdau. and her Infant dau. are both dead.
And there is now no Remaining Issue of sd. FRANCES ANN to enjoy the Property
I give to my grdau. MARIA, dau. of WILLIAM and ANN LANIER Negro Sidney and
grdau. SUSANNA, dau. of WILLIAM and ANN LANIER negro Jackson
wit: D. WRIGHT, ANN DICKSON, ANN PEARSALL
Signed: Wm. Dickson
Codicil: 20 Apr 1820
ANN DICKSON all Such articles of Clothing, bed Clothing, Curtains and all
Such other articles She has Made Since She Came here and all such as I have
Made her presents of and a bed in addition to one given her by Deed of Gift
& All such articles as She brought here when She Came to be Delivered to her
Such as she Claims; MILDRED DICKSON 3 Vollumes of Jarrets Sermons; grson
WILLIAM son of JOSEPH DICKSON four Volumns of Josephus History Containing
the Antiquities and Wars of Jews, two Vollumns of Miltons Poetical Work &
Salmons Geography; son JOSEPH all Money heretofore lent or Recd. by him from
me; JOSEPH GILLESPIE the money paid me for Toby Coopering for him; as I
have left the lands I sold to COL. DAVID HOOKS on persimmon to the Children
of my son JAMES I give the same Children all the money sd. COL. DAVID HOOKS
owes me for sd. Land To be Delivered as Soon as Collected to ELENOR DICKSON
Guardian of sd. Children; Extrs. to have power to sell negro Spencer given
to the Children of my son JAMES but not to Sell him out of the Neighborhood
or two far from his wife & Children; for the Tender Care and affection
together with the Service Rendered me & for which he made no Charge When I
got my lag broke and had it taken off I now give my friend WILLIAM MEAZEL
one broad Cloth pattern for a Coat which bought for myself some time past and
is not made and a waistcoat already made and a black Casamers Pantaloons that
is Cut out the Overalls will only answer to work in, in his Shop and the trimmings for the Coat & 2 1/2 yds of white homespun for a pair of Drawers;
dau. in law CATHARINE A. DICKSON her Choice of all my books and as many as
she thinks proper to accept & the twenty Dollars I lent her to her dau. PATSEY
wit: D. WRIGHT
signed: Wm Dickson

142. DICKSON, ZILPHIA (CR.035.801.4/3-16)
22 Dec 1854 - Oct Term 1860
grandchildren DAVID & CHAUNCY, sons of ALSA SOUTHERLAND negroes Sarah, Eastir,
Wright, Charles, Aaron, Abram, Denis, Sam, Lucy, Anthony, Jim, Matilda &
Rachel; grandsons to be furnished with a good liberal education as the means
of this Estate May afford
extrs: THOMAS H. McGEE, ALSA SOUTHERLAND
wit: D. REID, G. W. GRAHAM
signed: Zilpha Dickson

143. DOBSON, ELIZABETH (CR.035.801.4)
11 Jun 1845 - Jul Term 1845
dau. SALLEY GRIMESes Children [not named] 1 Dolar; dau. ALSA DUMPSEYs
Children [not named] 1 Dolar; sons JOHN, JAMES & PEORY negro Lidda and
residue of estate
extr: not named
wit: DAVID SOUTHERLAND, LAVINIA KILLPATRICK
                    signed: Elizabeth   Dobson

144. DOBSON, LEWIS (CR.035.801.4/A-124)
2 Dec 1822 - Apr Term 1826
wife HANNER all my house hold furniture, 1 horse bridle and saddle, 10
barrels of Corne, 300 wt. of pork, 1 blake stear; cousin JAMES 2 Cows and
earlings, my shoemakers Tools and my weareing Clothes, $20; residue sold to
pay all Just demands
extrs: cousin JAMES DOBSON, LEWIS HERRING
wit: LEWIS HERRING, LEMUEL M. WHITFIELD
signed: Lewis Dobson

145. DOPSON, HANNAR (CR.035.801.4)
25 Jan 1840 - Apr Term 1840
BUTHE HARREL 1 feather Bed and furniture, one half my waring Cloes, one half
Rest of My household property; CELEY GLISSON 1 feather Bed and furniture,
one half my waring Cloes, one half Rest of My household property; brother
WILLIAM TURNAGE Residue of Estate, lands and Notes
extr: brother WILLIAM TURNAGE
wit: GRIFFIN ─┼─ JONES, DAVID JONES
                        signed: Hanner ✕ Dopson

146. DOWD, EMANUEL (CR.035.801.4/A-107)
2 Apr 1778 - Jul Court 1779
WELIBY DOWD, JAMES DOWD & SARAH DOWD 1 shilling Starling each; JOHN DOWD
700 acres with the rest of my Estate only SARAH, my Wife to have a Loan
of the Same During Widow hood
extrs: wife SARAH & JOHN DOWD
wit: FLEET COOPER, JOHN COOPER
                        signed: Emanuell ℰ Dowd

147. DOWNIE, ALAXANDER (CR.035.801.4/A-127)
18 Jun 1798 - Oct Term 1799
true and trusty friend MARY McCANNE SENR All My Remaining Notes and Accompts,
my Bible and Morter, 1 old Cow Calld Crossey, My Bed and furniture; true
and trusty friend NANCY McCANNE My Dictionary and family Instructor, 1/4 of
My Cattle, A Book Cald Brown; true and trusty friend MARY McCANNE JUNR My
Religeous Courtship, A Divinity Book And Walkers Sermons, 1/4 of My Cattle;
SARAH McCANNE a young Cow Called Spotty and hir Calf; trusty friend JOHN
MCANNE DILWORTH A Book of Arithmitic, 1/4 of My Cattle, 1/2 My Close And
Hym Book, Raisor And hone; friend JOSHUA McCANNE WINGATE A Book of Arithmetic,
1/4 of My Cattle, 1/2 My Close And Slate; true and Trusty friend JOHN GILLMAN
the Confession of faith, a Book and What Money is in his own Hand; trusty
friend WILLIAM MCANNE two Books Viz Darvey and Vincint My Scale and Scilles
extrs: True and Trusty friends JOHN MCANNE & WILLIAM MCANNE
wit: DANIEL MURPHY, FRANCIS ✕ PICKET
signed: Alexr. Downie

148. DUACKS, WILLIAM (CR.035.801.4/A-132)
19 Jul 1780 - Jan Court 1782
wife MAGDELANE the Plantation where I Now live And all my household Goods;
dau. SARAH CAMMISON 1 bull; son PRESLEY 1 Cow & Calf; son WILLIAM 1 Cow &
Calf; son ROBERT 1 Cow & Calf; dau. SELAH 1 Cow & Calf; dau. RHODE 1
heifer; son HENRY the Plantation where I now live; daus. ELIZABITH & NANCE
3 head of Small Cattles; lend wife all the rest of my Estate during her
widow hood and then to be Equally Divided between my 5 youngest Children
SELAH, RHOADE, HENRY, ELIZABETH & NANCE

extr: RUES BLACKMAN
wit: WILLIAM ✝ DUACKS JUR, ROBERT ✝ DUACKS, RUE BLACKMON
                                      signed: William ✗ Duacks

149. DUNCAN, EDMOND (CR.035.801.4/A-108)
13 Sep 1799 - Oct Term 1799
wife GRACE 1 Horse Bridle and Saddle; sons WILLIAM, EDMOND & GEORGE and dau.
ANNA REAVES 5 shillings each and no more; the Ofspring of my dau. SARAH
ROACH dec'd to have no part of my Estate; Carpenters and Turners Tools sold
to pay debts; residue of my Estate to my wife during her natural Life or
Widowhood then to daus. MARY BROWN, GRACE DUNCAN & CATRON REAVES
extrs: sons EDMOND & GEORGE
wit: REUBIN ℞ WESTON, ZACHARIAH ∄ HARRIS
signed: Edmund Duncan

150. DUNCAN, ISAAC (CR.035.801.4/A-127)
15 Oct 1793 - Oct Term 1793
wife SUCKE all my oveble property with all my stock, all houshold goods and
working tools likewise all my lands and plantation for her life then all property to be sold and money divided amongst brothers WILLIAM, EDMUND & GEORGE
extrs: brothers WILLIAM & GEORGE
wit: SARA ∞ ROACH, CHARLOTTEY Ⅴ ROACH
signed: Isaac Duncan

151. DUNKAN, WILLIAM (CR.035.801.4/A-121)
7 Oct 1806 - Oct Term 1806
son EDMOND 250 acres on both sides of No East including the plantation I
bought of JOEL SASSER & between GEORGE DUNKAN & JOHN KORNEGAY; son JACOB
250 acres of land & plantation on which he now lives Joining JOHN KORNEGAY
near the foot way that crosses GEORGE KORNEGAY's plantation he bought of
JESSE REAVES, the corner of the Bass land, the N. E. Pecoson; son WILLIAM
250 acres above JACOB's adj. the Pecoson and a cross fence thro the Bass
plantation; son ISAAC 250 acres on the south side of the No Et at the mouth
of a branch that makes out of Thunder Swamp Pesocon adj. JAMES JOHNSTON, the
Gray Patent now belonging to FRANCIS OLIVER; son STEPHEN the land I bought
of WILLIAM HARRIS; wife ANNE residue of land including the plantation I
live on for her natural life and then to be equally divided between my three
youngest sons LEWIS, JOSEPH & JOHN CHARLES, also negroes Jim, Charles, Mary
& Hannah, three feather beds & firniture, one Desk, two Chests, two Tables,
six siting Chairs, the Bofat and firniture, Kitchen firniture, 6 Cows and
Calves, my lill mare & 2 year old Horse Colt, one Riding Chair & Harness,
40 head of Hogs, 100 barrels of Corn & she to raise & school my youngest
children in their minority; dau. ELIZABETH BOURDEN negro Lucey and all the
other things I have given her which I estimate at $200; dau. ROCHSELLAERY
CHRRY [?] negro Jenny and about $200 worth of other property which she has
received; dau. CATHARINE PIPKIN negro Dinah, all the other things I have
given her which I estimate at $140; dau. ANNE negro Tener, 1 Feather Bed
and firniture; dau. SARAH negro Harry, 1 Feather Bed and firniture; son
EDMUND has received of me what I estimate at $140; son JACOB has received
of me what I estimate at $150
extrs: wife ANNE, eldest son EDMUND
wit: FRAN. R. OLIVER, JOHN ROBERTS, WILLIAM DUNKAN JUNR
signed: William Dunkan

152. DUNKIN, JACOB (CR.035.801.4/A-133)
7 Apr 1812 - Jul Term 1812
wife FANNEY Land and plantation where I now liv, the hole of my houshold
& kithen furneture, 2 yong Mars, Riding Chear & Hunting Saddle, the hole
of my stock of Hogs & Sheep, fore Cous & Calvs or yearlings, one Heifer, my
Cart, all my plantation tools, one Bar of Iron, what Sault I have by meat
this time, & negro Jinny During her natural Life or as long as she shal
live a Widdo & she to Rase and School my Children to Read and Write & my
Suns to Sipher; at her death bulk of property to be Sold and money divided
between fore children JAMES, CULLIN, LUKE & SUSANNA
extrs: LAML. CHERREY, OEN CONNELEY
wit: LAML CHERREY, RUBEN ⌇ JOHNSON, STEPHEN DUNKAN
signed: Jacob Dunkan

153. DUNN, SAMUEL (CR.035.801.4/A-135)
28 Jan 1829 - Feb Court 1829
nephew SAMUEL DUNN HOOKS land whereon I now live adj. Reedy Branch, MICHAEL
BYRD, Poplar Branch, West side of the main Road, ELIAS FAISON, SAMUEL DUNN,
JAMES DUNN, Bell, Wolf, Joiner & Connerly reserving unto sd. SAMUEL DUNN
HOOKS 1/2 acres used as a familley Burying Ground whereon his wife is now
Buried, negroes Cato, Chloe, Violet, Clary and all her children, 2 horses
called Dolphin & Medler, 2 Cows & Calves, Stock of Hogs which he feeds near
RICHARD WOLFs, 1 Feather Bed & furniture, one fall Desk, 1/2 doz. Windsor
Chairs, 1 shot Gun, 1 Saddle & Bridle, 1 ax, 1 Horse Cart, one yoke of oxen,
1 Tea Table, 1 Common Pine Table; niece FRANCES, dau. of nephew JAMES DUNN
negro Dinah & her Two Children, 1 Feather Bed & furniture, 1 new Bureau;
niece ELISABETH, dau. of nephew JAMES DUNN negro Eliza; nephew JAMES, son
of nephew JAMES DUNN negro Stepney; neice SIVIL, dau. of DAVID HOOKS negro
Rachell & her Child Ann, 1 Work Stand, 1 Feather Bed & furniture; nephew
JAMES DUNN 415 acres I bought from my Brother WILLIAM which was formerly
owned by JAMES CLARKE, negroes Cam & Hanah & her 6 children Silvia, Alexander, Washington, Tilley, Esther & Mary; brother ROBERT my Gold Watch;
brother WILLIAM residue of estate both real & personal
extrs: brother WILLIAM and nephew JAMES
wit: JAS. H. HICKS, WM. B. BORDEN
signed: Samuel Dunn

154. EDWARDS, MATTHEW (CR.035.801.4/A-142)
29 May 1816 - Oct Term 1817
wife ANNE plantation and all lands Joyning on the South Side of Limestone
Belonging to me where I now live, all my houshold and Kitchen Furnetur,
working tools, stock of Hogs, Horses, Cattle and Sheep, negroes Nan, Luse
& Jirden; dau. SENE negro Luse after wife's death & if she die without
issue then to sons JAMES & FELIX; remainder given wife to son FELIX and
if he die without issue, it to be divided equelly Between JAMES, SUSANAH,
FANNE & SENE; son JAMES negro George & 380 acres on Cuffe Branch; son FELIX
negro Simon; dau. SARAH WILLIAMS 1 shilling Starling; dau. ELIZABETH PADGET
1 shilling Starling
extrs: wife ANNE, JOHN E. HUSSE
wit: ROBERT SOUTHERLAND, SEENY EDWARDS
                    signed: Matthew ⌇ Edwards

155. ELICE, WILEY (CR.035.801.4)
20 Sep 1837 - Apr Term 1838
JOSEPH ELICE $1; MAJOR ELICE $1; BENJAMIN DAVID, son of JANE JOINER My land
& all the property that I possess; JANE JOINER my Household & Citchen Furniture until BENJAMIN DAVID JOINER comes to the age of Eighteen years then it
belongs to him
extr: JOHN S. HILL
wit: DANIEL BOWDEN, GILBRON WOOLF
signed: Wll. Elis

156. ELIOT, WILLIAM (CR.035.801.4/A-136)
19 May 1784 - Jul Court 1784
eldest son WILLIAM 5 shillings specie; son ZACARIAH 5 shillings specie;
dau. ELIZABETH 320 acres whereon I now live, my riding mare, all my Cattle
and hogs & residue of my Estate both rale and Parsonal
extrs: WILLIAM NEWTON, FELIX FREDRICK
wit: ROBERT WILKINSON, THOMAS PHIPS
                              signed: William   Eliot

157. ELLISON, JESSE (CR.035.801.4/A-137)
25 Jun 1804 - Jul Term 1804
wife ANN all my land and personal Estate during her natural life to use and
raise my children and at her death to my children JORDAN, JESSE, CHARLOTTIE
& WILLIAM; dau. WINNEY WATSON 10 pds; dau. NANCY ALBERSON 1 Bed and furniture and one cow and calf which she hath already Received; son ACKISS one
horse, 1 bed and furniture which he hath already Received; my Executor do
cause to be made up to BRIAN WHETFIELD a good and lawful Right to all the
land my bond calls for
extrs: wife ANN & son-in-law MATTHEW WARD
wit: ISAAC KORNEGY, JESS ELLISON
                              signed: Jesse X Ellison

158. EVANS, DAVID (CR.035.801.4/3-77)
28 Mar 1858 - Apr Term 1863
wife REBECA all my property of Eveary description dureing her natural life
time an after her death to my daus. REBECA & BETSEY and there children
extr: not named
wit: A. MAXWELL, MARGARET TUCKER
                 signed: David X Evans

159. EVANS, JAMES (CR.035.801.4/A-138)
6 Dec 1801 - Apr Term 1802
wife ELIZABETH for her Natural life my House and all the part of my Plantation from the second bottom above my Orchard Down the Swamp adj. a 400 acre
survey, JAMES MAXWELL west of the Plantation, a small Branch, Gallimoor,
GEORGE ROUSE, THOMAS GARRISON and at her death the lower half is to go to
my son JAMES; son WILLIAM BURTON EVANS all my land lying South of my Plantation adj. the above described land, May, Tarekiln branch, JOHN DICKSON,
Maxwill, Millers old corner and McCartneys branch near Carrs foard; son
DAVID land lying above and adj. the other two tracts at the head of the
second bottom above the Orchard in the field adj. a small branch near Fanneys
field & Maxwell; son BENJAMIN 10 shillings; dau. REBEKAH 10 shillings;
dau. MARGARETT MAXWELL 10 shillings; son WILLIAM B. 10 shillings; son DAVID

10 shillings; son JAMES 10 shillings; dau. ELIZABETH 10 shillings; wife
ELIZABETH during her Natural life negro Esther
extrs: CHARLES HOOKS, JAMES DICKSON
wit: JNO. HUNTER, HOGAN HUNTER, JAMES FREDERICK
signed: James Evans

160. EZELL, MIKEL (CR.035.801.4)
27 Dec 1799 - Jul Term 1800
wife SARAH all my worldly estate during hur life time and at her death to be
eaquilly devided between MARY NIGHT, BENGAMIN EZELL, RUEBIN EZALL, WILLIAM
EZELL, SARAH RALLEY, GEORGE EZELL, NANCEY EZELL, HENRY EZELL, ELISABETH
SUTTON & FEDRICK EZELL
extrs: REUBIN EZELL & WILLIAM EZELL
wit: JACOB MATHIS, WILLIAM MATHIS
                          signed: Mikel   Ezell

161. EZELL, REUBIN (CR.035.801.4/1-1)
28 Feb 1823 - Feb Term 1830
wife SARAH plantation whereon I now live for her natural life and then to be
divided between my 2 sons JOHN R. & DENIS by a line which I myself have already
marked off; son SALATHAIL 100 acres on the No. Side of black Creek in Onslow
County; dau. DOLLY one bead, beadstead & the furniture therein to, one loom,
two chests; dau. LUCY one bead, beadstead & the furniture therein to, one
loom, two chests; daus. DOLLY & LUCY one cow each; son DENIS young horse
Cald Dimond which sd. horse will be two yeares old this ensuing Spring;
residue of estate sold and money divided Between my Children ELIZABETH WEST,
PATRICK, SALATHAIL, DOLLY, MARY CHESNUT, JOHN R., LUCY & DENIS
extrs: sons PATRICK & DENIS
wit: JOHN LINTON, JACOB MATHIS, ISAAC CRLTON
                          signed: Reubin   Ezell

162. EZZELL, PATRICK (CR.035.801.4/2-16)
11 Mar 1847 - Apr Term 1847
wife NANCY all my land & plantation whereon I now live for & during her life,
the Bradley tract adj. widow NANCY BRADEY's dower, the piney woods field,
THOMAS HERRING; son JOSHUA R. land at wife's death; wife NANCY negroes
Polly, Jack, & Tempy for her life time and then to son JOSHUA R.; son
JOSHUA R. negroes London, Peggy & Abram; dau. ELIZABETH ANN WILLIAMS negroes
George, Sary, Rose, Mary & Isaac; son JOSHUA R. 216 acres in Sampson County
on Baker's Branch adj. JOHN WEST & HENRY HOLLINGSWORTH; wife NANCY all the
household and kitchen furniture; dau. ELIZABETH ANN WILLIAMS $500 in notes &
money, a note of hand for $128 & interest against her husband, JAMES K.
WILLIAMS; wife NANCY 1000 pds Bacon, 35 Barrels corn, all the Fodder on
hand, horses Selim & Darling, 3 cows & calves, 3 sows & pigs, 15 shoats, 5 yews
& lambs, 1 horse cart, 4 plows & gear, 3 best hoes & 3 axes; son JOSHUA R.
5 yews & lambs
extrs: wife NANCY & son JOSHUA R.
wit: JAS. G. DICKSON, JESSE CARROLL
signed: Partrick Ezzell

163. FAISON, ELIAS K. "of Sampson" (CR.035.801.4/3-1)
14 Mar 1859 - Apr Term 1859
wife MARY E. Dwelling house and lot including all outhouses in the town of

Magnolia in the County of Duplin for her widowhood, then to my mother
MARGARET FAISON, all my Household and Kitchen furniture; my heir, if I
have one my lot in the town of Magnolia called my Office lot adj. the lot
before mentioned & negro _____; residue sold and money kept until heir is
21 years old, if no heir or he dies before age 21 then money goes to my
father ELIAS
extrs: ELIAS FAISON, ALFRED JOHNSON
wit: B. V. CARROLL, N. C. FAISON
signed: Elias K. Faison

164. FAISON, HENRY (A-147)
14 May 1788 - Oct Term 1788
Land whereon I now live to be divided into two Seperate Plantations by a line
from the main Run of Goshen Swamp, up the run of Turkey pen branch, DANIEL
CLARK's land, Reedy Branch & ROBERT BYRD's land & the half containing 475
acres with the houses and outbuildings to wife DEANA for her lifetime with
slaves Pompey, Jimmy, Rose, Inde, Amey & Lucy, eight cows and calves, five
Sows and pigs, six sheep, my Fearnaught mare, my Mark Anthony Mare, all my
Household furniture, one half of my plantation tools; 75 pds. to be raised
out of my Estate and expended in Repairing and furnishing my House for the
more comfortable Residence of my said Wife and Family; children POLLY,
ISOM, ELIAS, NANCY, PATSEY & FANNEY to have the other half of my land between
the said dividing line and Panther branch from the run of Goshen to DANIEL
CLARK's line containing 500 acres including my mills which land is to be
considered as a Destinct Plantation and is to be kept together along with
one half of my Plantation Tools, my whole set of Blacksmiths Tools, one half
of my piney woods Land, Stud Horse Fearnaught and all the rest of my Horses
and stock with negroes Sam, Jacob, Cudjo, Bet, Murriah, Celia, Nat, Milly,
Hannah, Eaton & Daniel for the use of my children until POLLY shall attain
the full age of Twenty one years or marry; son ISOM when he attains the
full age of Twenty one the said Mill Plantation containing 500 acres, one
half of my Piney woods lands and a full share of my Negroes, stock and tools;
remainder of my estate after ISOM has his share to be divided equally amongst
my children ELIAS, NANCY, PATSEY & FANNY when they reach the full Age of
Twenty one years; son ELIAS 475 acres left to my wife DIANA after her
decease and one half of my Piney woods Lands and should he attain the age
of Twenty one Years before the Decease of my said wife she to put into his
possession the part of the Land which lies between the Poplar branch and
ROBERT BYRD supposed about 40 acres; residue of Negroes, stock, Household
Furniture, Tools, etc. divided amongst all my children; should ISOM or ELIAS
die before the full age of 21 or without lawful issue, the Lands and other
Estate willed them to be Eaqually Divided amongst all my children; upon my
decease my good friend JOHN GRIFFIN to join his five Negroes with those I
have left on the Mill plantation and himself to take charge of the whole as
a conductor and Overseer; residue of my estate sold and all profits be disposed of in giving my children Education by Instructing them in Reading,
Writing and arithmetic sufficient and suitable for Farmers; my sons to be
strictly bred up to Industry in the Farming business; My Daughters remain
with their Mother until they attain to full age of Maturity or Marry That
they be Bred up to such Employment and Business and recieve such Education

as their said Mother may think most proper for them
extrs: good frends JOHN GRIFFIN & WILLIAM DICKSON
wit: DAV. GLISSON, STEPHEN BARFIELD, RESTON Ɏ POWELL, W. DICKSON
signed: Henry Faison

165. FAISON, ISHAM (CR.035.801.4/1-15)
1 Nov 1831 - Nov Term 1831
wife SARAH the plantation whereon I now live during her natural life but
should my son ELIAS arrive at age 21 before her death he should have
possession of 200 acres of the sd. land, 200 Barrells of corn, 4000 weight
of pork, $100 for and in lieu of one years provisions, 4 head of Horses,
10 head of Cattle, 10 head of Sheep, all the Stock of Hogs on my home
plantation, my stock of Geese, negroes Sam, Everett, Peter, Old Nance,
Harriet, Juliet, Bob, & old Jack, waggon & Gear, cart & oxen, all my
Farming tools & utensils, my Barouche & Chair with the Harness, all my
Houshold & Kitchen Furniture; stepdau. ANNE ELIZA PECK negroes China,
Young Nance & her child Levi, & Dublin, my Dion mare, 4 head of Cattle,
one Bed & Furniture; son HENRY 2 plantations in Sampson County, the Oates
plantation purchased of JOHN OATES & the plantation purchased of JOHN
WATKINS on Cabin Creek; son ISHOM plantation purchased of WILLIAM DUNN
together with a strip of land from the Home plantation at the mouth of
long branch within fifteen Steps of the Spring; son ELIAS whole of my home
plantation except strip mentioned above at wife's death; sons ISHAM & ELIAS
tract of piney wood land on Beaverdam branch in Sampson County; children
HENRY, ISHAM, ELIAS & FRANCES negroes Hinson, Uzzell, Larry, Virgil, Squire,
Kate, Ryal, Isaih, Nelson, Beck, Allen, Temp, Horace, Eveline, George,
Washington, Claresse and Andrew; dau. FRANCES negroes Rufus, Bryan, Bell
& Hannah; negroes Reuben, Jack, Jacob, Mill, Phillis and Harry sold &
money kept until son HENRY is 21 years old & then divided between children
HENRY, ISHAM, ELIAS & FRANCES
extrs: brother ELIAS & nephew JAMES H. HICKS
wit: JAS. LAWSON, SAMUEL A BOWDAIN
signed: Isham Faison

166. FAISON, MARTHA (CR.035.801.4)
15 Jul 1842 - Jan Term 1843
nephew ALBERT R. HICKS my plantation and land upon condition that he pays my
nephew ELIAS SHAW $1000 and if he declines I leave the plantation and land
to ELIAS SHAW upon condition that he pays ALBERT R. HICKS $1000 and if both
decline plantation and lands are to be sold and money divided between
ALBERT R. HICKS & ELIAS SHAW; neice MARY ANN MILLER negroes Rhody & all
her children & Tom, half of my wearing clothes, 6 windsor chairs; nephew
COLIN SHAW negro Isaih, young horse called Durham, 1 bed & furniture;
MARTHA FAISON FREDERICK negro Charlotte & all my silver plate; CAROLINE,
youngest dau. of MARIAH FREDERICK negro Rachel; MARTHA W., dau. of JAMES
HICKS negro Harriet; MARTHA FAISON, dau. of ISHAM F. HICKS negro Rebecca;
MARTHA FAISON, dau. of WILLIAMS HICKS negro Chelly; HENRY, ISHAM, ELIAS
& FRANCIS, children of my Decd. brother ISHAM FAISON negro Avey & all her
children; brother ELIAS FAISON 2 mules; CHARLES BRADLEY $300; FRANCIS
FAISON my looking glass and Beaureau; MARIAH FREDERICK $100 & the other
half of my wearing clothes; residue to JAMES HICKS, WILLIAMS HICKS, ALBERT R.

HICKS, ISHAM HICKS, COLIN SHAW, ELIAS SHAW & MARIAH FREDERICK
extrs: ISHAM HICKS, ALBERT R. HICKS
wit: GEORGE W. HUFHAM, CHARLES BRADLY
signed: Patsey Faison

167. FARIOR, JOHN "of the Parish of North Carolina" (CR.035.801.4-A-146)
nuncupative will 1 Apr 1812 - April Term 1812
dau. NANCY negro Peg & her children Cogdon & Ned
probate lists witnesses as JOHN FARRIOR JUNR & JAMES FARRIOR and was proved
on oath of JOHN FARRIOR JUNR.

168. FARRIER, MARTHA (CR.035.801.4/A-191)
27 Feb 1822 - Jan Term 1823
son HUGH negroes Sal & Mary & all the rest of my property
extr: son HUGH
wit: HUGH FARRIER, SARAH FARIOR
                    signed: Martha _U/_ Farior

169. FARRIOR, JOHN (CR.035.801.4/2-57)
22 Nov 1850 - Jan Term 1851
WILLIAM FARRIOR, EDWARD W. FARRIOR, JESSE B. SOUTHERLAND & JOHNATHAN W.
WILLIAMS to have control & management of all my house hold & kitchen, negroes
Jack & his wife Pege, Charley, Anthony, Ned, Sam, Jim, Frank & Peter, all the
lands adj. the plantation where on I now live including the dwelling House &
all out houses, the CHARLY WHALEY tract, all my lands including & adj. the
lake lands, 4 Cows & Calves or Yerlens & $1000 for the benefit & support of
my wife ELIZABETH and benefit, support and schooling of my 7 youngest children
(not named); children EDWARD W., DAVID & MARTHA $100 each over & above an
equal share with my eldest set of children (not named); eldest set of children the lands on the wist side of the North East River; residue of slaves
to oldest set of children after those of them receives equal to those that
have recd viz WM FARRIOR Recieved Sam, ELIZA SOUTHERLAND recd Seer, MARY
SOUTHERLAND recd Margaret and SARAH SOUTHERLAND Phebe and Dilce; JOHN DAVID
SOUTHERLAND & EDWARD SOUTHERLAND grandchildren & children of my dau. ELIZA
SOUTHERLAND be equal heir with the rest of her children; residue of my lands
including those Known as the Speculating lands sold
extrs: sons WM & EDWARD
wit: N. SANDLIN, CHARLES M. OGLESBY
signed: John Farrior

170. FARRIOR, MARGRET (CR.035.801.4/A-143)
28 Oct 1778 - Jan Court 1779
WILLIAM one bed & furnature; WILLIAM & JOHN all my goods and Chatteles
extr: not named
wit: MARY _+_ MAGEE, HANNAH BATS
                    signed: Margret _Æ_ Farrior

171. FENNEL, PENELOPE (CR.035.801.4/2-95)
11 Feb 1853 - Jul Term 1855
dau. LENORA A., wife of JOHN HENRY HEATH 120 acres whereon JOHN HENRY HEATH
now lives; extr. JAMES G. STOAKES in trust for LENORA A. HEATH all my hogs,
sheep, cattle and more; grdau. CLARRISEY W. HEATH one bed & furniture

extr: JAMES G. STOAKES
wit: J. B. B. MONK, HARDY STRICKLIN
signed: Penneope Fennel
Codicil: 10 Oct 1854
item in my said will giving to LENORA A. HEATH my land be considered null
and void in as much as I have sold said land the money from which is to
be used by my excutor for the maintainance of my dau. and her children
wit: T. NEWKIRK, H. NEWKIRK
signed: Pennelopa Fennell

172. FOLDS, JOSEPH (CR.035.801.4)
2 Dec 1802 - Apr Term 1812
see the will of JOSEPH WELTZ as the name "Folds" is used in the body of the
will but is signed and probated as Weltz

173. FORLAW, ELIZABETH (CR.035.801.4/2-99)
24 Mar 1841 - Jan Term 1856
As to the Property which was secured to me by a marriage contract entered
into and duly executed by me & my husband on the   day of June 1821 which
was regularly recorded & registered which embraces negroes Slaves Chloe
& her children Westbrook, Bill, Caroline, Cork & Penny together with the
increase of the females I lend to my husband during his natural life and
at his death to my children DAVID W., PRISCILLA W., ELIZABETH J., THOMAS,
ROBERT & NANCY
extrs: husband JOHN FORLAW, JEREMIAH PEARSALL
wit: EPHRAIM STRICKLIN, ELIZABETH (X) STRICKLIN
                              signed: Elizabeth Forlaw

174. FOUNTAIN, JOAB [also listed as JACOB] (CR.035.801.4/A-144)
24 Aug 1798 - Oct Term 1800
wife MARY plantation whearun I Now Live, one bed and firneture, 1/3 of my
house hold furneture, all the Stock of Catthel and Hogs that is in my own
proper mark; son JOAB 300 acres with a Smal Claring Lying on the head of
Gravly run, 1 Meir, 7 head of Cattel that is in his own mark, 1 Sow with
all the Hogs in the Same marke of the Cattel; son JOHN 500 acres with the
plantation wheare on I Now Live, 300 acres at my Dearth & 20 at the Darth
of my wife, 7 head of Cattel in a mark to him, all the Hog that is Called
hisen; dau. LYDA BROWN 5 shillings; dau. MIRRIM BROWN 5 shillings; dau.
TAMMEY one bead and feirneture, 6 head of Cattel marked for hir; dau. MARY
one bead and feirneture, 3 head of Cattel marked for hir; dau. SARAH
4 head of Cattel marked for hir, the bead at her mother Dearth; daus.
TAMMAY & MARY remaining 2/3 of my household firneture
extrs: JOB THIGPEN, JOHN FARRIOR
wit: GIDON HAWKINS, STEPHEN BRABHAM, JOB THIGPEN
                              signed: Joab ⨍ Fountain

175. FREDERICK, WILLIAM (CR.035.801.4/1-5)
25 Mar 1830 - Nov Term 1830
wife NANCY negroes Celia & her son John, Lucy, Nancy, Susy & Daniel,
1 year's provisions, 1 horse, my rideing chair & harness, household &
kitchen furniture, 3 cows and Calves, 2 sows & pigs, my stock of sheep;
at wife's death negroes Lucy, Nancy, Susy & Daniel divided between the
children of my son WILLIAM K; grdau. BETSEY JAMES, dau. of my son JAMES
FREDERICK dec'd $1; dau. CATHARINE HOUSTON my persimon land called the
Tanner Plantation; dau. POLLY WILKINSON negro Jackson; dau. JANE TIPLER

land on Stewarts Creek, lands on Buck branch, all household and kitchen furniture now in her possession which was purchased by me the second of November eighteen hundred and Twenty eight; son WILLIAM K. land whereon I now live & negro Ichmael in trust for his 2 sons, WILLIAM KENNON & PETER COFFEE until they arrive at the age of 21; negroes Lott & Lydia sold & money divided between daus. CATHARINE HOUSTON, JANE TIPLER & NANCY McDANIEL; grson PETER COFFEE FREDERICK my still
extrs: son WILLIAM K. & son in law JOHN HOUSTON
wit: BLANEY WILLIAMS, HARPER WILLIAMS
signed: Willim ᘛᘏᘜ Frederick

176 FREDRICK/FREDERICK, FELIX (CR.035.801.4/1-28)
4 May 1831 - Aug Term 1832
wife KATHARINE all my negroes & all my cleard land for her life time, all my house & kitching furniture, my mare & stock of all kind and at her death negroes to be sold & money divided between my daus. [not named] and three youngest Boys [not named] & three Boys to get stock & furniture; son PATRICK land on East side of the Big Branch Except the wheet patch field adj. the percoson path above Patrick's field, JOHN S. HILL & WILLIAM NEWTON decd.; son THOMAS KENAN FREDERICK land on Big Branch at the mouth of the little branch adj. the burnt percoson north of the land given PATRICK; sons JACKY & JAMES all remaining land; son WILLIAM 50¢; son NORICE 50¢; son FELIX 50¢
extrs: my good wife & ISAAC TALOR
wit: JOHN S. HILL, D. B. NEWTON
signed: Felix Fredric
Codicil: 6 Jun 1832
wife KATHARINE negro Betty for her lifetime & then sold & the money divided between my dau. ANNY TAYLOR & my 3 youngest sons [not named]; I take from my daus. NANCY MALPRUS, JANE GRIMES & CATHARINE GRIMES all rights to the negroes which I gave them in my will & give them $1 a piece
wit: JOHN S. HILL, D. B. NEWTON
signed: Felix Frederick

177. FUSEL, BENJAMIN (CR.035.801.4/A-146)
11 Aug 1783 - Jan Court 1784
sons BENJAMIN & JOHN two peceses of land 320 acres & 150 which will apear by the patents; wife ELIZABETH all my Live Stock & moveabels During Hir Widowhood
extr: not named
wit: DAVID JONES SNOR, JOHN 𝐽𝑅 RIVININGBARK, PETER 𝒫𝒴 YOUNG
signed: Benjamin 𝐵𝑓 Fusel

178. FUSSELL, ELIZABETH (CR.035.801.4/3-14)
20 Sep 1859 - Jul Term 1860 [very hard to read]
dau. ANNA JANE, wife of KILBY SALMON negro Sarah; son STEPHEN $500; son BENJAMIN negro Brister; dau. NANCY, wife of GEO. W. WILLIAMS negro Dinah which she is not to sell or convey without the consent of my brother STEPHEN WILLIAMS; son JOHN negro Hester
extr: son JOHN
wit: JOHN W. PETERSON, BIZZELL JOHNSON
signed: Elizabeth 𝒳 Fussell

179. GARNER, NATHAN SENR. (CR.035.801.5/3-29)
11 Mar 1857 - Jan Term 1861
eldest dau. LOUISA GRADY 194 acres below to little Juniper Branch adj.
BRYAN CASEY, $425; next eldest dau. MELILDA DAIL 120 acres whereon She
now lives, $500; next dau. CLARISA DAIL all my land lying below my Mill
between the Mill Branch and little Juniper Branch except one acre at the
east end of the Mill Dam, $575; dau. HARRIET REAVIS 172 acres whereon
She now lives, $400; fifth dau. AXY SIMMONS negro Nelly age 15 years, $500;
youngest dau. RACHEL negro Martha, $500 and if she die leaving no children
then her bequest to go to AXY SIMMONS; oldest son BASSIL $300; son HENRY
all my home tract lying between the Mill Branch and the Gum Branch down
the Run of the North East and up the lower line of the Herring Tract, 50
acres of the Herring Tract for Timber which is layed off up Gum Branch,
negro Ellect; youngest son SIMION 148 acres NEEDHAM SOUTHERLAND Tract;
residue sold & proceeds to sons BASSEL, NATHAN, HENRY and SIMEON
extrs: sons BASSEL and NATHAN
wit: D. JONES, N. B. WHITFIELD
signed: Nathan Garner

180. GARRISON, EPHRAM (CR.035.801.5/A-175)
27 Nov 1792 - Jan Term 1793
child POLLY 50 acres Being the piece Which my Mother Now Lives uppon,
1 Cow & Calf Except the Child Now in the Womb of my wife Shoud Be a Boy
which if it Lives & is a man Child then the aforementioned piece of Land
Shall Be my Son DAVID GARRISONs; son DAVID 100 acres bought of PHILLIP
ROUSE, 1 Cow & Calf Except the Aforementioned Child In my Wifes Womb
Shoud Be a Boy then the afore Said hundred Acres of Land to be my Son
THOMAS GARRISON's; son THOMAS 100 acres being the plantation which I Now
Live One, 1 Cow & Calf With the former Exciption Being made Concerning
the Aforementioned Child In the Womb Which it Shoud Be A Boy the Within
mentioned hundred Acres of Land Which I Now Live on to that Child And
Its Name to Be Called EPHRAM GARRISON; wife JENNEY my household furneture
& plantation tools, remainder of My Stock of Hogs, Cattle, Sheep & horses;
trusty friend ELIZABETH STRICTLING 1 Cow & Calf
extrs: wife JENNY, brother THOMAS, WILLIAM CARR
wit: WM MCANNE, JOSEPH MERRILL
signed: Ephraim Garrason

180A. GAVIN, EDWARD C. "of Sampson" (5-309)
30 Apr 1850 - 6 Mar 1909
plantation on which I now reside Containing Six hundred & fifty five &
three quarters acres be Sold with Exception of a portion I reserved for my
wife CHARITY the line of her portion to begin on Galonos Branch at the
mouth of the little branch to the first fork to the main road; money
arising from the Sale of the land be equally divided between my four
children SAMUEL JAMES, MARY BLENDA SMITH, MARGARET ANN HINES and SUSAN
MATILDA PIGFORD; one acre be reserved on the plantation where the Grave
yard now is west of the dwelling house between one & two hundred yards &
is Called the white grave Yard not be Sold; plantation on Stewarts Creek
Containing one thousand and twenty Seven & a half acres be sold and money
arrising be equally divided between my four children SAMUEL JAMES, MARY
BLENDA SMITH, MARGARET ANN HINES and SUSAN MATILDA PIGFORD; wife CHARITY
negroes Sylvia, Anna, Jane, Lously, Dick, Sylvia's son Tom & London and

after her death to be Sold and money arrising be equally divided between
my four children SAMUEL JAMES, MARY BLENDA SMITH, MARGARET ANN HINES &
SUSAN MATILDA PIGFORD; negroes Cherry, Mary, Walter, Candis, Lewis, Wills,
Reuben, Parker, Hasty, John, Bill, Aham, Hasty's son Tom, Dave, Mike, Penny,
Nehemiah, Mariah & Betsey be equally divided into five lots and one lot to
be sold & the money arrising to be lent to my dau. SALLY JANE TORRANCE and
the other four lots to son SAMUEL JAMES & daus. MARY BLENDA SMITH, MARGARET
ANN HINES & SUSAN MATILDA PIGFORD; wife CHARITY one horse & mule, one yoke
of oxen, two cows & Calves, five Ews & Lambs, Two Sows & pigs & a Sufficient
quantity of provisions of all kinds for her years suport, a Buggy & harness;
remainder of my Stocks & perishable property sold & money arrising be equally
divided between my children SAMUEL JAMES, MARY BLENDA SMITH, MARGARET ANN
HINES & SUSAN MATILDA PIGFORD; son SAMUEL JAMES not being a man of rational
mind & not capable of taking care of himself or property JAMES B. PIGFORD
to act as his Guardian and manage his own business; dau. MARGARET ANN HINES
not being a woman of a rational mind & not capable of taking care of herself
or property WILLIAM H. SMITH to act as her guardian; extrs. to pay MARGARET
ANN and WM HINES as heirs of JAMES HINES decd. the amt. due by me as guardian to the said heirs
extrs: son in law JAMES B. PIGFORD living in New Hanover & Son in law
       WILLIAM H. SMITH living in Sampson
wit: JOSHUA R. EZZELL, JOHN WEST
signed: Edward C. Gavin

181. GAVIN, SAMUEL (CR.035.801.5/A-155)
21 Dec 1761 - Feb Court 1762
wife PATIENCE use of all my Lands, negroes, Houses & Stock During Her Life;
son JOHN when he reaches 21 the plantation whearon I now Live, negro Cuff;
residue to sons SAMUEL, LEWIS & CHARLES
extrs: wife PATIENCE, THOMAS CARRILL
wit: HENRY HOLLINGSWORTH, JAMES BAKER
                         signed: Samuel   Gavin

182. GIBBS, BERSHABA (CR.035.801.5/1-68)
22 Aug 1833 - Jul Term 1835
body to be buried in a Christian lik maner at the decretean of my dau.
ELIZABETH THOMPSON; dau. ELIZABETH THOMPSON all my household Good &
Kitchin furniture, all my Stock of Every Kind and at her death it to be
divided in two Equal parts & one to be Given up for Equaly divisen betwen
the Lawful children of LAWRENCE THOMPSON & the other half to be Equaly
devided between the Lawfull children of THOMAS GIBBS
extr: dau. ELIZABETH THOMPSON
wit: SM. DAVIS
signed: Ba Gibbs

183. GIBBS, JOHN SENR. (CR.035.801.5/A-164)
4 Dec 1809 - Jan Term 1810
wife SARAH 70 or 80 acres of the Plantation where on I now live Beginning
at the Corner of the field that includes the House where the fence joines
below the Corn Crib & adj. LEVEN WATKINS, Cowhole Swamp including the Houses
and part of the Orchard Reserving Nevertheless to my Son CHARLES the Houses
where he now lives in with the Kitchen and Garden with one Acre Round the
House for a yard; wife SARAH negroes Dafne, Arthur, James & Cash, all my
Household & Kitchen Furniture, all my Plantation tools and Implements of
Husbandry, my Horse called Kitty, my mare called Strick, 5 head of Sheep,

two Cows & Calves, four Sows and their Pigs which Ranges over Cowhole
Swamp, one other large white Sow with five Pigs, all the Geese and Poultry
on the Plantation; son JOHN $1; son CHARLES $1; daus. SUSANNA BURNS,
TAMZARINE ROGERS & ZILPAH JERNIGAN negroes Dafne, Arthur, Jim & Cash at
wife's decease; dau. SARAH BENNETT negro Toney; dau. MARY BOURDEN negro
Simon; dau. CHARITY BOURDEN negroes Lucy, Marten & Edney, bed & furniture
already given her; if the foal the mare Strick is now with should live
I give it to my grandson JOHN GIBBS; residue sold & monies to go to all
my daus. SUSANNA BURNS, TAMZARENE ROGERS, ZILPAH JERNIGAN, SARAH BENNETT,
MARY BOURDEN & CHARITY GIBBS
extrs: sons JOHN & CHARLES
wit: WM DICKSON, LEWIS BARFIELD, THOMAS BENNETT
signed: John Gibbs Sener

184. GILLESPIE, JAMES (CR.035.801.5/A-178)
2 May 1804 - Apr Term 1805
son DAVID double cased Gold Watch, new boots & silver spoons, negro Frances
son of Satio as his share of the slaves settled by marriage contract on my
Late wife; son JOSEPH negroes Jack & Old Toney, 1 mule, 1 Stud Horse, 1
small survey of land adj. his plantation, $200, all my Coopers & Carpenters
tools, he to take charge of Guy & his wife & see that they are comfortably
maintained during their lives; son JOSEPH for his son JAMES negro Tom,
my case of pistols, 2 Cows & Calves; dau. LUCY negroes Daniel, Pensorey [?]
& Judy, 1 Feather bed & furniture, 1/3 part of all my table furniture, a set
of tea China, a set of silver tea spoons, Salora & her youngest child as her
proportion of the slaves setled on my wife; dau. ELIZABETH MORGAN negroes
Big Sam & his wife Cate & 2 children Leonora & Johanna, 1 set of large
Silver Spoons, one Set of Tea China & Silver Tea Spoons, 1 feather bed &
furniture, Moilcy & Tobey as her proportion of the Slaves Setled on my wife;
dau. JANE negroes Harvey, Nance & Mariah, 1 feather bed & furniture, 1/3
part of all my table furniture, 1 Set of Tea China, 1 Set of Silver Tea
Spoons, Warick as her proportion of the Slaves Setled on my late wife; dau.
MILDARD ANN negroes Litle toney, Bet & Ben, 1/3 part of my table Furniture,
one Set of Tea China & Six Silver tea spoons, 1 bed & furniture, Lot as her
proportion of the Slaves Setled on my late wife; lands in Tennessee sold
extrs: DAVID GILLESPIE, JOSEPH GILLESPIE
Codicil: 8 May 1804
CHARLOTTE MUMFORD 1 feather bed & furniture; JOSEPH MUMFORD silver watch
and they ever to be Considered as a part of the family
wit: JAMES MIDDLETON, ROBT. MIDDLETON, KEITLY MIDDLETON
signed: James Gillespie
Codicil: 30 Oct 1804
son JOSEPH negro Sam given to dau. ELIZABETH MORGAN and she to have $300
& she to enjoy all the profits from negro Pomp now in the possession of her
husband ARON MORGAN; $300 be laid out to purchase a young female slave for
my grandson JAMES WASHINGTON MORGAN
extr: COL. WM. DICKSON, EDWD. PEARSELL
wit: JAMES MIDDLETON, ROBT. MIDDLETON, KITTY MIDDLETON
signed: James Gillespie

185. GILLESPIE, JOSEPH (CR.035.801.5)
18 Jun 1835 - Jan Term 1837
wife JANE life estate in 1/2 of my plantation including 52 acres purchased
of WILLIAM ROGERS adj. the Avenue, DANIEL C. MOORE's fence, the Blacksmith's
shop, the head of Briery branch, long branch, Snake Branch, CLARESY McGOWEN's
fence, ALEXANDER DICKSON, the edge of the swamp, the Armstrong old Cotton
field, the Michael field, the east ditch of the low ground, the Herds
grase lot, the turpentine Cisterns at the Coopers shop, Long pond, BENAJAH
CARROL, Cowhone Branch, Matchet's Branch & at her death to my son SHADRACH
G. R., negroes Daniel Jr, Stuttering Nelly, Edy, Susy & Joe, my Jackson
Horse, my mare Polly Hopkins, my pleasure Waggon & Harness, 1 Yoke of Oxen
& cart, the Rockfish Stock of Cattle, 10 head of sheep, 3 Sows & pigs, 2
Beds & furneture, 1 Side Board, 1 Bureau, 2 Tables, 1/2 doz. chairs, 2 axes,
2 Grubing hoes, 2 Weeding hoes, 1 pr of Iron Wedges, 1 years provesions for
herself & family exclusive of Hirelings, 1/2 of my Cupboard, Side board &
Kitchen furniture; son JAMES negro George; son WILLIAM D. $50, lent him
for the purpose of Boarding, Clothing & Schooling his Children negroes
Junius, Clary, Anthony & Sam and they to go to his children JOSEPH, JAMES,
& CATHARINE; son DAVID his own note which I hold against him for $154,
negro Derry; son JOSEPH GEORGE W. the Gray mare which he rode away, Saddle
& Bridle, 1 bed & furniture, $200 with the interest from the hire of my
negroes Sophia & her child Charlotte, Daniel, Bristol & Bob; son CLEMONT M. P.
my Marsh Branch plantation, 1 bed & furniture, my Saladin Filly, saddle &
Bridle, negroes old man Bristol, old woman Nelly, Charles, Bill, Benny &
Mary Ann; son JOHN W. S. residue of my manor plantation, my JOHN HEATH
plantation, 1 bed & furniture; negroes Warwick, Spencer, Harry, Sally,
Christopher, Sarah, Lucy, Chloe, Tom, Matilda, Tamerlane, Dick, Flora &
Jim be hired out to support my infant children JOHN W. S. & SHADRACH GAIUS
ROWE; infant son SHADRACH GAIUS ROWE 1 bed & furniture, a note of TIMOTHY
NEWKIRK & one on JACOB WILLS worth about $880
extrs: nephew Doctor JAMES G. DICKSON, son CLEMENT M. P.
wit: J. M. MIDDLETON, D. C. MORE
signed: Jo Gillespie

186. GILLESPIE, SHADRACH G. R. (CR.035.801.5/3-59)
27 Aug 1860 - Oct Term 1862
brother JOHN W. S. plantation & all my land cleared & uncleared, my Library
of Books; mother JANE negroes Yam, Dick, Jim, Bill, Lewis, Matilda, Lavinia,
Mary, Martha, Catharine, Lucy & Laura, all my notes & money, household and
Kitchen furniture, farming utensils & stock
extrs: cousin Doctor JAMES G. DICKSON, brother JOHN W. S.
wit: J. B. B. MONK, D. D. WELLS
signed: S. G. R. Gillespie

187. GLISSON, BRYAN (CR.035.801.5/A-182)
2 Aug 1824 - Oct Term 1825
wife SALLY 240 acres where JOSEPH WALDER now lives, 1 Grea Mare by the Name
of doll and at her death or marrage to my son ABRAHAM; dau. ZILPHEA ANN
10¢; son BRYAN H. 10¢; two younges daus. SALLY JANE & SUSANNAH the BEN
CHREECH land, Cross road land & LUKE HERRING land by Estemation in all
three pieces 808 acres, 6 cows; dau. SALLY JEAN 1 feather bed & furniture;

brother ABRAHAM $150; brother STEPHEN H. $100; BRYAN, son of WM CHERRY
$60; WM. B. son of GEORGE F. KORNEGAY $60; residue of property to my
three youngest children; brothers ABRAHAM & STEPHEN H. my wearing Cloths
extrs: brothers ABRAHAM & STEPHEN H.
wit: SAML. DAVIS, DAVID ALBERTSON
signed: B. Glisson

188. GLISSON, JACOB (CR.035.801.5/A-166)
30 Nov 1805 - Jan Term 1806
wife MARY all my hole parishable property in Doors and Out Doors, all my
lands Excepting what is above the Little Branch in the field toward ALEXDR.
O DANIELS for her lifetime; JOHN GLISSON SENR all the rest of my Land
Lying East of the Little Branch runing west Side of my plantation adj.
JOHN GLISSON JUNR son of LEWIS GLISSEN in Goshen Swamp; LEWIS GLISSON all
the rest of my Lands Lying west of Sd. Branch; brothers & sisters ABRAHAM,
ISAAC, MICHAL, FREDK, RACHEL, GUFFORD, MARY SUMMERLING, CHARITY SUMMERLING
& PRUDENCE CHAMBERS 1 Shilling Starling apeace
extr: wife MARY
wit: O. ODANIEL, ALEX ODANIEL
                    signed: Jacob   Glisson

189. GOFF, JOHN (CR.035.801.5/A-168)
20 Feb 1809 - Jan Term 1810
son THOS. 5 shillings sterling; son JOHN 5 shillings sterling; son
WILLIAM 5 shillings sterling; dau. SIVEL JAMES 5 shillings sterling;
dau. ARRIBELAH WILLIAMS 5 shillings sterling; wife ELIZABETH all the
hole of my Estate Real and personal
extrs: wife ELIZABETH, WILLIAM STOAKES
wit: WM. WARD, TIMOTHY MURFFY
                    signed: John Goff

190. GORE, JOHN SENR. (CR.035.801.5/A-160)
28 Nov 1819 - Jan Term 1822
after my death, and my wife FRANCES GORE's, to be decently buried and all
my just debts to be paid; dau. ELIZABETH $1; son WILLIAM $1; grandau.
NELLY, dau. of WILLIAM 1 cow & Calf; dau. POLLY MILLER $1; dau. SARAH
BLANSHARD $1; son JOHN $1; dau. REBECAH $1; dau. NELLY HINES $1 and
the residue of my estate divided amongst her children after the death of
FRANCES GORE my wife
extrs: JONATHAN GORE, ISAAC GORE
wit: HENRY   BEST, D. K. LOVE
                    signed: John   Gore Senr

191. GRADDY, JOHN (CR.035.801.5/A-152)
9 Feb 1773 - Apr Term 1787
wife MARY 1 father Bed & furniture, 1 horse, Bridle & Saddle, 5 cows &
Calves and the plantation Whereon I Now Live Dureing hir Widdowhood; dau.
MARY GOODMAN 10 shillings proclamation money; son WILLIAM 10 shillings
proclamation money; son JOHN 10 shillings proclamation money; dau.
CHARITY HARRING 10 shillings proclamation money; dau. ANN CROOM 10
shillings proclamation money; son ALEXANDER 10 shillings proclamation
money; son LEWIS 10 shillings proclamation money; dau. ELESABUTH OUTLAW
10 shillings proclamation money; Son in Law ISAAC DAWSON 10 shillings
proclamation money; Son in law WILLIAM LAWS 10 shillings

proclamation money; grandson JAMES, son of my dau. ANN GRADDY 1 good father
Bed and furniture, 1 horse, Bridle & Saddle; son FRADRICK Land and plantation Where on I Now Live, remandir part of my house hold goods, Stock of
horses, Cattle and hogs, Blacksmiths Tools
extr: son FRADRICK
wit: WILLM WHITFIELD, BRYAN WHITFIELD
                        signed: John ⚏ Graddy

192. GRADY, ALEXANDER SR. (CR.035.801.5)
14 Jan 1819 - Oct Term 1825
wife ANNA all my Property During her lifetime and then to my children (not
named)
extr: not named
wit: A. O. Grady, Aleander Graddy Jr.
                        signed: Alexander 🐾 Graddy Snr

193. GRADY, ALEXR JR. (CR.035.801.5/2-83)
9 May 1846 - Apr Term 1854
sisters PUTNEY, NANCY, REPSEY & MARY all my lands that lies west of the new
road that leads from ALEXR GRADYS SR to A. O. GRADYs known as the FRED GRADY
100 acre track & the ABNER GRADY plantation adj. GOODMAN GRADYs & JAMES M.
GRADYs lands; oldest brother OUTLAW GRADY lands I purchased of PETER
KORNIGAY & KEENAN GRADY reserving the use of the houses and lands that I
purchased of KEENAN GRADY to his forther JAMES SR. so long as he lives or
is amind to stay on it whure he now lives which lands lie No of Burn coat
Et. of the long branch & joines the PETER KORNEGAY lands on the Et. side;
brothers OUTLAW & GOODMAN all the part of the ABNER GRADY lands whitch lies
East of the new road leading from ALEXR GRADYS SR to A. O. GRADYs whitch
said lands my father ALEXR GRADY SR has a life estate in, the lands to be
divided by a north - south line so as to give OUTLAW GRADY half lying next
to the ISLER KORNEGAY lands and GOODMAN the other half lying next to him
and down to the new road; brothers & sister OUTLAW, HENERY, GOODMAN,
HACK W., JAMES M, & ELIZZA ANN $1 each
extrs: brothers OUTLAW & GOODMAN
wit: J. W. OUTLAW, S. H. SIMMONS
signed: Alxr Grady jr

194. GRADY, HENRY "of Mount Pleasant" (CR.035.801.5/1-56)
3 Dec 1830 - Oct Term 1834
it has been an opinion of mine that a man aught to devise to his wife if
She Survives him all such property as he recieved with her in order that
She Should make such disposition of it as She Should please & as I have
Survived my first wife ELIZABETH & She never having in her life time Even
intimated to me how She Wished it disposed off and as I have taken a Second
wife out of the same family viz. her Niece ELIZABETH WHITFIELD I feel it a
duty En Cum bent on me to devise to her all such property as I received by
her aunt, negro Boron, 1 feather bed, 1 pr of Pillows, 1 Bolster, 1 pr of
Sheets, 1 Bed Cover, 1 Counterpin, 1 Chist in the East room up Stairs,
1 side saddle, also all property I shall receive from her father WILLIAM
WHITFIELD, also 1 undivided moiety of 1/4 part of 435 acres on Maple Swamp
where JACOB WILLIAMS now lives it being the land he conveyed to his sons
JOHN & OUTLAW WILLIAMS the sd. 1/4 being GEORGE WILLIAM'S interest, negro
Sary Commonly Calld Sal; son B. W. negro Larry; son B. F. negro Frank,

1 horse named Ball, 1 gray mare named Kate, 1 Feather Bed Stead & firniture
containing Curtains, 1 Bass Eight day clock, my Library of Books, all my
Scals, Weights, measures, Steelyards, mercantile Books, Letters, Pappers,
etc.; son ATLAS I. 1 feather bed & furniture; son STEPHEN M. 1 feather bed
& furniture, 1 pr. Silver Spectacles; dau. ELIZA ANN SIMMONS negro Pender;
dau. SUSA KORNEGY negroes Rose and her child Luce & Mary; dau. PATSEY
JACKSON 50¢; dau. LETTY WHITE 50¢; dau. HARRIET 2 Feather Beds, Steads &
firniture containing each a Set of Curtains, 2 trunks; residue sold &
proceeds devided amongst wife ELIZABETH & children A. O., B. W., B. F.,
A. I., S. M., & HARRIET
extrs: son A. O. GRADY & RICHARD MILLER
wit: JOHN MAXWELL, MARY MAXWELL
signed: H Grady
Codicil: 10 Aug 1831
son-in-law JAMES S. WHITE negro Luce & children Dinah & Julia, 1 feather
bed & furniture containing a set of curtains, Stead
wit: JOHN MAXWELL, MARY MAXWELL
signed: H. Grady

195. GRADY, HENRY G. (CR.035.801.5/4-27)
10 Aug 1858 - 9 Nov 1870
THEODOSIA, dau. of WILLIAM W. GRADY 161 acres where I now reside, my crop,
stock, all my furniture, provisions, & tools reserving however the use of
the same to my wife ELIZA during her natural life time
extr: SHERWOOD GRADY
wit: LEWIS JONES, WILLIAM A. JONES
signed: Henry G. Grady

196. GRAHAM, SALLY (2-80/CRX Box 243)
20 Sep 1849 - Jan Term 1854
sister ELIZA METTS negroes Doll & Betty; niece SARAH REBECCA KENAN &
SARAH R. KENAN's children (not named) my Beds, my Bedstids, Silver Spoons,
Beauros, Curtains and in a word all my Household Furniture, negroes Amanda,
Matilda, Jack, Simon, Betsey & Washington; niece MARY ELIZA GRAHAM negroes
Rachel, Emy & Lucinda; nephew STEPHEN GRAHAM negroes Albert, Julia and
her two children; CHAUNCEY W. GRAHAM negroes Louisa, Tom, Rachel and
Charity; nephew FREDERICK C. METTS negro Henry, my money and notes;
nephew WILLIAM PENN METTS negroe George; THOMAS STEPHEN KENAN & JAMES
GRAHAM KENAN my land and Houses
wit: JOHN J. WHITEHEAD, ALFRED BOYETT
signed: Sally Graham
niece SALLY GRAHAM STANLEY negro Jennettie; niece SARAH R. KENAN and her
children residue of my property
extr: not named
wit: JOHN J. WHITEHEAD, ALFRED BOYETT
signed: Sally Graham

197. GRAHAM, STEPHEN (CR.035.801.5/1-61)
12 Oct 1834 - Jan Term 1835
wife NANCY plantation whereon I now live & the Plantation on Stocking Head
Swamp, my Carriage or Gig, Riding Chairs, farming utensils, Carts, Horses,
Mules, Beds & Furniture, Household & Kitchen Furniture, $500 in Bank Stock
of the Bank of the State of North Carolina, all my Books; son CHANCEY

WILLIAMS my lands on the North Side of Goshen adj. JOHN CARR & the lands on
the East Side of the North East River to son STEPHEN; after wife's share
of Beds and Furniture residue to be divided amongst my Children CHANCEY W.,
STEPHEN, SARAH R. & MARY ELISA; ballance of my Bankstock Containing $2000
to my 4 children; DR. WILLIAM K. FREDERICK $100 as a compensation for his
Medical Services during my Sickness; lands lent to my wife to be divided
Equally between my 2 daus. at her decease; my 2 Old and infirm Negroes
Rachail & Hannah be Comfortably supported out of my estate; residue of
negroes to wife & 4 children
extr: not named
wit: WM. SWINSON, JAMES CARRELL, MARGARET SWINSON
signed: S. Graham

198. GRAY, JOHN "of the parish of St. Gabriel ... Planter" (CR.035.801.5/A-153)
3 Jan 1781 - Apr Court 1781
wife ELIZABETH the plantation whereon I now Live, my stock of Catle and hoggs
for her Naturall Life; son THOMAS 1/2 of my Land where I now Live Lying
Next to Grove Swamp to be Divided By a Direct Line from Burtons to Stoke's
Line, 1 feather Bead & furniture, my Coopers Tools, 1 2 or 3 year old heifer;
son WM. my Sorrell mare, the first Living Child that my Negroe Girl pleasant
may have, 1 feather bed & furniture, 1 2 or 3 year old heifer; dau. ELLEN
Negroe Girl pleasant after my wife's Decease, 1 feather Bed and furniture,
1 2 or 3 yr old heifer, 1 Box Smothing Iron; son JAMES the Other half of
the plantation I now Live on, 1 feather Bed & furniture, 1 2 or 3 year old
heifer; residue sold to educate my children
extrs: wife ELIZABETH, ANDREW McINTIRE, JAMES GILLESBE
wit: THOMAS #⌐ JOHNSTON, _____ BELL, ARABELA McINTIRE
signed: John Gray

199. GREEN, JAMES (CR.035.801.5/A-155)
2 Jan 1784 - Jan Term 1784
OFFERIAS HAGANS 125 acors that I purchist of SAMUEL BELL liing on the marsh
Swamp, 2 Cows & Cavs, 1 Sorrel mare; THOMAS HARDEN 125 acors that I purchist
of LEVY MANUEL Liing betwen the marsh Swamp and marsh branch, 2 Cows & Cavs;
RACHAL HAGINS 100 acors on which I now liv with All the rest of my Estate
With in Dores and without Dors
extrs: ROBRT BUTLER, WILLIAM BUTLER
wit: ARTHEOR BROWN, WILLIAM ✚ EVERIT, SARAH ⊥ NEMAN
signed: James ✚ Green

200. GREEN, JOHN (CR.035.801.5/A-176)
30 Mar 1807 - Jul Term 1807
wife ELIZABETH 1 bed & furniture, all my household furniture, 1 cow & calf,
1 Steer or heifer, 1 horse valued at $10, my house & plantation whereon I
now reside during her life only & at her death to my son TIMOTHY & my 4
daughters; son TIMOTHY 3 axes, 2 ploughs, 2 Iron wedges, 1 froe, 1 cross
cut saw, 1 Gauge, 2 Chisels, 3 head of Cattle, 1 sickle, 1 rifle gun; son
JOHN 5 shillings; dau. SARAH 1 bed which she now claims, 3 head of cattle;
dau. ANN 1 bed and furniture which she now has in possession, 3 heads of
Cattle; dau. PHEBE 3 head of Cattle, 1 bed & furniture, 6 head of sheep;
dau. ELIZABETH bed I bequeathed to her mother, 3 head of Cattle, 10 head

of young hogs
extrs: TIMOTHY GREENE, SAMUEL DAVIS
wit: WM. W. RIVENBARK
signed: John Green

201. GREEN, LOTT (CR.035.801.5/A-170)
28 Jan 1829 - May Term 1829
wife SARAH my house and Plantation with all the Land that I tend, all my
houshold furniture, all my Stock of Every Kind during her natural life;
son JAMES my tar Kill and all the Land not given to his mother; son
SAMUEL 1 Cow & Calf; dau. ANN WILLIAMS 1 2 yr old stear; it will be
understood that I have given my daus. MARTHA, REBECKAH and ELIZABETH all
that I intend for them
extrs: BENJAMIN FUSSELL, STEPHEN WILLIAMS
wit: DD. WILLIAMS, BENJAMIN FUSSELL
                              signed: Lott ✠ Green

202. GREY, JOHN (CR.035.801.5)
16 Jun 1855 - Apr Term 1863
sons JOHN, LEWIS, MORRIS and OWEN $1 each in adition to what I have hear
to fore given them; dau. REBECAR plantation that I now live on lying on
the North side of Turkey swamp & both sides of the Wilmington & Weldon
Rail Road suposed to be 75 acres, negroe Betsey & her children Dick, Henry
& Juliana all my stock & farming utensils, house hold & Kitching furniture
extr: DANIEL BOWDEN
wit: B. C. BOWDEN, HOWELL BEST
signed: John Grey

203. GRIMES, HUGH (CR.035.801.5/A-161)
2 Apr 1780 - Jan Court 1781
grandson JESSE 1 fether Bed & firneytuer; wife (not named) Rest of my
Estate which I now presess for heir Lifetime and at heir Deceas to be
Equaley Divid amongst my Children (not named)
extrs: sons JOSEPH & SAMSON
wit: JOHN WHITEHEAD, JOHN SULIVEN, BURWELL ✗ WHITEHEAD
signed: Hugh Grimes

204. GRIMES, JOSEPH (CR.035.801.5/A-158)
30 Dec 1779 - Jan Term 1790
wife ELLENDER the plantation whereon I now Live During her life, 10 Cows
& Calves, all my Stock of Hoggs & sheep & plantation utensialls; sons
CHARLS, JOHN, JOSEPH, JAMES & THOMAS all my Lands and tenaments to be
Equally Divid between them on the Arival of the Oldest son at the age of
21; if the Child that my wife is now pregnant with be a boy it shall
Bear an Equal Division with my other Children & if it should be a Girl
my Negroe wench Hanah to be sold and the money Instantly Laid out in a
young Negroe Wench for the use of said Daughter; sons to have an equal
share of my Neal Cattle except my Oldest son CHARLES who has a number
Equal to his share; negroe Jacob be sold at public Sail & the money
Aplied towards the payment of my Debts & the remainder appled toward
schooling my said Children; negroes Benard & Adam to be anually hired
extrs: JAMES GILLISPIE, SAMSON GRIMES
wit: _____ GILLESPIE, EDWD. PEARSALL, MARGARET PEARSALL
signed: Joseph Grimes

205. GRIMES, SAMPSON (CR.035.801.5/A-169)
27 Mar 1828 - May Term 1828
son JESSE 1/4 part of my lands at the lower part Joining the land that I gave
him; son JAMES 1/4 part of my lands at the upper part; son WILLIAM 1/4 part
of my land; dau. EASTER BRANCH 1/4 part of my land; daus. EASTER BRANCH &
NANCY STROUD & sons JESSE, JAMES & WILLIAM remainder of my property of every
kind
extrs: son JAMES, son-in-law ARCHELAEUS BRANCH
wit: JNO. WATKINS, TH. J. KINNEAR, SAMUEL SULLIVENS
signed: Sampson Grimes

206. GRIMSLEY, JAMES (CR.035.801.5/1-50)
29 Oct 1827 - Feb Term 1834
wife SARAH during here naterl life land on the No. Wt. Side of my plantation
from the cross fence by the well that is to water the Stock to poley Bridg
and to the back line including the house hold, 1 Horse, 1 Bed & furniture,
1 Cow and Calf, 1 Sow & pigs; dau. SARY BROCK all land on South Side of the
mirey Branch, 1 fether Bed & furniture, 1 cow & calf, 2 Sows & pigs which I
have Given heir Before; son JAMES 3 tracks of Land the Trip place, the
prise place & the ABEL DAIL place, 1 Horse, 1 bed & furnetur; son JOHN
the Salmon place & 30 acres laid of on the So Side of my plantation where
I now liv, 1 horse, 1 fether bead & furnitur; son ELISHE GORGE all the
remaining part of my land, 1 horse, 1 fether bead & furnitur; dau. POLLY
1 fether bead & firnitur, 1 Chest, 1 Saddle which 1 have given her be fore,
$1 in money; dau. MARGRET 1 fether bead & furnitur, 1 Hors; residue to
wife for her naterl life time & then to be equilly divided between JOHN,
ELISHE GORE & MARGRET
extr: JILES T. LOFTON
wit: M. KETHLEY, RICHARD KEATHLEY
signed: James Grimsley

207. GUFFORD, ANDREW (CR.035.801.5/A-170)
15 Oct 1805 - Oct Term 1805
sons STEPHEN & JAMES, dau. ELENDOR & grandau. HONNER all my hole Estate,
Lands, Negros, Debts & property
extr: not named
wit: O. O. DANIEL, J. GUFFORD, STEPHEN GUFFORD
signed: A. Gufford

208. GULLEY, WILLIAM (CR.035.801.5)
24 Apr 1802 - Jul Term 1802
wife CATY negro garl Sile; son JAMES first Child that sd. negro Garl has;
son HENRY second Child that sd. negro Garl has; wife CATY 1 feather Bead
& furniture, Beadstid & curtens, 1 hunting saddle, 2 cows & calvs, 1 Chist,
1 wheal & Cards; residue sold & money put into trust with rent from my
lands until my sons reach age 21, then money, land & all the rest of my
propirty divided Equally betwean them
extrs: LEVEN WATKINS, JAMES BIZZELL
wit: HARDY BIZZELL, LEVIN WATKENS, JAMES BIZZELL
                              signed: William ✗ Gulley

209. GULLY, WILLIAM (CR.035.801.5/A-157)
19 Feb 1819 - Jan Term 1822
dau. PATSEY 1 Featherbed & furniture with curtains, 1 cow & calf, 6 earthin
plates; son JOHN 1 sorrel mare calld fancy which he now has in pession,
1 feather bed bedstead & furniture, 1 cow & calf now in his pession; dau.
ELIZABETH BYRD negrow Girl Candos; dau. PITIENCE HINES negrow boy Hinton;
dau. EDITH FREDERICK negrow Allis; dau. NANCY GILMOORE negrow Girl Clarissa;
dau. MARY WILSON negrow girl Ally; dau. PATSEY negrow Woman Asha & her two
children Bristeo & July; son JESSE negrow Girl Anna; grsons. JAMES & HENRY,
sons of WILLIAM JR. decd. 1 silver dollar cash; grson WILLIAM son of
SALLY DANIEL $100; residue of estate to 6 daus.
extrs: sons-in-law JOEL HINES, THOMAS WILSON
wit: JOHN BECK, THOMAS BENNETT, POLLEY A. BYRD
                                   signed: William ⚓ Gulley

210. GURGANUS, EURIAS/URIAH "Planter" (CR.035.801.5/A-173)
20 Sep 1789 - Oct Term 1789
son BENJAMAN & JONATHAN land & Plantation whereon I now live with my wife
MARY to Live thereon & make what Lawful property She can until they Come to
the age of 21; sons JOHN & COOPER lands & Plantation on New River in Onslow
County; son JOHN 1 youn Horse by the Name of Scood[?]; son COOPPER 2 Cows
& Calves & 1 heifer 2 yrs old; son BIGAMON 1 horse colt; dau. SARAH 1 mair
named parrot; son JONATHAN 2 cows & calves; dau. BETSEY 2 cows & calves;
dau. NANCY 2 cows & calves; negro Mingo to be sold & money to be laid Out
to Buy a young wench to be hired out & the Profits to be for Raising the
Children till my three Daughters Comes to age then she to be sold & money
divided between daus. SARAH, ELIZABETH & NANCY; residue to wife MARY
extrs: GEORGE COOPER, RICHARD COOPER
wit: EDWARD PILCHER, RICHARD COOPER, DAVID COOPER
signed: Uriah Gurganos

211. GUY, JOHN (CR.035.801.5/3-77)
16 Jun 1855 - Apr Term 1863
sons JOHN, LEWIS, MORRIS & OWEN $1 each in adition to what I have hear to
fore given them; son JAMES $1; dau. REBECAR 75 acre plantation that I now
live on lying on the North side of Turkey swamp and both sides of the Wilmington and Weldon Rail Road, negro Betsey & her children Dick, Henry &
Juliaun, all my stock, farming utensils, house hold and kitchening furniture,
corn, foder, peas, rice and bacon
extr: DANIEL BOWDEN
wit: R. C. BOWDEN, HOWELL BEST
signed: John Guy
[Note: this will is almost identical to that of John Grey, #202]

212. GUY, LIMUEL (CR.035.801.5/2-136)
15 Jan 1857 - Jul Term 1858
son ALFRED all my lands on the N S of Turkey Swamp from the South Bank at
the canal adj. JOHN GUY & a track on S S of sd. Swamp at the mouth of the
Big Botom Just below my house to the Timber landing at the Rail Road & down
the Rail Road to the little Trust one prong of Turkey adj. STEPHEN VAN;
dau. ZILPHA wife of my deceased son STEPHEN GUY balance of my lands on the
South side of Turkey swamp & then to her children SARAH A. EZZELL, REBECCA
ELIZABETH GUY, MARY GUY, & DAVID THOMAS GUY with the exception that my wife

REBECCA have my house whare I now liv and all the land whar I now cultivate
myself for her natural life; wife REBECCA negro Sary & her child Margaret;
son ALFRED negro Sary & her increase at wife's decase; grdau. ZILPHA
STEPHEN GUY negro Margaret & her in crease
extr: son ALFRED
wit: D. BOWDLEN, BOWDE SOUTHERLAND
                    signed: Lemuel Guy

213. GUY, SAMUEL (CR.035.801.5/A-171)
16 Aug 1794 - Oct Term 1794
dau. NANCY BYRD the Cow & Calf and bed that I lent to her Soon after her
Marrieg; dau. FARABA STANDLEY the bed & three hogs I lent to her Soon after
her Marrieg; dau. MARY BUSSY Cow & Calf & bed I lent to her Soon after her
Marrieg; dau. PENNY BAKER bed and sow and pigs that I lent to her Soon
after her Marrieg; dau. SARAH PHIPS the feathers I lent to her Soon after
her Marrieg and a black & white heifer that she formerly Called hern; son
JAMES all the Land that Lies Joining his land from the fork of the Branch
of Turkey on the South E. Side of the same adj. JAMES REARDON; son JOHN
the Land that I now hold on the No Wt side of Turkey adj. the branch on
the upper side of the field at Sals Pocoson & JAMES GUY; son WILLIAM all
the land I hold on Turkey Swamp from the Second botom to JAMES GUY adj.
JAMES KENNANY; son LEMMUEL the remainder of my Lands; wife SARAH all my
Moveble Property and all my Noates and accompts
extrs: wife SARAH, JAMES REARDON
wit: FELIX FREDERICK, MARY   BULLS
signed: Samuel Guy

214. GUY, WILLIAM (CR.035.801.5/A-162)
22 Jan 1820 - Jul Term 1820
wife ELIZABETH 2 cows & calves, 2 sows & pigs, 2 ewes & lambs, 2 feather beds
& furniture & all the furniture she had at the time of Our marriage & a part
of the Kitchen furniture, 1 mare, bridle & saddle, $40, negroes Phillis &
Cudjo; son THEOPHILUS negro Cupid; son THOMAS negro Virgil; son JESSE
negro Derry; heirs of my son WILLIAM negroes Andrew & Milie; heirs of my
dau. ELIZABETH CHESNUTT negroes Grace, Rose & Sam; dau. POLLY MARTIN
negroes Sam & Rachel; dau. ANN PEARSALL negroes Clarissa [or Clara], Rebecca
& Candace; dau. ELEANOR ADAMS negroes Lucy, Willis & Cortiz; manor plantation where on I now live & my landed estate together with the residue of my
movable property & stock sold & money divided among my children
extrs: JOHN INGRAM, Esqr., JONATHAN THOMAS
wit: D. JERNIGAN, JAMES BYRD
                    signed: William Guy
Codicil
negro Nancy to be sold & money divided between all my children, not allowing
said Nancy to be sold out of my family
wit: D. JERNIGAN, JAMES BYRD
                    signed: William Guy

215. HALL, DRURY "of the County of Onslow" (CR.035.801.5/2-42)
5 Dec 1832 - Jan Term 1849
wife BLANCHY [name "Nancy" is marked through] all my estate both real &
personal during her natural life for the purpose of raising and Educating
my four children JAMES, SUSANA, SOLOMON & PENELOPE; at her death or marriage,

estate to be sold & money divided equally
extr: not named
wit: WM. JARMAN, STEPPEN BROCK
                          signed: Drury ⋈ Hall

216. HALL, JAMES EDWARD (CR.035.801.5/3-72/3-80)
18 Jul 1853 - Apr & Jul Terms 1863
present wife MARGARET L. all my estate real and personal and then to any
issue I have by her; if there is no issue, wife to have use of it for her
lifetime and at her death the plantation near Hallsville on which I now
reside to be held and owned by my sister CATHARINE P. & brother GEORGE
extr: wife MARGARET L.
wit: HANSON F. MURPHY, JNO D. POWERS
signed: J. E. HALL

217. HALL, MARY (CR.035.801.5/2-123)
25 Sep 1851 - Apr Term 1857
son LEWIS $1; dau. SUSAN MERRITT $1; dau. MARY WILSON $1; dau. RACHEL
MERRITT $1; son ALFORD negroes Rebecca & her three children (not named);
son HERRING negro Judy & her children Aberdean, Ollen & Mary, Molsey &
her child Everette & Lucy & her child Samuel; on account of the faith-
fulness of my old negro woman Moss that she shall stay on the premises
of my son HERRING & taken good care of, and be supported for and during
her natural life; son HERRING all my household & kitchen furniture
extr: JOS. T. MATTHIS
wit: GIBSON S. MATTHIS, DAVID WATSON
                          signed: Mary ✳ Hall

218. HALL, NICHOLAS (CR.035.801.5/3-45)
1 Dec 1860 - Jan Term 1862
wife CATHARINE negroes Jim & Harriett, all my Stock, Plantation Tools &
Implements, Kitchen & Household Furniture, all my land lying west of the
Main Road from Hallsville to Serecta & west of & adj. THOMAS HALL including
my dwelling House & all out houses, also negroes Dilly, Linda, Caroline,
Wright, Frank, Martha, Mary & Susan; son JAMES E. negro Dilly except the
life Estate of my wife & negro Sarah; dau. ELLEN, wife of JAMES M. SPRUNT
negroes Linda & Caroline except the life Estate of my wife; son-in-law
JAMES M. SPRUNT negro Wright except the life estate of my wife; dau.
CATHARINE PRISCILLA land whereon I now live except the life estate of my
wife with negroes Frank, Martha & Mary; grdau. SARAH CATHARINE FARRIOR
negro Susan except the life estate of my wife; extr. to sell all the
land lying East of the Main Road from Hallsville to Sarecta the sd. proceeds to be then paid over to my son GEORGE M.
extrs: sons JAMES E. & THOMAS
wit: E. J. HALL, W. T. HALL
signed: Nicholas Hall

219. HALL, SARAH (CR.035.801.5/A-193)
1 Oct 1786 - Oct Term 1789
grson JAMS T. RHODES 2 Cows & Calves, Bead, furniture & beadstead, one
Large New Chest, 6 Plates, 3 Pewter & 3 Earthen, 2 Pewter Diches & 3 Basons,
6 Spoons, 2 Punch bowls; grdau. MARY 1 Bead & furniture; grdau. MARTHA

WILLIAMS 1 cow & yearling; son DRURY 9 head of Cattle, 20 head of Hoggs,
3 head of Sheep, 1 Iron Pot & Hooks, 3 Earthin Plates, 5 Pewter Plates &
2 Dishes, 4 Basons, 1 Large Chest, 1 Bead & furniture, the Earthen Ware &
Small furniture not Other ways Given, 4 cheers; grson JAMS T. RHODES
3 House cheers, 1 year old Colt should he come Ever to receive it but If
not the same to my son DRURY; son DRURY 2 Linen wheels; negro Hannah
sold & money devided between DRURY HALL & JAMES T. RHODES; son DRURY
3 Tubs, 2 Pails, 2 Pigens, 1 frying Pan, all yarn Cotten & thread & cloath;
daus. MARY WILLIAMS & MARTHA WILLIAMS my wareing appearel, crop of Corn &
fotter & 1 flax hackle, 1 Iron Skillet; grson. JAMES T. RHODES 1 Iron
Spider, 1 cow & yerling
extrs: JOSEPH T. RHODES, JOHN UMPHREY
wit: CHRISTIAN _C_ WILLIAMS, SUSANNAH _R_ SMITH, JOHN UMPHREY, J. T. RHODES
            signed: Sarah _C_ Hall

220. HALL, THOMAS (CR.035.801.5/A-193)
5 Jul 1764 - no probate
wife RACHOL my plantation whearon I now Dwel untill my Son DAVID Shall
arrive to the full age of 21 with all Houshold Good & tools for Labour
apartaining; all my Stock, money & Debts to Be Equaly Divided a mongst my
Dear Children ELIZABETH, ELINOR, MARY, JEMIMA, NANSAY, SIVAL, DAVID &
LUCRESA
extrs: wife RACHEL, brother-in-law JOHN GOUFF
wit: HENRY HOLLINGSWORTH, ELIZABETH _9_ GOUFF
signed: Thoms. Hall

221. HALL, WILLIAM (CR.035.801.5/A-192)
20 Aug 1825 - Jan Term 1826
wife ELIZABETH negro Bess or Betsey for her natural life, her legal dower
of my plantation, 2 Beds & furniture; residue to my Grandchildren the
children of JAMES HALL, WM HALL decd., LEWIS HALL, NICHOLAS HALL, EDWARD P.
HALL, THOMAS P. HALL & ISAAC N. HALL; negro Bess sold at wife's death &
money divided out in manner as aforesaid
extrs: sons JAMES & NICHOLAS
wit: HENRY BAKER, J. C. MILLS, THOS. P. HALL
signed: William Hall

222. HAIRGROVE/HARGROVE, JOHN (CR.035.801.5)
12 Sep 1811 - Oct Term 1811
one mare, 4 head of young cattle & 10 head of hogs sold & money to go to my
Children, EDITH, LAMUEL & HENRY; wife MARGARET 1 Featherbed, plantation
whereon I now live for her lifetime then to be divided between sons LAMUEL
& HENRY; wife MARGARET negroes Dinah, Daniel & Lucy & all moveable property;
son LAMUEL negro Daniel at wife's decease; son HENRY negro Dinah at wife's
decease; dau. EDITH negro Lucy at wife's decease
extr: brother AARON
wit: S. GRAHAM, WM. MALLARD
            signed: John _X_ Hargrove

223. HANCHEY, MARTEN (CR.035.801.5/A-203)
13 Sep 1800 - Jan Term 1811
wife SARAH my hous and plantation for hir lifetime, all my hogs, cattle,
houshold furnature & plantation toles & my mare for hir use to Rase my
Small Children (not named) on; son WM. 100 acres above weats ford on both
Side of Island Creek; wife SARAH's dower of 100 acres to youngest son (not
named) at her death; residue of estate to all my children (not named)
extrs: DANIEL MURRAY, JOHN GILMON
wit: JOHN WHITTMAN, HENRY ALLON
                    signed: Marten   Hanchey

224. HARVELL, WILLIAM (CR.035.801.5/A-196)
22 Mar 1781 - Jul Term 1791
RUTH, wife of WILLIAM HARVELL decd. all my Lands and plantations where on
She now Lives, my Catle, hogs & 3 head of horses, all my housel furnerture,
then to all the Children (not named) except for GABREL & JAMES, sons of
WILLIAM HARVILL dect. who are to have 100 acres on the west side of Cuwiffle
extr: RUTH HARVELL
wit: RUTH X HARVILL, FREDERICK WILLIAMS, JOEL JOHNSON
                    signed: William   Harvell

225. HEARICK, JESSE (CR.035.801.5/A-206)
17 Dec 1778 - Apr Term 1789
wife MARY HERICK plantation Whereon I now live During her Life, my Riding
Horse Bridels & Saddels, 2 beds & furniture with the bedstids, Cords &
hides thereto belonging; dau. NANCY 1 bed & furniture & beadstid, Cow &
3 yr Old Heifer, 1 3 yr Old Stear, 1 Ewe; wife MARY remainder of my Sheep
for her livfetime & then to my Children (not named), 4 Cows & Calves, 2
3 yr Old Stears, 2 Year old Stears; son JESSE 200 acres on the Bever Dam
Swamp in New Hanr County, 1 Cow & year Old Stear; son RICHARD 200 acres
on the Great Swamp, 1 Cow & Calf; dau. MARY 1 Chist, 1 Speckeled trunk,
1 Cow & Cow year Old & 1 5 qt Bason; dau. ELIZABETH 1 3 yr Old Heifer,
1 2 yr Old Stear, 1 Dish; dau. THENCY 1 cow & calf; dau-in-law SARAH 1
3 yr old Heifer, 1 sow & piggs, 2 plates; dau. NANCY 1 small pot, 5
plates; wife MARY 2 potts, 10 plates, 7 basons, 3 Dishes, 1 pair Steelyards, all my working tools for her life & then to sons JESSE & RICHARD
extrs: wife MARY, brother-in-law THOMAS FORT
wit: RD. HERRING, ABNER FORT, LABAN TATUM
signed: J. Hearick

226. HEATH, JAMES (CR.035.801.5/1-27)
30 Jul 1832 - Aug Term 1832
all my Sisters (not named) to come & live on my Premises & have Posission
of all my lands, Tenements, negro Emily, stock, Household & Kitchen furnature
plantation utensils for their lifetime and after their Decease to be equally
Divided between my Brothers (not named)
extr: ALEXANDER HEATH
wit: WM. SWINSON, DOROTHY HEATH
signed: James Heath

227. HERRING, ALEXANDER (CR.035.801.5/A-202)
25 Jan 1819 - Apr Term 1819
wife REBECCA negroes Ned, Sharper, Weldon & Edy & her children Leah & Lizett,
my bay Horse Stump the Dealer & old Conjamingo, Riding Chair & Harness,
5 Cows & Calves, 10 good Ewes, 4 sows & 28 pigs, House hold & Kitchen
furniture, 60 barrels of Corn, all my fodder, also negroes Bob & Bett the
Children of Cate for her widowhood with the plantation & plantation tools
During the non age of my son LEWIS & when he becomes of the age 21 he to
take possession of sd. plantation; son LEWIS STEPHEN the Remainder of my
property of Every Discription
extrs: DAVID WRIGHT, DAVID HOOKS
wit: WILSON HODGE, B. BOURDEN
signed: Alax Herring

228. HERRING, ELISHA (CR.035.801.5/2-138)
7 Oct 1851 - Oct Term 1858
wife POLLY all my household & Kitchen furniture, my gig & Sulky, Farming
implements, carts, Wagons, stock & at her death to go to son ALEXANDER;
son ALEXANDER 3 beds & furniture, 10 sows & pigs, 6 cows & calves, 1 yoke
of Oxen & cart; wife POLLY negroes Dennis, Harry, John, Alfred, Phillis,
Clara, Eliza, Mary, Sylvia, Rachel, Nicy, Winny & little Alfred & at her
demise to my daus. PATSEY, NANCY, MARIA, POLLY & SUSAN; negro Jane & her
dau. Sena to sons ELISHA & ALEXANDER in special Trust for dau. POLLY;
negro George to heirs of my decd. dau. PATIENCE; wife POLLY to have all
the East side of my manor Plantation to the JESSE GULLEY tract & a small
Slip of the Gulley land on the west side of Maple branch; dau. PATSEY
negroes Curtis, Elias, Cassey, & Clara; dau. NANCY negroes Jo, Solomon,
Orris & Serena; sons ELISHA & ALEXANDER negroes Lovett, Lewis, Haley &
Jane & her dau. Sena in special Trust for my dau. POLLY, the wife of
WILLIAM JONES; heirs of decd dau PATIENCE negroes Theophilus, Alexander
& Lucy; dau. SUSAN negroes Jim, Rouse, Marinda & Needham; dau. MARIA
negroes Henry, Beck & Sinda; son ELISHA all my Gully & Sanders lands
containing 600 acres, negro Tom, all my Horses, Cattle, Hogs, Sheep &
plantation tools; son ALEXANDER my manor plantation including my wife's
dower at her death containing 702 acres, negroes Sary, Marinda, Nathan,
Rose, Daniel, Susanah & Washington
extr: wife POLLY
wit: BRYAN W. HERRING, MILLARD GLISSON
signed: Elisha Herring

229. HERRING, SAMUEL (CR.035.801.5/A-207)
5 Jan 1809 - Jan Term 1809
wife RACHEL 2 Cows, 2 Sows & 16 Pigs, 1 Bed & furniture, my Black Mare,
600 wgt of Bacon, 15 Barrels of Corn, fluke Plough, 1 Cutter, 1 Hoe, 1 Axe,
1 Linnen Wheel, 1 Woolen Wheel, 1 small Pot, 3 Chairs, 1 saddle; son
WILLIAM 1 Bed & furniture, 1 Gun; son FREDERICK 1 Bed & furneture; dau.
POLLY 1 Bed which she is to make out of new feathers now in my House & the
Saddle that was called SYLVIA's; son DRURY 1 Bed & furniture; dau. ALLY
money to Buy her a Bed; residue sold to pay debts
extr: JOHN ELIOT
wit: LEVI BORDEN, SOLOMON *8* ROUSE, LEWIS ROWSE
signed: Samuel Herring

230. HERRING, STEPHEN (CR.035.801.5)
21 Sep 1797 - Oct Term 1797
Plantation whereon I now live & the lands adj. be Eaqually divided by a line
from the main run of Goshen Swamp by the new Ricefield to the back line &
my son STEPHEN BRIGHT have the lowerpart adj. Hodges's line and my son
ALEXANDER to have the other part including the houses except for a life
right to my wife SARAH; negroes Cesar, Bet, Agga & Ned to remain with my
wife; wife SARAH to have use of all my household furnature, tools & Stock
for her natural life; dau. ALETHEA HARRELL negro Ned; remainder of the
property, stock & negroes loaned to wife be devided between my grson ELISHA,
the son of SAML HERRING & the children of ALITHEA HARRELL; son SAMUEL
5 shillings sterling; dau. ALETHEA HARRELL 5 shillings sterling; dau. CATY
CROOM 5 shillings sterling; children of CATY CROOM negro Jim; children of
my dau. SALLY GLISSON decd. former wife of DANIEL GLISSON to have 2 negroe
girls about 14 & 8 yrs old to be purchased for them by my son STEPHEN B.;
grson BRYAN GLISSON the young bay mare which I formerly gave him; dau.
PEARSIS GLISSON negro Jenny & her children, her first child Jack to go to
SALLY GLISSON, her first living child to HENRY GLISSON, her second living
child to CHARITY GLISSON, her third living child to HETTIE GLISSON; son
STEPHEN BRIGHT negroes Bob & Davy; dau. NANCY NEW negro Allen & a negro
girl abt 8 yrs old to be purchased by my son ALEXANDER & she to have the
use of negro Fillis until girl is delivered; son ALIXANDER negroes Squire,
Cate & Fillis, 1 Featherbed & furniture, 1 young sorrel horse
extrs: sons STEPHEN BRIGHT & ALEXDR
wit: WM DICKSON, JAMES STEWART [?], WILLIS HERRING, SARAH CROOM
signed: Stephen Herring

231. HICKS/HIX, THANKFUL (CR.035.801.6/A-185)
27 Oct 1784 - Jan Term 1785
grdau. ANN TILLIS 2 sows & pigs & 3 2 yr old hogs; grson HIX MILLS 1 bead
& sheet & blanket, one chest; dau. REBECCA MILLS 2 beds & furniture, the
rest of my puter & remaining hogs; grdau. THANKFUL MILLS 8 barrels of corn
& the remaining crop to my dau. REBECCA MILLS; 4 youngest grch. MARY, JAMES,
SHADRACH & FREDERICK MILLS each a cow & calf & the remaining part of my
cattle to REBECCA MILLS; grdau. THANKFUL MILLS all my sheep, the little pot
& hooks, 4 chairs; grsons JAMES & SHADRACH MILLS each 1 mare colt & the
remainder of my horse kind sold & the money divided into 3 parts, 1/3 to
SHADRACH, 1/3 to JAMES & 1/3 to MARY & FREDERICK MILLS; grdau. THANKFUL
MILLS 100 acres on Broad Branch; grson SHADRACH MILLS 100 acres on the No
Side of Limestone; grson HIX MILLS 2 surveys of land adj. the plantation
I live on; grdau. THANKFUL MILLS negro Leonia; remainder of estate to
REBECCA MILLS
extrs: ROUBERT SOUTHERLAND, JAMES MILLS
wit: TEMPLE LEILLOR, J. T. RHODES
                    signed: Thankful ✗ Hicks

232. HICKS, THOMAS (CR.035.801.6/A-186)
16 Apr 1775 - no probate
wife [not named] plantation whereon I now live, negroes Rose, Pleasant,
S. Kenders & Mingo, five cows and calves, a yoke of oxen, a riding horse,
two pots, all the puter in the house, her choice of the beds with the furniture, 20 head of hogs; only dau. REBECCA MILLS negroes Philip, Philis, Clove,
& her child, what cattle is in her [c]are at my dececese, the plantation where

she now lives to her and her present husband JAMES MILLS for her lifetime;
grson HICKS MILLS Plantation whereon I now live after the decease of my wife,
negro Saunders; grson LEONARD MILLS plantation were my daughter now lives
after her decease, negro Mingo; grdau. BOMLER MILLS bed and furniture, ten
head of cattle; grdau. THANKFUL MILLS bed and furniture, ten head of cattle;
grandchildren REBEKAH MILLS, ANN MILLS, LORENA MILLS, BETTY MILLS & SARAH
MILLS 10 head of cattle each; dau. REBEKAH MILLS negroes Rose & Pleasants
after wife's decease; remainder of my estate to be equally divided amongst
my living granchildren
extrs: wife, ROBERT SOUTHERLIN JUN.
wit: SHEARAD GRIMESLEY, MOSES HANCHEY
signed: THOMS HICKS

233. HIGHSMITH, JOHN (CR.035.801.6/3-125)
25 Aug 1858 - 4 Sep 1867
wife SARAH 497 acres whereon I reside for & during the term of her natural
life purchased of BRYAN LEE & ABRAM NEWTON; adopted grdau. ELIZABITH
CAROLINE, wife of OLIVER M. MATTHEWS land after wife's decease, negro Lucy
ae 9 yrs
extr: adopted grson OLIVER M. MATTHEWS
wit: W. R. WARD, BRYAN WILLIAMS
                   signed: John ✗ Highsmith
will was proved in open court by GEORGE F. DEMPSEY, JOHN J. WHALEY, JONAS
BOYETTE, RUFUS BENTON, JACOB BOSTICK, JAMES L. PIGFORD, WILLIAM H. MILLER,
WILLIAM THOMAS, BLANY WILLIAMS, D. T. McMILLAN, WM. D. PEARSALL, JESSE B.
SOUTHERLAND

234. HILL, BUCKNER L. (CR.035.801.6/3-18)
9 Feb 1860 - Jan Term 1861
JOSEPH R. HATCH slaves Old Hannah, Abby, Syvil & child Tony, Lucinda, Laura,
Martha, Orange, Phillis & children Rachel, Curtis & Charles, Kit, Frank,
Roxy & children Cassy & Louisa, Joe & Isham; CHARLES E. RHODES slaves
Nancy, her son Jim & Henry; ANN SMITH slaves Jacob, Lucy, Hannah, Leah &
Milly Children of old Milly & Bob for her natural life and then to her
children [not named] but should she die without issue, negroes to go to JOHN
SMITH, EDWARD SMITH & AMANDA HOUSTON (dau. of SARAH ANN SMITH); JOHN, son
of SARAH ANN SMITH slaves Billy & Fanny & their children Daniel, Henry &
Catharine; EDWARD, brother of JOHN SMITH slaves Calvin, Needham, Stanley &
Cullen; AMANDA HOUSTON slaves Louis & wife Litha & Margaret, Louis & Jackson
their children; JAMES RHODES of Alabama slaves Betsey & her children Stephen,
Anthony, Rhodes, Sarah & Fanny; DAVID EVERETT of Wayne County slaves Jonas
& Thena in trust for the benefit of LOUISA, wife of DANIEL E. SMITH; slaves
Council & Easter for the benefit of ANN, wife of BENJAMIN GRISWOLD; slaves
Peggy, George & Edward for the benefit of JULIA, wife of RICHARD HATCH;
KATE LEWIS formerly KATE RHODES slave Emily; BETTY, wife of DR. JOSEPH
BORDEN 19 or 20 shares of capital stock of the Wilmington & Weldon Rail
Road Company; ISAAC WRIGHT & HALSTEAD BOWDEN slaves Flora, Bryant, Catharine,
Old Mary, Margaret, Mingo, Julia & child Henry, Sylva & children Cassy, York,
George & Emanuel, Sina, Betsey, Tempe, Jeoffrey & Phillis & their children
William, Amelia, Solomon, Narcissa and Ivy, Martha & children Owen, Eli,
David & Mary Jane & Hepsy, Hester & Allen, Old Daniel, Robert & Grandison,
land on South Side of Bear Swamp where my new dwelling house is in Duplin

County, the Mill tract on the North side of Bear Swamp bought of W. D.
PEARSALL, all in trust for my son THOMAS B. HILL sometimes called THOMAS B.
STEPHENS and his wife BETSEY & should they die without issue 1/2 of the land
& slaves to go to BUCKNER, son of SAMUEL & ELIZA SMITH and 1/2 to LEMUEL D.
HATCH & wife MARTHA; ISAAC WRIGHT of Duplin slaves Sam and Binah & child
George, Chelly, Ned & wife Sarah & child Clarissa, Old Becky, Alvin & wife
Julia, the Bennett tract in Duplin bought of DR. THOMAS HILL, the THOMAS
HOOKS land purchased of THOMAS HOOKS adj. C. D. HILL & Mrs. Bird and lying
on or near Horse Pen Branch; slaves Alvin & wife Julia be allowed to choose
their new master As Alvin has been to me a faithful servant and contributed
much to my comfort; ISAAC WRIGHT & THOMAS B. HILL the Conolly tract in
Duplin County purchased from the heirs of JOHN CONOLLY SR., land purchased
of ZACHARIAH KORNEGAY on Poley Branch adj. DAVID WRIGHT & Mrs. Bird & the
lands formerly belonging to WILLIAM WRIGHT and the lands of JOHN C. BOWDEN;
THOMAS B. HILL all my crop, provisions, stock of every description, farming
implements and utensils, Household and kitchen furniture & black smith's
tools upon my Bear Swamp plantation; DR. THOMAS HILL the carpenter's tools
now in possession of Solomon & Peter and used by them; if THOMAS B. HILL &
his wife BETSEY die without issue, the Mill tract and the tract upon the
South side of Bear Swamp to go to BUCKNER L., son of DR THOMAS & FRANCES
HILL instead of LEMUEL HATCH and wife and BUCKNER SMITH; GORDON, husband of
BETSY WRIGHT and son in law of THOMAS H. WRIGHT (whose first name is not now
recollected) slaves Henry, Sarah & Elvy in trust for THOMAS H. WRIGHT & wife
PRISCILLA of Mississippi, also all my lands in the County of Carroll in the
State of Mississippi; brother DR. THOMAS HILL slaves Mary Ann, Thena, Beckey
Ann, Solomon, Big Squire & Sarah; BUCKNER L., son of THOMAS & FRANCES HILL
slaves Cassy & Peter her husband & children Edward, Robert, Sena, Peter &
Jackson & Louis & his wife Caroline; FANNY WEYMS slaves Green & his wife
Mary Eliza & child Edney & should she die without increase the sd. slaves
to HARRIET, dau of LEMUEL D. & MARTHA HATCH; BUCKNER L. H. WRIGHT slave
Louisa now in Mississippi; BUCKNER, son of WENTWORTH W. PIERCE slave Will
& wife Fanny & child Peter; DR. EDWARD W. WARD slave Patsey, dau of Old
Becky in trust for the benefit of JAKY JUSTICE or JAKY STEPHENS and at her
death to BUCKNER L., son of THOMAS & BETSEY HILL; JOSEPH R. HATCH land on
the west side of the main Public Road adj. the Wayne plantation which was
the residence of my late wife & myself purchased of RHODES CLARISSA HATCH
and adj. the land of R. C. HATCH & SAMUEL FLORRENS, also slaves Old Hester,
Old Peter & wife Sena; MARGARET J. HALL of the town of Wilmington 10 shares
of Capital Stock in the Wilmington & Manchester Rail Road Co.; ISAAC WRIGHT
1 share of capital stock of the Wilmington & Weldon Rail Road Company;
I hereby revoke bequest of slave to CHARLES E. RHODES and bequeath him to
JOHN SMITH; CATHERINE WITHERSPOON, dau. of LEMUEL D. HATCH slaves Becky &
her children Aleck & Washington; BUCKNER L., son of THOMAS B. & BETSEY HILL
slaves John, son of Milly; BUCKNER L. H. WRIGHT slave Easter now at the
Goshen Plantation, black in color, and aged forty years; BUCKNER L., son of
THOMAS & FRANCES HILL slaves Jackson & his wife Hannah & should he die without
issue slaves to CALHOUN, son of THOMAS & FRANCES HILL; extr. to dispose of
my cotton and turpentine on hand, my land known as my Sleepy Creek land on
Neuse River which I bought of WILLIAM A. WHITFIELD & money divided equally
between BUCKNER L., son of DR. THOMAS HILL & FRANCES and BUCKNER, son of
SAMUEL SMITH & MARTHA E. SHINE; CHARLES F. DEEMS $500; extrs. to keep up
the farms and carry on the farming operations on my Bear Swamp and the Goshen

plantations and on the land opposite by residence in Wayne for the present
year and until this (1860) year's crops have been housed; money arising from
the sale of the crops to be applied also to the purchase and Erection over
my grave of a monument Similar to the one about to be erected to the memory
of my late wife, the details as to which I confide to my friend CHARLES F.
DEEMS; residue of estate to BUCKNER L., son of THOMAS HILL & wife FRANCES
& BUCKNER son of SAML. SMITH & MARTHA E. SHINE; extr. my trusty friends
ISAAC WRIGHT & HALSTEAD BOWDEN of Duplin; extr. 2 acres of land upon which
is located the family burying ground and two acres of land whereon is located
the burying ground of my slaves always be continued and held for the purpose
aforesaid; revoke bequest of Easter to B. L. H. WRIGHT as she has been
previously bequeathed in trust for the benefit of ANN GRISWOLD
wit: L. P. WOLF, JOS R. PARKER
signed: B. L. Hill
Codicil: 25 Feb 1860
extr. not to pay out or deliver to any one of the heirs at Law of my late
wife ANNA M. HILL any of the legacies which I have left in my will until each
one shall release his or her claim against me or my estate; if ISAAC WRIGHT
should die without wife or issue, his land to go to BUCKNER L., son of THOMAS B.
HILL & his wife BETSEY
wit: L. P. WOLF, JOS R. PARKER
signed: B. L. Hill

235. HILL, JOHN (CR.035.801.6/A-218)
24 Jun 1802 - Oct Term 1807
wife JEEN All my Property and Rights of or to Property Real and Personal;
son FELIX K. Six Silver Dollars besides what he has already had of me and
Nomore; dau. CATHERINE LOVE Six Silver Dollars besides what she has already
had of me and Nomore; dau. SARAH Six Silver Dollares besides What I have
alreary give to her and Nomore; son JOHN Six Silver Dollares besides What
I have already give to him and Nomore; son JAMES Six Silver Dollares besides
What I have already give to him and no more; dau. ELIZABETH Six Silver
Dollares besides What I Gave her allreard and no more; son WILLIAM K. Six
Silver Dollars besides What is already Given to him and No more; son EDWARD
Six Silver Dollares besides what is already Given to him and No more
extrs: wife JEEN & KENAN LOVE
wit: THOMAS HILL, JAMES REARDON, JOHN SOUTHERLAND
signed: John Hill

235A. HILL, WM. L. (3-9)
15 Jul 1858 - Apr Term 1860
C. D. HILL's son WILLIAM L. and W. E. HILL's son EDWARD JOHN all the plantation
where I now live and all the lands I own adjoining to be equally divided when
the boys get to be twenty one two Square acres where the grave yard is located
is excepted; sons CHRISTOPHER D. and WILLIAM E. to have the use and rents of
all the above plantations gratis to manage as they think proper until the boys
get to be twenty one; son WILLIAM E. in case my wife ANN E. dies without a
will my Bizzell Plantation on Whiteoak Swamp and all the lands I own adjoining;
dau. MARGARET D. PIERCE negro Mandy and all Mandy's children and Farise Mandy's
husband, Amy and all Amy's children and Adam Amy's husband; sons CHRISTOPHER D.
and WILLIAM E. all the negroes at my home plantation, Bizzell plantation and
everywhere else, all my Bank Stock and Rail Road Stock and all the property I own
extrs: sons CHRISTOPHER D. and WILLIAM E.
wit: not named
signed: W. L. Hill

236. HOCKINGS, JOHN (S S Wills/DRB2)
29 Mar 1756 - Jul Court 1756
oldest dau. MARY a gray hors wich She now has in Possession; next oldest
dau. ANN a bay mear wich She now has in Possession; youngest dau. LATTESS
my Riding black mear; three daus. all my rites, Goods, lands and Chattels
extrs: three daus.
Loving Freends BENJAMIN FUSSELL & JACOB FUSSELL Overseers to take Care and
          See the Saim performed according to my true Intent and Meaning
wit: BENJN FUSSELL, JACOB FUSSELL, THOMAS DAVIS, RICHARD PENNEY,
          EDWARD ━━➤ SPEARMAN
                    signed: John 🖎 Hockings

237. HODGES, BENJAMIN (CR.035.801.6/A-197)
7 Jun 1823 - Jul Term 1824
dau. NANCY BOURDEN negroes Esther & Milley, $200, one horse worth eighty
dollars, four cows and calves, one bed and furniture, one chest, one table,
Six chairs, one bureau; dau. MARY HERRING negroes Clarry & Cass, one Mare,
bridle and Saddle, one bed and furniture, one chest, five cows and calves,
one bureau, $200; son HOLLOWELL the lands which I purchased of JANE HILL
estimated at 797 acres, negro Allen, one mare, bridle and Saddle, one bed
and firniture, three cows and calves, one bureau; son WILSON 200 acres I
purchased from KEDAR SIKES called the Ward land, negroes Joe & Lewis, one
bed and furniture, one desk, my grist mill and crushing mill, $100 of which
he has only the desk, bed and furniture in possession; son WILLIAM all the
lands and the plantation whereon I now live with all the improvements,
237 1/2 acres which I purchased from STEPHEN B. HERRING, negroes Rachel,
Black Jack & Sam, $200, one horse, bridle and Saddle, one bed and furniture,
one Side board, one still; dau. ELIZABETH negroes Abba and all her children,
Lencey and Daniel, one bed and furniture, one horse worth $100, one trunk,
one bureau; dau. SUSAN negroes Jack Ireland, Lucy, Harry, Isham & Clarry,
one horse, bridle and saddle, one bed and furniture, a half dozen windsor
chairs, one trunk, one bureau; dau. FRANCES negroes Chloe, Peter, Dinah,
Rose, Violet & Lena, one horse, bridle and saddle, one bed and furniture,
a half dozen windsor chairs, one trunk and one bureau; residue sold and
money equally divided between my daus. NANCY BOURDEN, MARY HERRING, ELIZABETH,
SUSAN & FRANCES
extrs: sons WILSON & WILLIAM
wit: DAVID D. BUNTING, JAMES RHODES, WILLIAM RHODES
signed: Benjn. Hodges

238. HODGES, HOLLOWELL (CR.035.801.6/2-40)
2 Dec 1848 - Jan Term 1849
wife SARAH & sons ISAAC, FRANKLIN & LEMUEL Tract of Land lying upon the
south side of Goshen, upon which I at present reside, together with the
Mansion house and Fixtures thereon - to be occupied by them jointly and in
common until the death of my said wife when the said Tract of Land and its
appurtenances are to be equally divided between the said ISAAC, FRANKLIN
and LEMUEL; wife SARAH & sons ISAAC, FRANKLIN and LEMUEL negroes Rachel,
Winny, Hannah, Maria and her two children Nance & Alick, Sidney and her son
Peter, Lizzy, Silas, Jerry, Squire, Daniel, Lina and Travis; wife SARAH &
sons ISAAC, FRANKLIN & LEMUEL all the Cattle, Horses, Hogs, Sheep and other
stock and all the Farming Utensils, Household and Kitchen Furniture and

Provisions; sons HENRY HOLLOWELL and WILLIAM THOMAS $1 apiece and no more
they having already received their respective shares of both my Real &
Personal Estate
extrs: wife SARAH & son WILLIAM T.
wit: J. H. SWINSON, JESSE C. PRIDGEN
signed: H. Hodges

239. HODGES, WILLIAM (CR.035.801.6)
17 Sep 1842 - Jan Term 1845
sister NANCY BOURDEN $50; sister MARY HERRING $50; brother HOLLOWELL the
lands which I now lives on at this time Estinated at 667 acres, negroes
Alfred, Ransin, Alvin, & Teaner; brother WILSON $5; sister SUSAN HUTCHINS
$5; sister FRANCIS COOPER $5; WILLIAM HODGES one horse, Saddle and Bridle
to be worth $100; WILLIAM H., son of FRANCIS COOPER one horse and Bridle
to be worth $100; residue sold and the money Equalley divided between my
Sisters and brothers To Wit NANCY BOURDAN, MARY HERRING, HOLLOWELL HODGES,
WILSON HODGES, SUSAN HUTCHINS, FRANCIS COOPER
extrs: brother HOLLOWELL & JAMES K. HILL
wit: C. D. HILL, JOHN SHINE   signed: William Hodges

240. HODGISON, ARON (CR.035.801.6/A-217)
5 Dec 1796 - Oct Term 1797
wife ANN negro Frank to bee hierd anuly for her soport deuring hir widowhood
After hir desease or mariage to be sold and the money to be devided Equally
betwen my two Sons to wit ARON & LEUIS; wife ANN my riding mair and gray
Horse, two Cowes and all and singilar of my household furniture Just as it
stands; I also desier that my wife should pay to my daughters CATTRON MILLS
fifteen pounds Out of the property left to hir; son JOSEPH one shilling
Sterling; son JOHN one shilling Sterling; the heirs of my daughter PHRABA
MCANN dseast one Shilling Sterling; dau. ESTER POWEL one Shilling Sterling
extr: wife ANN
wit: WM. WRIGHT, JOHN S. S. ASHFORD
                        signed: Aron [mark] Hodgeson

241. HOLDON, JEREMIAH (CR.035.801.6/A-183)
11 Jul 1774 - Jan Term 1785 [original damaged]
son ALEXANDER the Plantation whereon I now live with all Houses and Utensials
there unto belonging, negro Dover; friend JAN CAMBLE three Cows and Calves,
one Feathur Bed and furniture and the one [torn] of the [torn]; Grand Child
JOHN negro Phillis; son in law FREDERICK WELLS all my Cloaths and Wearing
Apperrel; FREDERICK WELL's Children [not named] three Cows and Calves to
each of them; son ALEXANDER Remainder of my Effects, the whole to be managed
and Settled by TIMOTHY MURPHY and [torn] who I make and ordain my Executors
wit: EDWARD DICKSON, JAMES DICKSON, PATRICK ROGERS
signed: Jeremiah [red wax covers surname]

242. HOLLEY, JAMES (CR.035.801.6/A-195)
19 Dec 1760 - 22 Mar 1761
eldest son JOHN the plantation whereon I Live Containing 100 acres Lying and
being on ye west side of Great Cohary, one Cow and Calf Namely a Red Cow &
White face of mine own proper mark; son JAMES Tract of Land Containing 150
acres Lying on great Cohary ye wt. Side of Rocky Mash, Likewise my gun;
dau. TAMAR two Cows and Calves Both of my own proper mark ye one a Black and

white Side and ye Other a Red Cow and an Iron Pott; child that my wife is
now Pregnat with yet unBorn whether male or female two red Brinded Cows with
white Backs Both of my own proper mark and an Iron Pott; wife SARAH ye Rest
of my Goods and Chattles whatever
extr: NATHANEAL WILLIAMS
wit: EDWD. BROWN, NOAH BARFOOT
signed: James Holley

243. HOLLINGSWORTH, ELIZABETH (CR.035.801.6/A-220)
17 Sep 1787 - Jan Term 1788
dau. SARAH negro Roze; son JACOB Two large pewter Basons, one dish and Six
plates; son HENRY my Stock of Cattle and Hogs, One Bead Beadstead & furniture;
dau. LYDIA One large Chest and Cap box, One woolen wheel and Cotton Cards and
one half of my Beading furniture not above Given and the Other half to my dau.
CELIA; dau. CELIA One Lining wheel, one pr of Cotten Cards and Hackle;
daus. CELIA & LYDIA all my pewter not above mentioned and Iron pots to be
Equally divided; son JACOB Six New House Chears and one Gin Case of bottles;
son HENRY Six New House Chears; all articles of my Estate not before mentioned to be Equally divided between my son HENRY & daus LYDIA & CELIA; daus.
LYDIA & CELIA my wearing cloaths
extr: JOSEPH T. RHODES
wit: JUSTUS MILLER, J. T. RHODES
                signed: Elizabeth   E   Hollingsworth

244. HOLLINGSWORTH, JACOB (CR.035.801.6/A-221)
26 May 1790 - Oct Term 1790
KEDAR HERRELs To Sons Viz JACOB & HENRY My Land Lying on Muddy Creek Being
In all Either three or four Hundred Acres To Be Equally Divided JACOB to Have
the Lower part Down the Creek & HENRY to Have the Upper part; brother HENRY
My Cloaths & Surveying Instruments; brother WILLIAM My Bed & furiture &
Saddle; sisters MARY FOUNTAIN & CELIA PICKET 18 pounds Being of a Note of
23 pounds Due to me from ELIN GARRISON to which 18 pounds to be Equally
Divided Between them & the Remainder of Sd. Note Being five pounds to be
paid to AUSTIN BRYAN for Satisfaction for his Troble
extrs: brother WILLIAM & Brother In Law KEDAR HERRELL
wit: WM. MCANNE, AUSTON BRYANT
signed: JACOB HOLLINGSWORTH

245. HOLMES, GORGE (CR.035.801.6/A-222)
10 Oct 1790 - Jan Term 1791
wife KEA [?] all my Estate Boath Reale & parsanal; after the death of my
wife all my Lands shad be Equilly devide between my five sons HARDY, FRED-
ERICK, WILLIAM, GORGE & JOHN; all my parsanalile Estate shad be Equlile
devided betwe my ten children [not named] after the death of my beloved wife
extrs: sons HANCE, FREDRICK, WM.
wit: ARTHUR BIZZELL, WILLIAM + BECK
                signed: Gorge H Holmes

246. HOMES, EDWARD (CR.035.801.6/A-466)
11 Jan 1761 - 23 Mar 1761
dau. MARY negroe Sarah; son JOHN negroes Charles & Hall; dau. DORATHA
negroes Nann & Joan; each of my Said Children a feather Bed; Remainder

Part of my Estate Be Equally Divided amongst my Children [not named]
extr: brother GABRIEL
wit: CANNON CASON, WILLIAM MAGEE, JAMES MOORE
signed: Edward Homes

247. HOOKS, THOMAS (CR.035.801.6/A-187)
7 Nov 1801 - Apr Term 1803
wife SUSANA during her life the Use and benefit of all that part of my Plantation which lies between Bear branch and Bear Swamp including all my Buildings,
Orchards & c., negro Lam & his wife Betty and all their Children, leaving
it in her discretion to give up any of said Negro Children at any time she
pleases to those of my Children who may have a right by this Will after her
decease, one yoke of work oxen (the youngest) and ox Cart, Six Cows and
Calves, Six Ewes and lambs, four Sows and pigs, two feather beds and furniture, two Iron Potts, one Skillet, a Tea Kettle, a frying pan, three Pewter
Dishes, three Basons, Six Plates, one Chest, one Case and nine bottles, two
Stone jugs, one pair of Cart and Irons, her Armed Chair and three Windsor
Chairs, half of all my Glass and Earthen ware and Knives and forks and Spoons,
half of all my Casks and Coopers ware of every nature, my sorrel horse & my
Mare called the Ritter Mare, all my Geese; son DAVID all my Lands which I
now at this time possess, negroes Lam and Bett after my said wife's decease,
one feather bed and furniture, 4 Cows and Calves, three Ewes and lambs,
negro Lucy, one hand Mill and one Grindstone; dau. SUSANA McGOWEN negroes
Jin & Candace both of which I heretofore gave & delivered to her; grson
THOMAS JEFFERSON McGOWEN negro Vina which I heretofore gave & delivered to
him; dau. POLLY SLOCOMB negro Sam; dau. LAVINIA SLOCOMB negro Manuel;
grson THOMAS WATKINS negro Daniel; son THOMAS negro Bob; son WILLIAM one
Silver Dollar; son CHARLES one Silver Dollar; Children of my son HILLARY
one Silver Dollar; dau. FANNY WATKINS one Silver Dollar; And whereas I
heretofore lent to my Daughter FANNY my Negro Wench Milley at the time of
her Marriage to JAMES WATKINS and the said Wench Milly having Since had
Increase Several Children, to wit, Jack, Hariot, Spicey, Leah and Mary Ann
I now give and bequeath the said Negro Wench Milly and her said five Children -
to the Children of my said Daughter FANNY WATKINS to wit NEEDHAM, THOMAS &
JAMES; Residue of estate lent to wife to be sold at her death and money
Eaqually divided amongs all my children WILLIAM, HILLARY, CHARLES, THOMAS,
DAVID, LAVINIA SLOCUMB, POLLEY SLOCUMB, FANNY WATKINS & SUSANA McGOWEN
extrs: friend WILLIAM DICKSON, son in law EZEKILL SLOCUMB, son DAVID
wit: WM A. HOUSTON, TEMPERANCE ⟨S⟩ PENNINGTON, WM. DICKSON
signed: Thos. Hooks
Codicil: 13 Jan 1803
Since the above Will was written my Negro Wench Betty has brot Girl Child
named Lucy which is not bequeathed to any one of my Children She is to be
valued by my Executors and by them delivered to any of my Children who will
choose to have her at such Valuation and the said Valuation Money to be
Eaqually divided amongst all my Children
wit: CURTIS HOOKS, HILLERY HOOKS, WM. DICKSON
signed: Thos. Hooks

248. HOOKS, WHITMEL (CR.035.801.6/A-216)
31 Oct 1795 - Jan Term 1796
Father THOS. my Black Mare; brothers & sisters WILLIAM, THOMAS, HILLARY
HOOKSes children [not named], CHARLES, DAVID, LEVINA SLOCUMB, POLLEY SLOCUMB,

FANNEY WATKINS, & SUSANNA one three year old mare named Pol, one Two year
old Do named Bounce, Nine head of year old hogs and one Sow
extr: brother CHARLES
wit: THOS HOOKS, SUSANNA BARFIELD, FRECH. BARFIELD
signed: Whit Hooks

249. HOUSTON, GEORGE E. SENR. (CR.035.801.6/2-70)
17 Feb 1852 - Apr Term 1852
son CALVIN J. the JOHN NEAL land purchased of JOHN MILLER supposed to contain
750 acres, negroes Mindis, Silva, Jim, Sam, & Kit, One Mare, Saddle & bridle;
son GEORGE E. JR. all the land East of Wards Road to J. PEARSALLs to the Main
Road known as the Witt Sand Road to the fork at WARD KORNEGAYs, negroes Bill,
John & Penny & Hester & her youngest child Harry, One horse, Saddle & bridle,
One bed & furniture; dau. SARAH ELISA and son in law JOHN MILLER negroes
Denny, Jimmy, Kit & Mariah, $750 which the Said JOHN MILLER owes me, negro
girl Hannah for her life and then to her children; son ALFRED One half of
all the lands whereon I now live Known as the Johnstone lands & TEMPERANCE
WILLIAMS lands subject to his Mother's Dower, all the Tract of land known as
the Holly Shelter land Supposed to Contain 640 acres, negroes Buck, Peggy,
Rose, Jerry, Martha, Jack & Amanda, One horse, Saddle & bridle, one bed &
furniture; son EDWARD W. the other half of the above discribed lands Subject
to dower, one smal tract of land Joining the lands of J. KENNEY, JAMES HOUSTON
and HARPER WILLIAMS Containing 127 acres, negroes Tom, Myma, Mustipher,
Rachael, Ned, Dick & Joe, One horse, Saddle & bridle, One bed & furniture;
dau. TEMPERANCE W. negroes Rhoda, Wright, Jilica, Caroline, Plinty, Bob, Huldy,
Betsey, Mike & Isaac, one bed & furniture, One piano; wife TABITHA dower in
the lands given My Sons ALFRED & EDWD. W. or the home tract, negroes not willed
viz. Manday, Denny, Sarah, Andrew, Matilda, Lewis & Jinny to Remain in Common
Stock for the Support & Maintanance of my wife, My household & Kitchen furniture, two horses, five Cows and Calves, One Riding establishment; dau.
TEMPERANCE Ballance of the Cattle; negroes Dave & Emanuel hired out to pay
debts during the lifetime of my Wife and at her death to ALFRED and EDWARD W.;
grson HENRY CLAY, son of GEORGE E. 141 acres whereon H. W. HOUSTON Now lives
at the death of said HENRY W. HOUSTON & wife
extrs: CALVIN J. HOUSTON, ALFRED HOUSTON
wit: JAS. PEARSALL, E. W. HOUSTON
signed: George E. Houston Senr.

250. HOUSTON, JAMES (CR.035.801.6/2-69)
16 Jan 1842 - Apr Term 1852
wife EZABEL my Lands, Houses and plantation where I now lives on the North and
east side of the big Branch and buckskin, allso apeice of land lieing in the
fork of buckskin and the Grove Swamp, all my household and kitchen ferneture,
all my stock of horses, Cattle, Hogs and Sheep, all my working tools; son
ROBART J. property left wife at her death to gether with one rifle & Shot gun;
dau. EZABEL McGOWEN one feather bed and firneture, two cows and calves; grsons
JAMES & DAVID G. McGOWEN land lieing on the North west side of The big branch
adj. Stoakes, SARAH JOHNSTON, WRIGHT WILLIAMS, the head of a small branch,
allso my interest and wife's write in the dower land of the Widow Armstrong,
one shotgun to each of them; son in law GEORGE McGOWEN one shot gun
extrs: son ROBERT J. & son in law GEORGE M. McGOWEN
wit: W. H. HANSLEY, J. G. MIDDLETON
                     signed: James Houston
                              Ezabella ✝ Houston

251. HUFHAM, JOHN (CR.035.801.6)
2 Sep 1832 - Nov Term 1832 [very hard to read]
son GEORGE W. $5; dau. HARRIET $50; dau. MARY NEWKIRK negroes Hannack and
her two children & Jack about Seven years old & to her eldest son JOHNATHAN
$400; dau. MARGARET A. negroes Esther and three of her children Jesse [?],
Rachel & Harriet [?] & $150, a bed and furniture; dau. HELEN M. negroes
Gracie & her children Bill, Tim, [?] & Virgil, a bed and furniture, $50;
son JAMES M. land on Clay Hill Branch adj. JOHN HIGHSMITH which I bought of
AUGUSTINE JONES, ELISHA POWEL, & Newton about 700 acres, negroes Sparks,
Andrew & Jack; wife [not named] plantation on which I now live, the mill
and my other lands which I have not left to my sons GEORGE and JAMES,
negroes Rachel and Violet, Peter, Faney [?], Gene about Twenty eight years
old, Comfort about thirty years old and Three of her children Peter, Susann
& Caithy [?] Ann, Cleery about seven years old and Betsey about seven years
old; son JOHN all the land which I have lent my beloved wife, negroes
George about nine years old and Jim about five years old; negroes lent to
wife to go to my three youngest daus. CLOARRISA CAROLINE, NANCY and [?] K;
If any of the negroes I have lent unto my wife NANCY becomes so unmanageable
as not to be controled with ease I leave such negro to my son GEORGE W.
extrs: GEORGE W. & wife NANCY
wit: WM. K. FREDERICK, JONATHAN BRADLEY
signed: Jno Hufham

252. HUNTER, ISAAC (CR.035.801.6/A-199)
12 Oct 1822 - Oct Term 1822
wife PATIENCE the Whole of my Lands together with all and singular the Residue
of my property (to do with as she shall see most proper to enable her to raise
and support my Dear Children) During her Natural life or Widowhood; son
ROBERT JOHN the Whole of my Land not to be taken into possession by him until
the Death or Intermarriage of his said Mother; youngest dau. PRISCILLA ANN
negro Winny aged Six months; daus. MARY ELIZA & PRISCILLA ANN All and every
Species of my Property that may remain
extr: friend ANDREW HURST
wit: RT. WILLIAMS, WILLIAM MECURDEY, TH. H. BRICKELL
signed: Isaac Hunter

253. HUNTER, HOWEL (CR.035.801.6/A-204)
9 Dec 1826 - Apr Term 1827
brother EDWARD $125; brother JOBE $100; brother WILLIAM my lands and $50;
brother NICOLAS $125; brother WRIGHT $10; MARTIN MANNING $10; nephew
HOWEL son of JOBE $150; HOWEL son of WILLIAM HUNTER $50; WILLIAM WRIGHT
HOLLINGSWORTH $50; FREDRICK PICKET the boy Now with me & bound to me $50;
JOHN MCANNE SR. $50; JOHN GOUGH $20; HEZEKIAH GRANT $15; BENJAMIN PADGET
$15; MARCANN MANNING $25; SALLY LUIZA MANNING $25; Next as I have bestowed
on Some of my Friends under age at present it is my wish And intention there-
fore that if one or all or any part of the afore mentioned minors Should dy
before they become the age of twenty one that then & in that case the afore
mentioned Sum or Sums herein Given to them To be Given to my four brothers
NED, JOBE, WILLIAM & NICHOLAS
extr: JOHN McCANNE
wit: WILLIAM MCANNE JUNUR, JOHN McCANNE JNR
signed: Howel Hunter

254. HUNTER, NICHOLAS "planter" (CR.035.801.6/A-213)
5 Jan 1791 - Jan Term 1791
sons HARDEY, NICHOLAS & EDWARD all my Lands and Improvements to be Equalley
Divided between them or the Survivors of them if they should require it at
the time the oldest may arive at the age of 21 years; negro Willm sold and
the money aplied towards the purchase of two young female slaves for my
daus. MARY & ANNEY; negroes Cezar, Jack & his wife Lucy be Hired out Anualy
and the monies arising from such Hire be Equally Divided between the whole
of my children [not named] at the time my oldest son shall be of Lawfull age
extrs: ALEXANDER DICKSON, EDWARD PEARCELL, WM. HUNTER
wit: JAMES GILLESPIE, HOLDEN MEGEE, EDWARD DICKSON
signed: Nich. Hunter

255. HURST, WILLIAM Be (CR.035.801.6/A-201)
24 Jul 1826 - Oct Term 1826
wife FRANKEY B. my mare Named Pol Robinss sucking Colt, one Cow and Calf
and Heffer, white sow and pigs & Eight shoats and my house Hold and Kidchen
furniture; son JAMES B. $5; son SAMUEL B. $5 if he applys; son JOHN B. my
Two year old sorrell mare; grson. WILLIAM B, son of JOSEPH B. $50; residue
of estate sold to pay my Just debts and the residue to be Devided between
WILLIAM B. & JOSEPH B.
extr: not named
wit: SENEY ✗ HARREL, THEO. BARFIELD
signed: Wm. Be. hurst

256. HURST, WILLIAM B. (CR.035.801.6/2-130)
28 Mar 1850 - Jan Term 1858
wife ZYLPHIA B. one third part of my real estate including the dwelling house
and all the outbuildings where I now reside, one years support, two horses,
2 cows and calfs, two sows and pigs, all the fowls, all my household and
Kitchen furneture, one cart and gear, two ploughs and gear and the other
farming tools, negroes Irvin, Jeffrey, Black Edy and child Ann & Rhody and
child Esther; at wife's death, the negroes are to be divided into two equal
parts and given to my son HENRY B. & dau. FANY the wife of NICHOLAS FARRIOR;
dau. FANY negroes Yellow Edy and her two children Frank and Peter; son
GEORGE WILLIAM all my real estate, 600 acres upon which I reside, also 90
acres adj. the same which I purchased of JOEL LOFTEN, negroes Hepsey & Offy,
two feather beds and their necessary furniture; son HENRY B. & dau. FANNY
FARRIOR residue of my property of whatever kind, negroes Jim, Washington,
Lewis & little Edy
extrs: son HENRY B. & son in law NICHOLAS FARRIOR
wit: W. B. WRIGHT, ALSA SOUTHERLAND
signed: Wm. B. Hurst

257. HURST, WILLIAM H. (CR.035.801.6)
__ Mar 1837 - Jul Term 1837
brother JOHN J. negro Brister & the residue of my property of every Kind in
trust for the comfortable Support of my uncle HOGAN HUNTER for and during
the terms of his natural life and at the death of my said uncle I wish a
Sufficiency of my estate appropriated for the comfortable Support of my
negro woman Lucy Senr.; residue of estate at uncle's death sold and money
divided betwen my Sister SARAH A. HILL, sister CATHERENE CALVIN's children,

sister NARCISSA S. HURST, brother ANDREW J. and brother JAMES R.; negro
Satira sold and money divided betwen my mother and all of my brother &
sister; balance of my negroes divided between my mother and all of my
brothers & sisters
extr: brother JOHN J.
wit: CHARLES WINDERS, HENRY WINDERS
signed: William H. Hurst

258. INGRAM, ABNER "Planter" (CR.035.801.6)
25 Sep 1778 - Oct Court 1782
wife FEREBAH negroes Dyce & Abram, Ten Cows and Calves, One Horse and Mare
and Stock of Hogs and What Money I have bye me and all my household Goods
And Furniture and plantation Tools; son SAMUEL my Uper tract of Land,
Five hed of Cattle, One Mare Cald Litefoot, negro Elias; dau. ELIZABETH
negro Alse, Five hed of Cattle; dau. FEREBAH five hed of Cattle And the
first child that the Negro wench Brings that I left to my wife; son JOHN
the plantation whereon I now live, five hed of Cattle and the Second Child
the aforesaid wench brings; residue Equally devided Amongst my Childring
my Eldest Son SAMUEL ariving to Twenty One years old
extrs: brother JOHN & wife
wit: NATHAN WILLIAMS, WILLIAM WILLEFORD, RICHARD WILLEFORD
                                          signed: Abner _Ingram

259. ISHAM, JAMES (S S Wills/DRB2)
2 Nov 1752 - Jul Court 1753
dau. MARGARET negroe Jupiter, one Feather Bed and Furniture belonging thereto
and should she die before She arrives to Age or Marriage to her Brothers
JAMES & CHARLES; son JAMES one Feather Bed and Furniture belonging thereto,
the Moity of my other Negro Roger when he shall arrive to the Age of one
and twenty years Which Said Negro shall then be Valued and Equally Divided
between my Sons JAMES and CHARLES and Roger to be Hired out untill sd.
CHARLES Shall Come of Age and Money arising there from to be applied for the
use of the sd. JAMES & CHARLES and no Other use Whatsoever; my Black
Stallion and three other of my Horses with my Sadle and Bridle to be Sold
and money arrising there from to be Lay out to purchase Lands or Plantation
for the use of my wife JANE until my Sons JAMES or CHARLES shall come of age
and then to be Valued and Equally Divided between my said sons; wife JANE
residue of my Estate Reall and personall
extrs: wife JANE, brother in law EVAN ELLIS, EDWARD HARRISON JUNIOR
wit: WM. HOUSTON, WM MccREE, JOHN DUNN
signed: James Isham

260. IVEY, JOHN (CR.035.801.6/A-224)
3 Oct 1792 - Oct Term 1792
wife LEAH negro Cush with all my Stock of every kind, Houshold Goods and
Plantation tools, negroes Isaac & Lucy; at wife's decease Isaac to be sold
at the discretion of my Executors (he having the liberty to Chose a master)
& the money given to my Grandson DEMCEY son of SAMUEL CARR & MARY his wife
& Lucy given to my Niece ELIZABETH, the dau. of LEMUEL IVEY (late of North-
folk County Virginia deceased); grson. JESSE BROWN negro Jane; grdau.
SARAH HARROD, the dau. of DAVID BROWN and PATIENCE his Wife both deceased
negro Harry; negro Woman Called Phillis be set Free, she complying with

the Law in that Care provided; negroes Anthony and Demcy sold, they having
liberty to chose Masters and the Money from the Sale of Anthony I give to
my dau. SARAH PARKER and the Money from the Sale of Demcy to be Equeally
divided between my wife LEAH & daus. CHARITY SMITH & MARY CARR
extrs: wife LEAH & friends FRANCIS OLIVER & NICHOLAS BOWDEN
wit: NICHOLAS ✗ BOWDEN, SAMUEL BOURDEN
signed: J. Ivey

261. JAMES, JAMES (CR.035.801.6/A-227)
14 Mar 1790 - Oct Term 1796
son THOMAS E. all the Lands I Purchased for JAMES PEARSALL amounting in the
whole to 355 acres; son GABRIEL H. land I Purchased from ALEXANDR DICKSON
& plantation & Land Known by the name of Pearce's place; wife MARY I will
that she live at the Cross rodes, The Mantion House or run ovr to the place
called the Cool spring (at her Option); wife MARY and children MARY TEACHEY,
THOMAS E., ELIZABETH, DORETHY, ANN, GABRIEL HOLMES, REBECCA & CATHRINE R.
my whole estate of negroes; negro Sall to live with my children in her old
age and they to give her comfortable food & Clothing suitable to her age;
wife MARY all my Household furniture, stock of every Kind & plantation Tools,
negro Judy; friend THOMAS SHEPPARD 20 Silver Dollars 2 years after my death;
one dollar be given to the Daughter of JAMES BAILEY of Bladen County, sd.
Bailey was formerly a merchant at Had park
extrs: wife MARY, friends JEREMIAH PEARSALL, JAMES CARR, GABRIEL HOLMES
wit: THOS. ROUTLEDGE SENR, WILLIAM JOHNSTON, JOSEPH JOHNSON
signed: James James

262. JAMES, JOSEPH (CR.035.801.6/A-246)
28 Feb 1781 - Jan Ct 1782
wife ELIZABETH the house & plantation where on I now live to Gather with all
and Every thing Else I Possess under the Son During her Natural Life or
widow hood; dau. ELIZABETH SUTTON one Shilling Stirling; dau. MARY SINGLETON
one Shilling Stirling; dau. REBEKAH MOORE one Shilling Stirling; son ELIAS
one Shilling Stirling; dau. MARGOT one Cow and Calf; dau. RACHEL one shilling
stirling; son CHARLES all the rest of my Goods & Chattels and he is to take
care and maintain his mother during her Life or widow hood
extr: son CHARLES
wit: JOSEPH WILLIAMS, JOHN ⱳ WILLIAMS, ROBERT ✗ KNOWLES
signed: J. James

263. JAMES, REBECCA (CR.035.801.6/A-238)
6 Mar 1824 - Apr Term 1824
mother MARY negroes Joe, Milly & Chole and at her death to my nephew and
Niece JOHN ISHAM STEPHENS and MARY ELIZA STEPHENS; mother MARY my mare,
feather bed and furniture and at her death my brother GABRIEL H. to have my
mare and my neice REBECCA JAMES my bed; nephew JAMES TEACHEY $100 to be
raised by the hire of negro Joe
extr: nephew JAMES TEACHEY
Wit: J. GRAHAM, A. MORGAN
signed: R. James

264. JERNIGAN, THOMAS (CR.035.801.6/A-244)
16 Mar 1786 - Jan Term 1788
wife JANE negroes Mingo, Patience & Tiller all my Cattle consisting of 22 head,
all my Hogs, One black Mare, three Feather beds and Furniture, all my other
Household and Kitchen Furniture and Working tools; wife to give negro Patience
two years Schooling and she to be Free at Wife's decease; sister ANNA BOYETTE
negro Tiller at wife's decease; wife JANE all my Property except what I have
given to others
extrs: friend ABRAHAM MOLTON SER & JOHN MOLTON
wit: ABRAHAM MOLTON, KEDAR BRYAN, FREDERICK RIVENBARK
                                        signed: T. Jernigan

265. JERNIGAN, WATSON (CR.035.801.6/2-77)
15 Aug 1853 - Oct Term 1853
all Lands, negroes and every other species of property sold to pay just debts
and residue equally divided between my beloved wife DICY and nephew CALVIN
extr: wife DICY
wit: JOS. G. DICKSON, DAVID JONES
signed: Watson Jernigan

266. JOHN, THOMAS (CR.035.801.6/A-240)
3 Mar 1762 - May Court 1762
wife MARY all the Household furniture & a note of hand of BENJAMIN EVENS
for 10 pounds, 10 pounds due to me from JACOB FUSSEL & 6 pounds pr annum to
be paid hur by my Executors; daus. SUSANNAH, MARGRET & MARY 20 pounds each
Proclamation money; son THOMAS 5 pounds Proclamation Money; sons DAVID &
JOHN all & singular my lands messuages & Tenaments with my Negroes, horses,
Chattls, moveables & Immoveables of what kind soever to me belonging
extrs: sons DAVID & JOHN
wit: WM. PITMAN, WM. CASE, THOMAS MORRIS
signed: Thom. John

267. JOHNSON, AMOS (CR.035.801.6/A-229)
25 Sep 1801 - Apr Term 1802
dau. MARY HARRIS & heirs of my dau. KEZIA HARDISTY my plantation on North
River in Carttret County; dau. MARY HARRIS negro Toney; dau. KEZIA HARDISTY
negroes Pleasent, Zilpha & Jack; wife SAPPHIER one fleather bed & firneture,
one cow & calf, one Duch oven, one Seader chest, two plates, one bason, one
square table, meat fat & bread Corn for the Season insueing - two two year
old hogs, one Sow & pigs, three gees, some cotten, one Linnin wheal & at her
death to return to my Daughter in law SARAH LANIER; four youngest Children
[not named] shall find my wife a suficient Suport Dureing her life or widowhood; son WILLIAM the plantation where on I now live, 200 acers bought from
WILLIAM PICKET, 75 acres on the south of Cypress Creek, negro Jim, all my
hogs raised a bout home, one cart & wheels, one ox chain, two plows, four
hoes, two axes, one large chest, one cubbard; friend GEDION ARTHUR my
black smith tools & bellos, 160 acers on the East Side of Cypress Creek that
I bought from CHARLES GRIMES, one feather bed and firneture, two two year old
heffers; dau. VIRGINEA QUIN negroes Tonna & Chloe, five Cows and Calves, six
ews; dau. PEGGEY WALLER 175 pounds which was the price of peter which Waller
has recieved 125 Ł of the money, one feather bed & firneture that I lie on;
grson AMOS WALLER negro Hannah; daus. MARY HARRIS, VIRGENNA QUIN, & PEGGY

WALLER negroes Rachel & Venus;   dau. SARAH MURREY negroes Bees & Tamer;
daus. SARAH MURREY, VIRGENNEA QUIN & PEGGEY WALLER my horses;   grson AMOS
HARRIS 200 acers lying on the East side of Cypress Creek joining the Lake
that I bought from JAMES LANIER, three Cows and Calves, one yoke oxen,
30 acers of the same land whereon sd Scarborough now Dweles my desire is
that NATHAN SCARBROUGHT shall have the use of the land for sevin years
after my Deceas;   REUBEN MEEKES shall live where he now Dweles Seven years
after my Deceas on my Land on the back
extrs: NATHAN WALLER, son WILLIAM, ARTHUR MURREY
wit: WM. HOLLINGSWORTH, BIRD LANIER
signed: Amos Johnson

268. JOHNSON, BENJAMIN (CR.035.801.6/2-45)
11 Aug 1843 - Apr Term 1849
wife MARY the Plantation on which I now reside being on the East side of
Stewarts Creek, the turpentine trees on this land I reserve and will them
to be rented out towards paying my debts and the ballance after to be
appropriated towards the education of my children and after her death the
land to be divided between my children JOHN, SARAH ELIZA, MARGARET SUSAN
& MARTHA ELLEN;   oldest son WILLIAM land lying on the other or west side of
Stewarts Creek in four years or at the time he becomes of age;   wife MARY
three beds, bedsteads, and bed clothes, all the kitchen furniture with the
loom and all such house hold furniture as she may choose to select;   son
WILLIAM my bay colt called Sorry
extr: friend HOWELL BEST
wit: THOMAS MORISEY, JR., JNO. D. LOVE
signed: B. Johnson

269. JOHNSON/JOHNSTON, JOHN (CR.035.801.6/2-1)
18 Sep 1838 - Oct Term 1845
wife SARAH JOHNSTON all my plantation whereon I now live so as to include
my dwelling and all out houses & the crop that is growing on it, my young
mare calld Blaze and Pedlar Wagon, my stock of Cattle, all my hogs, my
household & Kitchen furniture;   LOUIZA JOHNSTON one Bed and its necessary
furniture at the descretion of my Wife;   dau. NERCISSA JOHNSTON one Bed
and its necessary furniture at the descretion of my Wife;   dau. HEPSY ANN
JOHNSTON one Bed and its necessary furniture at the descretion of my Wife;
old mare & cold & Shop Tools sold;   wife SARAH JOHNSTON residue of estate
and at her death to be equally devided between my children viz. NEEDHAM,
SALLY, ISAAC, BETSEY JEAN, KITTY ANN, LANY, LOUIZA, NERCISSA & HEPSEY ANN
extr: friend JOHN CARR
wit: G. J. BARON, M. O. CARR
signed: J. Johnson

270. JOHNSON, THOMAS (CR.035.801.6/A-234)
9 Jan 1813 - Jul Term 1814
sons BENJAMIN & SLOAN all my property Real and personal and they to support
and maintain their mother JANE during hur life
extr: son BENJAMIN
wit: JOHN R. POWERS, SLOAN JOHNSON
                    signed: Thomas   Johnson

271. JOHNSTON, BENJAMIN (CR.035.801.6/A-239)
15 Nov 1823 - Feb Term 1828
land on which I now live lying on each side of Turkey Swamp together with
negroes Charles, Lier, Bett, Mitten & Moses, Horses, Cattle, Sheep & Hogs,
my House hold and Kitchen furniture and farming utensils sold; brothers
JOHN AMBERT, JAMES ROBERT & WILLIAM $1 each; sisters FRANCES, SYTHA, JANE
& RACHEL $1 each; ANN OWENS, dau. of LEWIS RYALL $1; BENONLY RYLAND $1;
ELISHA JANACUM negro John; residue to my niece FRANCES wife of WILLIAM
LOCKAMY, niece JANE, wife of JOHN SPEARS & POLLY RYLAND except for Four Cows
and calves and one heifer to FRANCES LOCKAMY
extrs: THOMAS KENAN, THOMAS BOYKIN
wit: JOHN GUY, LEMUEL ✝ GUY, ROBT GROVES
                              signed: benjamin ⌐ᵰᶜ Johnston

272. JOHNSTON, HANNAH (CR.035.801.6/A-235)
10 ___ 1777 - Jan Court 1783
son JOHN JUR. the plantation I Now Live on Granted me By Deed from WILLIAM
McREE provided he give or cause to be Given to my dau. HANNAH 300 acres to
Be at Stewarts Creek and dau. ELIZABETH 300 acres Belonging to or Joining
this plantation Where it may be Thught most Convenient and should he fail in
this my plantation to go to HANNAH & ELIZABETH shear & shear Alik; my Thirds
Be Divided Between them shear and sear alike Excepting three Cows & Calfes to
B Given to other Three Children [not named] one a piec; my three Grandchildren [not named] to get a too yeere old heifar a piec
extr: not named
wit: DAVID MURDOCK, JOHN JOHNSTON, CHAS. WARD
signed: Hannah Johnston

273. JOHNSTON, JAMES (CR.035.801.6/A-249)
17 Dec 1801 - Jan Term 1802
wife JANE the third of my lands together with the Houses whereon I now live
during her natural life, all my personal Estate and if my wife be with Child
that Child should have one half of my personal Estate but if she Should
not be with child I gives my brothers WILLIAM and ROBERT all my lands together
with the house and improvements whereon my Father lived; sisters JANE, SARAH
& EZABEL the price of my bay mare which I Sold to OWEN RIGBEY for $135
extrs: EDWARD PEARSALL, brother WILLIAM JOHNSTON
wit: ANNE MEGEE, SARAH ⅄ McCULLOUGH, EDWD. PEARSALL
signed: James Johnston

274. JOHNSTON, JOHN "of Burncoat" (CR.035.801.6/A-233)
nuncupative will
taken in Court 20 Oct 1795
THOMAS SHITTON Sayeth That sometime last Winter he heard Deceased say he
intended that all his Estate except his Land should be Sold and that the
Monies be laid out to purchase Land which together with the land he then
possessed should be Rented out early and the Monies be applied for the Use
of the Poor in Duplin County; Mrs. BURKE, a Woman who Attended the sd. JOHN
JOHNSTON in his last Sickness Sayeth that She had often heard him say that he
intended all his Estate should be for the use of the poor in Duplin County;
MILLS MUMFORD sayeth he had frequently heard JOHN JOHNSTON say that he would
leave all he had to the use of the poor in Duplin County
Test: WM DICKSON Clerk of Court

275. JOHNSTON, JOHN (CR.035.801.6)
21 Aug 1833 - Apr Term 1840
BENJAMIN son of JEREMIAH PEARSALL 1/3 part of my Estate real & personal;
EDWARD JOHN son of JNO. PEARSALL & EDWARD son of THO. H. WRIGHT 1/3 part
of my Estate real & personal; MURDOCK & CHARLES W. sons of ANDREW & ANN W.
JULIAN 1/3 of my Estate real & personal
extrs: JAMES PEARSALL, WM. CARR
wit: JAS. PEARSALL, EDWARD PEARSALL
signed: John Johnston

276. JOHNSTON, JOSEPH (CR.035.801.6/A-247)
5 Sep 1794 - Jan Term 1802
son WILLIAM 320 Acre Survey that lies below the mouth of the Big Branch and
the other side of Buckskin; son ROBERT the Big Branch Survey of 125 acres
and 100 acres to be taken off the new Entered Land; son JAMES the manner
plantation with all the Improvments and all the rest of my Lands; residue
to be Divided Between my daus. SUSANNAH, JANE, SARAH & ISSABEL Except Two
Cows and Calves, the Mare and Colt and side saddle and a Loom are for SUSANAH
over and above the other girls
extrs: JOHN ROBINSON, CHARLES WARD, EDWARD PEARSALL
wit: CHA. WARD, EDWD. PEARSALL, JOHN JOHNSTON
                              signed: Joseph   Johnston

276A. JONES, ELIJAH (3-69)
11 Aug 1858 - Jan Term 1863
wife ESTHER all of my property both Real and personal; dau. NANCY one
hundred and forty acres to be cut off at the south end of my land adjoining
STEPHEN B. WINDERS; son JOEL the balance and residue of my land; dau. MARY
GRIMES negroes George and Hester; dau. NANCY negroes Betsey and Hannah;
son JOEL negroes Harry and Rachel and Isham, my Coopers tools, Carpenters
tools and my farming tools; after the death of my wife my stock of horses,
cattle, hogs and sheep together with my household and kitchen furniture sold
and dau. NANCY to have one hundred dollars and the remainder equally divided
between dau. MARY GRIMES and son JOEL
extr: son JOEL
wit: D. JONES, C. Y. F. JONES
signed: E. Jones
Codicil: 23 Mar 1860
dau. NANCY one Bed with its necessary furniture, seventy five dollars to buy
her a horse, my large Bible with her School Books; son JOEL young mare Pink,
one saddle and bridle, One feather Bed and its necessary furniture, his
school Books; remainder of my beds and their furniture devided between my
two daughters and son after wife's death
wit: D. JONES
signed: E. Jones

277. JONES, ELISHA (CR.035.801.6)
14 Mar 1840 - Apr Term 1840
son DANIEL negro Stephen & the PETER PARKER land; son ELIJAH negroes Rachel,
Harry & Bet; son MATTHEW negro Moses; MATTHEW's children negro Esther; son
JOEL negroes Isham & Edea; dau. SALLY SULIVAN negroes Hannah & Penney & her
last two children; dau. MARY CREECH & her children negroes Hester & Allen;

dau. ZILPHA JONES & her children negroes Lucy & her child & Jack; dau. NANCY
PRICE & her children negroes Marenda & Ned; sons ELIJAH & JOEL land and
Plantation whereon I now live including the Plantation where ELIJAH JONES now
lives; son MATTHEW $100; residue equally divided between all my Children
extrs: sons DANIEL & ELIJAH
wit: DANIEL ⤳ PARKER, J. SWINSON
signed: Elisha Jones

278. JONES, JESSE (CR.035.801.6/A-237)
nuncupative will
taken 9 Sep 1815
JAMES WILKINSON of Cumberland County made oath that on Tuesday the Fifth day
of this inst. that JESSE JONES Being sick told this deponant that he had a
negro Woman Cate near Newbern who was Runaway and a certain man not Remembering
his name was to have the service of her ten months for catching her and she
was then to be kept by OWEN CONNERLY until he calld for her and it was his
wish that Connerly was to keep her as he had Rather he would have her than
any Other
JAMES WRIGHT, J. P.

279. JONES, JOHN (S S Wills/DBR2)
15 Mar 1759 - 12 Jan 1759
wife ANN all my Cattle and my Rideing horse and Sheep and all my house hold
Goods and hogs; wife AN my plantation Where on I Now Live During her Life;
son WILLIAM after my wifes Deseas my plantation Containing one hundred acers
Where I Now Live, my young mare and Gun; son THOMAS my plantation Containing
one hundred acors Where on ANN WILLIAMS Now Liveth; dau. PATTE my young
Sorrell horse; daus. CATTHERN, ELESABETT, MARY ANN & SARE five Shillings Each
extrs: wife & JOHN JONES
wit: WILLIAM WHITFIELD, ANN ⤳ JONES, ANN ⤳ WILLIAMS
                                         signed: John ⤳ Jones

280. JONES, JOHN (CR.035.801.6/A-231)
13 Jun 1796 - Oct Term 1796
wife ELIZABETH all my household furnture to Support upon and Raise my Children
and Give them Reasonable good Schooling and at her Death Equally Divided
Between my sons JOHN & LEWIS; the place where I now Live to Be sold and the
Money Laid out to purchase another place as good as my Exrs can Get as I Dont
want them to stay here
extr: Brother in Law LOFTIN WORLEY, THOMAS SHELTON
                              signed: John ⤳ Jones

281. JONES, MARTHA (CR.035.801.6)
16 Nov 1830 - Feb Term 1831
friend JAMES HARPER land and plantation whereon I now live containing by the
Estimation of CALVIN DAVIS County surveyor 163 acres; my Bear Marsh land sold
and money Divided into three Equal lots to go to MARTHA ELIZABETH heir of
WINIFRED SWINSON, PENELOPE WHITFIELD & POLLY CASEY; friend JAMES HARPER all
my Stock of Cattle, hogs, Sheep, my household and Kitchen furniture; JESSE
SWINSON JUR $5; friend JAMES HARPER my horse Tom and colt Sweeper
Extr: D. JONES
wit: JESSE ⤳ BROCK, FREDERICK ⤳ DAIL
                         signed: Martha ⤳ Jones

282. JONES, ROBERT (CR.035.801.6/A-243)
11 Apr 1828 - Aug Term 1828
friend JAMES HARPER n&gro David; friend WINNIFORD SMITH $25; wife MARTHA
all the Residue of Property During her natural life & then to Friends JAMES
HARPER & WINNIFORD SMITH
extrs: WRIGHT SMITH, WILLIAM WHITFIELD
wit: JOHN BROW
         signed: Robert   Jones

283. JONES, SOLOMON (CR.035.801.6/A-242)
30 Jul 1830 - Aug Term 1830
wife SARAH one years provisions; son JONAS the young Hourse named Shake-
Speare; dau. SARAH BOYET and her Children [not named] negro Bob; son
EDWARD $1; Ballance of my property disposed of and money Equally Divided
between wife SARAH, EMMA JONES, EDNA SMITH, ANTHONY JONES, JONAS JONES,
EDWARD JONES too Sons HAYWOOD & MARSHALL & my Little son FREDRICK and NANCY
JONES
extrs: son EDWARD, LEVI SWINSON
wit: THOS. HILL JR., JAMES GRIMES
signed: Solomon Jones

284. JONES, STEPHEN (CR.035.801.6)
18 Sep 1835 - Apr Term 1838
MARINA MARTIN my wife's niece negro Tener about 6 weeks old, one feather bed
and its necessary furniture, $100; wife NANCY one half of all the land which
I may die siesed or possessed of, one half of all the negroes; nephew FRANCIS
B. JONES all my land & negroes with one half at my death and the other half
at my Wife's death; perishable property sold and money equally divided
between my wife NANCY and my Nephew FRANCIS B. JONES
extrs: wife NANCY, nephew FRANCIS B. JONES
wit: M. O. CARR, H. KORNEGAY JUN
signed: Stephen Jones

285. KANEGAY, ABRAM (CR.035.801.7/A-263)
13 Aug 1825 - Oct Term 1825
wife ANNA all my property; three eldest daus. [not named] $1 each; 3 sons
& youngest dau. [not named] remaining part of estate after my wife's death
extr: friend HENRY KANEGAY
wit: JOHN BROWN, JOHN B. WHITFIELD
                 signed: Abram   Kanegay

286. KEATHLEY, JONATHAN (CR.035.801.7/A-271)
2 Dec 1821 - Jan Term 1822
son JOHN $296, Two Cows and Calves, Two Sows and pigs or the value of Cattle
and Hogs in money; son MARK Two Cows and Calves, Two Sows and Pigs, one
feather Bed and furniture; son JONATHAN Two Cows and Calves, Two Sows and
Pigs, one feather Bed and furniture, one horse by the name of Strap & one
feather bed and furniture at the death of his mother; wife NANCY for her
natural life Time Two Cows and Calves, Two Sears for her support, Two Sows
and pigs, one feather bed and furniture, negro woman Jan, all the Household
and Kitchen furniture; residue of estate sold at wife's death and money

divided amongst my daus. [not named] Counting in Sixty five Dollars for one
Horse, sadle and Bridle which my Daughter CHARITY HERRING have
extrs: sons RICHARD and MARK
wit: EDWD. ALBERTSON, JONATHAN KEATHLY, JOHN DANIEL
signed: Jonathan Keathley

287. KENADAY, DAVID (CR.035.801.7/2-39)
18 Sep 1845 - Oct Term 1848
wife LACCY all my property consisting of lands, Stock, Plantation tools, corn
& Fodder, Household & Kitchen Furniture, notes and money; dau. ELIZA after
the death of my wife one Bed and Furniture, one Loom and Slays and Gear thereunto belonging, one Sow and pigs, one Chest, one Wheel and Cards; dau. SUSAN
wife of HENRY CARLTON $3; dau. KIZEY JANE wife of BRYANT EVANS $3; son
WILLIAM MARSHALL all the residue of my property after my wife's death
extr: not named
wit: H. BOURDEN, LEWIS McCULLIN
                    signed: David   Kenaday

288. KENADY, DEMSEY (CR.035.801.7/A-262)
5th day 12th month 1783 - Apr Court 1784
my Books to be Equally Divided amongst all my Children [not named]; my
Moveable Estate to be sold and my wife RHODA to have as much as my Executors
Shall think Necessary; residue of money to be Applyde to the Use of Raising
and Schooling my Younger Children [not named]; all my Lands to be Rented Out
Untill my Youngest Child Arrives at age 21 with 1/3 part of the rents to my
wife; dau. RACHEL 20 shillings only Except her part of the Books; children
to Remain with their Mother or to be Bound Out among friends as Executors
Shall think best for their Education
extrs: friends WILLIAM LANCASTER, JOHN KENNEDY
wit: JOHN MOORE, JOSEPH PARKER, ABSALEM A KINCY
signed: Demsey Kenady
[note: from the dating of this will, it would appear Kenady was a Quaker]

289. KENEDAY / KENEDA, THOMAS (CR.035.801.7/2-64)
17 Jun 1840 - Apr Term 1851
wife NANCEY the plantation whearon I now live, two Cows and Calves, twenty
head of Hogs, one fether Bead and furniture, negroes Toney, Aamey & Cloo;
sone JAMES $10; sone JOSEPH $10; sone JOHN $10; sone DAVID one half of my
Broad Branch land; sone FELIX the oather half of my Broad Branch land; sone
DANIEL negroe Toney; sone ROBERT land adj. WILLIAM BROWN at the fourd of the
Branch which Runs through the field to the lain in forunt of the House whair
I now live to the foot of the Roling path; sone HENERY Balance of my land
whair on I now live; dau. RILLEY SOUTHERLAND negro Mornin & hir four Children
James, Teanor, Drendor & Marey; dau. DELLEY SOUTHERLAND negro Hammons; dau.
SALLY WILLKINS negro Lucey & hir two children John & Tim; dau. KITTEY negroe
Ories, one Bead and furniture; dau. NANCEY KENADA negro Jinne, one feather
Bead and furniture; dau. SUSAN negro Mary, one feather Bead and furniture;
dau. REBECAH negroes Bryant & Abel & $40; negro Sam sold to pay my Just Deb
and any money remaining to Be Equely Divided between sones ROBERT & HENERY &
dau. REBECAH
extr: not named
wit: DAVID SOUTHERLAND, WILLIAM BROWN
                    signed: Thomas   Keneda
[See Codicil on next page]

Codicil; 17 Jun 1840
sone HENERY one Horse, one Bead and furneture; when negro Sam is sold daus.
NANCY & SUAN are to have $20 each; sone DAVID my blacksmith tools; dau.
REBECAH the feather Bead and furniture after the Death of her mother
wit: DAVID SOUTHERLAND, WILLIAM BROWN
                            signed: Thomas   Kenaday

290. KENAN, ELIZABETH (CRX Box 243/A-259)
2 Oct 1789 - Jan Term 1790
grdaus. SUSANNAH LOVE & ELIZABETH MORRISSY negro Charity, all my beds and
furniture, all my wearing apparrell; son JAMES Two Cows and Calves, one
stear of six years old, 1/2 of a still; dau. JANE MORRICY all the remainder
part of my stock of cattle, half a Dozen of silver Tea Spoons; grdau. NANCY
TURRANCE negro Sedy; dau. ELIZABETH TURRANCE one small Table, 5 shillings;
dau. PENELOPE CLINTON 5 shillings; son MICHAEL J. one half of a still, 5
shillings; dau in law NELLE 5 shillings
extrs: RICHARD CLINTON, GEORGE MORRICEY
wit: DAN HICKS, JAS. THOMSON, SERVICE HICKS
                          signed: Elizabeth   Kenan

291. KENAN, JAMES (CR.035.801.7/CRX Box 243/A-257)
2 Jun 1807 - Jul Term 1810
wife SARAH my House wench Easter and all her Children; son DANIEL LOVE
two yellow men Slaves Aleck & Moses, my Plantation and all my lands joining
the same, also all my other lands of every Kind; son THOMAS negro wench
Polley & her child Henry, all & Singulor a Tract of land Patented by my self
and Sold apart to BENJAMIN JOHNSTON and JAMES TONANS; dau. SARAH negro wench
Thena and all her children; dau. JANE negro wench Hagar and all her children
& negro boy Isaac; grdau. SARAH NORMENT negro Ireland; residue of my estate
to my wife SARAH and at her death to be Eaqually divided amongst my children
the shares drawn by my daus. ELIZABETH PRICE & SUSANNA GREEN to go to their
children [not named]; if CATHARIN KENAN should Survive my wife She shall be
maintained out of my Estate
extrs: sons THOMAS & DANIEL LOVE
wit: DANIEL LOVE, WILLIAM TUTON, LEVI BORDIN
signed: Jas. Kenan

292. KENAN, SARAH (CRX Box 243/A-255)
16 May 1816 - Apr Term 1819
sons THOMAS & DANIEL L. negro Esther and her youngest child George for the use
and benefit of my dau. ELIZABETH; sons THOMAS and DANIEL L. negro Polly for
the use and benefit of my dau. SUSANNAH; son THOMAS negro Edmond; son DANIEL
L. negro Billy; dau. SARAH MORIS negro Moses and at her death to her son
GEORGE; dau. JANE HALL negro Baalam and if she has no children he to go to
my grson THOMAS D. son of THOMAS; grdau. CATHARINE E. PRICE one Bed Bedstead
and furniture; grdau. SARAH HOLMES $10; my six children the residue of my
estate
extrs: sons THOMAS & DANIEL L.
wit: JAMES LAUSON, ANN STANFORD
signed: Sarah Kenan

293. KENAN, THOMAS (CRX Box 243/A-253)
13 Jun 1762 - no probate
wife ELIZABETH the plantation whereon I now live containing 338 acres together

with all houses outhouses and other Improvements whatsoever and at her death
or marriage to my two youngest sons THOS. and MICHAL ye Lower part of ye
said plantation to be divided by a branch known by the name of Iluiar Branch
to THOMAS and the upper part to MICHAEL and my son THOS upon his attaining
his age of 21 years to pay unto MICHAEL 40 £ proclamation money to make their
devise more equal; wife ELIZABETH negroes Tom, Anthony & Floir and at her
death or marriage to my three daughters ARABELLA, ELIZABETH & PENELOPE; such
of the Floris children and future increase as shall not be particularly devised to my four daus. AREBELA, ELIZABETH, PENELOPE & JANE; son THOMAS negro
Caesar; son MICHAEL negro Ira; dau. JANE negro Hannah; wife ELIZABETH
residue and remainder of my real & personal estate
extrs: wife ELIZABETH & DAVID THOMSON
wit: EDWD MATCHET, EDWARD CANNONE, JOHN MATCHET
signed: Thos. Kenan
codicil: 6 Nov 1765
negro Derry given to my son MICHAEL I now give to my son in law RICHARD
CLINTON and give negro Moll to my son MICHAEL instead
wit: WM HOUSTON, ISAAC HUNTER
signed: Thos. Kenan

294. KENNADAY, JOHN (CR.035.801.7/3-115)
30 Nov 1859 - Fall Term 1866
wife MARY all my lands including the plantation whereon I now life with the
dwelling house and all out houses and at her death to be divided as equally
in Value as possibly among my children & grandchildren JOHN B., JESSE MILLER
& wife ELIZA JANE, HENRY WHALEY & wife SARAH, JAMES W., ISAAC SANDERSON &
wife SYLVIA, JESSE T. & the children of my dau. MARY ANN HOUSTON & the children of my dau. ZILPHA TILGHMAN; wife MARY negroes Jack & Fanny & her children,
two beds bedsteads and furniture, one Horse and Buggy & harness, two cows &
calves, one sow & pigs, two plows & gear, four ewes & lambs, all the kitchen
furniture; son BRYAN $75; son-in-law MICHAEL TILGHMAN & wife ZILPHA $1;
son JESSE T one bed bedstead & furniture; son-in-law ISAAC SANDERSON & wife
SYLVIA one bed bedstead & furniture, one cow & calf; friend JAMES LAWHORN
& wife NANCY 1 cow & calf
extrs: friend HOUSTON MAXWELL, son JOHN B.
wit: JOHN D. SOUTHERLAND, JOHN SMITH
                        signed: John ⚔ Kenneday

295. KING, HENRY (CR.035.801.7/A-260)
19 Nov 1762 - no probate
wife ANN negro Robin, one feather bed and furnetude, one Rone Pacing mare
and her Riding Sadle and Bridle, three head of Sheep & my Two Work horses
for the use of the Plantation; son HENRY negro Ned, one fether bed and
furnetude, one head of sheep, three cows and calves, three head of other
Catle, my Pacing mare Colt Named Sparkle, three Sows and Pigs, 100 acres of
Land Lying below whare I Now Live on the Six Runs Swamp; son STEVEN the
first child that my Negro Weoman Named Cloe has that Lives to be Two years
ould, three head of Sheep, three Cows & Calves, three hed of other Cattle,
three Sows and Pigs, one Gray mare and a yearling horse colt, my plantation
where on I Now live; dau. MARY the Second Child that the above Named Cloe
has to Live to be Two years ould, three head of sheep, three Cows and Calves,
three head of outher Catle, one bay mare, one feather bed and furnetude,
three sows and pigs; son CHARLS the above Named negro Woman Cloe, three

head of sheep, three Cows and Calves, three head of other Catle, three Sows
and Pigs, one feather bed and one Shot Gun, one bay horse, one black mare,
a yearling horse; one Gray horse, the 100 acres bought of Mr ALEXANDER
MEEDLER Lying on Boun Ridge Swamp Sould to Pay my Debts; wife ANN residue
of estate; that Part of Negroes that fals to me after my mother's Dearth
to be Equally Divided between my four Children
extrs: wife ANN, MICHAEL KING, ABRAHAM FFORRIS
wit: JOHN YARBROUGH SEN., JOHN KING, JAMES YARBROUGH
signed: Hnry King

296. KNOLES, ROBART (CR.035.801.7/A-264)
26 Apr 1792 - Jul Term 1792
wife ELISABETH all my movable property with the full possession of my lands
and plantation during her continueing my widow or untill the Children become
of age then the land to belong to EMANUEL & JAMES and the Movable property
to be Equally devided between FRANCIS, ELISABETH & WILLIAM
extrs: JAMES KNOLES, STEPHEN WILLIAMS
wit: AARON WILLIAMS, JOSEPH WILLIAMS, DANN   BOWEN
         signed: Robt. ✗ Knoles

297. KNOLES, ROBERT (CR.035.801.7/2-93)
19 Mar 1855 - Jul Term 1855
wife SUSAN 1/3 part of all my lands laid off so as to include my mansion
House and all outhouses, one cow & calf, one sow & pigs, one bed & furniture
which it is understood in the family she claims, 1/3 part of all my other
property & effects; dau. ANNA JANE, wife of DAVID REGISTER the upper or
Northern part of my land whereon I reside, one bed & furniture, one cow &
calf, one sow & pigs, 1/3 part of all my other property; dau. SUSAN all
other of my land, one bed & furniture, one Cow & calf, one sow & pigs
extr: WILLIAM R. WARD Esq
wit: GEORGE W. WILLIAMS, JOHN T. WILSON
signed: Robt. Knoles

298. KNOLS, JOHN (CR.035.801.7/A-268)
29 Nov 1802 - Apr Term 1804
sun WILAM 1 shiling searling; dau. MEREY 1 shiling Starling; dau. DARKIS
1 shiling starling; dau. BARBERY 1 shiling starling; dau. ELIZABETH
1 shiling starling; wife FRANKEY rest of my estate and at her death to Be
Equel Ley Devided Amung suns JAMES, DAVID, JOHN & STEPHEN
extrs: DAVID CARLTON, wife FRANKEY
wit: AUSTIN BEESLEY, AMUS ✗ TUCKER
         signed: John 🗲 Knols

299. KNOWLS, ROBART (CR.035.801.7) [badly damaged]
Second Year of our Sovearn Lord George the year of our Lord one thousand
       seven hundred sixty two - Aug Ct 1762
dau. MERAY one Shilling Starling; son JOHN ten [torn] what he had all
Redday; wife FR[torn] plantation and all the movales whatsoever; [torn]lemon
Knowls the plantation and to there heirs [torn] ROBART and ANDREW KNOWLES
one half of the Real [torn]
extrs: JAMES MURRAY Esquer, WILLIAM ST[torn]
wit: WILLIAM MARFORD, JOHN 🖎 WILLIAMS, JOSEPH WILLIAMS, CLIFTEN BOWEN
signed: Robrt Knowls

300. KORNEGAY, GEORE (CR.035.801.7) [original missing from folder]
21 Nov 1773 - 29 Nov 1773
wife SUSANNAH negro Hannah, six cows & calves, three sows, a young mare,
one third part of my plantation & one third part of my crop now standing for
her support of my two children [not named], one linnen wheel, all the household goods which was her own before, my riding horse Cromwell; son DANIEL
350 acres adjoining my son DAVID's land & ROBART ORME, one mulatto girl Pegg,
negro Anthoney; son ELIJAH 300 acres in Dobbs County on falling creek on
the south west side of Thunder Swamp, negro Rachel; increase of sd. negro
Rachel to be equally divided between sons DANIEL & ELIJAH and are to be in
my wife's care & use for the benefit of schooling my said children; son
ELIJAH six cows & calves; eldest son JOHN 200 acres of land including the
houses and a part of the plantation whereon I now live to be divided by a
direct line from the river to the back line, 400 acres whereon my son JOHN
now lives, negroes Tom, Will & Ben, 40 acres of land in the fork of the
Beaverdam, all the cattle, horses and mares that is in his proper mark, 3
ewes & a ram; son JACOB all the land adj. his line on the Southwest side of
the Northeast branch containing 640 acres, negroes Pompey & York, all the
cattle and horses that is in his mark or brand; son GEORGE 150 acres in the
fork of Beaverdam on the Northeast, 50 acres over Spring Branch towards Munts,
negroes Boston & Pope, all the cattle and Stock that is in his mark or brand,
350 acres on the horse pen branch; son WILLIAM 50 acres on Buck Marsh,
negroes Jack & Prep, all the cattle and horses that is in his mark or brand;
dau. MARY DEBRUHL all the cattle and horses that is in her mark or brand;
sons JOHN & DAVID the great distill which is now on my plantation; son JOSEPH
500 acres in three patents on the Northeast of the Capefare adj. Johnson,
negroes Toney & Peter, a part of my stock not divided between my sons JOSEPH,
DAVID & ABRAHAM; vessel sold at public vendue & money divided between sons
DANIEL & ELIJAH; the tarrkiln which is now standing be finished in order
for the tarr to be sold & also the turpentine and millstones and the remainder
part of my cyder & money divided between sons DANIEL & ELIJAH & for the trouble
and time that they with their negroes and horses shall be at in helping to
burn the tarrkiln into tarr they shall have all the brandy & cyder & the hides
and leather made this present year; sons JOHN & DAVID my large canoe; suns
JOSEPH, ABRAHAM & DAVID all my household Goods of what nature within doors
and without with all horses, cattle and sheep not willed before and if JOSEPH
doth not return within three years then his part to ABRAHAM & DAVID; sons
JOHN, JACOB & GEORGE to be trustees and guardians of my sons DANIEL & ELIJAH
and they may bind them by Indentures to some Tradesman according to the best
of their judgement and the consent of my wife according to law
extrs: sons JOHN, JACOB & GEORGE
wit: JOHN GRANADY, MORGAN SMITH SANDERS, RUBEN ℞ ANDREWS
signed: George 𝐆𝐊 Kornegay

301. KORNEGAY, GEORGE SENR. (CR.035.801.7/A-266)
31 Jan 1808 - Oct Term 1808
son GEORGE the land he lives on, negroes Toney, Charles, Bob, Honer & Cato;
dau. SEVILE & her husband JOHN KORNEGAY one mare, Saddle & bridle, One bed &
furniture, four Cows & Calves all of which they have previously recd., negroes
Esther & all her Children & Jack during my life and then to be under the Care
of my Son DANIEL for the support of sd. SEVILE and after her Decease to be
Devided Amongst her children [not named]; son DANIEL the land he lives on,

negroes Jenny, Silocy & All her children & Jim, three Cows & Heffers & yearlings; son DAVID the land he lives on, negroes Violet, Will, Guff, little Tom & Matthew, $100; sons BASEL & JACOB Residue or Remainder of my Negroes; wife MOORENE one Horse named Snip, my Riding Chair; son BASEL to pay son JACOB $500 out of my Estate; sons BASEL & JACOB Residue of my estate; son BASEL my stock of Cattle
extrs: sons BASEL & JACOB
wit: READEN BOWDEN, ABRAHAM JOHNSON
signed: G. Kornegy

302. KORNEGAY, ISAAC (CR.035.801.7)
3 Sep 1836 - Apr Term 1838
son HARGETT 390 acres Including the plantation whereon he now lives, negro Henry; dau. NANCY negroes Matilda & Olly; son ISLER 270 acres, negro Mike; son ISAAC 250 acres, negro Ned; son LEWIS WILLIAMS 185 acres, negro Friday; dau. HESTER negroes Ginne & Austin; son IMMANUEL negroes Wiley & Charles; dau. POLLY negroes Old Easter, Celah & Harriot; son AHASUERUES negroes Aaron & Alfred; dau. ELIZA negroes Moses & Elsey; wife ESTHER negroes Hary & Caty, horse called Jackson, two cow & calves, one feather bed and furniture, one Cart, one yoke of oxen and waggon; daus. CAROLINE & CLARRISSA negroes Clary, Henry, March & Alexander when either of them Shall marry or arrive at the age of twenty years; residue of property to wife ESTHER to educate and raise my sd. two children; daus. CAROLINE & CLARRISSA one feather bed and furniture and two cows each
extrs: trusty friends JOHN CARR & JOHN COLWELL
wit: CHARLES MILLARD, ISAAC MILLARD
signed: Isaac Kornegay

303. KORNEGAY, LUKE (CR.035.801.7/A-251/A-269)
9 Feb 1819 - Jul Term 1819
brother & sister JAMES CARRAWAY & wife MARY $200; brother HENRY $210; NATHAN GARNER & wife PENELOPE $200; brother ABRAHAM $300; mother MARY all my negrows to wit Nead, Milley & her children, two Cows and Cals, two Sows and pigs; brother BRYAN the hole of my Lands and my Negrows after my Mothers Deaced
extr: brother BRYAN
wit: ROBT. WILLIAMS, MUTILDY ✗ PRICE
signed: Luke Kornegay

304. KORNEGAY, MARGARET S. (CR.035.801.7)
nuncupative 19 Sep 1840
taken by JAMES K. HILL & JEREMIAH PEARSALL acting justices of the peace; MARGARET HURST and DAVID S. HURST swore that on Tuesday the 15th Inst. MARGARET S. KORNEGAY departed this life and that shortly previous to her deccase she called upon these affiants to witness her declaration touching the future disposition of her property, ROBERT K. son of ANDREW HURST & wife MARY to have negro London now in the possession of THOMAS W. KORNEGAY of Tuscaloosa County, Ala.; her notes also in possession of THOMAS W. KORNEGAY of Tuscaloosa County, Ala. to be equally divided between her brothers DAVID L. & THOMAS W. & sister MARY E. HURST

305. KORNEGAY, MARY (CR.035.801.7/A-265)
10 Sep 1826 - Oct Term 1826
son BRYAN negroes Green, Adam & Neady; son HENRY negroes Lucy & her children
Sene & Gim and Cassey & Rachel; dau. PENELOPE GARNER negroes Gim, Tuffey
& Agnes; dau. MARY CARRAWAY negroes Sally & her child Charles also Gorge;
grandchildren MARY NORRIS, NANCY JONES, ZACHERIAH, HENRY, WARD & MARTHA
$100 each at age 21; LOVY BLAYLOCK $1
extrs: sons BRYAN & HENRY
wit: CHARLES WILLIAMS, Mc. WILLIAMS
                    signed: Mary ✖ Kornegay

306. KORNEGAY, SARAH (CR.035.801.7/3-2)
15 Apr 1859 - Jul Term 1859
son HENRY R. all the property that his father [not named] left unto him,
one Choice sow and pigs; dau-in-law GINNETT $8; grandson ROBERT DANIEL
One Ewe and lamb; Mare and Buggy sold and $100 kept for my grson. JOHN WM.
until he becomes 21; grdau. JULIA HATCH $15; grandchildren LOUSY ANN &
GEORGE E. $10 each; grson. JAMES ROBRT. $10; dau. MARY A. HERRING $10, One
Bed and set of Curtains in my room for her life and then to my grdau. MARY
ELIZABETH HERRING; grdau. MARY ELIZABETH HERRING one Looking glass, one
dressing table, One pair Smoothing Irons; dau in law MARGARETT $10; dau-in-
law SARAH A. $10; dau. in law JANE SOPHIA one bed and furniture with a sett
of checked curtains and after her death to her dau. MARTHA TENNESSE; residue
to be sold to pay Doctors Bills and all my Just debts; remainder of money
to my son WM M.
extr: son JOSEPH
wit: H. KORNEGAY, SIMMONS KORNEGAY
                    signed: Sarah ✚ Kornegay

307. KORNEGAY, THOMAS H. (CR.035.801.7/2-91)
nuncupative 16 Oct 1854
WILLIAM KORNEGAY, LETTY KORNEGAY & THOMAS M. GRADY state sd. THOMAS H.
KORNEGAY died on Oct. 8, 1854 & that previous to his death he bequeathed
mother KITTY all of his crop of Every discription; sister CATHRINE E his
horse; before JAMES G. BRANCH & GEORGE SMITH two of the acting Justices of
the Peace

308. KORNEGAY, WILLIAM SENR. (CR.035.801.7)
1 Jan 1837 - Apr Term 1837
wife KITTY negroes Joe, Prince & Pege & her children Allen, Sarah, Stark,
Ede & Rachel, Hanner & her children Dilse & Willis, five feather Beds, steads
and furniture, two mares called Blaze & Puss, 60 Barrels of corn, 20 Bushels
of peas, 3000 pds of pork, all my blades & Top fodder, 1 Barrel of lard, 100
pds of sugar, 30 pds of coffee, 20 gallons of Molasses, all my farming tools,
five cows and calves, One yoke of Oxen, five sows and pigs, all my household
and Kitchen furniture, all my stock of year old hogs, One grinstone, 20
Bushels of Rice, One Bay horse named Arch and at her death sd. property to
be divided among my 5 youngest children WINNEY, NANCY THOMAS, THOMAS HILL,
KITTY ELIZA & WILLIAM HENRY; son ABRAHAM one horse named Jesse, two cows and
calves, 5 Barrels of corn; children of my son ABRAHAM [not named] negro Dave;
dau. ELIZABETH GRADY two cows and calves, $20; son WILLIAM negro Peter, two
cows and calves; dau. ZILPHE CHAMBERS twenty five dollars; dau. POLLY BOSTICK

negroes Ede and Hanner; son GEORGE W. all the land on Burncoat that I
formerly gave to my son WILLIAM, the land where DAVID KING lives, One grey
mare, two cows and calves, four sows Called the Blizzard sows, One bed &
Stead and furniture, One shotgun, negro Sam; dau. CHARLOTTE SMITH five
dollars; grdau. ZILPHA ANN SMITH three hundred dollars kept on Interest
untill She arrives at age twenty One years; son THOMAS HILL all my lands on
the East side of Poly Bridge Branch at the head of said Branch to the end of
a large ditch not far from my corn cribs to a small ditch crosing the Road
about one hundred yards below my negroe house to a large ditch in a flat
Branch to the Miller Road on the Edge of Goshen to the Main road Just below
my landing just over Goshen Bridge, One year old colt; son WILLIAM HENRY
all the Balance of my home land and plantation including my dwelling house
and Out houses
extrs: son WILLIAM, soninlaw WHITFIELD GRADY
wit: S. MILLER, J. M. LARKINGS, H. KORNEGY
signed: Wm. Kornegay

309. LAND, RENATUS (CR.035.801.7/A-273)
24 Mar 1778 - Apr Term 1798
wife [not named] all my plantation and Lands with all the Rest of my Estate
During of her Natural Life; son ROBERT all my plantation and the Lands that
Lies above the plantation; son JOHN URIAH the remaining part of my Lands
that is to Say between the plantation and STEPHEN LANIERs Line Which In
Cloods all my Lands Except 50 acres Lying upon the Long Branch which I give
unto ELEANDER MERIDA that is if he Doth Live with and Be have him Self well
with my wife till he is of meture age Like wis fifteen Dollars worth out of
my Estate; all the Rest of my Estate to be Equally Devided Between my
daus. [not named] Except the working tools which I give to my two sons
extrs: wife, JOB THIGPEN, AMOS JOHNSON
wit: JOHN HALSO, JOHN LANIEAR, JOB THIGPEN
                                     signed: Renates 𝓡 Land

310. LAND, ROBERT (CR.035.801.7/A-275)
9 May 1780 - Jan Court 1782
wife [not named] the plantation whereon I now live; son SHADRICK the plantation at my wife's death; son RENATUS the Tract of land where he now lives
being 230 acres; son HENRY a Tract of land containing 175 acrecs adj. land
bequeathed to my son RENATUS; son SHADRICK 25 acres adj. Betwixt the line
of the aforesaid Plantation & Cypress Creek Swamp; son JOHN the remaining
part of my Land that is part sold out to LAMB LANIER; son SHADRICK my mare
Colt; son JOHN the Young Horse Called Pompey; son HENRY my young Horse
Called Badger; daus. FRANCIS & ELENOR my Young mare Called Fill; sons
HENRY, JOHN & SHADRICK a Yew & Lam each
extrs: wife, sons HENRY & JOHN
wit: JOS. LOCKHART, THOS. LANIER
signed: [signature covered by red wax]

311. LANIER, ISHAM (CR.035.801.7)
27 Dec 1843 - Oct Term 1844
wife NANCY my plantation where I now Live and all the appertainances there
unto belonging; son HOSE FRANKLIN the plantation from the upper Corner of
the field across the Swamp to Glissons lower field all from there dwon the

Swamp; grsons JAMES MARIAN & BENJAMIN FRANKLIN the upper part of my planta-
tion; wife NANCY & son HOSEA FRANKLIN two shares in negroe Jim & molatto
Henry; grsons JAMES MARION & BENJAMIN FRANKLIN the other two shares; dau.
DICY CASTEEN 1/4 part of the work & Labor of negro Tame; dau. KISIAH CASTEEN
1/4 part of the work & Labor of negro Tame; dau. PEGGA JANE 1/4 part of the
work & Labor of negro Tame & one Feather Bed; son ISHAM 1/4 part of the work
& Labor of negro Tame; wife NANCY one Cow and two hifers; son HOSEA FRANK-
LIN all my guns and shooting utentials; wife NANCY all the Pork, Corne,
Cotton, Rise, Pease and Potatoese that I have at the time of my death, one
bed two stids and Furniture, one Bofat, one desk, one Cheste, all my household and kitchen Furniture, one Loom, Four oxen, one Carte, all my Plows,
hoes, axes and plantation tools, one pare of spoon molds, nuney six head of
sheep, all my hogs, turkeys and Chickens; grsons JAMES MARION & BENJAMIN
FRANKLIN 100 acres on the back swamp; wife NANCY all of my bees
extr: not named
wit: THOS. LANIER, BRYANT MAREDDY
                signed: Isham ✗ Lanier

312. LANIER, JESSE (CR.035.801.7/A-277)
4 Mar 1829 - May Term 1829
wife ZILPHEY My maner plantation in Cluding all my land on the uper side of
Rood, also all my house hold & kitchen Firniture, all my Stock of Cattle &
hoges; son PEARSELL land at hir death; dau. ELIZEBETH one bed & firniture
extr: JAMES WILLIAMS
wit: JAMES WILLIAMS, HOLDIN ✗ LANIER
                signed: Jesse ✚ Lanier

313. LANIER, JOHN (CR.035.801.7/A-272)
17 Mar 1799 - Apr Term 1799
son JESSE the Land and plantation Whereon I now Livie and all the Land adj.
that tract; sons LEWIS & JAMES a track of 300 in the pinewoods; the remainder
to Be Eaquealy devided and all the Remander to Be de Vided at the descretion
of BYRD, BENJN and JOHN My Sons Betwen my Four youngest daughters [not named]
and My Loving Wife [not named]
extrs: sons BYRD, BEN & JOHN
wit: BIRD LANIER, [second witness name is unreadable on the original will
            and not listed on the will book copy]
signed: John Lanier

314. LANIER, THOMAS (CR.035.801.7/A-274)
7 Jul 1784 - Jul Term 1787
son JAMES 200 acres part of that Survey that ROBERT LAND took up upon Cypress
Creek of the ct. Side below where I now live Except 75 Acres upper part;
sons JESSE & STEPHEN 139 acres whereon I live; dau. ANNE MURRAY 5 Shillings
Specie in full; children JOHN, FANNY, JESSE, STEPHEN & ELIZABETH all the
Rest of my personal Estate of what Nature or Kind soever; my Children to
bear an equal portion of my Funeral expenses (except my dau. Ann Murray)
extrs: brothers JOHN & BENJAMIN
wit: JAS LOCKHART, JOHN FARRIOR, WM ✖ McCANN
signed: Thomas Lanier

315. LANIER, ZILPHA (CR.035.801.7/1-20)
10 Mar 1832 - May Term 1832
son PEARSALL all the, Catle and hogs that is in my mark Except one cow that
is my dau. ELIZABETH, one bed & firniture, all my house hold & kitchen
firniture provided he will take ELIZABETH & seport hir with him as She is
not able to work to seport hir self & if he will not I want the property
to be Sold & put to the use of Seporting hir but PEARSALL is to keep the
bed that I have mentioned; should BETSEY die before it is disposed of I
want my dau. ZILPHA & my grdau. THURSAY to have all except one bed &
firniture which I want sold and the money equaly devided between my other
daus. MITTY, JAIN, SPICY & SEALY; grasone OBED one unmark yearlin and the
bees that is at Hiziekiah's I want to be taken next taking time and the
honey to be Equally devided betwixt him and the family hear and the bees
hear after to be his oun rite and property; sons HOLDEN & PEARSALL one
cart, one Cross Cut Saw and all the plantation tools; son PEARSALL one
Shot gun and a loom at Hiseys; dau. ELIZABETH a chist; THURSEY 1 woolen
wheel & 1 linen wheel; dau. ELIZABETH a pare of cards
extr: not named
wit: JOHN J. JONES, CRAY PADGETT, THOMAS LANIER
                              signed: Zilpha ⤢ Lanier
Codicil: 12 Mar 1832
son PEARSALL the corn & Bacon for the use of the family and to no other use

316. LEE, JOSIAH (CR.035.801.7/A-245)
10 Mar 1805 - Apr Term 1807
son JOHN one horse Cretor; next ouldest Son JESESE one hourse cretor;
next ouldest Son JSHUA one hourse cretor; next ouldest Son THOMAS one
hourse cretor; daus. SARAH, ELIZABETH, ANNEY, WINNEY & DORAS 5 Shillings
a pese; Rest of my propities to ANNEY my wife during her life time and
then the land to be Equelly devided betwixt the three younges sons REUBEN,
JOSEPH & BENGAMIN
extr: not named
wit: JAMES NEWTON, ELISHA POWELL, JESSE LEE
signed: Josiah Lee

317. LINTON, JOHN (CR.035.801.7)
9 Mar 1842 - Oct Term 1842
three youngst daus. POLLY, ELIZABETH & KITTY the North Side of my plantation
on which I reside on the west and on the out side line Runing East so as to
make a large mulbry tree in the old field a four and aft which stands No Wst
of the Graveyard for MILY CRED WELLS and East to his Out Side Line including
the house and all the appertainances during a single life; after the death
or marriage of my daus. the whole of my posesions to my son WELLS
extr: JACOB TAILOR
wit: JAMES G. STOAKES, JOHN SMITH
                    signed: John ⌎ Linton

318. LOVE, DANIEL (S S Wills/DRB 2)
6 Nov 1752 - Jul Court 1753
Debts & funerall Charges be paid out of the mony I have here with me by
JAMES McREE & JAMES PAXTON; estate divided between my wife CATHARINE & my
two children SARAH & JAMES; wife CATHERINE to have remainder of my money
with my negro boy Toney & Horses
extrs: wife CATHARINE, WILLIAM McREE, JOHN SMITH
wit: GEO. BRICE, RICHD. COCKBURN, JAMES PAXTON
                         signed: Daniel ⌐ Love

319. MCANNE, HUGH SR. (CR.035.801.7/A-321)
6 Dec 1792 - Jan Term 1796
wife MARY have my house and plantation, all my hogs, My Catle with this priviso
that My four daus. [not named] have their Equal Divide of all my Cattle when
they See fit to Depart the family by mariage, wife to manage Stock & plantation
for the Good of My Small Children [not named], the Bay Horse Traveller and the
Gray Mare Phinix, the kitchen and Household furniture and plantation tools,
one bed and furniture; my Sheep to be Divided Equally amongst my five youngest
Children & Eldest dau. [not named]; dau. AGNES one feather bed & all the Sheep
by the name of hers; son WILLIAM 50 acres on Goshen part of a 300 acre tract
Recovered by my brother WILLIAM from the Estate of HENRY EUSTACE MCULLOCH of
England, one bed and furniture already In his possession; dau. MARY one
feather bed and furniture and one Cow and Calf Now In her possession; dau.
MARGRET one feather bed and furniture, one Linen wheel, one Cow and one Steer
and one yearling her own purchase and Now In her possession; dau. JANE one
feather bed and furniture & one Sow and pigs; son JOHN the part of My land
where the plantation is up to a bottom above the plantation to the Swamp line
to the old Schoolhouse Spring branch, one bed and furniture and all the hogs
In his Mark also my young filly; son JOSHUA the Rest of My land, one Bed and
furniture, all the hogs In his Mark
extrs: son WILLIAM, friend HUGH MCANNE
wit: THOS. MCANNE, JOHN GILMAN
                    signed: Hugh Y MCanne Sr.

320. MCANNE, MARY (CR.035.801.7/2-76)
13 May 1852 - Jan Term 1853
JOHN CARR MALLARD in trust negro Sam with the labour, hire or profits to my
brother JOSEPH CARR; JOHN CARR MALLARD in trust negroes Lewis, Mary, Mary
Ann & Ned & all other property that I may have together with all my notes
for the support of my dau. MARGARET L. HALL and at her death to be sold and
the money divided as follows 1/4 to the Treasurer of the American Bible
Society, 1/4 to the Treasurer of the Presbyterian board of Publication, 1/4
to the Treasurer of the Presbyterian board of Education, 1/4 to the Treasurer
of the Presbyterian board of domestic Missions in the Presbytery of Fayetteville (the old school Presbyterian boards as they are usually termed are
here in meant and intended)
extr: not named
wit: JAMES DICKSON, OZBORN CARR
signed: Mary MCanne

321. MCANNE, WILLIAM SENIOR (CR.035.801.7/A-543)
10 Sep 1793 - Oct Term 1793
son NATHANIEL 125 acres on Goshen formerly the property of HENRY EUSTACE
MCULLOCH; son WILLIAM land on Iland Creek In New Hanover County Known by
the name of Jamisons old field, his bed and furnature, all the money he has
Received from my Estate; dau. JANE one Bed and furniture & to her son WILLIAM
negro Hagar; son HUGH land and plantation I now live on, my Wench Philis and
hir two youngest Children Ned & Limrick, my Snap horse and old mare and colt
by the name of nick, the Remainder of my Cattle and hogs, all my plantation
tools, household and Kitchen furniture; dau. SARAH one feather Bed and
furniture and to the first Child She Shall have In Wedlock negro Nell; son
THOMAS 125 acres upon Goshen formerly the property of Sd. MCulloch, negro
Sam, my Bay horse Statesman, what Cattle he has Reserved and all the Hogs

In his mark also one feather bed and furniture;   brother HUGH 50 arces upon
Goshen
extrs: son HUGH, ROBERT SLOAN, JOHN CARR
wit: WILLIAM MCANNE JUNR, RICHARD CHASTEN
signed: William MCan

322. McCANNE, WILLIAM (1-30/A-313)
12 May 1832 - Aug Term 1832)
two oldest sons FITZHUGH and JAMES a certain tract known by the Old Place
or Reedy Meadow Land on the river Bank Ratliffs corner south side of the
Little branch along Mulbery Branch to the upper end of the Island to Big
pond to the run of reedy meadow near Deep hole;   son JOHN apiece of land
in my father's old line running parrallel to the fence up to the head of a
little bottom above Sd. JOHN to the poley bridge in the road along the run
of pastor branch;   dau. POLLY land above JOHN over the middle of the old
hog pen made formerly by JOHN in a meadow to the back line between me and
JOHN McCANNE SR. to the road, one cow and calf on Fussells Creek;   son
WILLIAM one hundred acres in the big pecosin patented by me and a small
pice Including Duns Landing namely 15 acres, about twenty acres the remainer
of the Eighty acre floyd survey;   son JOSH piece of Land Including his field
in my father's old Line running with Johns Dividing line parralel with the
upper corner of the Dual field on the Little pocosin;   son OTHNIAL all the
Rest of my Land Including where I live, one small Dark bay mare, household
and Kitchen furniture, Plantation Tools provided he stay on the plantation
and provide for and takes care of his mother;   dau. SUSAN the other cow and
calf runing on fussells Creek;   dau. NANCY CHERRY hir yearlin & c.;   my
books, Saw, clock, sheep, Shop tools, steel traps, old gun and mutch trash
too tedious to mention sold to pay Debts and any Rems to be Eaqualy Divided
between my three daus.
extrs: son [not named] & son JAMES
wit: ELI X   GRANT, HUGH ⋏   PICKETT
signed: William McCanne

323. McCURDY, WILLIAM (CR.035.801.7/A-297)
no date - Oct Term 1806
dau. JANE all my money & obligations for money which may be found and all
accts & debts of every kind which is due me Except five silver dollars which
I give to my son THOMAS;   son WILLIAM all my wearing apparel;   dau. JANE &
son WILLIAM all my land and all the residue or remainder of my property of
every kind to be equaley divided between them But shoad the sd. JANE or
WILLIAM die without any heir of their bodies the whole of my estate to fall
to the surviver of them
extrs: JAMES WRIGHT, CHARLES HOOKS
wit: THOS WRIGHT, JAMES WRIGHT, JE. WRIGHT
                              signed: William ✝ McCurdy

324. McCURDY, WILLIAM (CR.035.801.7)
20 Feb 1838 - Apr Term 1838
JOHN & HENRY, sons of HENRY WINDERS all my land Except one acre for a Grave
Yard at the Graves;   IRY D. HINES & LOTTY HINES, the Heirs of NANCY McCURDY
that was former Wife of DANIEL HINES $50 Each;   CATHARINE, dau. of JAMES
WINDERS deseased Negro Girl Citty;   ALMIRER, dau. of JAMES WINDERS Negro Girl

Hager; MARY ANN, dau. of WILLIAM NEWTON Negro Man Balaam; SALLY, dau. of
ZEBEEDEE HOLLENSWORTH Negro Woman Betty; JOHN, son of JAMES HILL Negro
boy Liaz; WILLIAM, son of HENRY WINDERS Negro Boy Moses; ELIZER, dau. of
ZEBEEDEE HOLLENSWORTH Negro Boy Ben & $150; negro Woman Clarry to be Sold
with all my other property, JOHN L. HILL to have $100 out of the Money And
the Balance to be Equally devided between ELIZER HOLLENSWORTH, JOHN HURST,
CHARLES HURST & HENRY, the son of HOLOWAY HODGES
extr: friend JOHN L. HILL
wit: BH. WILLIAMS, HARRIS LANIER
signed: Wm. McCurdey

325. McGEE, ANN "widow of the late THOMAS McGEE" (CR.035.801.7/3-74)
14 Jan 1860 - Apr Term 1863
CORNELIUS McMILLAN Negro Violet and child; JOHN C. McMILLAN Negro Dick;
DANIEL T. McMILLAN Negro Frank and one Beauro; GEORGE J. McMILLAN $15; ANN
REBECCA LENNON one Bed and its furniture also my Mattress; CATHARINE KELLY
one bed and its furniture; CORNELIUS McMILLAN rest residue and remainder of
my Estate, property, goods and effects of every nature, kind and description
extr: CORNES. McMILLAN
wit: BONEY WELLS, JOSEPH K. BONEY
signed: Ann Megee

326. McGEE, WILLIAM "Planter" (CR.035.801.7/A-320)
29 Aug 1822 - Jul Term 1827
wife ELIZABETH my Negroes Esther, Guy and Kate, all my Stock consisting of
horses, cattle, hogs & sheep, all my plantation Tools, household and Kitchen
furniture; after the death of my beloved wife property to be equeally divided
between my 8 children [not named] and ZILPHA DICKSON
extr: son THOMAS
wit: SAML HANFORD, A. MOREAU
signed: Wm. McGee

327. McGOWAN, WILLIAM (CR.035.801.7/A-309)
5 Oct 1792 - Oct Term 1792
I do Will and ordain that the Estate be kept Together undivided and that my
Children Together with the Slaves belonging to me be kept at the making naval
Stores of my lands untill a Sufficiency be made to pay Debts Except Such time
as may be necesary for the Said hands to Work in the Crop for the Support of
the family; son JOHN after Debts are paid negro Will and the Lands I have
Given him by Deed is to be his full Share Except 4000 Weight of good pork
which I am in Debt to him and my Executors hereby Required to pay at 30
Shillings Each hundred Weight and Spanish Milled Dollars at Twelve Shillings;
son WILLIAM all that parcell of Land on the Grove Swamp Joind ANDREW McINTIRE
& JOHN McGOWEN below JAMES GILLESPIE Computed to be about 150 acres; son
ROBERT all that parcell of Land on Persimon Branch which I Bought from JAMES
EVANS & 25 acres I Bought from RICHARD WILLIAMS & 100 acres to be Laid off
to him Joind out the Land for which I have the State Patent; son EDWARD a
Certain part of my mannor Plantation bounded by the run of Fredericks Mill
Branch at the mouth of a Branch that Runs on the upper Side of my oldest
field, the mouth of a Small Drain that Divides my Little Newground field
from my Little old ground field & WILLIAM FREDERICK, 70 acres of piney Land
Joining the Same to Begin at or near the head of the miry Branch; land in

Newhanover County purchased of FRANCIS BRICE to be offered to my Brother
George at 70 £ Current money and Should he not Comply Land to be Sold or
Divided for the Bennifit of the Children [not named]; wife MARY do have
Quick and Peaseable Possession of my Mannor Plantation and all the Lands
Joining thereto During her natural Life and at her Decease to my son DAVID,
negro Roze, Two Good Feather Beds and furniture, negroes Dick & Nancy;
residue of negroes and estate to remain with my Wife for the purpose of
Raising and Schooling my young Children [not named]
extrs: wife MARY, son JOHN, Brotherinlaw JAMES DICKSON
wit: JAMES MIDDLETON, JAS. McINTIRE, JOSEPH DICKSON
signed: Wm. McGoen

328. McGOWEN, WM. (CR.035.801.7/3-13)
24 Sep 1853 - Jul Term 1860
son WM. JR. 50 acres of the tract of land I now live on including all his
improvements where he Now lives; dau. ZILPHA $60, One bed & furneture, One
Cow & calf, two Sheep, all the poltry on the farm; residue of estate sold
and money devided between all My Children Now living & the Children of My
Son JOSEPH decd. Viz CATHARINE SHUFFIELD, ZILPHA, JAMES, NANCY STANLEY,
SUSAN HALL, WM. JR. & MARY STOAKES
extrs: JAMES McGOWEN, WM. McGOWEN JR.
wit: JAS. PEARSALL, J. W. MURRAY
            signed: Wm. ✕ McGowen

329. McINTIRE, ANDREW (CR.035.801.7/A-342)
22 Sep 1783 - Jan Term 1784
Kinsman ANDREW son of JAMES McINTIRE all my lands and Improvements, Eight
Negroes Derry, Warwick, Ireland, Sam, Little Cato, Cesar, Daniel & Cate,
all the rest of my Estate Real and personal Not other Wise Desposed of
alway reserving unto the said JAMES McINTIRE the sole use And possession
of same untill ANDREW may arive at the full age of twenty one Years; Negro
Ireland be hired out Yearly for a term of Seven years and money applied
to the Express purpose of Educating sd. ANDW.; Niece AREBELLA CLINTON
Negroes Luce & Bella, one Side Saddle and all the Cloaths that belonged
to my late wife [not named]; Brothern JAMES of the Kingdom of Ireland 40 £
sterling; sister MARTHA the like sum; Negro Cato & Sall his wife, my horses,
Still and Household furniture sold to raise same; WILLIAM BEST five Cows
and Calves, one Good featherbed and furniture; JAMES McINTIRE all the
residue of my stock of Every kind, one young Mare and all my [torn]
extrs: ROBT. DICKSON, WILLIAM McGOWAN, JOSEPH DICKSON
wit: CHAS. WARD, JOS. MAXWELL, JAMES GILLESPIE
signed: And. McIntire

330. McLENDON, JESSE (A-317)
9 Mar 1782 - Jul Court 1782
wife ELIZABETH the land and plantation on which I now live, stock of all
Kinds, Housing Stuff of all sorts; WILLIAM BULL and ESBEL his wife the
plantation where they now live During their natural Lives and then sold and
money Eaqually Divided amongst the five Boys HENRY, THOMAS, JESSE, WILLIAM
and DENNIS McLENDON; dau. MARY the Cattle Formerly called hers, one Feather
Bed and Bolster and two sheets, one Linen Wheel, Four pewter and two Earthern
plats; dau. ANN the Cattle Formerly called hers, one Feather Bed and Bolster
and to sheets, one Linen wheel, Four pewter and two Earthern plates; dau.

SALLY the cattle called hers, one Feather bed and bolster and two sheets, one
Linen wheel, four pewter and two Earthern plates; land near ABRAHAM GILBERT's
line sold and the money applyed to Schooling the Children HENRY and THOMAS
six months Each JESSE twelve months WILLIAM, SALLY and DENNIS [torn]; land
on north side of Charry between PETER BARBERY and JOHN HARRIS sold and money
applied to pay Debts
extrs: ELIZABETH McLENDON, WILLIAM BALL
wit: JOHN BRYAN, PETER BARBRE, SIMON McLENDON, JOHN CLARK
                              signed: Jessey X McLendon

331. McREE, WILLIAM "of Goshen Settlement" (S S Wills/DRB 2)
13 Mar 1751 - 2 Apr 1751
son JOHN 6 Merchanable Cows and Calves the same to be Delivered to him when
he Comes unto this Province to Demand them; son JAMES 5 shillings Sterling;
son WILLIAM 5 shillings Sterling; son ROBERT 5 shillings Sterling; dau.
SARAH McREE alias SMITH 5 shillings Sterling; dau. ALACE McREE alias WILLIAMS
5 shillings Sterling; grson. WILLIAM WILLIAMS one Two Years Old Heifer;
grdau. DORATHEA WILLIAMS one Two Years Old Heifer; son SAMUEL this Plantation
that I now live upon Containing 500 acres, six Cows and Calves, One Feather
Bed and Furniture & his Sheare of the Furniture belonging to the House; dau.
SUSANNAH all my Money that is now in the Country, remaining Part of my black
Cattle young and Old, One Feather Bed and Furniture with one Half of the
Household Furniture But she now being in a weak and low Condition and more
likely to Die than live so that if she dies with this present Sickness that
she is now under I do Order that he Part shall be and Remain in the Hands of
My Dear Son WM.
extrs: son WM, son in law JOHN SMITH
wit: WILLIAM Q KENNAN, SARAH 'SC McALEXANDER, ELIZABETH CHAMBERS
signed: William McRee

332. MALLARD, ASA (CR.035.801.8/3-31)
28 Aug 1860 - Jan Term 1861
wife MARTHA all my land, stock of Cattle & hogs, crop of corn, peas & potatoes,
household & Kitchen furniture, farming utensils & all other property; eldest
son WILLIAM WRIGHT portion of land on which he now resides provided he will
pay $100 as hereafter appropriated & if not the land to be sold & he to re-
cieve 2/3 of the proceeds & 1/3 to my daus. hereafter named his portion to be
on the run of Cook's Branch adj. NANCY MALLARD containing 45 1/2 acres; son
ALFRED JAMES the portion of my land on which I reside in the Percosin old field
adj. Thomas containing 14 acres; sons ASA BURNET & JOHN WESLEY residue of my
land with the house in which I reside & four acres around excepted & bequeathed
to my daus. MARTHA CATHARINE, SYMADOTIA, LANEY SERENE, LUCY, SARAH PRISCILLA
& ELLEN JANE as long as two of them remain unmarried and no longer and my
two sons to pay my daus. the sum hereafter appropriated & should they refuse,
land sold and sons to recieve 2/3 of the amount of the sale & 1/3 to be divided
equally between my daus. ELIZABETH A. wife of SAMUEL EVANS, MARTHA CATHARINE,
SYMMADOTIA, LANY SERENE, LUCY, SARAH PRISCILLA & ELLEN JANE; dau. ELIZABETH
ANN wife of SAMUEL EVANS One Milch Cow, $50 to be paid out of the $100 I have
levied upon my son WILLIAM WRIGHT; should any of my daus. marry after the
death of my wife they to receive $50 each from my sons ASA BURNET & JOHN
WESLEY; at my wife's death all my unmd. daus. shall recieve my house &

kitchen furniture & my sons ASA BURNIT & JOHN WESLEY shall recieve my stock
of hogs & cattle & farming utensils, all my tools
extrs: GIBSON S. CARR, son ASA BURNET
wit: G. S. CARR, JOHN E. FUSSELL
signed: Asa Mallard

333. MALLARD, GEORGE (CR.035.801.8/A-332)
nuncupative dated 27 Mar 1798
PHILL SOUTHERLAND made Oath that GEORGE MALLARD Caled sd. Southerland last
night to write his will; he appeared in a very Low State but in his proper
Senses to the best of his Knowledge; to dau. MARY land; at which time the
Cough Took him of a Sudden and Never appeared to be Capeble of Making any
Further Will and Died about Teen aclock or Som Earlyer this Day; sworn
before ROBT. SOUTHERLAND

334. MALLARD, JAMES (CR.035.801.8/2-101)
7 Dec 1855 - Jul Term 1856
wife NANCY all of my lands except 45 acres, all my money, notes & accounts
except $200, Stock of all Kinds, household & Kitchen furneture, negroes
Susan, Netter, Shade, Betsey, Patrick, Manson, Jo, Daniel & Amanda; son in
law WILLIAM MURRAY and his Sons MURDOCK WILLIAMS & ROBERT FRANKLIN negroes
Chaney, Jerry, Susan, Hulda, Hillory, Eliza, Calvin, Mary & Robert to be
devided among them when the eldest son MURDOCK WILLIAMS arrives at 21 years;
grson. ROBERT FRANKLIN MURRAY provided he attains the age of 21 land which I
purchased of JOHN CARR MALLARD containing 45 acres, negroes Netter, Betsy,
Jo & Amanda & should he not attain the age of 21 then land & negroes to go
to son in Law GIBSON CARR & his wife EMILY, also $200; son in Law GIBSON
CARR & wife EMILY all my lands & negroes Mary, Charity, Clarra, Zilla, Ada,
Sarah, Lenon, Isham, Alfred, Shade, Susan, Patrick, Manson & Daniel, all
money, notes & accounts, stock of all kinds
extr: son in law GIBSON CARR
wit: JAMES CARR, JAMES W. BONEY
                    signed: James ⚘ Mallard

335. MALLARD, JOHN (CR.035.801.8/A-319)
23 Dec 1811 - Apr Term 1812
wife MARY two beds and ther furneture, My House and plantation and as Much
of the furneture as She Shall Se preper; son WM. $150, one Gun, one ax now
in possession; son JOHN 146 acers now in his possession; son JAMES 180
acers now in his possession; son GORGE one Mear, & $160; youngest son ASA
all the Rest of my Lands, one gun and one Cow and Calf; dau. NANCY $10; dau.
SARAH one bed and its Furneture, one Cow and Calf now in hir possession; dau.
CATHREN one bed and Furneture, one Cow and Calf now in hir possession; dau.
DORCAS one bed and Furneture, one Cow and Calf; at wifes Decese ballance of
Stock of all kinds with my house hold Kitchen and plantation furneture to
SARAH, CATHERN, DORCAS and ASA
extr: sons WILLIAM & JOHN
wit: JOHN GILMAN, WIMBERT BONEY
signed: John Mallard

336. MALLARD, JOHN (CR.035.801.8)
10 Dec 1852 - Jan Term 1855
wife BARBARA house and plantation, household and kitchen furniture, plantation tools, my mare and stock of all kinds, my boy Jack (if Jack will not be

governed by his mistress I then wish him to be hired out sold or swaped),
privilige of making Turpintine, splitin Rails and fire wood on any part of
the land, and at her death Land and Jack to be equally devided between all
my children JOHN C., DICKSON, POLLY ANN, BETSEY, SUSAN & BATHSHEBA; sons
JOHN C. & DICKSON $200 each which they have already Received; dau. POLLY
ANN, BETSEY, SUSAN & BATHSHEBA $200 each
extrs: sons JOHN C. & DICKSON
wit: JAMES CARR, OBED W. CARR
signed: John Mallard

337. MALLARD, JOSEPH (CR.035.801.8/A-327)
4 Apr 1827 - Jul Term 1827
all my Lands be sold one piece lying on Maxwell Swamp which I purchased from
THOMAS HEATH & his Sister BETSEY ANN, two of the heirs of WILLIAM HEATH decd,
also another piece lying in & on Hill Swamp with my Stock of Horses, Cattle,
hogs & sheep, House hold & kitchen furniture, plantation tools except one
Feather bed & common cest [?] which I give to my grdau. CATHARINE DICKSON;
money arising from the sale to be equally divided between all my Children
[not named] except dau. MARTHA who I give $30
extr: worthy friend WILLIAM MALLARD
wit: A. MORGAN, JCOB HEATHE
signed: Joseph Mallard

338. MALLARD, WILLIAM (A-294)
22 Feb 1826 - Nov Term 1827
wife REBECCA all my land and plantation untill my dau. MARY ELIZA come of age
the equeally divided between my wife and dau., negroes Letty & Prince, one
horse chair & Harness, Three cows & calves, Three Ews & Lambs, one Sow & pigs,
all my plantation Tools, Two feather beds & furniture, as much of my house
hold and kitchen furniture as will be necessary for her convenience; dau.
MARY ELIZA negroes Sarah, Stephen & Lewis which I purchased from JAMES MAX-
WELL for the Sum of Five hundred Dollars the sd. Maxwell has liberty to take
back Said Lewis by refunding Three Hundred Dollars in four years from the
17 January 1826, feather bed & furniture
extrs: friend AARON MORGAN & wife REBECCA
wit: THOMAS HEATH, D. C. MOORE
signed: Wm. Mallard

339. MASHBURN, JAMES (CR.035.801.8)
6 May 1840 - Jul Term 1840
wife SARAH negroes Dick, Hannah, Edith & George and at her death to be equally
devided amongst all my children; dau. ELIZABETH PAGE negro Esther, 50 acres
on the E side of Bull Tail Swamp adj. JESSE LEE, JAMES JOHNSON & JAS. HARRELL
including the place on which she formerly lived; son HENRY negro Amos, 100
acres on the East side of Mill Branch adj. WM. HARVELL & WILLIBY POWELL being
the land on which he ones lived; dau. MARY PAGE negro Peggy; son DANIEL
negro little Dick, 50 acres adj. the 50 acres above mentioned given to CHARLES
PAGE lying on the East side of sd. tract; son JAMES negro Dilsy, 102 acres
being the balance of my land that lies in the fork of Bull Tail and Powell's
Swamp; son JOSEPH negro Hannah daughter of Hannah, 200 acres being the Survey
that includes the plantation whereon I now live; wife SARAH the above mentioned
200 acres including the plantation & Houses & all the priviliges thereunto
belonging, my mare & saddle, two Cows & Calves, my Household & Kitchen furniture,

beds & their furniture & plantation tools of every description; son DANIEL
my Horse; balance of land say 149 acres, my yoke of Oxen and balance of
Stock of every description to be sold to pay debts
extrs: Soninlaw CHARLES PAGE, son HENRY
wit: GEO. FENNELL, ENOCH JOHNSON
                    signed: James ⟡ Mashburn
6 May 1840
N. B. residue from sale of lands after debts are paid to go to dau. ELIZABETH
PAGE
wit: GEO. FENNELL, ENOCH JOHNSON
                    signed: James ⟡ Mashburn

340. MATCHET, JOHN "planter" (CR.035.801.8/A-324)
27 Apr 1774 - Jul Term 1774
son JOHN plantation I now live on With all the Improvements, negroes Old
Iscac, Moll, Fridy & Hanna, all my Cattle & Horses & Hogs Except the old
Mair; son WILLIAM the Uper field & land, negroes Young Iscac & fillas;
wife SARAH negro Jain and then to son JOHN, Bed and Bed Cloathes and all the
Rest of my House Hold furneture; if HENNERY MATCHET Com Over from Irland,
he to have 50 pds Raised off the Estate or his Use of the Uper field to live
on for Two Years
extrs: FELIX KENEN Esq., CHARLES WARD
wit: CHARLES WARD, JOHN AUSTINE, WILLIAM BURRLL
signed: John Matchet

341. MATCHET, SARAH (CR.035.801.8/A-308)
24 Sep 1790 - Oct Term 1790
debts to be don out of the Rent Corn that is due from NATHAN GRAY and WILLIAM
GRAY for this years Rent; Rest of my warlay Estate to Son WILLAM
extrs: son WILLAM , JAMES PERSEL
wit: NATHAN WALLER, JOHN CHAMBERS
                    signed: Sarah ⟡ Matchet

342. MATHEWS, JACOB (CR.035.801.8/2-74)
23 Jul 1851 - Oct Term 1852
son NICHOLAS P. negroes Charles & Joe which he has in his possession; grson
KEDAR negro Columbas; grson SAMUEL JAMES BARDEN negroes Rile and Macolm;
grandchildren ROBERT, CATHARINE & NICHOLAS W. BARDEN negroes Penny and child
and Macolm; dau. BARSHEBA CARLTON negroes Stays, Olive, Sam, Oliv's two
children; dau. SUSEY land whereon I reside containing four hundred acres
including my mill & negroes Jack, Sal and Lindy; dau. NANCY CARLTON-negroes
George, Ann and Henry; Whereas I received as tenant by the courtesy in
right of my deceased wife from the proceeds of sale of the lands of her
brother PEYTON R. PARKER decd late of Sampson County three hundred and
seventy odd dollars to which the heirs at law of my said deceased Wife SUSY
will be entitled at my death; residue of estate consisting of negroes Dave,
Rile Senr & Stannorb, stock of all Kinds, tools, furneture unto my children
and grandchildren [not named]
extr: son in law JOHN CARLTON
wit: SALATHEL EZZELL, JOHN K. GROVES, PATRICK MURPHY
signed: Jacob Mathews

343. MATHEWS, JAMES (CR.035.801.8/A-304)
22 Feb 1821 - Apr Term 1822
dau. ANN LANGSTON negraw Milley, one bed and furniture; dau. MARY STEWART
negraw hanah which she has a Deed of Gift for, one Bed and furneture Which
she has had; dau. CHARITY negraw Cassee, on Bed and furnetire; dau. RACHEL
negraw Charlot reserving the first Child the said Charlot has to be three
years old to my sone MICHEAL, one Bed and furneture; sone MICHEAL one Bed
and furnitire; sone JAMES part of my Land and plantation all on the south
side of poley Bridg and the Bowin Marsh Branch, negraw Ede; sone JOHN all
my land and plantation on the North side of the poly Bridg and Bowan Branch,
negraw Jim, one horse Named Dolin; wife [not named] negraw Rose and after
her Death to my sone HERRING & the Ramander of my property and after hur
Death to be Divided among my daus. [not named]; son RICHARD 106 acres, one
Horse Bridle & saddle which he has had
extrs: wife ELIZABETH & son JOHN
wit: EDWD. OUTLAW, ELIZABETH OUTLAW
                        signed: James ⚡ Mathews

344. MATTHIS, EDMOND (CR.035.801.8/A-315)
18 Apr 1783 - Oct Court 1783
wife MARY all my lands with the profits there unto belonging and after her
disease to son HARMON; dau. SARAH LANIER 5 pds. Sterling; son JOHN negro
Peter; son RICE negro Isaac; dau. TOMZAN GOFF negro Clo; dau. ELIZABETH
ELKINS negro Jan; dau. JEMIMA FENNEL negro Hager; dau. MARYANN negro
Clarry; dau. SABRA GOFF negro Amey; son EDMOND negro Reddick; son JAMES
negro Esseck; dau. EDAH negro Milee; dau. ESTHER negro Hannah; son THOMAS
negro Duplin; son LAZARUS negro Toomer; dau. OLIFF negro Teen; son ZACHEUS
negro Sam; son HERMAN negro Briston; wife MARY whole of my estate during
her life and then to be equally devided amongst my children all
extrs: wife MARY, sons JOHN & RICE
wit: JONATHAN PARKER, PEREGO JOHNSTON, JOHN ⚡ BLANTON
signed: Edm. Matthis

345. MAXWELL, ELINOR (CR.035.801.8/1-35)
31 Oct 1832 - Feb Term 1833
dau. MARGARET PEARSALL negross Luke & Mary, one bed & furneture, my Silver
teaspoons & Tea Trey; dau. SARAH STANFORD negroes Phereba & child Rachel
and girl Kelly, one bed & furniture, one mahogany table, my saddle & bridle;
dau. DORETHY ANN MOAN negro Laura & child Bill; dau. CASSANDER MOON negro
Eliza Ane, my riding chair & harness; extr. sell negro Harry and with money
arising together with fifty dollors from the sale of Crop, stock, & c. purchas
a negro girl and he execute a deed to dau. CASSANDER from sd. girl; son
DICKSON SLOAN $300 in cash now in my house & $150 to be raised from sale of
crop, Stock & c; grdau. CLARRISSA McGOWEN one bed & furneture; grdau. ANN
ELIZA SLOAN on bed & furneture; grson. DAVID MOON my bay colt; residue to
pay debts and remaing money to children DICKSON SLOAN, CASSANDER MOON,
DORETHY A. MOON, SARAH STANFORD & MARGARET PEARSALL
extr: brother JAMES DICKSON
wit: GIBSON SLOAN, SUSANA ⚡ DICKSON
signed: Eleanor Maxwell

346. MAXWELL, JAMES (CR.035.801.8/A-346)
27 Feb 1811 - Apr Term 1811
son HUGH negro Billy, 175 acres, 100 acres of which joins to ROBERT DICKSON's
line & JAMES EVANS lines and the other 75 acres including his house and
improvement joining his own, and JAMES EVANS lines; son JOHN negroes Becke &
Cloe, my bay Major Colt; son DAVID negroes Dick, Cain & Biddy, 450 acres
begining at the branch at Powells field at the old Murphy footway up the
branch by the school House through the glades to Millers line, WILLIAM CARRs
line, JOHN CRANFORDs line, EPHRAIM GARRISONs line, HENRY MAXWELLs line including WILLIAM MURPHEYs old field, 1/2 of my stock of Cattle, hogs & bees,
plantation tools, household and Kitchen furniture, bacon and corn that is
now on my plantation, one feather bed and furniture; son ARCHIBALD negroes
Jack & Hannah, 1/2 of my Stock of Cattle, hogs & bees, plantation tools,
household and kitchen furniture, bacon and Corn that is now on my plantation,
one feather bed and furniture, the remainder of my lands including my mannor
plantation; all my books be equally divided between my Sons DAVID and ARCHI-
BALD; DOLLY ANN, dau. of JOHN & ELEANOR MAXWELL have the bed & furniture
that I now lie on and my Wifes saddle; JAMES son of HENRY MAXWELL decd &
MARGARET one bed and furniture and my firetab colt; my Sorrel Union Mare,
chair & harness be Sold and money arising be placed in the hands of JOHN
MAXWELL together with $100 to buy a negroe boy for said JAMES MAXWELL minor
extrs: son JOHN & Friend JOSEPH GILLESPIE
wit: JOHN CARR, DAVID CARR, ANDREW McINTIRE
signed: Jas. Maxwell [red wax seal]

347. MAXWELL, JOHN (CR.035.801.8/A-341)
12 Dec 1813 - Jan Term 1814
wife ELINOR negroes Sylvia & Harry, my black mare & Bay Horse, yoke of oxen
& Cart, five Cows and Calves, ten head of Sheep, my Cupboard & furniture,
Two good feather Beds and furniture, Six Sows & pigs, Thirty hogs two years
old next fall & $100 & provision sufficient for herself & family for a year,
my Chairs and tables, one half of my Kitchen furniture, plows, hoes, axes &
plantation tools, my riding Chair & harness, my hand mill; Step Son DICKSON
SLOAN my bay filly foaled about last April; children DOLLY ANN, SARAH,
HENRY & MARGARET negroes Beck, Dave, Chloe, Charles, Cade, Larry, Kitty &
Balaam their part of sd. Negroes as they arrive of age; son HENRY $150 to
assist to educate him; wife one large Wheel & Cards, one Linnen Wheel and
her riding Saddle; residue of estate to be equally divided amongst my
children DOLLY ANN, SARAH, HENRY & MARGARET
extr: friend JOSEPH GILLESPIE
wit: AMOS SHAFIELD, A. CHAMBERS
signed: John Maxwell

348. MERCER, JOHN "Planter" (CR.035.801.8/A-290)
21 Feb 1775 - Jan Term 1781
wife RACHEL the use of my maner plantation During hur Life and then be my
Son ABSALAM's all Above the Indian run, my Stock and house hold goods of all
kinds; son WILLIAM all my Land on houses Branch With all the Cattle and
hogs in his mark; son JOSHUA all my Land Below the Indian Run; dau. NANCE
five Cows and Calves; grdau. NOANCEY BROCKSON five cows and calves; dau.
DEBORY one Sow and pigs; son JOSHUA fifty pounds procd mony to Be paid him
at the years of twenty one; sons ABSOLAM & JOSHUA Be Brought up in A

Christtian Manner; residue Be Equaly Devided Between wife RACHAEL and my two
youngest Sons ABSOLAM and JOSHUA when they Come of age
extrs: wife RACHAEL, son WILLIAM, GEORGE SMITH
wit: GEORGE SMITH JUNER, JOHN ✚ WHEEDEN
signed: John Mercer

349. MEREL/MARIL, JOSEPH (CR.035.801.8/A-307)
20 Dec 1794 - Jan Term 1795
wife ELIZEBETH MEREL the whole of my Land and Estate of Cattel, horses and
hogs and Tulls and haus furnetud During her Life and at her Decase to fall
to my Son WILLIAM MAREL
extrs: wife ELIZEBETH MEREL, Brother in Law THOMAS CARRESON
wit: WILLIAM FARRIAR, DAVIE SOUTHERLAND
signed: Josep Maril

350. MERRIT, ABSOLUM (CR.035.801.8/A-306)
29 Mar 1802 - Oct Term 1803
son THEOPHILUS 5 shillings; son ABSOLUM 200 acres, a cow and yearling which
he has recieved; dau. REBECAH a feather Bed and furniture, two pewter Basons
& a Dish, a Cow and Calf and a two year old heifer which she has received;
son MICHAEL 100 acres Lying between the flat Branch & Birch Branch, one Cow
and calf and a pot; daus. BARBARA and BEDIE my old plantation on Stewards
Creak and a feath. Bed each; son McKINSEY the mill and 200 acres Joining,
a Cow and Calf; wife [not named] the Mare and colt and Cattle and the profits
arising from the mill During her widowhood to Support her and the young children [not named] as alson the hogs and a Bed, all the working tools; dau.
CELIA Cattle or Money to the amount of ten pounds, all the house hold goods;
daus. BARBARA and BEDIE a Cow and Calf to each; the Cart Wheels for the use
of my wife and little Children
extrs: NATHIEL MERRIT, DANIEL MERRIT
wit: STEPHEN SMYTH, ELIZABETH ✗ MERRIT, UNITY ✗ COOK
signed: Absolum ✗ Merrit

351. MIDDLETON, AMOS (CR.035.801.8/1-3)
6 Dec 1829 - Feb Term 1830
nephew WILLIAM BRYANT MIDDLETON Negroe Lott; niece MARY ELIZA Negroe Maggy;
nephews OWEN & ALFRED my Plantation to be equally devided between them;
Ballance of property sold to pay Just debts and Ballance to Sisters ELIZABETH
BROWN and SARAH HOBBS and Brother JAMES
extr: Brother LIBIUS
wit: WM. K. FREDERICK, JAMES MAXWILL
signed: Amos Middleton

352. MIDDLETON, DAVID SENR. (CR.035.801.8/A-349)
10 Jun 1819 - Oct Term 1819
wife SELAH have quiet and peaseable possession of all my lands on the South
side of the grove swamp where I now live bequeathed by my father [not named]
to me also a certain tract purchased from GEORGE GIBBENS on the south side of
the groves adjoining the aforesaid lands during her natural life then to my
son DAVID; wife SELAH Slaves Elias, Venas, Ester, Rachael and little Worrick
son of Ester; wife SELAH negraws Clary & Caty during her lifetime then to my
son DAVID; wife SELAH negraw Hannah then to my son JAMES; wife SELAH mare
by the name of Jim and a young filly by the name of Geen, two sows and pigs,

tow Cows and Calvs, four Ewes and lambs, my yoke of oxen bought of JOHN
COOPER, my big ox chain and big ox Cart and yoke, two bar plows and two
flukes, two axes, two weeding hoes, two grubing hoes, one pair Iron wedges,
two beds bedsteads & furneture, one small red chest, one unpainted Chest,
one set of Silver tea spoons & one set of silver Table spoons marked DSM
square at the Ends during her natural life then to dau. KITTY; one Coffee
mill, one side saddle and bridle, one half of my Kitchen furneture, one
fourth of all my Coopers ware Consisting of tubs, pigings, pails, barrels,
Hogsheads & c., my Jugs, dimyjohns, bottles, & c. be divided Equeally between
my wife and my sons JAS. and DAVID; wife SELAH my wire sive and at her death
to sons JAMES and DAVID; wife SELAH riding Chair and harness; son JAMES
500 acres on Stuerts Creep purchased of AARON MORGAN, 740 acres Deeded to
said JAMES in a former Conveyance ajoining the same, slave Balaam, big
Worrick, Quash, Sall & Bob, my Black smiths tools, my old shot gun and pistol,
my Silver watch, Two horses which he has allready rcd., one bridle and sadle,
one large chest, one large trunk, my blue bed sted bed and furniture, one set
of Silver Teaspoons, one set of Table Spoons marked JM; son DAVID my manor
plantation with all my lands on both sides of the grove swamp also the lands
Joining on Marsh branch with Exception of wife's life in the manor plantation
and Gibbons plantation, slaves Jack, Allen, Harry, Dillaway, Catoe & Margret,
my new shot gun, red chest with out a back, my writing desk, my side board,
one Chest unpainted which my wife is to Keep in possession until DAVID arives
at the age of twenty one years, my rideing mare by the name of Cute, one bed
bedstead and furniture, one set of Silver Table Spoons marked DSM round at
the end; dau. KITTY slaves Phillis, Rose, Dick, Daniel, Kent, Morris,
Claryan & Eliza, $1000 raised out of the residue of my Estate, one bed
bedsted and furneture, one new trunk which she has got, my big red chest,
my large dining Table with the split in the leaf, one small dress table
which she has got, one young mare, bridle and saddle the mare by the name of
Mountain buty; my siting chairs Equally divided between my wife & children
JAMES, DAVID & KITTY; son DAVID old mahogany table; son JAMES my new Cart
and one yoke of oxen, one bar plough and one fluke, two axes, two grubing
hoes, two weeding hoes, one small ox chain, one pair of Iron wedges, one
Scythe and cradle; my Carpenters tools divided between sons JAMES & DAVID;
residue of property sold to raise $1000 for KITTY and ballence to be Equeally
divided between wife and JAMES, DAVID & KITTY; dau. KITTY one set of Tea
Spoons Marked DSM a match for a set I lent my wife; my children DAVID and
KITTY have a good English Education
extrs: Brother ROBERT & son JAMES
wit: THOMAS PHILLIPS, ROBT. MIDDLETON
signed: David Middleton

353. MIDDLETON, ISAAC SENIOR "Planter" (CR.035.801.8/A-299)
31 Mar 1820 - Apr Term 1820
wife JANE negroes Dick and Dilsey, Ceasar and Esther, one mare by the name of
blare, one horse by the name of Statesman, Six Cows and calves, one yoke of
oxen and cart, Twelve head of Sheep, all my hogs that use on this side of the
grove, four ploughs, two bars & two flukes, two grubing hoes, two weeding
hoes & three axes, all my houshold and Kitchen furniture; son SAMUEL the
land and plantation where he now lives a dividing line run between my Son
SAMUEL & my son ISAAC begining at the mouth of the Spring branch to the fork
up the south prong to the head of the said branch to Samuel's upper corner

formerly Shepheard's corner, negroes Balam, Peg and Pegs youngest child, one
horse, one Cow & heifer, one feather bed & furniture, all of which he has in
possession except Peg'& her child; son ISAAC balance of my land on the South
side of my mill Swamp except one acre adjoining to the mill, negroes Lewis
and Hannah, one mare & colt, one cow & heiffer, one bed & furniture, all of
which he has in possession except the girl Hannah; son LIBEOUS the Plantation and land where he now lives a diving line to be run between my son
LIBEOUS and my son JAMES begining at the Grove Swamp at the mouth of a small
branch thence along the fence to the back line, negroes Tone and Kate, one
horse, one Cow & heifer, one feather bed & furniture, my blacksmiths tools
all which is in his own possession except the blacksmith Tools; son AMOS
all my Land on the east side of the grove Swamp, negroes Lot & Mog, my gray
mare, one cow & heifer, one bed & furniture; dau. ELIZABETH BROWN negroes
Tener, Jenny & Joe, one horse, one Cow & heifer, one bed & furniture all
which she has in possession except negro Joe; dau. SARAH HOBS negroes Fan,
Chilsey & Albert, one horse & heifer, one feather bed & furniture all of
which she has in possession except negro Albert; wife my house and plantation during her natural life and then to son JAMES; youngest children JAMES
& ANN negroes Daniel, Esther, June, Anthony, Alex, Eliza & Charles which
negroes to Remain on the plantation untill my children come of age or Marries;
negro Cesar lent to wife to belong to dau. ANN; negroes Sampson, George and
Hagar sold to pay debts with enouth of the money to son LEBIOUS to pay for
three Lots of land ajoining the Land on which he lives now belonging to
DORATHY CASSANDRIA and MARY QUINN and balance of money divided between my
six oldest children [not named]; perishable property sold and money divided
between my two youngest children
extrs: JAMES CHAMBERS, son LEBEOUS
wit: A. MORGAN, JOHN J. MIDDLETON
signed: Isaac Middleton

354. MIDDLETON, JAMES (CR.035.801.8/A-278)
4 Sep 1801 - Jul Term 1805
wife MARY Quiet and peaceable possession of all my lands and Buildings during
her Natural Life with the following Exceptions son DAVID to have use and
Benefit of part So of the Mare Branch Below the Lane as it now Stands and
down to the sd. DAVID's line for a Term of five years, the Barnfield as the
fense now runs reserved to son ROBERT; wife for her Natural Life Slaves Sam,
Ned, Amy & Pegg and at my wife's decease Amy to be the property of dau. SARAH
NIXON and and Child or Children Amy Should have Before the Death of my wife
to be Eaqually the property of SARAH NIXON, ELENER HERRING and KITTY, my daus.,
Pegg to be property of ELENOR HERRING, Sam the property of ROBERT and Ned the
property of DAVID; wife negro girl Hesse and at her Death to be property of
dau. SARAH NIXON; wife MARY all my stock of Hogs that are in my own Mark,
all my stock of Sheep Except two Ewes & Lambs to Son ROBERT and Two Ewes &
Lambs to dau. KITTY, three Horses viz. Roebuck, Lightfoot & Tibby a filly that
came of my Mare named Fancy, five Cows & Calves, one yoke of Oxen & one Ox
chain and as many of the Dry Cattle for her and the family's Support for Two
years, three axes, one pair of hand Mill stones and at her Death to be the
property of my son ROBERT, three plows almost new, one Barr and two Flukes,
three of the Best Weeding hoes, two Grubing hoes, two pair of Iron Wedges
which articles at her death is to be divided among all my Children, one Wire
Seive and at her Death to sons DAVID and ROBERT and the Longest Liver of the

two to have the Said Seive Entirely, one new flower Search and at her death
to be the property of my Soninlaw DANL NIXON; DANL NIXON my Walking Cane
as a Testimony of my Regard and esteem for him; wife one case and Bottles
& three Reap hooks, one Ox Cart and at her Death to be the property of my
son ROBERT, all my Houshold furneture that is now Belonging to my Dwelling
House, two Beds and furneture and at her Death to be delivered to my son
ROBERT & dau. KITTY, to each one bed; if ROBERT Marry or Go to Housekeeping
Before the Death of his Mother he to have half dozen Windsor Chairs, my
small Mahogany Table, my Square pine Table, all my Barrels, Hogsheads and
Such Cooper Ware to be Eaqually Divided Between my Wife and Sons DAVID and
ROBERT, all my Jugs and two Demi Johns to be valued and DAVID to have one
share and My Wife and ROBERT one share; all my Kitchen furniture of Every
Kind be Divided Between my Wife, Son ROBART and dau. KITTY; wife to have
5 or Six Cows or heifers with her Stock until Son ROBERT & Daughter KITTY
arrive at Lawfull age or Marry then they are to Recive Each Two Cows and
Calves; Executors to buy out of the Moneys now in hand three Mahogany
Tables the Size of my Smallest one or thereabouts and deliver one to my
Son DAVID, one to my dau. ELENOR HERRING and one to my dau. KITTY; son
DAVID all the Lands that I own in the County of Newhanover, slaves Quash,
Pompey, Jude & Warrick, one old pair of Cart Wheels Iron Bound, my Lot of
Blacksmiths Tools reserving my wife and Son ROBERT the Priviledge of geting
their work done when they can Get Workmen to do it, one old cross cut Saw,
one new Whipsaw Jointly to DAVID, ROBERT & my wife, my Rifle Gun, my half
that is in an old Still Between me and WILLIAM RIGBY SENR.; son ROBERT all
the Land that I Possess at this time in the County of Duplin, slaves Ochre,
Billy, Miley, & Jack, one Mare Called Dolly, one Horse Colt called Buckenoar,
one Saddle and Bridle, One Feather Bed & Bedstead and Bed furniture on his
arriving at Lawful age, half a Dozen of Pewter Plates, two Pewter Dishes, two
Pewter Basons, half Dozen of Spoons, half Dozen of Knives and forks, my Copper
Still & Worm Reserving to my Wife and Son DAVID the Privilege of Distilling
therein their Cider or other Stuffs for Liquor when the Said ROBERT is not
useing her in Distiling his own fruit my wife & son DAVID paying their proportion of the Dutys, all my Books Except the Large Testement Which I Give
to my dau. KITTY, my Shot Gun with the Copper Bond Round the Briton [?],
my Carpenters and Coopers tools, my Sun Dial, one pair of old hand Mill Stones,
my currying Knife Remain on the Plantation and the longest Liver of my two Sons
to have it, one Case and Bottles, two Reap Hooks, one Horse Cart, one Barr
Plow, one Fluke, two axes, two grubing hoes, two weeding hoes, two pair of
Iron Wedges, two pair of Sheep Shears; dau. SARAH NIXON of Onslow County
Slaves Sarah and her two Children Jack & Miley, Claray & Chelsea, a Certain
Mare, Saddle & Bridle, a Bedstead and a Bed and furniture which she hath
already Recd.; dau. ELENOR HERRING Slaves Violet and her child Bitty, Little
Sarah & Chloe, a certain Mare, Saddle and Bridle, a Bedstead, a Bed and furniture which she hath already Recd.; dau. KITTY Slaves Toney, Nancy, Harriot
and her Child Edy, & Lot, a Mare that Shall be worth Eighty Dollars, a Saddle
and Briddle which She hath already Recd., a bedstead, a Bed and furniture
when of Lawfull age or Married, one half Dozen of Pewter Plates, Two Pewter
Basons, two Pewter Dishes, half Dozen of Spoons and half Dozen of Knives and
forks; grandson JAMES, son of DAVID my Writeing Desk; three hundred Dollars
for the purpose of Educating my Grand Sons that is to Say to JAMES MIDDLETON
one hundred Dollars, to JAMES NIXON one hundred Dollars, BRIGHT MIDDLETON
HERRING one hundred Dollars; wife MARY & daus. SARAH NIXON, ELLENER HERRING

& Kitty and daughter in law CELAH MIDDLETON to Reseave from my Executors Each Twenty Dollars to Buy a Suit of Mourning on account of my Death; son DAVID & daus. SARAH NIXON & ELENER HERRING Each another Bed to what they have already Recd; if son ROBERT die under Lawfull age without Lawfull Issue the Lands herein Granthed to him to be property of my grandson JAMES and should he die to my son DAVID; residue sold and Moneys arising Eaqually Divided Between my Wife and all my Children
extrs: sons DAVID & ROBERT & Friend JOSEPH DICKSON
wit: JOSEPH GILLESPIE, PETER FREDERICKS, JOSEPH DICKSON
signed: James Middleton

355. MIDDLETON, JAMES JUNR (CR.035.801.8/A-292)
29 Mar 1799 - Jul Term 1801
wife SARAH to have Quiet and Peaceable possession of the Land and Plantation whereon I Live including the mill; son ISAAC whole of my Lands in Duplin County after my wife's Decease; lands in the Cumberland Settlement on the Western Waters sold; son ISAAC slave Liberty; all the slaves of which I am now possessed, my Stock of Every Kind, Household furniture and plantation Tools Remain in the possession of my wife and at her Death to be Divided amongst all my daughters [not named] Eaqually Except my youngest dau. POLLY who is to recieve Two Shares
extrs: son ISAAC, Uncle JAMES MIDDLETON, Friend JOSEPH DICKSON
wit: JOSEPH DICKSON, MARY MIDDLETON, DAVID MIDDLETON
signed: James Middleton

356. MIDDLETON, LEBEUS (CR.035.801.8/2-85)
5 Jul 1854 - Oct Term 1854
wife ADELINE a part of the plantation on which I now reside including the dwelling house Beginning at the Grove Bridge, to the mouth of the Lane up the Lane in the direction of the Lawn, to the upper corner of the Boyette field to the back line; son WILLIAM BRYANT ballance of my lands except 25 acres on Muddy Creek, the lands lately purchased from ALFRED MIDDLETON on the North East side of the Grove Swamp and a piece purchased of JAMES SOUTHERLAND lying between Alsa's Swamp & a branch of Cypress Creek on the Buck Swamp, all the land whereon my wife ADELINE has a life Estate; grandson SAMUEL ORLANDER son of WM. B. lands lying on Alsa's Swamp & Cypress creek purchased of JAMES SOUTHERLAND, also a tract lying on Muddy Creek purchased of HENRY BROWN; grandson LEBBEUS MIDDLETON COOPER lands purchased of ALFRED MIDDLETON on the North East side of the Grove Swamp adjoining the lands of FRANCIS WILLIAMS; wife ADELINE negroes Hardy, Lewis, Esther, Clarissa & Rose, one bead and furniture, slaves William, Daphiny, Lucy, Alice, Melissa, Alonzo, Harriet, Clew, Primus, Amelia, John & Amanda for her natural lifetime and then divided among my children; son WM. B. slaves Kate, Esther, Ned, Ailsey, Mingo, Esther, June, George, Jenney, Amanda, Merinda, Julia, Asha, Kenan, Toney, Dick, Isaac, Clerry, Sanders, Mariah, Joanna & Lotte; old negro man Toney to be taken care of by my son W. B.; dau. MARY E., wife of WM. COOPER negroes Julia, Allen, Peggy, Lunga, Albert, Jasper, Dolly, Rane, Abel, Lestina, John, Civil, Mary, Sampson, Luisa & Lisha; dau. MARTHA ANN negroes Nick, Rilly, Huldah, Abram, Christiana, Dick, Cass, Daniel, Sarah, Phoeba, Pleasant, Owen, Isaac, Miley, Margiana, Lisha, Henrietta, Caledonia, George, Susan, Finetta, Jane & Winnifred, one good bed & furniture; grandson CHARLES HENRY MOORE negroes Henry, Hasseltine, Catharine, Sarah, & Marshall to be delivered to him upon

his attaining the age of twenty one And in case he shall die before that age
negroes to WM. B. MIDDLETON, MARY E. COOPER and MARTHA A. MIDDLETON; son
WM. B. Blacksmith tools, my Saw mill Irons, Tools and fixtures; residue
sold and surplus money to W. B., MARY E. COOPER and MARTHA A; I lend as a
public burying ground Two acres of land including the present family burial
place And I request my family and friends to improve and preserve the same
from encroachment and trespassers
extr: son WILLIAM B.
wit: ALSA SOUTHERLAND, W. J. HOUSTON
signed: Lebbus, Middleton

357. MIDDLETON, MARY (CR.035.801.8/1-24)
11 Jul 1829 - Aug Term 1832
son ROBERT one Bed & furniture; dau. SARAH NIXON one Bed & furniture; dau.
ELEANOR HERRING one Bed & furniture; grandson JAMES & my friend JEREMIAH
PEARSALL & their legal Representatives negro Sarah in trust for the use &
benefit of my dau. ELEANOR HERRING of Sampson County & in trust that she may
be permitted to use said property for her benefit during her life but in no
case to be Subject to her debts or contracts & after her death to be the
property of her youngest child ELEANOR; grandson JAMES & my friend JEREMIAH
PEARSALL & their legal Representatives negro girl Eliza In trust for the Seperate use & benefit of my dau. CATHARINE SIMMS in trust that she may be permitted to hold, occupy & enjoy Said property during her natural life but in
no manner or wise to be subject or liable to the debts of her or her present,
past, or any future Husband, and after her death to be the property of her
dau. SARAH ANN; Friend and House Keeper ELIZABETH TURNER one Three year old
Heifer; balance of my property of every kind sold & the proceeds be disposed
of as follows 1/4 to my Son ROBERT, 1/4 to SARAH NIXON & 1/2 to my grandson
JAMES & my friend JEREMIAH PEARSALL in Trust for the use and benefit of my
dau. ELEANOR HERRING & CATHARINE SIMMS
extrs: grandson JAMES MIDDLETON, JEREMIAH PEARSALL
wit: JERE PEARSALL, KITTY PEARSALL
                              signed: Mary   Middleton
Codicil: 14 Dec 1831
grandson DAVID H. MIDDLETON my Silver ladle & Silver Tea Spoons; grandau.
MARY K. MIDDLETON my Silver Table Spoons; Housekeeper & friend ELIZABETH
TURNER $40; grandson BRIGHT HERRING my Horse Cart, four ewes & one Ram
Sheep; NANCY, dau. of BRIGHT HERRING one cow & calf; STEPHEN, son of BRIGHT
HERRING one cow & calf
wit: EDWARD JONES, JERE. PEARSALL
                              signed: Mary   Middleton

358. MIDDLETON, SUSANNAH (CR.035.801.8/A-298)
24 Nov 1801 - Jan Term 1802
son JOHN JAMES the whole of my property; should JOHN JAMES die before he
arrives to the age of twenty one years my property to be equally divided
between my brother ROBERT JOHNSTON & my Sisters SARAH JOHNSTON & ISABELL
JOHNSTON, except one featherbed to my brother JAMES JOHNSTON the same that he
now has in his possession
extrs: JEHU WILKINSON, brother JAMES
wit: OWEN RIGBY, LEWIS CHAMBERS
                              signed: Susannah   Middleton

359. MILLARD, ELIZABETH (CR.035.801.8)
10 Feb 1831 - Jul Term 1840
daus. NANCY & MARY negro Tildy, one bay mar & riding Cheir, all my house holde
and Kitchen furniture; son ISAAC one bay Colte, one Chist, negro Henry;   all
my stock of hogs and Cattle to be Sold and money Equally devided between
KENAN, CHARLES & ISAAC MILLARD & SARAH CRADDOCK
extr: son CHARLES
wit: ISHAM SOUTHERLIN, BENNETT MILLARD
                    signed: Elizabeth ✗ Millard

360. MILLARD, JESSE (CR.035.801.8/A-302)
17 Jul 1822 - Oct Term 1822
wife BETSEY deuring her naturel life or widower hood all my lands liing on
the house side of the   rode begining at JOHN BENNETTs line runing as
the Rod Runs to JOSEPH DICKSONs line; son ISAACE all the Same land which I
lent my wife; wife BETSEY slaves Stephen and Tome, all the parte coming
frome her fathers Estate, one horse take her choice, one bed and fernerture,
three cow and calf; Stephen I wish Sold and money and property I left wife
be Equely Devied amunk all heirese at her Deth; son KENON all my Cerry
track land after his takeing up my note Due JORGE CHERRY for thate land;
son CHARLY all my lands on the South Sid of the rode begining at JOHN BEN-
NETs line Runing Downe the Rode to the fork then downe the Rode as Runs to
JOSEPH DICKSON for which he must pay ISAACK five hundrede Dollars when he
Comes to be twenty one years of age, one fether bede and furneture & the
price horse; ISAACK one fetherbede and furneture; dau. SARAHE negro Nice,
one fether bed and ferneture; dau. EADY negro Manuwell one feather bed and
fernuture; dau. NANCY negro Alforde one fether bed and ferneture; dau.
MARY negro Jordan one fether bed and funeture; Bass lands solde and Executors
make all the Rest of the Girls Negros Equl to that of SARAHs and ballae of
money eqely Divied amonkst all girls; wife two sows and pigs, the safe,
all geese; balance of property Sold and money Equally Divied amonkst my
four daus.; if the Negro boy which i leave my dau. EADY is in persesion of
HONRY SHEROD if is not got She must be made Equeal with Mary
extrs: sons KENON & CHALS
wit: PETER WOOTEN, JOHN BENNETT
signed: Jesse Millard

361. MILLARD, KENAN (CR.035.801.8/2-24)
28 Apr 1847 - Jan Court 1848
brother ISAAC my house plantation whereon I now live, negroes Phillis &
Caty; I lone my brotherin law JOSEPH WILLIAMS and his wife NANCY my CHALES
BENNETT Land for Ten years and then to my nephew KENAN WILLIAMS, one leather
Trunk; nephew JESSE my GEORGE REASON Tract lying in Wayne County; my LYDIA
SMITH Land and NANCY REASONS Land sold and money Be Equally divided betwen
CHARLES MILLARD and my three Sisters NANCY WILLIAMS, MARY GLISSON & SARAH
PORTER; my CALVIN SIMMONS Land sold & money go to SARAH PORTERs two Sons
that She had by GEORGE CRADDOCK Names not Recollected; crops on the Bass
Land and NANCY REASONS Land and Stock of all kinds sold, all my Timber
Gathered together and Inspected and Negro Moses sold and money equally
divided between NANCY WILLIAMS, MARY GLISSON, SARAH PORTER and CHARLES MILLARD
extrs: brother ISAAC & Brother in law JOSEPH WILLIAMS
wit: D. JONES, WILLIS WILLIAMSON
signed: Kenan Millard

362. MILLER, RICHARD (CR.035.801.8/2-53)
18 Dec 1849 - Apr Term 1850
wife [not named] I lend a 4 horse farm during her natural life time, negroes
Frank & his wife Herma and her two Boys Ames & George, Mary and her dau.
Harriet and her Son Sip, big Clary and her three daus. Luce, Jane & Linda,
Daniel & Malvine; Ben & his wife Mila, Old Sarah & John I wish Kept & supported on the farm; wife 5000 lbs of Bacon, one barrel lard, 3 Barrels
flour, one Barrel fish, one barrel Sugar, one bag coffee, one barrel Molasses,
150 Barrels Corn, 10 bushels Salt, 30 bushels peas, all my Slips, 4 Horses
her Choice, all the poultry, all my House and Kitchen furniture, my Barouch
& harness, One Waggon and gear, 6 Axes, 6 Grubbing hoes, 2 Spades, 2 Shovels,
2 forks, all the weeding hoes, grind Stone, and all the Blacksmith tools;
sons RICHARD ELIAS, STEPHEN HENRY & JOHN WILLIAM all the lands I possess
except my Interest in my Brother GEORGE's land in Florida that I wish sold
and money applied to the benefit of all my children [not named] and they
pay over to the two Girls MARTHA FRANCIS and MARY WINIFRED one thousand
Dollars each when they arrive at age of twenty one years or marry; ballance
of my property converted into money for the benefit of my children jointly
extrs: Doctor JAMES H. HICKS, WM. W. MILLER
wit: JERE PEARSALL, T. M. GRADY
signed: Richard Miller

363. MILLER, SARAH "Widdow of RICHARD MILLER Late of Duplin County
           Carpenter" (CR.035.801.8/A-317)
9 Sep 1766 - no probate
sons GEORGE & ANTHONY all the Worldley Wealth I dye possessed off
extr: not named
wit: WM. HOUSTON, BENJAMIN RHODES, NED WORLEY
                          signed: Sarah   Miller

364. MILLS, ANN "Being Advanced in Years" (CR.035.801.8)
8 Mar 1825 - April Term 1837
sons RICHARD, BENJN & WILLIAM CHASTEN 5 shillings each; dau. MARY BROCK
all the Rest of my Estate
extr: son in law DAVID BROCK
wit: ARTHUR W. HALSO, JOHN G. MCANNE
                    signed: Ann   Mills

365. MILLS, ELIZABETH (CR.035.801.8/A-296)
8 Dec 1821 - Jan Term 1822
grandau. KITTY CARLINE NEWKIRK negro Sanders and he to Be heired out or
Sold If it is hir choice and money arising is to By a Negro Girl for hir
and If Such Girl Shold Be Bought hir first living Child is to go to the use
of my grandau. RACHAL NEWKIRK; grandau. ELIZABETH ANN NEWKIRK my large Chist
at this time in my posesion; grandau. MARY NEWKIRK one fether bed and furniture which is in the posesion of my dau. REBECAH NEWKIRK; Afectnate friend
POLLEY WADE one feather bead and furneture; grandau. KITTY CARLINE NEWKIRK
my fether Bed and furneture which I Now lie on, my Disk; all my household
and Kitchen furnitur, all my Stock of hogs, horses and Cattle and all my
farming utensals and working tools be Sold and money arising go to the use of
my grandau. KITTY CARLINE NEWKIRK
extr: Trusty friend and Neighbor DAVID SOUTHERLAND
wit: WM. B. SOUTHERLAND
                    signed: Elizabeth   Mills

366. MOBLEY, OLLEN/OLLON (CR.035.801.8/3-11)
22 Sep 1850 - Apr Term 1860
wife MARTHA all my Estate her lifetime; land where I now live unto JAMES RILY
SHOLAR; land lying on poly bridge branch called the Mobly Tract to HANNAH
SHOLAR and TISH E. SHOLAR; JOHN STILES the WILLIAM SHOLAR tract lying on the
watering hole branch; TISHY E. SHOLAR two Choice cows and calves in my stock;
SOLOMON J. L. SHOLARS one cow and calf; JOHN STILES one cow and calf, one bed;
rest of my Estate sold and money Equally devided between DAVID SHOLAR, HANNAH
SHOLAR & TISHY E. SHOLAR
extr: DAVID SHOLAR
wit: WM. SHOLAR, JAMES H. SHOLAR
signed: Ollon Mobley

367. MOLTEN, ABRAHAM (CR.035.801.8/A-335)
23 Nov 1784 - Jan Term 1791
wife SARAH 1/3 of my lands on Stewarts creek and back branch which I purchased
from FELIX KENAN, JAMES KENAN and JOSEPH WILLIAMS so as to include the House
and plantation on the South wist side of back branch where I now live; son
JOHN that part of my land on Stewarts Creek runing out with THOMAS JOHNSTONs
line to his upper back corner; son MICHAEL land which I patened of two hundred
Acres Joining Glissons line and my own to the south west of my plantation;
remainder of my land Equally divided as to possess my son MICHAEL of the
plantation & buildings wst of back branch & the upper half of the plantation
Est. of sd. Branch and the remainder to my son ABRAHAM; son JOHN Negro Ben;
son ABRAHAM negroes Ishmael, Jupiter & Pompey, one good feather bed and
furniture, one Horse called Driver; son MICHAEL negroes Harry, Cesar & Chloe,
one good feather bed and furniture, one young horse named Virtue, one other
Horse Called Spider; dau. PATIENCE negroes Jack, Airy & Sall, one good bed
and furneture, one mare called Juliet; grandson ABRAHAM HALL twenty pounds
Specie; grandson MOLTIN DICKSON twenty pounds Specie; grandson JAMES HALL
negro Peter; dau. ELIZABETH negro Rachel; son in law WILLIAM HALL 5
Shillings Sterling; son in law JOSEPH DICKSON 5 Shillings Sterling; son in
law JESSE PEACOCK 5 Shillings Sterling; wife SARAH negroes Ismail, Pen &
Chloe during her lifetime and then to son MICHAEL; remainder of my estate
be wholy and intirely the property of my wife SARAH
extrs: wife SARAH, trusty & worthy friends JAMES KENAN & JOSEPH DICKSON
wit: JONATHAN THOMAS, MARY ⮌ QUIN, SALLY THOMAS
signed: Abraham Molten
Codicil: 25 Nov 1784
son JOHN one hundred and five acres of Land on the No. E. Side of Stewarts
Creek which I purchased from JOHN ROBINSON Late of Wilmington Decd.
wit: KEDAR BRYAN, THOMAS ✝ JOHNSON, JOHN JOHNSTON
signed: Abraham Molten

368. MOLTEN, JOHN (CR.035.801.8/A-287)
23 May 1790 - Jul Term 1790
father ABRAHAM my Suit of Black Cloathes; daus. MARY & SARAH my Silver Tea
Spoons, the apparrel and Cloathing of Every nature or kind which did Belong
to my Deceased wife [not named]; dau. SARAH, ELISABETH and CATHRINE the
Feather Bed that I used to Lie upon Known and called by the Family my Bed
together with its Furneture Compleat includeing the Bedstead and Cord So
long as they live Single and under Lawfull age; Old Celah Remain unsold or
hired and She Remain with my dau. for their use and Bennifit to Nurse Wash
Spin Wait uppon and do all and Everything Necesary for the Support and

Maintenance of my Said Children; Aunts [not named] of my Children Distribute
the Buckels and Rings that Lately Was my Wifes Sugar Tongs and the Trunks
that my wife usually Kept her cloaths in; Executors to sell all my Stock
of Horses, Cattle and Hogs, Plantation Tools, Household Furniture and Kitchen
Utensils and the moneys arising Together with the money due me from THOMAS
JOHNSTON used to Discharge my Just Debts and the Over pluss Eaqually Divided
amongst my children; Should such Monies arising be found insufficient to
Discharge My Just Debts Negro Ceasar should be sold; unsold negroes be
hired out yearly to the best advantage and money applied in Schooling and
Cloathing my said Children; negro Ben Which is my property at my Father's
Decease be Eaqually Divided Amongst the whole of my Children; executors to
make over to THOMAS JOHNSTON a Deed or Deeds for all Such lands as I have
Sold to him
extrs: worthy Friend JOHN JAMES Esqr. of Newhanover County, JOSEPH DICKSON Esq,
        THOMAS JAMES, Brother MICHAEL
wit: KEDAR BRYAN, RIGDON BRYAN, JANE DICKSON, ANN BRYAN
signed: Jno. Molten

369. MOLTEN, TAMER (CR.035.801.8/A-286)
2 Sep 1761 - May Court 1762
dau. MARY SCOT one Spice morter, ten Shillings procklamation Money; son
JONITHAN CARR Twenty Shillings procklamation Money; dau. MARGET JONES one
Iron pot rack, one Brass hackel; grandau. TAMER JONES twenty Shillings
procklimation Money; dau. WINNY CARR one feather bed and furniture, two
Cows and Calfs, two Sows and five Shotes that I bought of CANNON CASON, one
puter Dish, two puter plates, one puter midlesised bason, one Lining Wheal,
my Saddle and my Executor to get it New Cevered; son THOMAS CARR all and
Singular my Land
extr: THOMAS CARR
wit: SAMUEL WEBSTER, JOSHUA CHESNUTT, MARTHA ✝ CHESNUTT
                                    signed: Tamer ⚏ Molten

370. MONK, ELIZABETH ANN (CR.035.801.8/2-16)
8 Dec 1846 - Apr Term 1847
son LEVI THOMAS KENNADY one bed and furniture, one Mahogany Table, looking
glass to be Kept until he arrives at full age; son WILLIAM HENRY KENNADY
one bed & furniture, Side board & clock to be kept until he arrives at full
age; residue of my property Sold together with my legacy left me by my
deceased husband JNO. W. MONK and money devided between my two sons
extr: THOMAS B. HEATH
wit: JACOB TAYLOR, A. G. MALLARD
                    signed: Elizabeth ✗ Ann Monk

371. MONK, JACOB (CR.035.801.8/1-12)
4 Apr 1831 - Aug Term 1831
wife SARAH the use of my house and plantation with all my lands that I possess
except the Tract called the Marsh land lying back of the Big Marsh for her
natural life also the use of all my personal Estate; dau. FANNY wife of
RAIBURN EZZEL all the part of my lands lying on the west side of the branch
call the Cook Branch with the middle prong that runs between the Tom field
and the Elijah field to JOHN MONKs line and on to JAMES WILSONs line to
include all the swamp of said Branch and a strip of high land on the East
of said Branch wide enough to run a fence upon; son BRUSTER all my land on

the East side of the Branch called the Cook's Branch; dau. NANCY MERRITT $1;
all my personal Estate sold and mony equally divided among my children JOHN,
BRUSTER & FANNY EZZEL; extrs to sell my Tract of land called the Marsh land
extrs: son JOHN, trusty Friends DICKSON SLOAN Esqr. & JOHN BRYAN
wit: ALEXANDER ✗ MERRITT, ABNER ⟋⟍ MERRITT
signed: J. Monk

372. MONK, JOHN WILKINSON (CR.035.801.8/2-6)
23 Jan 1846 - Oct Term 1846
wife ELIZABETH ANN 1/3 part of all the lands of which I may die seized of
including the homestead and plantation with all out buildings during her
natural life, the best one of my horses, the best cow and calf, the best
sow and pigs, one thousand five hundred pounds of good pork or one thousand
pounds of good bacon, forty barrels or two hundred bushels of good ground
corn, the best one of my beds with all its necessary furniture including bed
stead and bed clothing, the sum of fifty dollars to purchase Sugar and coffee;
rest of my personal estate including my negroes, & stock of all Kinds be sold
and wife to be paid one third part of the monies; brother JAMES BREWSTER all
my lands of every description reserving my wife's one third and two thirds
of the proceeds of the sale; my executors shall lay off one acre of land
around a posimmon tree about one hundred and fifty yards to the Eastward of
my present residence which acre of ground I hereby reserve forever to the use
of a burying ground or graveyard and my Executors to make a good Substantial
paling or fence around the said grave yard and to procure for my grave a
suitable gravestone
extrs: brother JAMES BREWSTER, my worthy friend JAMES DICKSON (late Clerk
          of Duplin County Court)
wit: ISAAC B. KELLY, H. J. JARMAN
signed: J. W. Monk

373. MOODY, JAMES SR. (CR.035.801.8/3-4)
16 Feb 1858 - Jul Term 1859
negros Jane aged about twenty four years, Knowel aged about nine years &
Solomon aged about Seven years to be free; all my land, Stock and all the
rest of my estate to SILAS M. TURNER as trustee to the use of Jane, Knowel
and Solomon
extr: SILAS M. TURNER
wit: RICHARD LEE, SIMPSON HARPER JR.
                    signed: James ⟋⟍ Moody Sr.

374. MOOR, JOHN (CR.035.801.8/A-338)
14 Jul 1771 - no probate
wife MARY During her widowhood negroes Ceasar, Tom, Nan, Dorcas, Doll, Davy
and then to be Eaquelly Divided among daus. ANNIS, SARAH, BACKEY, MARY,
SUCKEY & BETSEY; sons JOHN & JAMES all the Lands Below the Spring Branch
Joining Mr. Hills land; sons ORSON and MAURICE all the Lands above the
Spring Branch and up the Great Branch Bounding on Mr. Bells Land Including
the plantation where I Now live; sons WILLIAM, JOHN, JAMES, ORSON & MAURICE
negro Venus when MAURICE Coms to the age of twelve years old; my beloved
Children [not named] all my horses, Cattle, hougs & sheep; son WILLIAM One
Feather Bed; Loving wife the remaining Part of my household Furniture;
Turbevill land Be Sold to Discharge Debt Due Mr. McColloth; land beginning

at or near the School house runing Down to Bare Swamp and the Horsepen
Branch Disposed of to Discharge the Debt Due Mr. McColloth
extrs: ABRAHAM MOLTEN, HENRY CANNON
wit: JAMES KENAN, OWEN KENAN, WILLIAM GUY
signed: John Moor

375. MOORE, DAVID C. (CR.035.801.8/3-85)
2 Oct 1860 - Jan Term 1864
wife ELIZABETH one half of that portion of my negroes Known as Megee Negroes
excepting those I purchased from THOMAS H. MEGEE which I do not consider as
Megee Negroes, $100, two horses, four cous & calves, sows & pigs, one buggy
& harness, one wagon & gear and a sufficiency of my farming utensils & my
house & lot in Magnolia for her lifetime and after her death to my children
LEVI, MATTHEW & MARY ELEN; sister RACHEL and my four children LEVI, MATHEW,
MARY ELEN & THOMAS a bed & furneture each; wife ELIZABETH the remainder of
my houshold & kitchen furneture with the exception of the Piano Forte which
I give to my dau. MARY. ELEN; grandson CHARLES HENRY Son of CHARLES H. &
SARAH E. MOORE Decd. negroes Charlotte, Rose & Durry; son THOMAS M. one half
of that portion of my negroes known as Megee Negroes including Martha & her
three Children excepting those that I purchased from THOMAS H. MEGEE namely
Aaron, Mary & three children; remaining portion of my negroes to my children
LEVI, MATHEW & MARY ELEN; sister RACHEL three hundred dollars; the whole
of my lands and tenaments sold except my house & lot in Magnolia and proceeds
equally divided among LEVI, MATHEW & MARY ELEN; executors to pay my Son
THOMAS' tuition untill he completes his education & pay the same while study-
ing a profession if he desires to do so; LEVI & MATHEW shall be Guardian
for my son THOMAS M.
extr: LEVI & MATHEW
wit: D. G. MORISEY, S. R. BOWDAN
signed: D. C. Moore
Codicil: 18 Aug 1863
since my sister RACHEL has died I now revoke that part of my will concerning
her and divide legacy equally among my children
wit: D. G. MORISEY, S. R. BOWDAN
signed: D. C. Moore

376. MURPHEY, TIMMOTHY (CR.035.801.8/A-325)
7 Apr 1787 - Apr Court 1787
wife BARBARY slaves Jack an old fellow, Blainey, Black Jupiter, Yellow
Jupiter, Lucy, Jean and Child Called London and after her Decease Equally
Divided Amonst all the Children of my Friend WILLIAM MURPHEY & ELISABETH
his present Wife Except his Son TIMOTHY which is to be otherwise provided
for; wife BARBARY Dureing her Natural life all my Horses, Hogs, Cattle,
Sheep, poultry, Household Stock of Every nature or Kind, Kitchen furniture,
Plantation Tools & c and at her Decease Equally Divided amongst the Children
of WM. MURPHEY aforesaid and ELISABETH his wife; WILLIAM MURPHEY negro Grace
and her two Children Stephen and Hannah; TIMMOTHY Son of WM MURPHEY Slaves
Jack, Cato, Arthur, Chloe and Celah and Should he Die without heirs of his
Body then Equally Divided amongst the Surviving Children of the Said WM
MURPHEY and ELISABETH his wife; Friend TIMOTHY BRYAN negro Jerry, one
hundred acres in Newhanover County nigh the Mouth of Rockfish; DANIEL,

a Son of FRANCIS GIBSON a Small Tract on a branch of Stockinghead be the place
whereon the Said FRANCIS GIBSON now lives; JACOB son of HENRY WELLS Dec'd.
Five Shillings Sterling Money of Great Brittain
extrs: wife BARBARY, JAMES KENAN, WILLIAM DICKSON, JOSEPH DICKSON
wit: JACOB WELLS, WILLIAM ✗ KNOWLES, WILLIAM WELLS
                            signed: Timmothy ✗ Murphey

377. MURPHEY, TIMOTHY (CR.035.801.8/A-328)
9 Feb 1827 - Apr Term 1827
wife MARY my household goods and chattles, plantaion tools likwise my Stock
of Cattle and hogs, one horse, negro Tener, Ten pounds current money; dau.
SUSAN STALLINGS Ten Shillings; son DAVID Ten Shillings; dau. ELIZA ANN
BRICE Ten Shillings; son WILLIAM Ten Shillings; son HENRY Negro Sam; dau.
JEMIMA Ten Shillings and the next child Teiner may have; dau. PHEBE Ten
Shillings and the next child Teiner may have; son TIMOTHY W. negro Charls;
dau. MARY JANE Teiner and her last child that She may have and if so be her
increase exceed what has been mentioned I wish them equaly divided between
my children DAVID, WILLIAM, HENRY, JEMIMA, PHEBE, TIMOTHY W. & MARY JANE;
Negro Sam to be hired out until my Debts are paid then to be to the use of
my wife MARY During her lifetime then to be equaly Divided be tween the above
mentioned children
extrs: wife MARY, WILEY STALLINGS, HENRY MURPHEY
wit: JNO. HUFHAM, WILLIAM ○ SELLARS SENR.
signed: Timothy Murphey

378. MURPHY, BARBARA (CR.035.801.8/A-331)
1802 - Jul Term 1802
Yellow Jupiter have leave to Choose his own Master and that he shall have
The mare and Colt and three Cows and Calves and one yearlin, one plough, one
ax, one drawing knife, one hoe, one Cart, Six plates, four boles, two mugs,
one pot
extr: brother FREDERICK WELLS
wit: JOHN MATTHIS, MARY ✗ MURPHY, MARY ✗ BROWN
                            signed: Barbara ✗ Murphy

379. MURRAY, DANIEL (CR.035.801.8/3-94)
28 Aug 1858 - Jan Term 1865
wife BARBARY full privalidge of Two Hundred acreas wheare I now reside so as
to take the house and fenced Land, two horses, my cattle and hog Stock, my
house hold and chichen Furnture, my Carte and farming utencheals and Tools
of all kinds, one Yoake of Oxen and my stock of Bees, my present crop during
her natureal life and then to my son DANIEL H.; Ten Dollars be equally
devided among all my Children Viz NATHAN, JAMES, DAVID, THOMAS, DANIEL H.,
MARGRET A. CASTEEN, ELIZA & MARY C. other property being Conviend to them
by deeds of Gifts
extrs: son DANIEL H. & brother HIRAM
wit: JAMES W. MURRAY, AARON W. MURRAY
signed: Daniel Murray

380. MURRAY, HOSEA (CR.035.801.8/3-36)
13 May 1856 - Jul Term 1861
wife RHODA negro Old Chaney, one grey horse, one buggy & harness, all my
Silver plate, two cows & calves her own choice; grandchildren ANN VICTORIA &

JAMES children of my deceased dau. ELIZA MOORE negroes. Mariah, Bernette,
Hannah, Nancy, Maggie, Little Amy, Westley & Anness, Little Tempy, Little
John, Hannah's last child name not known, Little Norman, Annes, Howard,
Quince & Isaac; ANN VICTORIA one feather bed; dau. CHARITY, wife of
ALFRED MOORE negroes Maggie, Aly, Lindy, Susannah, Bob, Lucy, Patrick,
Tempey, Norman, Leah, Julia, Wingate, Elon, Hannah, Silvia, Jere, Matilda,
Shepard, Bunyon & Old Amy; dau. HULDAH, wife of GEORGE MOORE negroes
Kitty, Washington, Mary, Harriet, Nelson, Clarissa, Polk, John W., Phillis,
George, Kenan, Grace, Carolina, Little Mahala, Candis, Williams, Elizabeth,
Peter & Mahala; son JONATHAN negroes Isaac, Hillary, Murdock, Esther, John,
Sophia, Kitty, Cornelia, Etna, Marlin, Little Chaney, Silvia, James, Harriet,
Adeline, Thursay, Jenny Lind, Noah, Sam, Washington & Jessee, one Boat, one
Handmill, one set Blacksmiths tools, all my farming utensils and plantation
tools and all the rest and residue of my property
extrs: son JONATHAN, my friend JAMES DICKSON
wit: HONSON F. MURPHY, HIRAM MURRAY, W. J. HOUSTON
signed: Hosea Murray
Codicil: 8 Dec 1858
wife RHODA to have the slaves living on the plantation where I now reside
for her natural life also such of my household and kitchen furniture, horses,
carts, farming utensils, stocks necessary for her convenience, comfort &
support; dau. CHARITY MOORE negroes Maggie, Alie, Lindy, Susannah, Lucy,
Patrick, Norman, Leah and her youngest child Julia, Wingate, Elon, little
Hannah, Sylva, Matilda, Shephard, Jerry, Bunyan and old Amy; grandchildren
ANN VICTORIA & JAMES MOORE negroes Mariah, Bernette, Hannah, Quincey, Maggie,
Annie, Wesley, little Anniss, little Tempie, little John, Howard, Cassie,
little Norman, Anness, Isaac, Laura, Nancy, little Amie & little Sophia;
JAMES DICKSON one of the Executors left out and my friend S. S. SATCHWELL
be my Executor in his place
wit: HIRAM MURRAY, JOHN A. BONEY, DANIEL **W** BONEY
signed: Hosea Murray

381. MURRAY, JAMES (CR.035.801.8/A-333)
7 Apr 1794 - Oct Term 1797
wife [not named] all my hole estate Dureing her widdohood; son JAMES negro
Sutton; son ARTHER negro Sam, my Desk, half my waering apperel; my dau.
ELESABETH MASHBORNs children is to Draw their mother's Shear with the Rest
of my daus. SARAH JAMES, ESTER PICKET & CHARITY WILLIAMS; son ARTHER the
Bed and furnetude he lieth on and the plantation tools
extrs: JOBE THIGPEN, JOHN FARIOR
wit: JOB THIGPEN, STEPHEN **Q** HANCOCK
signed: James Murray

382. MURRAY, JAMES "of Newhanover County" (CR.035.801.8/A-305)
2 Dec 1826 - Feb Term 1828
son in Law AMOS WALLER Eight Shillings; children NICANOR, ETHALINDY STALINGS,
RHODY, DANIEL & HIRAM all my Perishable property to be Sold & Equally devided
extrs: son & son in law HIRAM & HOSEA MURRAY
wit: JONATHAN JOHNSON, DANIEL **X** BRADSHAW
signed: James Murray

383. MURRAY, JAMES "Planter" (CR.035.801.8/3-15)
14 Dec 1859 - Jul Term 1860
wife CATHORUN all my house hold and kitchen furneture, Two hundred pounds
bacon, Seven Barrels Corn, One Cow and Sucklin, one Sow & pigs, five Shotes,
Two Ewes & Lambs, my Stock of Bees, Twenty five Dollars; All my property
not named Sold Except my Boy Tom who Shall be hired out on the first day
January Anually at the vilage of Chinkepin at Auction during the naturel
life time of my wife And not to be Suffered to go on the Water; CATHORIN
ANN dau. of ZEBULON LANIER boy Tom at death of my widdow
extr: JAMES CAVENAUGH Esqr.
wit: WM SHOLAR, SAML. C. JONES
signed: J. Murray

384. MURRY, ARTHUR (CR.035.801.8/A-344)
22 May 1814 - Jul Term 1814
wife SARAH 100 acres on which is the plantation bounded by WM PICKETT &
Burton's Lines & the river, negroes Bes, Sam, three head of Horses, saddles,
bridles and plantation tools, one grine stone, Eight sows & pigs & twenty
five kilable hogs at the Ensuing Season, seven Cows & Calves, two four year
old Steers, two three year old steers, one yoke of oxen & Cart, with my stock
of Bees, House holde & Kitching furneture with the corn & Bacon now remaining;
to my youngest son that Comes of age [not named] two peaces of land Lying on
the wolf pond & fishing branch containing 327 Acres, 50 acres Lying in the
river Swamp against Bowzars old Landing, 130 Acres on the other Side of the
river Joining WM. PICKETT also the widows 100 acres after her death being
607 Acres in all vallyed at five hundred Dollars; son NATHAN land Lying on
fussels Creek & perrys branch two peaces containing 250 acres vallyed at four
hundred & seventy five Dollars & $25; rest of the Heirs [not named] that has
not been mentioned five Hundred Dollars to be raised out of the remainder of
my Estate when they Come of age; Peter & Frank to be hired out on the 1st.
day of Jany next to help school my five yong Children [not named]; Unwiled
stock to be sold and all my Just debts paid
extr: not named
wit: F. PICKETT, JOHN BURTON
signed: A. Murry

385. MURY, BETHOLEMY "Plantar" (CR.035.801.8)
18 Nov 1780 - Jan Court 1781
SARAH SPRINGS all my household goods debts and Moveable Effects
extr: not named
wit: JOSEPH COOK, SHADRACH STALLINGS
                        signed: Betholemy Mury

386. NEAL, JOHN (CR.035.801.9/A-366)
10 Jun 1804 - Apr Term 1805
dau. ELIZABETH REED three Cows and Calves; son in law ANDREW REED ten
shillings; son JOHN all my Lands, negroe Andrew Noel, all the Remainder of
my Stocks of Horses, Cattle and Hogs, all my houshold & Kitchen furniture and
plantation tools, what money I have due me by note or accts and what crop I
have growing; Negroe Andrew Noel the use of two Cows and Calves to give him
milk untill he arrives at the age of nine years old
extrs: son JOHN, friends ANDREW McINTIRE, GEORGE HOUSTON
wit: EDWD. HOUSTON, A. McINTIRE
signed: John Neal

124

387. NEATHERCUT, LOFTIN (CR.035.801.9)
11 Jan 1842 - Jul Term 1844
wife NANCY during her natural lifetime the lands & premises whereon I now reside Begining in Anthonys branch at the mouth of a short drain, to the main road, to Cow hole, the head of the long pond, G. F. NEATHERCUTs corner, all the perishable property which I may die possessed of; daus. BETSEY & ELIZA two cows & calves each; son GEORGE F. five dollars in addition to what I have given him; son JOHN H. five dollars in addition to what I have given him; son MARSHAL MONEY two cows and calves; dau. CHARITY BARFIELD five dollars in addition to what I have given her; daus. BETSEY, ELIZA, TEMMY & KITTY all my lands lying on the great branch adjoining MERRIT BAR-FIELD, all my money, all the debts due me, my perishable property of every kind at the death of my wife
extr: son GEORGE F.
wit: J. H. JARMAN, A. O. GRADY
                    signed: Loftin ʒ   Neathercut

388. NEW, JOHN (CR.035.801.9/A-357)
15 Mar 1780 - Jul Court 1780
dau. BET 2 Cows & Calves; dau. TAB 2 Cows & Calves; son JOHN 2 Cows & Calves; son WILLIAM 2 Cows & Calves; dau. PEGGY 2 Cows & Calves; son GEORGE 2 Cows & Calves; dau. WINNY 2 Cows & Calves; wife MARGARET all the rest & residue of my Estate of every kind during the term of her natural life & then equally divided amongst all my children
extrs: NOEL PENNINGTON, ROBERT SOUTHERLAND
wit: CATHERINE K KENAN, RICHD. BROCAS, W. KENAN
                    signed: John Ħ New

389. NEWKIRK, TIMOTHY (CR.035.801.9/3-5)
31 Jan 1859 - Oct Term 1859
friend JAMES G. STOAKES my land Beginning on the Run of Bens Creek where my line and Said Stoakes crosses said Creek thence a straight line to BETSY WELLS line so as to include the Bryan old house; nephew TIMOTHY JR. son of my brother JOSEPH the plantation on which I reside including my dwelling house, Saw mill, grist mills & the lands Known as my old place; friend JOHN D. POWERS my plantation known as the Wells place for the occupancy Support and maintainance of Certain Negroes which I have Conveyed to Said Powers and at the decease of said Negroes the plantation belong to the children of Said Powers by his present wife FRANCINIA (except forty acres around the dwelling of JNO. Q. A. BONEY on which he at present resides which I bequeath to the children of Said Boney); residue of land sold; brother BRYAN SENR negroes Mingo, Eveline wife of Mingo and her children Beatty, Aga, Mingo and Victoria; brother BENJAMIN R. slaves Ivey, Candace wife of Ivey and her children Milton, Lewis, Alvira and Lucy & Isaac; JOHN A., BENJA. H., GEORGE B., & HARRIET ADELAIDE WAYNE children of my brother JACOB F. slaves Eliza and her children John, Harriet, Aga and Pence; nephew TIMOTHY JR. slaves Jere, Francinia & her child; nephew JAMES L. slaves Tom and Levi; niece THANKFUL wife of NATHANIEL BONHAM slaves Aly and her child; nephew BRYAN B. slaves Stephen, Jim O. & Pearsall; niece MARY ANN wife of CHESTER R. VANN slaves Joe Lewis, Molsay and her child; nephew ABRAM N. MATTHIS negro John; TIMOTHY NEWKIRK, son of ABRAM N. MATTHIS negro Nancy; sister MARY MATTHIS negroes Bill and Sarah; nephew THOMAS BEATRY MATTHIS negro Mansfield;

sister ANN JANE WILLIAMS negros Crosby & Amanda; nephew DAVID H. WILLIAMS
negro Jim; neice RACHEL ANN dau. of ALBERT G. HALL negro Katharine and her
two children; niece FRANCINIA wife of JOHN D. POWERS slaves Calvin, Fennell
and Elisabeth; niece HELEN C. wife of JULIAN P. FAISON slaves Becca and her
two children; JOSIAH STALLINGS of the State of Mississippi slaves Abram,
Edmund and Sam; JOSIAH STALLINGS in trust for the use and benefit of KEDAR
STALLINGS slaves Henry and Spencer; friends WILLIAM BRICE and wife slaves
Sylvester and Rachel; TIMOTHY NEWKIRK P. WELLS negro Caroline; friend
HANSON F. MURPHY negro Sophia; friend CORNELIUS T. MURPHY negro Helen;
friend JOHN WILLIAM STOAKES negro Isaiah; friend DANIEL SOUTHERLAND negro
Joe Crocket; niece ANN JULIA wife of DR. J. B. SEAVEY negroes Adelaide and
Caroline; nephews BRYAN N. and SAML. A. WILLIAMS negro Mima and her two
children Usher & Jim; friend DR. DAVID D. SLOAN of Sampson County negro
Jordan; friend AMANDA wife of JOHN WILSON negro Isabel; friends JOHN W. &
SHADRACH G. GILLESPIE negroes Bryant and Livinia; friend BONEY SOUTHERLIN
negro Essex son of Insane Jane; My Stock of all Kinds, Crop, household and
Kitchen furniture and all personal property sold to pay debts and Surplus
equally divided among all my brothers and sisters [not named] or their legal
representatives except my sister PENE HAWES
extrs: trusty friends JAMES G. STOAKES, HANSON F. MURPHY, JOHN D. POWERS,
          CORNELIUS T. MURPHY
wit: JACOB WELLS JR., M. J. TAYLAR
signed: T. Newkirk

390. NEWTON, ISAAC (CR.035.801.9/A-358)
19 Nov 1798 - Jan Term 1799
sons ENOCH & ISAAC all my Lands Devided as followeth Beginning at the run of
the Swamp he now lives on Crossing through the part of the plantation call'd
the long field to the Back line All below this line to be ENOCH's and all
above to be ISAAC's; son ISAAC Negroe Grace and her first child that shal
live to be one Month to ENOCH, the Second Child that shall live to be one
Month old to my dau. ESHER And her third Child that shall live to be one
Month old to my dau. ANN; dau. ESTHER one feather Bed and firneture; dau.
ANN one feather Bed and firneture; son ENOCH one Mare Colt; all the hogs
and Sheep to be equally divided between ENOCH and ISAAC, ENOCH to have one
third of my stock of Cattle and ISAAC have the other two thirds of the Cattle
and the mare and young horse; all my household furniture Equally devided
among my four youngest children [not named]; plantation tools Equally devided
between my sons ENOCH and ISAAC; And as for those of My Children that have
married I leave to them the following sums and no more Except my Blessing
SARAH ALDERMAN Five shillings, PHEBE HERRING five shillings, MARY WILLIAMS
five shillings, ELIZABETH BONEY five shillings, DORCAS MORGAN five shillings,
the heirs of my two daus. Deceased MIRIAM JAMES and JEMIMA WILSON five
Shillings each; wife JEMIMA my house plantation and all the above mentioned
Estate during her widowhood
extrs: AARON WILLIAMS, ENOCH NEWTON
wit: DAVID ALDERMAN, DANIEL ALDERMAN, THOMAS   LANEAR
                                                  signed: Isaac   Newton

391. NEWTON, MARY (CR.035.801.9/A-353)
25 Apr 1822 - Jan Term 1823
son JAMES three Children DANIEL B., JULIOUS & MARY ELIZA forty acurs adjoining
ther own lands But before they are to have poseshion of this land they must

pay to my dau. KITTY two Dollors per acur; son WILLIAM's two Children
MARY ANN and WILLIAM W. forty Acurs Joining their Fredrick land and the land
of DANIEL & JULEOUS and ELIZA and also to Join the old plantation belonging
to myself But before they are to have poseshion of this land they must pay
to my dau. KITTY two Dollors per acur; son MAJOR all the rest of my land
which is about Seventy acurs lying Joining his land to be laid of as to
Include all the Building that is now about to be Erected on my land But
Before he can have poseshion of this land he must pay to my dau. KITTY two
Dollars per acur; dau. KITTY the hole Rest and Residue of my Estate whither
Real or personal whatsoever or where soever
extr: son MAJR
wit: JAMES WATKINS, JAMES ✝ CANIDO
                            signed: Mary ✝ Newton

392. NEWTON, PATRICK (CR.035.801.9/A-353)
4 Feb 1793 - Apr Term 1793
wife MARY negroes Tom and Pat during her natural life and then to my daus.
ELVY and SUSANNAH; Mother BRAMBLY PARKER fifteen Acres of Land Lying in the
Parting Branch where She now Lives during her Life and then to be returned
to my sons; sons JAMES, ISAAC, WILLIAM and MAJOR all my Lands and Rights
of Lands When WILLIAM becomes to the age of Twenty one years; daus. ELVY
and SUSANNAH negroes Doll, Dorcas, Peter and Moses; wife MARY one bed and
furniture, two Cows and Calves, all Household furniture; son JAMES one Bed
and furniture; sons ISAAC, WILLIAM and MAJOR two Cows and Calves Each;
daus. ELVY and SUSANNAH one Bed and furniture; Remainder of my property
to be sold and any Remains to be applied to Educate and Raise my Children
extrs: Colonal WILLIAM DICKSON, JAMES REARDON, MARY NEWTON
wit: MORRIS MOOR, THEOPS GUY, JOHN NEWTON
signed: Patrick Newton

393. NEWTON, SARAH (CR.035.801.9/A-364)
3 May 1821 - Oct Term 1821
son ABRAHAM one feather bed and firneture to be left with my son WILLIAM
till ABRAHAM comes for it; grandau. ELIZABETH my yong Hors, one Cow and
calf, one feather bed and firniture, one woolling whel, one chiesh, one bed
stead, one small pott; son WILLIAM my marand colt and hunting saddle, all
my stock of Hoggs; grandau. CLARY MARIA TATOM one Heifer three years old;
grandau. SARAANN TATOM one feather bed and firniture and stead; daus.
ELAZABETH TATOM and SARA HIGHSMITH my Bofat and table firnitur; grandau.
ELIZAHELA one ewe & lam; Hors I gave to my grandau. ELIZAHELA be sold and
the money kept out on intrest
extrs: Brother JAMES NEWTON, ALFRED WARD
wit: MARY POWELL, DUNKIN BELL
signed: Sarah Newton

394. NITHERCUT, NANCY (CR.035.801.9/A-78)
30 Aug 1849 - Oct Term 1853
son MARSHAL M. all my property which I may die possessed of consisting of
Hogs, Cattle, Sheep, geese, chickens, One bed and furniture, One pot, Crockery ware, Knives & forks, Stock of provisions on hand, Crops of Corn, peas,
potatoes & c. all the debts due me and at his death should he die without

a wife or children to my sons GEORGE F. & JOHN H. & dau. ELIZABETH
extrs: sons GEORGE F. & JOHN H.
wit: A. A. GRADY, ALEXR. GRADY JR.
                    signed: Nancy ⌘ Nithercut

395. NORMAN, RICHARD (CR.035.801.9/A-360)
19 Jan 1807 - Jan Term 1807
wife PATCY the hole of my Estate ore as such as she can keep together to
raise my children [not named]; when all my children comes to the age of
twenty one years my Land to be Equaly divided between the hole then Living;
If it should so happen for all my Children to die without a Lawful heir
I bequeth My Land to my Brother in Law ISAAC MIDDLETON; Executors to make
a deed for all my Land on the Est side of Paster branch to SAMUEL MIDDLETON
on the payment of twenty two dollars
extr: ISAAC MIDDLETON
wit: JOHN HUNTER, POLLY ┼ GARRISON
                    signed: Richard ⚡ Norman

396. NORMENT, THOMAS (CR.035.801.9/A-362)
18 Sep 1799 - Oct Term 1799
wife CATHERINE the Lands and plantation wheron I now live with all the lands
adjoining containing about two Thousand acres, negroes Young Derry, Cork,
Sall, Silva and her Child & Nepton, one third part of furniture, horses,
cattle, hogs, sheep and Corn, my sorrel mare and chair, two trunks, two tables,
learge Looking glass; dau. SALLEY negroes Ben, Peg and her five children;
dau. BETSY JANE negroes Mingo, Phyllis, Bob, Nance, Josh, Tom and Mary; rest
and residue of my estate to be sold to Discharge Debts and ballance equally
Devided betwen my wife and two daus.
extrs: Friends KENAN LOVE, JAMES WRIGHT, THOMAS WRIGHT, DAVID WRIGHT
wit: K. LOVE, WILLIAM BEST
signed: Thos. Norment

397. NORRES, JESSY (CR.035.801.9/A-363)
6 Mar 1806 - Apr Term 1807
wife MARY one bay mare and two Colts one year old, all the Houshold furneture
& plantation tools, the Land I now Live on & the Land I bought of JOSHUA
MURRAY, ten cows with Calves & all the money I Have for Her Life time; son
JOSEPH the Land I now Live on; dau. MOLSEY the Land I bought of the sd.
Murray; son ISOM 150 acres Lying Gining His own Land; son REUBEN 100 acres
Lying in Onslow County, one Cow and Calf; sons LEWIS & JAMES 349 acres on
Mill Branch and one Cow and Calfs each; Remainder of my property I leave in
the Hands of my wife MARY to School the unlearned parte of my Children
extrs: wife MARY & ASA MURRAY
wit: ASA MURRAY, LEWIS NORRIS
                    signed: Jessy ✦ Norres

398. NORRIS, ISOM (CR.035.801.9/A-354)
5 Feb 1817 - Apr Term 1817
wife EUNICY all of my houshold furniture and working tools and stock of all
Koinds, one hundred and ninty six acres where I now Live to hir natural Liftime
then the lan to my sone RIEL Lying in and on the south side of island Creek
where I now live
extrs: JAMES CAVANAUGH, JOHN GREER
wit: JOHN MALLARD, REUBEN NORRIS
signed: Isom Norris, James Cavenaugh, John Greer

399. OATES, JETHRO (CR.035.801.9/A-374)
30 Aug 1780 - Jan Term 1781
Eldist dau. LYDDA STEVINS negroes Ben & Jena, Five Cows and Yearlings, one
Feather Bead and firniture; Next Eldist dau. AMY KING negroes Simon & Grace,
Sevin Cows and two 2 year old Stears, One Feather Bead and firniture; wife
ORTESHA All the Rest of my Estate, Lands, tenaments, Negrows, Goods And
Chatteles Not to Be Removed out of the County Dureing of her Natral life
and afterwards to be Equally Devided Amongst my Children JESSE, JETHRO,
ELIZABETH, MICHAEL, SUSANNAH & JOHN
extrs: ARTISHA OATES, STEPHEN KING, ROGER SNELL, MICHA KING
wit: JAMES OATES
signed: Jethro Oates

400. OATES, SUSANNAH (CR.035.801.9/3-43)
17 Feb 1851 - Oct Term 1861
children of my dau. ELIZABETH A., wife of WILLIAM W. FAISON one thousand
one hundred dollars; negro Woman Milley sold and monies arising equally
divided among my sons DAVID, JAMES and LEWIS and my grandson JETHRO son of
my son the late JETHRO; dau. ELIZABETH A., wife of WILLIAM W. FAISON all
the residue of my personal estate of whatever description; dau. ANNA M
50¢ and to her husband JETHRO OATS 50¢
extr: son in law WILLIAM W. FAISON
wit: JOS. T. RHODES, JON. W. HILL
signed: S. Oates

401. ODANIEL, ALEXDR. (CR.035.801.9/A-370)
10 Mar 1816 - Apr Term 1816
wife ANN all my Lands and all my horses, all my Cattle, hogs, Sheep and Stock
of all Sorts, all my household furnitue, Kitchen furnitue, plantation tools
During her Life time; son WILLIAM one feather Bed and furnitue and two Cows;
dau. CHARITY one feather Bed and furnitue and two Cows; should wife Marry
the Best one of the horse Creature, the Stock of all Sort and all the parishable property of all Sorts sold and the money put on Intrust, Nun of my oak
timber to be made any use of only for plantation use nor no trees boxt for
turpentine & all my lands rented out untill my youngest Son [not named]
Comes of age to be twenty one years then Lands to be Sold and moneys arising
Equilly Devided Between my wife ANN's Children [not named] that is now alive
or in the woumb
extrs: JAMES PEARSELL, OWEN ODANIEL
wit: O. ODANIEL, CHARITY ✕ HERRING
signed: Alex. ODaniel
N. B. At my mother [not named] Death all property that will fall to me in her
Lands Consising of one fourth part of fib, June, Claben and James, and Stock
of Cattle be Sold and money arising Equilly Devided among all my Children
[not named]
wit: O. ODANIEL, CHARITY ✝ HERRING
signed: Alex. ODaniel

402. ODANIEL, OWEN (CR.035.801.9/1-54)
3 Aug 1833 - Oct Term 1834
dau. SALLY WORLEY beside what I gave her Son [not named] at her request and
her Husband [not named] by deed and bill of Sale her poshonable part of my
parishable Estate with the Rest of my heirs; dau. CHELLY KORNEGY Deased or

at least to her children CHARLOTTE negro Mike when maried or at twenty one
years of age, CHARITY negro Jim when maried or at twenty one years of age and
ANNE negro Squier when maried or at twenty one years of age also her poshonable
part of my parishable Estate when Sold Equilly divided among the heirs of her
body the daus. to recieve there Shear at Sixteen years old; dau. ELIZHA GRADY
her poshonable part of my parishable Estate with the rest of my heirs; dau.
POLLY BROWN Citizen of Georgea State negroes Bill, Toney & Dilsay also her
poshonable part of my parishable Estate whith my other heirs; grandau. NANCY
JANE SMITH of Georjea Stat negro Jackson and a poshonable part of my parishable Estate with my other four heirs besides what I gave her by bills of
Sales for to Recieve it when maried or twenty one years Old
extr: not named
wit: Z. SMITH JURY, Z. SMITH
signed: O. ODaniel

403. OLIVER, FRANCIS (CR.035.801.9/A-371)
28 Oct 1807 - Jan Term 1808
eldest son ISAAC has recieved property estimated at seven Hondred dollars and
as I have lately recieved certain Intelegence that he is dead and has left
a son by the name of FRANCIS if the said seven Hundred dollars should be less
than an equal division among my Children he is to share in the surplus; son
JAMES three Hundred and fifty dollars; dau. ZILPAH KORNEGAY Three hundred
dollars; dau. SALLY WOOTEN Three hundren and Thirty dollars; dau. ANNE
negro Juda, one Horse, Saddle and bridle, one feather Bed and firniture and
one Chest estimated at three hundred and sixty five dollars; son JOHN negro
Hardy, one young hors commonly called his, a Saddle and bridle, one feather
bed and firniture when he arrives at the age of twenty one years or Marrys
estimated at three hundred and sixty dollars; dau. LUCRETIA negro Miley,
one Horse, bridle and Saddle, one feather bed and firniture when she comes
of age or Marrys estimated at two Hundred and forty dollars; dau. REBEKAH
one Hundred and fifty dollars in cash, one Horse, bridle and Saddle, one
feather bed and firniture estimated at three Hundred dollars and negro Willis
should be sold in order to discharge the said Legacy; Wife SARAH all my lands
during her natural life and then sold and Money equally divided between my
sons JAMES, JOHN and BENJAMIN; wife SARAH negroes Anthony, Rose and Lucy
with all the residue and remainder of my estate for raising and schooling my
dau. RACHAEL and son BENJAMIN and when they come of age or Marry they to have
Rose, Lucy, Lewis and the surplus from the sale of Willis if any; residue
sold at wifes death and money arising applied towards making the shares of
all my Children equal as near as may be and surplus divided amongs my Children JAMES, ZILPAH, SALLEY, ANNE, JOHN, LUCRETIA, REBEKAH, RACHAEL and BENJAMIN
and my grandson FRANCIS
extrs: wife SARAH, son in law DAVID KORNEGAY, son JOHN when he arrives at
        the age of twenty one years
wit: LEVIN WATKINS, LEVIN WATKINS JR.
signed: Frans. Oliver

404. OLIVER, JOHN (CR.035.801.9)
21 Jul 1842 - Oct Term 1844
wife [not named] during her life time all my lands on the South side of the
Northern prong of Dark branch and the whole of my negroes until my daus.
FEREBY or SARAH shall arrive at lawful age or marries; son JAMES all my Lands
subject to the loan to my wife & negro Glasco; dau. MARY negroes Anthony,

Violet and her two children Lucy and Hester also enough of my other negro property at the death of my wife to make her equall in value to her two younger Sisters the above considered to be worth thirteen hundred dollars; remainder of my negroes put in the possession of my wife Kept in common stock until one of my two daus. comes to lawful age or marries the one third in value set off to her and so with the other when she comes to lawful age or married; the property set off to my son JAMES A. is valued at twenty one hundred dollars, at the final division among my daus. if their portions fall short of that sum he is to pay over to them within two years a sum sufficient to divide my property among my children all equal
extrs: JEREMIAH PIERSALL, Brother BENJAMIN
wit: W. D. PEARSALL, FEREBY PEARSALL
signed: J. Oliver

405. OLIVER, SARAH (CR.035.801.9)
8 Oct 1836 - Jul Term 1838
son FRANCIS five Shillings; heirs at law of ZILPHA KORNEGAY one eighth part of my estate; heirs at law of SARAH WOOTEN Viz. MARCH BYRD five cents, OLIVER WOOTEN one sixteenth part of my estate; heirs at law of LUCRETIA MORRIS five shillings; ANN WILLSON one eighth part of my estate; dau. REBECCA MORRIS five shillings; son BENJAMIN one eighth part of my estate; son JOHN all the balance of my estate
extrs: son BENJAMIN, JOHN CARR
wit: DANIEL GLISSON, WILSON BOURDEN
                            signed: Sarah ✗ Oliver

406. OUTLAW, EDWARD (A-369)
22 Mar 1759 - no probate
wife [not named] a third part of all my moveable estate Excepting my negroes my plantation whereon I now live and my negro Flora; son ALEXANDER after my wife's decease my plantation whereon I now live, one horse and mare that is called hisin; son JAMES negro Jack, one young mare of his own Brand; son EDWARD negro Toney, the first Colt that comes of a mare that Runs up the mash; son WILLIAM the first child that my negro woman Brings that liveth to be two years old and then the next colt that the before mentioned mare Brings after my son EDWARD has his; my child that my wife now Gose with the next child that my negro woman Brings that livith to be two years old; daus. ANNA, ELIZABETH and MARY after my wife has her part all the rest of my movable Estate Equally Divided amongst them; my water mill and fifty acres of Land whereon She stands sold
extrs: wife PATIENCE, son ALEXANDER
wit: SAMUEL ALBERTSON, WILLIAM GRADDY, WILLM. WHITFIELD
signed: Edward Outlaw

407. OUTLAW, EDWARD SR. (CR.035.801.9/2-118)
8 May 1854 - Apr Term 1857
son JAMES MONROE the plantation whereon I now reside, negroes Phillis, Tom, Henry, Lewis jr, Daniel, Ben, Allen, Rose (Phillis's dau) & Etha, my Stock, plantation tools, all my household and Kitchen furniture reserving for my wife ELIZABETH the use of the above property during her natural life; son in law ALEXANDER S. ROUSE negroes Mariah, Hannah, Andrew, Kate, Simon Sr, Hannah, Suckey, Ben, Balaam, Rose (Suckey's dau), Andrew & Sylva reserving to the use of my wife ELIZABETH during her natural lifetime Mariah, Hannah,

Andrew & Kate;   three grandchildren daus. of JAMES decd negro Isham, one bed
& furniture
extrs: son JAMES M & 'son-in-law ALEXANDER S. ROUSE
wit: JAMES OUTLAW SR., A. O. GRADY
signed: Edwd Outlaw
Codicil
sons EDWARD, WILLIAM JR., GEORGE & BRYAN R. one dollor each
wit: JAMES OUTLAW SR., A. O. GRADY
signed: Edwd. Outlaw

408. OUTLAW, ELIZABETH (CR.035.801.9/1-7)
24 Jun 1830 - Nov Term 1830
dau. CHARITY GRADDY one bed and furniture; sons in Law JACOB WILLIAMS,
TIMOTHY GRADDY, HENRY GRADDY & WILLIAM WHITFIELD fifty cents each; sons
JOHN & LEWIS fifty cents each; sons EDWARD, ALXD. & WILLIAM the Rest of my
property, my Stock of all Kinds, my Beds, household and Kitchen furniture,
plantation tools, Desk, bophat, hand mill, the hire of my negraws in the hands
of EDWARD OUTLAW
extr: not named
wit: J. A. SWINSON, JAMES OUTLAW, WM OUTLAW
                              signed: Elizabeth   Outlaw

409. OUTLAW, JAMES (CR.035.801.9/A-367)
17 Apr 1826 - Jan Term 1827
son in law JACOB WILLIAMS who Married my oldest dau. MARY negro Lewis with
the Rest of the property that I have heretofore given him & twenty shillings;
son in law TIMOTHY GRADY who Married My dau. PATIENCE negro Rose & her Children, the property he has heretofore had & twenty Shillings; son in law HENRY
GRADY negro Boson whith what he has heretofore had & twenty Shillings; son
in law ALEXR GRADY negro Jenny together with what I have heretofore given
him; son in law WM. WHITFIELD negro Abbe together with what I have heretofore
given him; son JOHN my land on the South Side of the No East & above the
Miry Branch One hundred & Seventy Acres together with What I have given hir
heretofore; JOHN's children PATIENCE, MARY, OLIVE, LEWIS, ALEXANDER, SALLY &
EDITH my land on the So Side of the No East & below the Miry Branch down to
MARK KEETHLYs to be divided among them as they Come of age or Marry; wife
ELIZABETH while She remains my Widow all the Residue of my Negroes Old &
young & My Stock of all kinds and after her death My Negroes to be equally
divided among my Sons EDWARD, ALEXR., WM & LEWIS; wife ELIZABETH all my
household furniture & plantation tools
extrs: sons EDWD. & WM.
wit: JNO A. SWINSON, JNO MATHEWS, HAMMOND HARDISON
signed: James Outlaw

410. PARISH, WILLIAM (CR.035.801.9/A-385)
1 May 1759 - 22 Mar 1761
son THOMAS One Hundred Acres Including the Plantation I now Dwell upon
Prevoiding he suffers and Pemits his mother my wife ANN to Dwell there on
as sole Owner During her life; son WILLIAM lands on Raleys Brach; sons
JEREMIAH, HENRY, EDWARD and CHARLES three Hundred acres Lying between Rabey's
Branch and Goshen Swamp; wife my riding horse and a gray mare; son HENRY
a gray mare; son JEREMIAH my Riffle Gun; wife ANN all my Cattle; dau. JUDITH

one Cow; dau. SARAH one Cow and yearling; dau. NANNY a yearling heifer;
wife ANN everything to me appertaining not mentioned in this will; son
WILLIAM a Gun; son JOHN my gray mare
extrs: wife, son JOHN
wit: JOSEPH RD. HICKSON, ELIJAH SLOCUMB, ELEANOR HICKSON
                                    signed: William ⟨mark⟩ Parish

411. PARKER, JOHN (CR.035.801.9/A-382)
27 Mar 1785 - Apr Term 1788
son PETER one hundred Acers of Land Whereon I Now Dwell, one Two year old
horse, 2 Cows, one year old and a Calf; wife ELIZABETH one mare, one horse,
two Cows & three year old Creatures, three Two year olds, one heiffer, one
steer, one bull Dureing the Term of her life then to be Equally Divided
among all my children [not named]; dau. SARAH one Cow one year old and a
calf; dau. RACHEL one Cow and one Two year old hieffer & a calf; dau.
MARY one Cow and one year old hieffer; wife ELIZABETH Nine head of sheep
Dureing the term of her life then to be Eaqually Dividded among All my
other Children [not named]
extr: not named
wit: DEMS TAYLOR
        signed: John ⟨mark⟩ Parker

412. PARKER, WILLIAM (CR.035.801.9/A-375)
2 Mar 1779 - Apr Term 1780
dau. MARY JENKINS one shilling Sterling; dau. ELEZABETH TICE [?] one shilling
Sterling; grandau. EASTHER CHERRY one shilling Sterling; dau. JERUSHEA one
hundred Acrees on Goshen Swamp being a part of the Land Whereon I now Live
and the feathers of an ould bed; wife SUSANA the rest of the afforesaid
track Lying up the mill branch With the Improvements, my horses, Cattle and
hogs, Sheep and houshold goods
extrs: wife SUSANA, dau. JERUSHEA
wit: THOS. CHESSHER, JESSE BROCK
        signed: William ⟨mark⟩ Parker

413. PEARCE, SNODEN (CR.035.801.9)
12 Dec 1820 - Jan Term 1821
son WILEA Land on the Easte side of the new Roade after they death of his
mother in Cluding the mannor plantation; son SAMPSON all the land I percess
laying between the New Road & old Road after the death of his mother; son
HUGH all my Land laying over the old road on the West side; son ALEXANDER
the Bed he lays on and firneture dureing his lifetime & $25; dau. MARY $5;
son HUGH all they Stock of catle & hogs on my primises marked with a smove
Crop in the right ear I disclame; son WILEA one cow & calf, one 2 year old
Heffer marked with a crop & Slit half moon in the rite ear; son SAMSON one
cow & calf & 2 year old heffer marked with a crop & slit & half moon in the
left ear; wife CYTHE 2 cows & calves, one 3 year old heffer & one 2 year
old Heffer, one feather bed & furniture, all my plantation tools & plowing
teem, 10 Hogs
extr: DARLING DAUPHIN
wit: JAMES DAUPHIN, WM. ALEXANDER PEARCE JR.
signed: Snoden Pearce

414. PEARSALL, EDWARD (CR.035.801.9)
4 Oct 1836 - Jan Term 1837
wife ANN during her natural life time one third part of my Lands in valuation
including my dwelling & yard, Grist Mill, Cotton Gin, Slaves Frank & Beck
his wife & their Child Kitty & Jerry, my Ox Cart, Riding Chair & harness,
two Beds & furniture, two Horses, three Cows & Calves, ten head of Sheep,
four Sows & Pigs; son WILLIAM J. two hundred Dollars which he has already
recieved negroes Martha & Clara; son JEREMIAH negro Virgil which he now has
in his possession & Andrew; son THOM. U. one third part of all my Lands in
value after the demise of my wife & negro Alfred; son EDWARD O. one third part
of all my Lands in value after the demise of my wife & negro Garry; son
JOHN D. one third part of all my Lands in value after the demise of my wife &
negro Candace; daus. MARY & SUSAN A. negro Sam & his wife Isabel, Rachael
& Sophia and Executors to have power to make Sale of Sam in case he misbehaves
himself so that they think it would be beneficial to sell him; Negroes lent
to wife at her death to be equally divided between those of my Children who
are not entitled to my Land under this Will viz. WILLIAM, JEREMIAH, MARY
& SUSAN; daus. MARY & SUSAN a Bed & furniture; wife a Sufficience of my
Household & Kitchen furniture
extrs: friend JOHN CARR, JEREMIAH PEARSALL
wit: JOS. H. HICKS, W. O. CARR, JERE [?]
signed: Edwd. Pearsall

415. PEARSALL, HUGH (CR.035.801.9)
20 Jul 1839 - Oct Term 1839
wife MARGARET Slaves Buck & Warsaw and during her lifetime Polly and until
oldest living Child comes to lawful age or marries negro Anny, all the cleared
part of the plantation whereon I now live with priviledge of getting any
Timber that may be needed except the cutting of Turpentine Box Trees, two
Beds & furniture with all the rest of my Household & Kitchen furniture, my
plantation & farming Tools, my Gig & harness, my side Saddle & bridle, two
of my horses, four cows & calves, my stock of Sheep & Geese, my Ox Cart &
fifty dollars and she to be the legal owner in her life time of Slaves Luke
& Mary; sons JAMES D. & WILLIAM F. all my Lands on Bear Marsh purchased
of WILLIAM RHODES & BRYAN SOLLIS to be divided equally when oldest comes of
lawful age, one feather Bed & furniture each; dau. SARAH A. Lands lent to
my Wife after her decease, my Mahogany Tables, half dosen table & tea Spoons
each, one Bed & furniture; son JOHN H. eleven hundred dollars to be kept in
interest till he comes to lawful age, one fourth part of my negroes but as
he is partially deprived of the sense of hearing & speech, my Executors are
to hold said property in trust for his benefit and when he comes to lawful
age if Executors consider him compitent to manage his business properly they
to deliver the same to him; whole of my Negroes not given to my wife to be
equally divided among all my children as they come to lawful age or marry
till which time the Negroes to be hired & my Bear Marsh land rented and the
proceeds kept in Common Stock for the raising & education of all my Children;
my Stock, Waggon & my Crop of Turpentine be sold and proceeds put with what
notes & c I may have & my interest in trade with WILLIAM D. PEARSALL as a
fund; wife my clock & Watch, five Sows & pigs and a years support for herself and family
extrs: brothers JEREMIAH & II .IAM D.
wit: EDWD. PEARSALL, WILLIAM McGOWEN
signed: Hugh Pearsall

416. PEARSALL, JAMES (CR.035.801.9/A-376)
26 Sep 1812 - Jan Term 1813
wife ANN during her natural life three Hundred and twenty acres Pattented
by RICE EVANS which I purchased from DAVID MURDOUCK to include my dweling
house, a part of my Cleared Land and forty three acres of pine woods lying
in frount of the plantation I purchased of JOHN GRIMES pattented by JOSEPH
GRIMES, negros Jack, Betty & Eady, my riding Chear, harness and horse, all
my Household and Citchen furniture; sons EDWARD, JAMES, JEREMIAH, JO DICKSON,
HUGH & WILLIAM DICKSON all the Lands that I posses in this County and in the
State of Tennessee; son EDWARD one hundred Dollars with the three Negroes,
one horse, bed and other things I have given him by deed of Gift; dau.
MARY McGOWEN negroes Sal, Big Sam, Little Sam and Seal, sixty Dollars
togather with some other property given her that is not named; son JAMES
negroes Nancy & Arthur, one mare, one bed and one hundred and fifty Dollars;
son in law JAMES McGOWEN negroes Silvey, Bob & Bil, one bed and some other
articles already recieved; dau. ELISABETH negroes Caleb & Cate, one Hundred
and fifty Dollars, one feather bed and firniture; seven youngest children
ANNE, JEREMIAH, LUCY JANE, JO. DICKSON, HUGH, FERABY and WILLIAM DICKSON
negroes Old Daniel, Charles, Old Clow, Penney, Young Clow, Charlotte, Hagar,
Ben, Muro, Daniel, Old Phillis, Buck, Warsaw, Young Daniel, Sidia, Jacob,
Henry, Belford, Young Phillis, Rose, Flora and Simon; daus. LUCY JANE and
FERABY one hundred dollars each
extrs: sons EDWARD & JAMES & friends JAMES HALL & THOMAS MOLTEN
wit: S. GRAHAM, EDWD. PEARSALL, HENRY JOHNSON
signed: J. Pearsall

417. PEARSALL, JAMES (2-141)
18 Oct 1858 - Jan Term 1859
wife ANN use of all the lands whereon I now live west of my Road with the
avenue including all my buildings to my old field up a Ditch to the old new
ground fince to the cotton field fence and the big low field the marsh fence
so as to include my low Pasture and improved low grounds to JEREMIAH PEARCELL'
line with all the timbered land west of the Cypress run as her dower, negroes
Arthur, Virgil, Daniel alias Dick, Julia, Barbara & Grace & child Liberty,
Jackson, Polly and her children Martha and Sarah, two Horses, one rolling
establishment, five cows and calves, two ewes and lambs, Six Sows and Pigs,
one Yoke of Oxen and Cart, three Beds and furniture, all my household and
Kitchen furniture, One Loom and Gear, four Plows and Gear, the necessary
provisions for herself and family for one year, two hundred dollars in
cash, My Books I wish divided amongst my wife and Children; dau. SUSAN C
and son-in-law JAMES LARKINS one tract of land worth one thousand dollars,
boy Swan worth Six hundred dollars, girl Hannah worth four hundred dollars,
Cash advanced at Sundry times twelve hundred dollars, one bed and furniture,
one Cow and Calf thirty dollars which they have already recieved, negroes
Steuart, Jerry and Adaline all worth one thousand and Seven hundred dollars
all amounting to four thousand and nine hundred and thirty dollars; son
EDWARD my Molton Lands East of the Ward's Road with a Small piece I bought
of JOSEPH D. PEARSALL on Green pudding excepting a small piece adjoining
the Quinn lands south of the LUKE HUGGINS old place worth three thousand
dollars, boy Calvin worth six hundred and twenty five dollars, girl Clary
worth five hundred dollars, girl Rachel worth four hundred dollars, one
mare, Saddle and bridle worth one hundred dollars, one bed and furniture
and one Gun worth thirty dollars to the sum of four thousand six hundred and

fifty five dollars, also my watch; dau. MARY ANN and son in law OLIVER
GILLESPIE boy Howard worth six hundred and twenty five dollars, girl Rachel
and child Penny worth six hundred and twenty dollars, girl Mary worth four
hundred dollars, boy Allen worth three hundred and fifty dollars, boy Turrisman worth two hundred dollars, boy Alexander worth four hundred dollars with
Cash and notes advanced at Sundry times amounting to six hundred and sixty
five dollars, one bed and furniture, one Cow and Calf, one Sow and Pigs worth
thirty five dollars amounting to the Sum of Three thousand and three hundred
dollars and my will is that MARY W. GILLESPIE be made equal with SUSAN C.
LARKINS, MALINDA BONEY, LUCY J. MIDDLETON and MARTHA RHODES out of my Estate;
dau. MELINDA and COL. WRIGHT BONEY girl Sophia worth five hundred and fifty
dollars, boys Bill and Harry worth Eleven hundred dollars Cash and notes
advanced to the amount of twelve hundred and fifty dollars, one bed and
furneture, one Sow and Pigs worth thirty dollars amounting to the sum of two
thousand nine hundred and thirty dollars; dau. ZILPHA and husband DAVID B.
NICHOLSON boy Curly worth six hundred dollars, girl Matilda worth five hundred
and fifty dollars, girl Rose worth four hundred dollars, girl Elizabeth worth
six hundred and fifty dollars, cash advanced for land nine hundred dollars,
one bed and furniture, two sows and pigs, one Cow and yarling worth forty
dollars amounting to the Sum of three thousand Six hundred and ninety dollars;
son JOSEPH all the tract of land I now live upon worth Six thousand dollars,
boy Haywood worth six hundred and fifty dollars, girl Candace and her two
children Leah and Chloe worth Six hundred and fifty dollars, one horse,
Saddle and bridle, one bed and furniture, one Gun worth one hundred and twenty
dollars to the sum of six thousand nine hundred and twenty dollars; dau.
CATHARINE C. and Son-in-law DAVID J. MIDDLETON boy Lewis worth six hundred
and fifty dollars, girl Chloe worth four hundred dollars, girl Fanny worth
four hundred and twenty five dollars, boy Austin worth two hundred dollars,
girl Milberry worth two hundred and fifty dollars, one bed and furniture,
two Sows and Pigs, three Cows and Calves worth fifty dollars to the Sum of
two thousand Six hundred and fifty dollars; dau. LUCY J. NICHOLSON a tract
of land on Maple Swamp Known as the ROBBIN WILLIAMS land valued at one thousand
five hundred dollars, boy Alfred worth six hundred and twenty five dollars,
Girl Silva and child Jinny worth six hundred and twenty five dollars, boy
John worth four hundred and fifty dollars, girl Laura worth three hundred and
fifty dollars, one bed and furniture, One Cow and Calf, one Sow and Pigs
worth thirty five dollars, one thousand dollars in notes, the use of boy
Jackson one year amounting to the Sum of four thousand five hundred and eighty
five dollars and said LUCY J. having a son by the REV. JAMES L. NICHOLSON my
will is that the proceeds of said land which I have Since Sold and girl Laura
by the property of JAMES L. NICHOLSON JR. son of LUCY J. NICHOLSON as agreed
upon by DAVID J. MIDDLETON and myself previous to his intermarriage with the
said LUCY J. NICHOLSON and should JAMES L. NICHOLSON JR. die the property to
go to his mother LUCY J. NICHOLSON; dau. MARTHA widow of HENRY RHODES decd.
land lying on the East Side of Maple Run and west of the main Road Known as
the Williams Land, Grady land and Quinn Land and a Small piece East of the
Main Road and adjoining the Quinn Land I purchased of JA. D. PEARSALL South
of LUKE HUGGINS old place Containing six hundred and sixty seven acres valued
at three thousand dollars and after her death to all her children [not named],
Hagar worth two hundred and fifty dollars, Joanna worth four hundred dollars,
boy Bob worth four hundred dollars, boy Milo worth two hundred dollars, girl
Caroline worth four hundred dollars, one bed and furniture worth twenty

dollars amounting to the Sum of four thousand six hundred and Seventy dollars; residue of my negroes including those I have loaned my wife ANN set apart to make EDWARD PEARSALL,' JOSEPH PEARSALL, SUSAN C LARKINS, MARY A GILLESPIE, MALINDA BONEY, LUCY J. MIDDLETON and MARTHA RHODES as near equal in property as possible with every other description of property not devised or given away
extrs: son EDWARD, son-in-law DAVID J. MIDDLETON
wit: THOMAS J. CARR, JAMES DICKSON
signed: Jas. Pearsall
Codicil: 2 Jan 1859
I hereby revoke the disposition made of my boy Daniel; I loan to my wife ANN boy Daniel during her natural life and after her death said boy to go to my grandson JAMES L. NICHOLSON; children of my dau. ZILPHA NICHOLSON five hundred dollars in addition to the sum I have already given them
wit: BENJ. OLIVER
signed: Jas. Pearsall

418. PEARSALL, JOSEPH D. (CR.035.801.9/A-379)
2 Apr 1827 - Nov Term 1828
sister FEREBY all my Land in Duplin County if she marries & has a living child and if she dont marry and have a Child the Land at her Death to be sold and the money arising devided equally betwen my Brothers & Sisters; the balance of my proberty of every Kind sold & money arising equally divided between my Brothers JEREMIAH, HUGH and WILLIAM D. and Sisters ANN OLIVER and LUCY J.
extr: brother JEREMIAH
wit: ANN PEARSALL, SINGLETON HUGGINS
signed: Jo. D. Pearsall

419. PERCE, SARAH (CR.035.801.9/A-397)
3 Oct 1790 - Jan Term 1791
ISOM NORRES 6 head of Cattle, 1 bed and furnertur, 1 sow, 1 little whele, som spun truck and som to spin; SARAH BABY 2 Caps and four rows, 1 half of spons [?]; MARY wife of JESSE NORRES all the rest of my Clothing
extr: JESSE NORRES
wit: WM. McCANNE, JAMES MURRAY
signed: Sarah Perce

420. PETERS/PETTERS, SAMUEL (CR.035.801.9/A-395)
18 Sep 1783 - Apr Court 1784
son JAMES one hundred accors lying on the west Side of little Coharey after the death of my wife ANN, one cow and Calfve, one Bright Bay Mare, Sadle & Bridle, two sows and piggs, one Shot Gun; son SAMUEL one hundred accors lying on the East Side of litle Cohary Joyning NATHAN WILLIAMS, one Gray mare, Sadle and Bridle, one Cow and yearling, one Barren Cow, two Sows & piggs; dau. CHRISTIAN 30 wight of new feathears, two Sows and pigs, nien head of Gees; son JOHN one hundred accors with the Improvedments Lying on the uper Side of NATHAN WILLIAMS on the said side of little Coharey, one cowe and Calfe, one Sow and piggs; dau. ELIZABETH Nien head of Gees; wife ANN All the Rest of my perrishable astate in and out Doors and after her Death Equily Devided amongst the Children REBEACA, JESSE, ELIAS, DAMARIS of heir Body in my life time
extrs: wife ANN, WILLIAM BASS
wit: JOHN SIGERIST, RICHARD BASS, LEVI DUDLEY
signed: S. Peters

421. PHILLIPS, JOHN (CR.035.801.9/A-392)
5 Mar 1793 - Oct Term 1795
wife DOROTHY Possession of the Buildings Where I now Live and one third of
the Land and Plantation where I now Live on the South Side of the Groves Swamp
Dureing her Natural Life and then to my son THOMAS; wife DOROTHY negro Doll
and at her Decease to my daus. FRANCES & MARY; plantation tools, plantation
utensils, Houshold furniture and Cattle to remain with my wife for her natural
Life and then Equally Divided amongst all my Heirs; wife DOROTHY one Mare
Called Ball, one Feather Bed and Furnature; Remainder of my Horses and Mares
to my daus. FRANCES and MARY; dau. FRANCES negro Jenny, one Feather Bed
and furniture; dau. MARY negro Teener, one Feather Bed and furniture; son
THOMAS one hundred and thirty Seven Acres on the South Side of the Grove
Swamp where I now Live, negro George; dau. RUTH BEST negro Chelsea; son
JOHN negro Nimrod; son BENJAMIN negro Isom, one hundred acres at the Run of
the Grove Swamp opposite the mouth of the Huckleberry Drain; son JOHN all
that part of my land from the Huckleberry Drain to the mouth of Ashe Branch
Joining BENJAMIN for one hundred acres; sons BENJAMIN, THOMAS and JOHN to
equally share in the Remainder of my Land on the north side of the Grove
Swamp above BENJAMIN PHILLIPS place Called the Gore place
extrs: wife DOROTHY, son THOMAS
wit: JOSEPH DICKSON, WILLIAM RIGBY SER., WILLIAM RIGBY JUNR
signed: John Phillips

422. PICKETT, DAWSON (CR.035.801.9/A-383)
5 May 1829 - May Term 1829
wife ASENAH two cows & calves, two baron cows for beef, my blinde mare, two
fether beds steds & furniture, two plows, four weeding hoes, two grubing
hoes, two axes, one had saw, two jimblets, two augurs, one draw knife, one
chisel, two Iron pots, one skillet, one Dutch oven, one half Doz. siting
Chears, all my Crockery ware, three pewter basons, one dish and all the
spoons, one pare dog irons, one Loom & geer, one hand mill, one wooling
wheel & cards, one Large Chest, one table, one small tin trunk, one Looking
glass, one Clawhammer, one saddle & bridle, one Cart, three sows & pigs,
one hackel, one pare steelyards, ten two year old hogs & five year old do.
all the wooden ware, one meal sifter during her natureal Life then Equally
divided between her children DICY, LARKINS & DARKIS; wife ASENAH negro
Candice during her natural Life then to my son LARKINS; dau. DICY one Cow
& calf, one fether bead stid and furniture, one mulato girl Mary, one hundred
acres being half the tract known by the name of the Harel Land divided by a
Line running from Muddy Creek to the Land where I now Live, fifteen dollars;
son LARKINS negroes Dick, Sook, London & my half of the Sholar negroes,
one cow & calf, one yong baron cow, one shot gun, Land where I now Live;
dau. DARKIS THIGPEN mulato girel Martha, one Cow & Calf, one fether bead,
one hundred acres where She now Lives ajoining my dau. DICY; grandchildren
ELIZABETH & PENELOPEY SHOLAR one hundred and fifty dollars Each to be kept
in interest untill they come of Lawful age and they to be scooled on the
interest & should my dau. ANN SHOLAR have another child it to have fifty
dollars
extr: FRANK PICKETT
wit: SARAH GRANT, HEZEKIAH PARKER
signed: Dawson Pickett

423. PICKETT, WILLIAM SENR. (CR.035.801.9)
1 Jul 1840 - Oct Term 1840
wife HESTER remain in possession of and use all my Lands in Duplin & Newhanover
and all my Slaves until my Son WILLIAM R. or dau. MARY J. arrives at lawful
age or marries then my Lands & Negroes divided into three parts one share to
each of my said Children and at the death of my wife the remaining third in
her possession equally divided between my Son & dau.; wife HESTER all my
stock of Horses, Hogs, Sheep & Cattle on the Home & White Oak Plantations,
my farming & plantation tools, Carts, riding carriages, Household & Kitchen
furniture, Clock, Growing crop & provisions on hand; son FREDERICK negro
Isaac & Sarah, with sundry other property given him heretofore; son WILLIAM R.
my watch & Trimmings, my Rifle & Shot Gun; grandau. ANN JANE negro Mahala;
grandau. MARY JULIA negro Matilda; grandau. OLIVE negro Martha; grandson
JAMES negro Ben; grandson ANDREW J. negro Jerry; Cattle at Henderson's &
Jone's & my Guns not mentioned Sold; my money, Notes & accounts with proceeds
of the Sale be equally devided between my wife & children WILLIAM & MARY my
children's part to be kept at interest till they come to lawful age or marry;
Should one or more of my Negroes set off to my Wife & infant Children mis-
behave as to be unprofitable to my said family my executors are requested to
hire them out & if necessity requires sell such as one for the benefit of my
Wife & children
extrs: son FREDERICK, friend JEREMIAH PEARSALL
wit: WM. T. JOHNSTON, THOMAS BURTON, BASIL BURTON
signed: Wm. Pickett Sener

424. PIGFORD, TIMOTHY (CR.035.801.9/A-387)
24 Jun 1823 - Oct Term 1823
wife ELIZABETH Two Hundred and Sixty six acres including the plantation where
on I live with all the improvements thereon and after her discease to be
Equally divided Between My Children ENOCH, SARAH, ANN, RIGHT, MARTHA, JURUSHA,
JEAN, WILLIAM, ELIZABETH & ALFRED; part of a Tract Lying in Newhanover County
the Right of which Lies in my Brother SOLLOMON be sold and the money Convey
towards the payment of my debts, also one grey horse; Live stock of Cattle,
horses & Hoggs, poultry of Every description, plantation tools, household
Firniture of Every nature or Kind to wife ELIZABETH and after her decease
to be Equally divided Between my abovementioned Children; should Mortgage
of Negrow Peter Be paid at any time hereafter money to be Conveyed to the Use
of paying my debts and schooling my above named Children
extrs: DAVID WELLS, SOLLOMON PIGFORD
wit: J. B. LaROGUE, T. TEACHEY
signed: Timothy Pigford

425. POPE, THOMAS "of Halifax County" (CR.035.801.9/A-380/Halifax Will
Book 1 page 78)
4 Jul 1760 - Jun Court 1762
Youngest Son THOS. plantation whereon I now live with all the Land thereto
belonging; son JAMES all my Coopers Tools, one gun, and the Cow with all her
Increase that is now Call'd his; son OBEDIAH all my Black Smiths Tools, one
Cow and Calf, one Sow and piggs, one Gun, one disk, four Spoons; dau. SELEY
One feather Bed and furniture, one old Iron pott; wife CONSTANCE all and
every thing that I had with her whether here or else where to her only, the
third of the Plantation whereon I now live during her natural life; remainder

not Given out in Legasies be Equally Divided amongst my Children ANN CLARK,
THOS. POPE the ELDER, ROBT., PATIENCE BENSTON, MARY BAILEY, JESSE, JAMES,
OBEDIAH, THOS. POPE the YOUNGER & SELEY
extrs: sons WILLIAM, THOS the ELDER
wit: PHILLIP *P* BAILEY, RICH. *┼* BAILEY, JESSE *X* POPE, RICHD. JONES
signed: Thomas Pope

426. POTTER, DANIEL (1-8)
12 Feb 1831 - Feb Term 1831
wife [not named] all the land on the East Side of Sandy Run to the Maner
Meadow to Wallars line to RACHEL DAVIS line, One Gray Horse, One bed & its
Necssary furnetere, Six Siting Chairs, One pot & Oven, 1 Sow & Pigs, One Cow
& Calf, all the Crockery ware, 2 Tables; son DANL. land after wifes death;
son DALHAM all the land on the East side of the Ready Branch & Sandy Run
Begining at ROBT CARRs across the Bridge through the Meadow to Carters line,
two Cows and Calves, two Sows and pigs, 1 Pot; son WM. all the lands I bought
on the West Side of the Reedy Branch, 2 Cows & Calves, One Sow & pigs, One
Pot; son DANL. JR. all the land I bought of Bushee on the East Side of Maner
Meadow, 2 Cows & Calves, One Sow & pigs, One pot; daus. BEADY & ELIZABETH
200 Acres where MAJOR POTTER Now lives, One Cow & Calf each; ballance of my
parishables sold to Satisfy a Debt that I owe to CONSIDER BUSHEE
extrs: sons DALLAM & WM.
wit: JNO DAVIS, JOSEPH WALLER
                    signed: Danl. *X* Potter

427. POWELL, BRITTAIN (CR.035.801.9)
23 Aug 1838 - Oct Term 1838
wife [not named] all my stock of Cattle and hogs, house hold & kitchen furniture and Crop and untencels of ever Kind during her natural life after which
be equally divided between daus. MILLA JOHNSON and MARY C. BLAND; grandson
AMOS JOHNSON negro Brittain; grandau. MARGARET ANN JOHNSON negro Redick;
dau. MARY C. BLAND negro Richard; son JOHN fifty cents; dau. LANY BIVAN
two dollars; dau. ELIZABETH two dollars; dau. MARTHA two dollars; son
ELISHA One dollars; son ISAAC fifty cents; son JACOB fifty cents
extr: ALFORD WARD Esqr
wit: A. WARD, DAVID WELLS
                    signed: Brittain *┴* Powell

428. POWELL, FERABAY (CR.035.801.9)
6 Jun 1844 - Jul Term 1845
grandsun MARSILLEY BURNIM one cow and calf, one bead and furnitur, on chel [?]
and tobel; grandau. FERIBAY BURNIM four Head of catel, tw pots, one fryin
pan, one chess, one feather Bead and furnitur; grandau. NANCY BURNIM one
bead and furnitur; grandsun JOHN FUTEREL BURNIM thre head of catel; all my
Stock of Hogs and the ballance of my proprity Sold and Equal divided betwe
my Four aires
extr: Sun in law WILLIAM BURNIM
wit: JOSEPH B. HURST, JAMES B. HURST
                    signed: Ferabay *XI* Powell

429. POWELL, MARY (CR.035.801.9/2-13)
6 Mar 1847 - Apr Term 1847
son in law JAMES BLAND bonds I hold against him viz one note for Twenty two

Dollars dated the 24th December 1841, One bond for Thirty three Dollars dated
the 19th April 1845, One bond for One Hundred Dollars dated 24th April 1846;
grandson ISAAC Bonds which I hold against him One note for Forty six 60/100
Dollars dated the 24th December 1842 One bond for Forty three Dollars dated
26 January 1845 One bond for One Hundred Dollars dated 24th April 1846;
children ELISHA, ISAAC, AMELIA and JACOB One dollar each; I will to mysel
a decent barial
extr: WILLIAM R. WARD
wit: CHARLES PAGE, ELIZABETH   PAGE, MARY   POWELL
                                       signed: Mary   Powell

430. POWELL, PATRICK (CR.035.801.9/A-388)
22 Jul 1769 - 2 Aug 1769
oldest Son GEORGE land and plantation where I Now live When he comes to Age
and Not befor But the Rest of My Children [not named] Shall have an Equal
Share of Sd. land and Plantation to help them for a Muntenance to Such time
As he comes to Eage and then Sd. land and plantation Shall all devolve to
him; wife MARY MAGDELON One third of all My Moveable Effects viz Horses,
Cowes, Swine, Shepes And all other My Household Effects & furniture of Every
kinds Together with all my Debts Oing to Me with all Ampliments of farming
whatsoever; Other tow Thirds Equally Divided Amongst My four Childering
Now in being [not named] And likewise the Child that My Wife is Now big of;
it is my Will And I Order that my Wife and Childering Shall all live together
upon My Plantation to Such time As My Wife Shall Marey this She Shall have
No longer right to live here But My Plantation Shall be Employ'd to the
Munteance of the Childering to Such Times as My Son GEORGE comes of Eage;
it is my will that all My Childering And my Wife Make No Division but all
live together to Such Times as My Wife Should Marey Or that the Childer
Shall Come to Eage
extrs: wife MARY MAGDELENE & ALEXANDER HOLDEN
          ROBERT DICKSON Overseer and Garden to See My Childering Justly
          delt with
wit: JOHN DICKSON, CHARLES WARD, RICHARD MILLER
                              signed: Patrick   Powell

431. PROWSE, JOHN "Schoolmaster" (CR.035.801.9/A-398)
16 Jan 1791 - Jul Term 1791
wife ELIZABETH my Estate both Real and personal during her natural life or
widowhood and then the whole to my son THOMAS
extrs: SAMUEL BOURDEN, Soninlaw ISAAC SPENCE
wit: FRANS OLIVER, TIMOTHY SPENCE, JOSEPH   SCREWS
signed: John Prowse

432. PUMPHREY, SILVENUS "Planter" (A-399)
6 May 1778 - Jul Court 1778
wife ANN Neagros Pharoh & Mary, two horses with her riding and Bridels, maner
plantation and household furniture and Stock of all kinds So long She Remains
my widow; dau. NANCY Neagro Deno, two Cows and Calves, one cow and Earling
& three two year olds, one bed & furniture; if Neagro Mary Should have any
more Children my dau. SALLAH to have the first Live Child she Brings and the
Rest of hur incriase Be devied Betwixt my sons JOHN and JESSE; sons JOHN &
JESSE two hundred & fifty acres Belonging to the plantation; three youngest
Children JOHN, SALLA & JESSE three Cows and Calves a piece; son JOHN my gun &

Riding Sadle, one puter dish, one puter Bason & 2 plates; dau. SALLE one
feather Bed & furniture, one puter dish, one Bason & two plates; son JESS
on puter dish, one Bason and two plates
extrs: wife ANN, JAMES OLLINS
wit: GEORGE SMITH, SAML. ALBERSON
                        signed: Silvenus ʃ Pumphrey

433. QUINN, EASTER (CR.035.801.10)
22 Apr 1839 - Apr Term 1844
dau. CATHERINE negro George it being all my interest in the negroes of my
deceased husband DAVID QUINN
extr: neighbor ROBERT DICKSON
wit: JAMES DICKSON
                signed: Easter ✗ Quinn

434. QUINN, JESSE (CR.035.801.10/3-12)
30 Aug 1859 - Apr Term 1860
wife MARTHA negro Sarah; son WATSON F. all of my lands; dau. ESTHER GARNER
negro Grant; negroes Tom, Lize, Levi & Jim together with my Stock, crop &
provisions be Sold to pay my just debts and the balance to be equally devided
among all my children
extrs: son JESSE B., Soninlaw JOHN MAXWELL
wit: JAMES G. BRANCH, ARCHILAUS BRANCH
signed: Jesse Quinn

435. RAINER, STEPHEN (CR.035.801.10)
14 Jul 1842 - Oct Term 1842
wife [not named] land where on I now live, all my Stock of Catle, Hogs, Sheep
and one horse, also my Chekens and all my plantation tools of every kind, all
my House hold and Kitchen firniture and at hir decease to the hole of my
Heirs [not named] to devide amongst them Selves; residue to be sold by my
Sone MARSHALL including the Lands on the big branch, the old Mare and the
old ax
extr: Sone MARSHALL
wit: JOHN J. JAMES, CHARITY JAMES
                signed: Stephen ✗ Rainer

436. RHODES, ANN (CR.035.801.10/2-37)
8 Feb 1847 - Oct Term 1848
brother JOSEPH T. slaves Rebecca, Rose & child Luui, Chelly, Harriet and
Sarah; brother JOHN F. slaves Boston, Easter & child Bill, all my Land which
lies on Goshean Swamp and adjoins JOSEPH T. RHODES and JOHN F. RHODES and
formerly owned by WM HODGS Containing four Hundred and twelve acres; brother
in law JOHN SHINES and his wife sister MARTHA one Dollar each; all the Residue
of my estate sold and surplus over and above the payment of debts divided and
paid over to my brothers JOSEPH T and JOHN F.
extr: WILLIAM FARRIOR
wit: JOHN W. HALL, JOHN D. ABERNATHY
signed: Ann Rhodes

437. RHODES, BENJAMIN (CR.035.801.10/A-416)
16 Jan 1804 - Oct Term 1805
wife RACHEL negroes Roze, Daniel, Charlotte, all my Household furniture, my

142

stock of Horses, Hogs, Cattle, Sheep & Poltry, my Plantation tools Dureing
her Natural Life, also the use of my Plantation whereon I now life containing
One Hundred & fifty acres, negroes Peter, George & Franck; son JOSEPH T.
negro George at the death of his mother; son JACOB negro Peter at the death
of his mother; dau. NANCY POWELL negro Mingo; son JOHN F. land and Plantation whereon I now live after decease of his mother; grandson JOHN BROCK
one Hundred & fifty acres lying on the North side of Limestone opposite and
above Wallers Mill Except a part Sold to SAMUEL WHALEY; grandau. ELIZABETH
MILLER negro Franck after the death of my wife, Bed, bedstead and furniture
whereon I lie; negroes Charlotte & Daniel and all the remaining part of my
Estate after the death of my wife Equaly divided to my sons JOSEPH T. &
JACOB & daus. RACHEL NEWKIRK & NANCY POWELL, allso my grandaus. MARY & ANNE
JEAN, daus. of my dau. MASSEY BRICE decd. and there share kept in the Care
of my Executor until they become of the age of Twenty one years or are maryed
extr: son JOSEPH THOMAS
wit: NATHAN WALLER, JAMES T. RHODES
signed: Benjamin Rhodes

438. RHODES, JOSEPHUS [JOSEPH] THOMAS (A-421)
26 Jan 1816 - Jul Term 1820
housekeeper MARY WILLIAMS land whereon I now live and all the land on the
waters of Muddy Creek during her lifetime, negroes Anthony, Chelay and her
children Hariot and Squire, Two Horses, my stock of cattle and hogs, one
years provisions, my Beds, Bedsteads and furniture, loom, Springs, wheels,
plantation Tools, Household and Kitchen furniture, the work and use of negroes
Pompey, Philus, Ned, Lewis, Aleck, Jack and Jo; son JAMES THOMAS land and
plantation on Goshen, negroes Jupiter, Nell, Daniel, Beck and Hannah; niece
ELIZABETH BOSTICK negro Peggey; negro Arthur in possession of my brother
JOHN to labor for said JOHN F's wife and children; one Hundred acres on the
north side of Limestone bought at Sherrif's Sale commonly called the Murray
Place to brother JOHN FELIX and after his death to my nephew JOSEPH; negro
Gerewy wait in the house to my wife or housekeeper called MARY WILLIAMS:
son JAMES T. negroes Pompey, Phebe and Aleck after the death of my wife or
housekeeper; grandson [not named] negroes Lewis, Jack and Jo After the death
of my wife or housekeeper; grandson JOSEPH T. negro Gerewy After the death
of my wife or housekeeper also the land and plantation whereon I now live and
Two Hundred acres on Mudd Creek; negro Peter, his wife Heziah and their
children Pearce, Caster, Zilpha, Killis, Sam and Jinsey sold along with two
hundred and Ninety acres on Limestone and Every other Tract of land on the
waters of Limestone on the North side to pay debts and reside devided between
my nephews JOSEPH NEWKIRK, JOSEPH POWELL and JOSEPH RHODES; wife or housekeeper MARY WILLIAMS my stock of Sheep, my fowls, a yoke of oxen and cart,
the Gear and Slays belonging to the loom; son JAMES T. negro George and he
to take and support an old negro named Roze as long as she lives; wife or
house keeper MARY WILLIAMS my riding chair and harness, one mare, saddle and
side saddle; grandson JOSEPH T. Two hundred acres lying betwen Muddy Creek
and Limestone it being part of Four Hundred acres
extrs: brother JACOB R., ANDREW McINTIRE Esq.
wit: NATHAN WALLER, AMOS J. WALLER
signed: Josephus T. Rhodes

439. RHODES, MARY (CR.035.801.10)
19 Oct 1834 - Jan Term 1836
brother JESSE WILLIAMS negroes Squire, Dave and Hannah, 430 acres that he

now lives on, one horse named Tom; MARY JANE, dau. of MARY PICKETTE negro
Sarah, one bead, beadstead and furneture that I now lie on it to remain in the
hands of the mannager of this will till she arives at age; neace MARY PICKETTE's
Children slaves Misier & Jim; WM. DOSSEN son of JOHN S. PICKETTE one Cow &
yearlin; neace MARY PICKETTE one chest, two Iron pots, one tin kettle, one
dutch oven, one bead beadstead & clothing, one dozzen Silver Spoons half large
and the other half Small, three Hundred Dollars to buy a peace of land to live
on; neace MARY dau. of Brother JOHN WILLIAMS one bead, bead Stead and firniture; neace MARY dau of Brother LOT WILLIAMS one bead, bead Stead and firniture; brother JOHN WILLIAMS fifty Dollars; brother LOTT WILLIAMS fifty
Dollars; neffeues RIGHT, NICHOLAS & WM JACKSON Sons of WM HUNTER Desd fifty
Dollars to be Equally devided; rest of my property Sold and the ballance to
my Brother JESSE WILLIAMS
extr: JOHN FARIOR
wit: WM. COTTLE, BENGAMIN H. WALLER
                    signed: Mary   Rhodes

440. RHODES, SOLOMON (CR.035.801.10/A-407)
19 Dec 1799 - Jan Term 1800
wife SARAH my beds and all the furniture thereunto belonging; wife SARAH
& dau. RACHEL to Equally devide my Stock of hogs and Cattle, also my Household furniture and my dau's. dividend sold at six months Credit and money be
put at Interest; wife SARAH my Plantation Tools
extr: JOSEPH THOMAS RHODES
wit: BENJAMIN RHODES, JOSEPH T. RHODES
                    signed: Solomon   Rhodes

441. RINCHEY, ADEM (CR.035.801.10/A-404)
12 Feb 1789 - Apr Term 1791
grandson SAMUEL son of JOHN & MARGRET COX one half of all my Lands in The
Fork of Aleder & Maxwell Swamp Containing one Hundred acres; grandson JOHN
son of JOHN & MARGRET COX one Hundred acres in the Fork of alder & Maxwell
Swamps; child MARGRET COX my land a Bove for the Benefet of Her Lifetime;
dau. SEARAH all my Plantation that I now Live on Containing one hindred acres,
one Bed & Furnture, one Hors & Sadell, one Sabell [?], three Cows & Cives
Tow Sow year ould, one Half of all my hogs; my Three Sons & Daughter JOHN
COX, JOSEPH COX, JAMES COX & SERAGH RINCHEY all The Rest & Resedue of my
Movable Estate
extrs: JAMES GILLESPIE, JAMES MAXWELL
wit: HENRY MAWELL, HUGH MAXWELL
                    signed: Aadem   Rinchey

442. ROGERS, JOHN (CR.035.801.10/A-419)
31 Aug 1797 - Jan Term 1800
wife SARAH my stock of Hogs, Plantation Tools and household Goods, also the
Plantation whereon I now live with one Hundred and fifty acres; son JOEL
plantation after wife's decease; son ISAIAH one Hundred and fifty Acres at
my uper Corner Joining Taylors Lands and estending down the Swamp including
Swamp Land and piney woods; son ASA one Hundred and fifty Acres on my lowir
line on the Run of Goshen Swamp and extending up the Swamp to the Back line
in the piney woods; son DAVID Residue and Remainder of my Lands; dau. HANNAH
BROCK one Cow and Calf; grandau. MARY dau. of said HANNAH BROCK one Heifer

yaerling; son JOHN & dau. SARAH BROCK each of thim five shillings Current
Money; son WILLIAM five shillings;° dau. MARY SCREWS one two years old Hifer;
dau. ELIZABETH one Linnen Wheel, one smoothing Iron and after hir Mother's
decease one Bed and Firniture; wife Residue and Remainder of my Personel
Estate
extr: LAMUEL BOWDEN
wit: SOLOMON ⅄ BLIZZARD, FRANS. OLIVER
                              signed: John ⅄ Rogers

443. ROGERS/ROGGERS, MARY (CR.035.801.10/2-4)
26 Mar 1829 - Jan Term 1846
grandson WILLIAM BRIANT NETHERCUT all of my Estate
extr: JOHN NETHERCUT
wit: JOHN FAROR, LEWIS ⊥ WALLER
                              signed: Mary ⅄ Roggers

444. ROGERS, STEPHEN (CR.035.801.10/A-408)
29 Feb 1804 - Apr Term 1804
wife NANCY all my Real Estate & perrish able property an entry of Land
adjoining RICHARD BRADLEY be Secured for my wife; brother MARK has two
hundred & ninety one dollars in has hands if in case he Should deny it it
can be proved by THOS. BENNETT & wife & ELIZABETH McGEE & old Mr. WHITEHEAD
extrs: PETER CARLLIN, THOS. McGEE, JOHN HUNTER
wit: B. ARMSTRONG, ANCRAM AVERITT
signed: Stephen Rogers

445. ROGERS, WILLIAM "Planter" (CR.035.801.10/A-409)
1 Jan 1770 - no probate
wife COMFORD all my lands and Stock of Evry kind and all my household good
and working Tools for the Saport of hurself and my Childering She yealding
and paying to Each and Every of thim ELIAZER, WILLIAM, ZACHARIAH, ANNALINA,
ELISABETH & MARY the Sum of forty Shillings prock mony when they Come of age
and that She larn the Children to Read and Right if in hur power
extr: not named
wit: WILLM GOODMAN, WM ⊥ TAYLOR
                              signed: William ⅄ Rogers

446. ROGILES, TAMMEY (CR.035.801.10/A-410)
16 Sep 1827 - Nov Term 1829
dau. ZILPH B. HURST one Dollar; son STEPEN ROGERS one Dollar; son JOHN
ROGERS one Dollar; MARK ROGILES Childrin one Dollar Each; CHARLES ROGILES
Childrin one Dollar Each; dau. SARAH BURNS one Dollar; son ELISHA ROGILES
all my part of the property that fill to me from the death of my husband
MARK ROGILES, one feather bed and furneter, Eight hogs year oles, three head
Cattle and Cow and Calf, one heffer, one wheel and Cards, all my Crope as it
now Stands
extr: son ELISHA ROGERS
wit: KENAN MILLARD, ISHAM SOUTHERLIN
                    signed: Tammey ⅄ Rogiles

447. ROUSE, GEORGE (CR.035.801.10/A-418)
11 Feb 1810 - Apr Term 1810
wife RHODA My House and Plantation, hous and Plantation Furneture hir Life

time or widowhood with all my Stock of Cattle and hogs Except one Two year
old heifer I Bequeth to NATHAN's Son DAVID;   remainder Equaly Divided among
my three youngan Sons GEORGE, RUBAN & DAVID
extrs: JOHN CARRE, JOHN GILMAN
wit: JAMES ALLEN, JAMES ✝ HARREL
                          signed: George ⚬ Rouse
                                   Rhoda ⚬ Rouse

448. ROUSE, HENRY (CR.035.801.10/2-55)
19 Jan 1839 - Apr Term 1850
wife REBECCA During hir natural life time all my lands & as well also as all
of my parishable or whole property or Estate for hir improvement or consupsion
& mintianance; the boy [name JAMES MITCHEL is marked through here] now living
with me at the decease of my Wife one hundred & twenty Six acres containing
the house & plantation, my mare, also an eaqual Divid of all My perishable
property; DOLLY MITCHEL the Girl now living with me one hundred Acers of
land and an Eaqual Divide of all the parrishible Estate with hir afore sd
Brother JAMES Except the mare Especially Willed to him
extr: JOHN GREEN
wit: WILLIAM CHASTEN, JOHN CHASTEN
                          signed: Henry �H Rouse
N. B. JOHN CHASTEN and WM. CHASTEN By HENRY ROUSE request Be gardean
                          signed: Henry ⊢⊣ Rouse

449. ROUSE, PHILLIP (CR.035.801.10/A-415)
10 Oct 1784 - Oct Court 1784
son MARTAIN one horse, bridle and Sadle and gun, twenty five head of Cattle
Consisting of Cows, Calves and other young Cattle, ten head of sheep, two
Kittles, two falling axes, one bed and furnerture, two basens and seven
plates with all my Stock of hogs more or less, one hand mill, one pair of
Iren wegges, one plow; ELIZABETH my youngest Daughter two Cows and Calves,
six new plats, one set of tea Cups and sosers, one feather bed and furnerture, one fring pan, one mug
extr: not named
wit: EPHRAIM GARRASON, ADONIJAH GARRASON
                          signed: Phillip ℗ Rouse
PRESSELLAH MURPHY one pot, one bason, two plats;
BARBARY SHEPARD one shilling starling

450. ROUTLEDGE, NICHOLAS R. (CR.035.801.10/A-401)
13 May 1765 - no probate
wife ANNE the manner plantation whereon I now live with all my other lands
during her life and after her Death to be the child she is now big with,
negroes Lony, Isaac & Cate, all my creature Horses, cattle and hogs, all my
Household goods and furniture and plantation Tools;   dear child yet my wife
is now Big with negroes Jupiter, Priour, Seley, Sarah & Phebee but in case
the child should Die before it should come of age of maturity negroes to be
my wife and at her disposal
extr: wife ANNE
wit: FELIX KENAN, GEOR _____, CATHERINE ✕ KENAN
signed: Nicholas R. Routledge

451. ROUTLEDGE, THOMAS SR "in my Seventy third year" (CR.035.801.10/A-411)
10 Aug 1801 - Oct Term 1801
son THOMAS eleven hundred and three acres on Duck River in the state of
Tenessee reserving one third thereof to be given to JOHN DICKSON Esqr of
Cumberland in this state for his Surveying the said Land or the value thereof
if my Son should sell and dispose of same or Should DR. WILLIAM DICKSON dispose of it as he is impowered to do; grandson THOMAS son of THOMAS the
plantation on which I live containing in part two purchaces by estimation
three hundred & Seventy three acres, negroes Rachel & her Son Tom & Candice;
grandau. CATHARINE negro Diana and her son Peter; negroes Jack, Young
Pompey, Sam, Isaack and Fanny be hired for three years and the money arising
to support my son THOMAS' family and after the expiration of sd three years
five Negroes to my son THOMAS; old Pompey continued at the turpentine
untill the trees that are now boxed be fully done but if it should happen
that the turpentine not produce a sufficient profit he to be hired as the
others; dau. SARAH LEDDON two pounds in purchasing her a mourning Suit;
negro Boson in my possertion under mortgage from JOHN MACHET be hired out as
the others and money arising to be applied in paying debts; all my Stocks
of horses, cattle, hogs, crop, sheep to remain on the plantetion for the
use of my Son's family; son THOMAS two hundred acres lying on Persimmon
Swamp
extrs: son THOMAS, step Sons JAMES PEARSALL & EDWARD PEARSALL
wit: JAMES GILLESPIE, ANDREW McINTIRE, JOHN WILKINSON
signed: Ths. Routledge

452. ROUTLEDGE, THOMAS JR. (CR.035.801.10/A-406)
22 Jan 1825 - Oct Term 1825
uncle AARON MORGAN my plantation situated on the Grove swamp in special trust
and confidence that he will apply the rents and profits arising there from
to the Support and maintenance of THOMAS ROUTLEDGE and his wife MILDRED my
father and mother and after the death of the said THOMAS and the said MILDRED
I give the said Plantation to my three brothers NICOLAS, EZEKIEL MORGAN &
EDWARD PEARSALL; AARON MORGAN negro Clarissa in special trust and confidence
that he will apply the hire and profits arising from her labour to the support
and maintenance of sd THOMAS ROUTLEDGE and his wife MILDRED so long as they
live and then to my three sisters MARIAN, DORITHE PEARSALL and MARGARET
ELEANOR; negro John and all my stock of every kind sold
extr: AARON MORGAN
wit: JAMES W. MORGAN, THOS. H. WRIGHT
signed: Thos. Routledge

453. ROUTLEDGE, WILLIAM "Late of Wilmington" (CR.035.801.10/A-402)
8 Nov 1794 - Jan Term 1795
dau. MARY Ten Shillings; dau. ELLINOR Ten Shillings; dau. ELIZABETH Two
thirds of what my Estate may amount unto when she shall attain to the age
of Eighteen years or marries; dau. ANN WILLIAM EVANS the other one third
part of my said Estate for her particular Care in nursing me in my last Illness; aunt CATHRINE ROUTLEDGE my riding Chair and harness with a double
Seat which Mr. Jackson of Wilmington will deliver as an acknowledgement for
her Exhonary Care she has shewn in my Illness; if dau. ELIZABETH not live
to the age of Eighteen years or marrys then Two thirds to my uncle THOMAS
extr: uncle THOMAS
N. B. After the Death of my aunt CATHERINE and uncle THOMAS my dau. ANN

WILLIAM EVANS have my riding Chair and harness
wit: DAVID MURDOUCK, EDWARD DICKSON, EDWD. PEARSALL
signed: Wm. Routledge

454. RUNNELS, SHADRACH (CR.035.801.10/A-414)
26 Aug 1782 - Oct Term 1783
wife MARY Two Cows and Calfs, one feather bed and furniture and one Mare and
Colt; son ROBERT One Hundred Acres Lying on the west side of Bearskin Swamp
Joind JACOB CRUMPLER's Line, One Cow and Calf; son WILLIS One Cow and Earling,
One pot, Two Basons, four plates, One Dish, Ten Spoons
extr: WILLIAM BUTLER SENR.
wit: DANIEL COOR, MYAL TURNER, ELIZABETH **✦** PORTER
                                    signed: Shadrach **✝** Runnels

455. SALMON, WILLIAM (CR.035.801.10)
7 Jun 1816 - Jul Term 1818
dau. TABBITHA BROCK one Cow and no more; dau. MARTHA BRANCH one Cow and no
more; wife MARY all the rest of My property Lands, Stock of every kind and
houshold Furneture and tools of every kind
extrs: JOHN WATKINS Esqr., BENJAMIN BOWDEN
wit: JOHN JOHNSTON, BRINKLEY **✦** BLIZARD, LEAVIN **⊞** BROCK
                          signed: William **ᴎ** Salmon

456. SAMPSON, JAMES (P.C. 521.1 Benjamin Grady Collection)
27 Oct 1783 - Dec Term 1784
MARY Wife of WILLIAM BLUNT and Daughter of CALEB GRAINGER Deceased One Young
Negro Wench; all my Wearing Apparell to be divided amongst my Houshold Negroes;
negro Moll her liberty and freedom immediately upon my death as reward for her
long & faithfull Services; Mullatto Hannah dau. of the aforesaid Moll her liberty and freedom immediately upon my death as reward for her constant & deligent
attention to her deceased Mistress in her Illness & her great Care & attendances
on myself when sick; grand nephew JAMES son of my Nephew JAMES SAMPSON the Planta
tion whare on I now live called Sampson Hall (reserving the Burying Ground) containing about one thousand Acres bounded by lands of RICHARD CLINTON, GABRIEL
HOLMES, JAMES SAMPSON & Vacant lands, slaves Chloe, Joe, Darcy, Molly, Arthur,
Peggy, Johnny, Ben, Tommy, Statira, Billy, Candice, Betsy, Beckey, Aaron, Old
Toney, Polly, Juland, & Harriot, all the plantation tools whenever he may attain
the age of twenty one Years & not before But in case he should die before he
attains that age the same to go to the next surviving Eldest Son lawfully begotten
of my Nephew JAMES SAMPSON & on default of any such then unto any Dau. or Daus. of
the same JAMES SAMPSON may have But in case JAMES SAMPSON should die without any
lawfully begotten then unto RICHARD CLINTON; the Children of RICHARD CLINTON
[not named] the rest and residue of all the Slaves I may die Possessed of exclusiv
of Six Young Negroes (one half to be Males, the other half Females) to his dau.
ANN & the Remainder equally divided amongst the other Children of sd. RICHARD
CLINTON by his present Wife PENELOPE; RICHARD CLINTON my Grist Mill & the lands
thereunto belonging, all the Lots & Lands I may die possessed of in this state,
all my Smiths Tools, my Silver hilted Sword & Watch; nephew JAMES SAMPSON &
RICHARD CLINTON my Still Worm & Tub, Barrels & all other Utensils thereunto
belonging; executors if they think necessary to sell & dispose of all my Household & Kitchen Furniture, riding Carriages, Horses, Cattle, Hogs & Sheep to paymer
of my debt But in Case they shall not think it necessary I bequeath the same unto
my Nephew JAMES SAMPSON & RICHARD CLINTON; JOHN HAY Esqr. Five Guineas to purchase a Mourning Ring; RICHARD CLINTON all the rest & residue of my Estate Real
& Personal; I do request that my Nephew JAMES SAMPSON & RICHARD CLINTON should

live in Peace & Harmony
extrs: JOHN HAY, JAMES SAMPSON, RICHARD CLINTON
wit: JAMES M[torn], RICHD. BROCAS, LEWIS MOORE
signed: James Sampson

457. SCOTT, JOSEPH (CR.035.801.10/A-445)
20 Dec 1770 - Jan Court 1781
son JOSEPH one Doller; dau. JEEN CHESNUT one Doller; son JONATHAN all the
Stock that is at DAVID WALKENSONs Except the Stears that is from two years
old and upwards, Negro Will; dau. JERASHA one feather Bed and Sum furniture,
two Cows and Caffs; son NEHEMIAH Plantation that I now Live on and all the
Land that belongs to it, negro Jim, my Still; dau. PEGGY one feather Bed and
Sum furniture, Two Cows and Calfs; dau. ADER one feather Bed and Sum furniture, Two Cows and Calfs; dau. ASHEA one feather Bed and Sum furniture, Two
Cows and Calfs; dau. MARY one feather Bed and Sum furniture, Two Cows and
Calfs; wife [not named] negro Jinne and all the Stock that belongs to the
Plantation with Negro Jimmy for the Maintenance of the Children upon the
Plantation; all the Rest of my Estate Equally Divided Amongst my Nine Child-
ren JOSEPH, JONATHAN, NEHEMIAH, JENNE CHESNUTT, JERUSHA, ADER, ASHEA, MARY
& PEGGY
extrs: son JONATHAN, JONATHAN CARR
wit: JOSHUA CHESNUTT, MARTHA ✚ CHESNUTT
signed: Joseph Scott

458. SHEFFIELD, JOHN (CR.035.801.10/1-10)
28 Mar 1831 - May Term 1831
Just Debts paid out of my Perishable property and the Ballance to be Equally
Divided between my three Grendchildren EDITH, JOHN and WILLIAM Children of
JAMES SHEFFIELD EDITH to Inherit one half of all my Estate Real and personal
and JOHN & WM to inherit the other half when ever they arrive at the age of
Twenty one years; land be Sold & the mony thense arising to be divided
betwen EDITH, JOHN and WILLIAM EDITH to Recieve one half and JNO & WILLIAM
the other half
extr: WILLIAM SWINSON
wit: WILLIAM JOHNSON, MARY ✗ JOHNSTON
                                  signed: John ✗ Sheffield

459. SHEPARD, THOMAS JR. (CR.035.801.10/2-59)
29 Mar 1849 - Apr Term 1851
wife MARY JANE land on the Newbern road at DAVID SOUTHERLANDs line to the
black smith shop, round the negro graveyard to the Kenansville Road to LEBEUS
MIDDLETONs line to Forlaws line to STEPHEN HERRINGs line up the branch to
DAVID I. SOUTHERLAND's including my dwelling and all out buildings at the
cros x roads, thirty barrels of corn, twelve hundred lbs of bacon or eighteen
hundred lbs of pork, two hundred pounds of lard, two barrels of flour, sixty
pounds of coffee, one hundred pounds of Sugar as her Years provisions, all
my household and kitchen furniture, two ploughs, two Grub hoes, two weed
hoes, two axes, 2 iron wedges, four cows & calves, 2 Sows and pigs, 6 ews
& lambs, 1 cart or waggon, one horse, one Buggy & harness, negroes Boston &
Julia; dau. MARY ARMSTRONG negroes Louis, Joe & little Ben; grandau.
GEORGEETTA SHEPARD One Hundred dollars when she shall arrive at the age of
21 years; dau. CATHARINE KELLY negroes Liberty, Jenny Ann & big Ben; dau.
CAROLINE SOUTHERLAND negroes Louisa, Augustus & Isham; son THOMAS E. negro

Peter & my blacksmith tools; infant dau. SARAH ELLIS negroes Randolp & Mary,
six hundred Dollars, negroes Julia & Boston, household and Kitchen furniture;
executors ISAAC B KELLY and DAVID I. SOUTHERLAND Land I purchased of JAMES
LAWHORN in trust for my dau. ANN WHITFIELD and her children [not named] not
to be subject to the payment of any debts of her husband THOMAS W. WHITFIELD;
children of ANN WHITFIELD a note of hand on DAVID I. SOUTHERLAND of six Hundred
Dollars; residue of my property with negro Old Mary to be sold and land not
included in my wife's dower be rented out & the money applyed to the raising
schooling & clothing of my infant dau. SARAH ELLIS
extrs: ISAAC B. KELLY, DAVID I. SOUTHERLAND
wit: STEPHEN GRAHAM, D. GILLESPIE
signed: Thos. Shepard
Codicil; 26 Oct 1850
In as much as my Wife is pregnant the negroes I gave my dau. SARAH ELLIS
with a note of hand of Six Hundred dollars on JOHN CARR & JOHN GREEN and
fifteen hundred Dollars bee divided betwen my dau. SARAH ELLIS and my child
unborn
wit: STEPHEN GRAHAM
signed: Thos Shepard
Codicil: 27 Jan 1851
In as much as I have another child born I revoke the codicil of 26 Oct., 1850
and will that the negroes I gave my dau. SARAH ELLIS with a note of hand of
six hundred Dollars on JOHN GREEN and JOHN CARR and one thousand Dollars be
equally divided betwen my daus. SARAH ELLIS & CHARLOTTE on their arriving at
the age of twenty One Years
wit: D. GILLESPIE, STEPHEN GRAHAM
signed: Thos. Shepard

460. SHOLAR, LEVY (CR.035.801.10/A-454)
15 Sep 1822 - Oct Term 1822
my hole Estate be sold and when my Just debts are Collected son EPHRAIM one
hundred & seventeen Dollars, son ISHAM Seventeen dollars and after this an
Equal devision to take pleas between my three Heirs
extrs: sons ISHAM & EPHRAIM
wit: N. MURRAY, JAMES MURRAY JR.
                signed: Levy   Sholar

461. SHOLARS, SOLOMON (CR.035.801.10/A-435)
27 Oct 1824 - Nov Term 1828
son WRILEY my yong hors; son MOSES my yong filly; son JAMES the Coalt that
my mare is now in fold with; all my Children that is now with me [not named]
one Cow and Calf, one sow & pigs, two Ewes & Lambs & one fether bead; wife
MARY all my Estate in Land, all my Stock of Cattle, hogs & sheep & my two
oldest mares With my house hold & Kitchen furneture and plantation tools;
my Crop of turpintine to be Cared to Wilmington & Sold; at the Death of my
wife all my Land be sold & the money Equally divided between my five sons
[not named] and at the same time all my other property sold and devided
between my six Daughters [not named]
extr: son WRILEY
wit: WM   RICHERSON, F. P. H. KETH [?]
signed: Solomon Sholars

462. SHUFFIELD, JOHN (CR.035.801.10/A-427)
22 Nov 1790 - Jan Term 1791 [original missing from folder]
son EPHRAIM Eighty acres including the plantation he lives on being part of
a tract of two hundred and Fifty acres I bought of THOMAS GRAY and lying on
the third and fourth lines of the patent; son WILLIAM Eighty acres joining
the piece I give to EPHRAIM lying on the fourth and fifth lines of the paten;
wife ELIZABETH Residue of my lands together with the plantation I live on
and after her decease sold and the money arising eaqually divided between
my sons WRIGHT, ISHAM, BRYAN, WEST and ARTHUR and my wife's son WILLIAM
GRADDY; young sorrel mare sold and money arising divided equally between
my daus. NANCY SCREWS, POLLY, LOUISA, CATHARINE and TABITHA; wife ELIZABETH
remainder of my personal Estate to the raising and schooling of my youngest
children and after her decease sold and the money divided between my sons
and daus. WRIGHT, ISHAM, BRYAN, WEST, ARTHUR, NANCY, LOUISA, POLLY, CATHARINE,
TABITHA and my wife's son WILLIAM GRADDY
extrs: FRANCIS OLIVER, LEVIN WILKINS
wit: FRANCS. OLIVER, LEVIN WATKINS, WILLIAM ✗ HARRIS
                                        signed: John ✗ Shuffield

463. SIKES, WILLIS (CR.035.801.10/A-433)
31 May 1816 - Apr Term 1817
all my debts paids which I hope will be without Selling a Small Negro Boy
Called Fred now Living at CHARLES GIBBS the Said Boy I do Give Sincerely to
my Brother FREDERICK for Certain Reasons that I Could Render besides Brotherly
affections but Shall not as I hope all of my Relations will be Satisfyd that
my wish Should be fulfilled
extr: not named
wit: not named
signed: W. Sikes
proved by oath of BRYAN BOURDEN & ALEXANDER HERRING; THOMAS MOLTON named
administrator

464. SLOAN, DAVID "Planter" (CR.035.801.10/A-447)
1 Sep 1784 - Jul Court 1785
wife MARGRATE all my goods and Chattels, lands, house, Improvements, Hoursses,
Cattle, Hogs and Sheap, negras hir life; oldist Son JOHN one Shilling; son
DAVID Brown field and all that Belongs to it, one feather Bed and firniture,
one tow years hors, negro Mingo; son GIBSON the plantation whare I live now,
one feather Bed and firniture, negro Tome, one year old Colt; dautir MARGRAT
one feather bed and firneture, negro Lum; dautir SUSANNA one feather bed and
firneture, negro Frank; dauter POLLY BROCK negro Back
extrs: MARGRAT SLOAN, LEWIS BROCK, DAVID SLOAN
wit: ROBART STON, JACOB ⅋ BARNET, WILLIAM 𝓙𝓙 McCANNE
signed: David Sloan

465. SLOAN, DAVID (CR.035.801.10/A-430)
8 Jan 1801 - Jan Term 1807
wife ELEANOR use of my House and Plantation and all my Other Lands I am now
possessed of and after which they shall disend to my son DICKSON and dau.
CASSANDRA; wife ELEANOR negroes Davi, Silvia, my Young Bay mare, four Cows
& Calves the pick of all my pen, one good feather bead and furniture, one
third part of all my Hogs; wife ELEANOR during her widowhood My Buofat and

furniture which after shall devolve to my son & dau. DICKSON & CARSANDRIA and one feather Bead and firniture which shall devolve to my Children in manner above; son DICKSON & dau. CASSANDRIA all my Lands in the State of Tennessee five hundred acres part of 1000 Acres on Yellow creek Patined by JAMES MIDDLE-TON, five hundred Acres part of 2500 Acres Patined by DANIEL WILLIAMS on the head of Yealow creek, negroes Daniel about Ten years old, Isaac about Eight years old, Edmond about two years & a half old and Chancy about one Month old when said heirs comes of age or are Lawfully married, Two Hundred pounds in Money to be put to Interest by my Executors or laid out for two young Negroes
extrs: JAMES MATHIS, ANDREW THALLY
wit: not named
unsigned
proved on oath by James Dickson Senr & Gibson Sloan

466. SLOAN, DAVID SNR. (CR.035.801.10/A-425)
3 Oct 1820 - Oct Term 1820
wife NANCY and my Eldest son DAVID all my personal Estate to be used as they may think proper to Raise and Support the rest of my family and what is left to be Equal divided among all the heirs [not named] only one Cow and Calf to be given my grandau. SUSEY POWELL and that is to be reducted out of JOHN POWELL's share
extrs: wife NANCY, son DAVID
wit: SAMUEL EVANS, JACOB WELLS JUNER
signed: David Sloan Snr.

467. SLOAN, JOHN (CR.035.801.10/A-444)
18 Aug 1824 - Jul Term 1827
my Son and dau. JACOB BRYANT & his wife MARY half of all my land with the all of all my pirsonal or parishable Estate consisting of Stock of Various dis-criptions, all of all of my household & citchin furniture, the crop now on the Ground of Every discription with the plantation tools; son WILLIAM the other half of all my lands
extr: son in law JACOB BRIANT
wit: JOHN POWELL, JOHN McCANNE
signed: John Sloan

468. SLOAN, ROBERT (CR.035.801.10/A-547)
19 Aug 1834 - Jan Term 1840
son DAVID Manor Plantation on the North Side of the Run of Beaverdam, my plantation on the East Side of Maxwell Creek Joining OZBORN CARR, a piece of land on the South Side of Island Creek, my Cummings land on the South Side of the Run of Beaverdam; dau. MARY HOWARD all my lands in New Hanover County on Holly Shelter and Ashes Creeks together with the Mills and timber there-unto Belonging; dau. SUSANAH NIXON land on the South Side of the run of Beaverdam Known by the name of the Holden Survey and an entry Joining to it; all my Stock and other property Sold to fund a legacy for the children of my dau. MARGARED DICKSON Decd to wit ROBERT SLOAN DICKSON, BARBARY ANN CHAPMAN, WILLIAMS DAVID DICKSON, MARTHA DICKSON and EDWARD DICKSON also negro Rosella; son in law WILLIAMS DICKSON negroes Charles, Mary, John, Bill, Nance, Mariah, Luce and all of her children that She has heretofor had; son DAVID negroes Jim, Laney, Willis, Charles, Rhoda, Sam, Manirva, Temperance, Mariah, Aleck and Abram; dau. MARY wife of JAMES HOWARD negroes John, Daniel, York, Clarricy, Mariah and all of Mariah's children that she has heretofore had &

Jin and her children Anthony, Bryan, Ady & Alfred; dau. SUSAN wife of
WILLIAM NIXON negroes Garret, Ned, Henry, Pheriby and all of her children
that she has heretofore had & John, Dick & Hannah and her children Isham and
Sarah; after my death negroes Bill Lancaster, Joe Jr., Primus, Tom, Ephraim,
Muriah, Sall, Silvia, Nance, Joe Jr., Winsor, Ceasar and Isreal after the
portion of my dau. MARGARET's children shall have been made be divided into
four parts with one fourth part each going to my son DAVID, dau. MARY HOWARD,
dau. SUSAN NIXON and the children of my dau. MARGARET DICKSON
extrs: son DAVID, Son in Law WM. H. NIXON
wit: JAMES DICKSON, W. CARR JR.
                     signed: Robert 𝒮 Sloan

469. SLOCUMB, SAMUEL (CR.035.801.10/A-448)
23 Nov 1767 - no probate [original damaged]
wife MILDRED all my whole Estate During her Life and after her Death to be
sold and one third of the money I Bequeath to her of all Except the Lands and
that I will to be sold and all the Money Equally divided amongst my Children
[not named] and the Children's part to be Let out on Interest till they are
of age to Receive it
extrs: wife MILDRED, Brother JOHN CHAS. SLOCUMB
wit: JOSEPH SLOCUMB, ARCHD. CLARK
not signed

470. SMITH, ELIJAH (CR.035.801.10/1-14)
22 Jul 1831 - Aug Term 1831
wife NANCY my plantation and all my land, all my parishable Estate her life
time, then my parishable Estate be Sold money kept at Intrist for my Children ELIZA, ANDREW JACKSON and PENNEY SUZAN Children that I had by my last
wife
extr: wife NANCY
wit: DAVID WOODARD, OWEN ODANIEL
signed: Elijah Smith

471. SMITH, GEORGE JUNER (CR.035.801.10/A-437)
9 Mar 1799 - Apr Term 1799
wife NANCY five Cows and Calves, one Hors by the name of Rebel, one Mare by
the Name of Lilley, use of My maner Plantation and timber, Negroes Venus,
Charry & Abram, my Stocks of all kinds, all my household funiture and plantation
Tools During her Natrel Life; son JESSE two Hundred and Thirty Acres Being
part of Fore Hundred and Sixty Acres at the Back line and Runs to the Rivr to
be Divided By a Row of Markd Trees it being the part that includs the plantation,
allso Eighty Acres Between Sander [?] and Cabble Branches, the first live Born
Child that Charry Bears, one young mare, one Cow & Calf, one Shot Gun; son
JONES two Hundred and thirty acres the other part of the Before mentioned land,
the next live Born Child that Either of the wenches has, One Cow and Calf, One
young Mare; dau. NANCY negroe Luce, one Cow and Calf, one Feather Bed and
firniture; three youngest Sons BRYAN, GEORGE & DAVID one Cow and Calf a piece,
Two Negroe Children a piece of the wenches baring them; Negroes lent wife to
be Equally Dived Betwixt all my Children which I have Before mentioned after
her Decease; Rest of the property I lent her Equally divided amongst all my
Children; if Wife Dies Before my Children Comes of age Son JESSE Should keep
the Children and give them Shchooling and to keep Chana and Abram while the

Children Comes of Age and Son JONES to keep Venus and her Children untill my
Children Comes of Age
extrs: JOHN JONES Esqr of Onslow County, FREDERICK SMITH, son JESSE
wit: THOS. SHELTON, LOFTIS WORLEY
signed: George Smith Jener

472. SMITH, HENRY (CR.035.801.10)
7 Feb 1843 - Apr Term 1845
dau. JENNET WILLIAMS fifty cents; wife CATHERINE all the rest and residue
of my property of every discription and kind whatever
extr: wife CATHERINE
wit: JOHN SWINSON, JAMES DICKSON
signed: Henry Smith

473. SMITH, JONES (CR.035.801.10/1-22)
15 Mar 1832 - May Term 1832
wife [not named] my plantation where I live and Negroes Tener, Hanna, Worrick
& Bill, all my household furnitue, Stock of Cattle, hogs, Sheep, all my Stock
of horses and at her Death all sold but my land and Equelly DiVided between
my Children Expect negroes Worrick and Bill and them to be long to my Sons
JOHN and JONES; dau. NANCY negro Ginney; dau. MARY negro Sarah; dau.
ELIZABETH negro garl bought from Sell of my property; sons JOHN and JONES
Lands and mill on panter Swamp, lands from the green pond and to the first
prong of Cabbin branch and ballance of my piney woods land joining Messor [?]
Lands with the line to BRYAN SMITH land; dau. SUSEY JANE negro Hanner after
wife's Death; sons EDWARD and JONAS my plantation Where I live after my
wife's Death and the piney woods up to the green pond; son GEORGE five
Shillings; son JAMES my mill Stones now at the rock where they ware Cut,
also a new mill form and to be put to grinding to the panter Creek mill;
wife to have the Use of the panter mill her lifetime
extrs: sons GEORGE & JAMES
wit: O. O'DANIEL, BRYAN SMITH SENR.
                        signed: Jones   Smith

474. SMITH, ROGER (CR.035.801.10)
11 Jan 1794 - Jan Term 1795
father JOHN one horse, two Cows and earlings, one gun, Two Sows and pigs,
three head of Sheep, one pot, one chest, one ax; mother SARAH one mare,
five head of Cattle, three head of Sheep, five barrels of Corn, one bed and
furniture, one pot, one ax, one case; the rest of my household furniture
equally Divided between the two
extr: mother SARAH
wit: RICHARD HART, JAMES   MOODY, ELESABIT   KERNEY
                        signed: Roger   Smith

475. SMITH, ZACCHEUS SR (CR.035.801.10/3-80)
30 Jan 1856 - Oct Term 1863
son ZACHEUS plantation in New Hanover County purchased of THEOPHILUS SWINSON,
my EDWARD A. HOUSTON plantation on Buckskin, negro Allen, two Cows & calves;
son ABIJAH negro Morris, five cows & calves, half my Stock, hogs; son IVY
all my lands on which I reside, negroes Joe, Linday & Arch; four Cows &
Calves, one half of all my Stock, hogs, one horse named Tom, one bed &
furniture, one hand mill, one set Black Smiths tools, one half of my household

154

furniture, one half of my kitchen furneture, all my farming tools, Carts &
wagons; dau. LUCY DAVIS Lot. No. 38 in the Town of Saracta; dau. CLARISSA
negro Priscilla, one black mare named Trimmer & Cold Tredwell, one yellow
mare named lightfoot, four cows & calves, one bed & furniture, one half of
all my household furneture, one half of all my kitchen furniture, one Buggy;
grandson MARTIN F. two cows & calves; balance of my property, Stock, provisions on hand & every other article of every description equally divided
between my four children ZACHEUS, ABIJAH, IVY & CLARISSA
extrs: sons ZACHEUS JR. & IVY
wit: JOHN R. MILLER, A. O. GRADY
signed: Zaccheus Smith Ser
Codicil: 7 Apr 1863
grandson MARTIN F negro Ervin about 4 years of age & Son of Linday and her
other child Roda about 2 years of age to my son IVY, Hannah about 7 months
old, daughter of Priscilla to my dau. CLARRISSA
wit: D. H. SIMMONS, A. O. GRADY
signed: Zaccheus Smith Ser.

476. SNELL, JAMES "Planter" (CR.035.801.10)
4 Aug 1762 - Aug Court 1762
wife ELISABATH negro Nat, my horses and mars, my Catell and my hogs, my bed
and furneture, all the rest of my house-hold goods and furneture; the Child
that my wife is Now big with negro Ben and if the Child doth die before it
Comes of age Negro to go to my brother ROGER; the Child as my wife is Now
Big with one Hundred and fifty Acors Ling one ye East Side of the Six Runs
Swamp below ABRAHAM HERRINGs joining ABRAHAM HERRINGs Land; brother ROGER
negro Lue, all the Rest of my Estate that is now in my Mothes [not named]
hands
extrs: ROGER SNELL, GEORGE BILL
wit: WILLIAM BYRD, JOHN YARBROUGH, ANN [mark] WILLIAMS
signed: James Snell

477. SNELL, ROGER (S.S. Wills/DRB2)
27 Oct 1758 - 2 Jun 1759
son JAMES Negro Boys Ben and Nat, one hudred and fifty acors lying one the
East Side of the Six runs [torn] ABRAHAM HERRINGs, one feather bed and furniture, one gun, Negro Lue after my Wife's Deceas, my Carpenters and Sue makers
tools; dau. PARTHENY negroes Sezer & Lonon, one feather Bed and firnitude;
son ROGER Negroes Andrew, Green & Harry, one feather bed and furnetude, my
plantation where one I now live with one hundred acers of Land there to
Belonging, one Rifel Gun, one Set of Coopers tools; wife ANN Negroes Lue,
Betey & Bes, all the Rest of my goods and Chattels and house furniture and
after her deceas to be disposed of in manner as follows; dau. MARY KING
negro Bes; dau. REBACA HERRING negro Betey; son in law ABRAHAM HERRING
one hundred and fifty acers of Land with the Plantation he now lives one;
dau. ANN KING negro Need; all the good and Chattels and hoas furneture as
I have lent my wife at her deceas to be Equally devided betwen Sons JAMES &
ROGER & dau. PRITHANEY; son in Law MICHAEL KING all my Lands that is Not
her before mentson
extrs: MICHAEL KING, GEORGE BILL
wit: JOHN KING, JOHN CANEDAY, JESSE BELL
signed: Roger Snell

478. SNOW, WILLIAM "Trader" (CR.035.801.10/A-434)
22 Feb 1762 - Apr Court 1762
friend WILLIAM PITMAN àll my houshold furnature & Plantation tools; wife
[not named] one third of my Estate; daus. ELISABETH & MARGRET ye other two
thirds of my Estate
extr: WILLIAM PITMAN "Trader"
wit: A. ROUTLEDGE, JAMES BRYEN
signed: Wm. Snow
Codicil: 27 Feb 1762
white Linin to be Purchased for 8 Masons to attind my funaral and Gloves &
Other nesesarys for sd. purpose as my Earnest wish & Desire is that I may be
Intar'd In a Masonik manner
wit: A. ROUTLEDGE, JAMES BRYEN
signed: Wm. Snow

479. SOLLIS, BRYANT (CR.035.801.10)
25 Sep 1851 - Apr Term 1857
wife NANCY whole of the land that I now possess and on which I now live with
my dwelling house and all out houses, negroes Moses, Sarah, Needham, Bob &
Boston and at her death or marriage negroes to go to my sons LUTHER B. &
BENAJA; wife NANCY all my beds and bed clothing, house hold and kitchen
furniture, farming tools of every description, all the domestic fowls and
poultry with all my horses and stock of every description, one ox cart, one
horse cart, one buggy, all the crop growing on my plantation where I now live
and all the provisions on hand; PHERABA JONES a piece of land taken off the
land I purchased of EDWARD O. PEARSALL beginning at the public road near the
corner of the fence to the head of the bottom near thee house whare she now
lives to Pearsall's back line to Poley Bridge Branch to the public road for
her lifetime and then to her dau. CLARISSA forever; CLARISSA JONES one
hundred dollars for schooling & c.; SENY A. BOURDEN peice of land beginning
at PHERIBA JONES's first corner on the Pearsall line to a branch near JESSE
SWINSON's at the mill branch to Wilsons corner to JESSE FLOWERS line to the
big Mill branch to Poley Bridge Branch for her lifetime then to SARAH ELIZA-
BETH   BOURDEN forever; SENY A. BOURDEN negro Mary for her lifetime and
then to SARAH E. BOURDEN; SARAH E. BOURDEN one hundred dollars for schooling
& c.; all notes and money to be kept at interests untill oldest son LUTHER
arrives at age of twenty one and then divided between my two sons LUTHER B
& BENAJAH
extr: WILLIAM H. TOLAR
wit: WM H. TOLAR, JESSE   FLOWERS
                        signed: Bryant   Sollis
Will was contested by WILLIAM W. BOWDEN and wife ANN A. Jury consisting of
SALATHIEL UZZELL, THOMAS B. HEATH, WILLIAM OUTLAW JR., WILLIAM R. WARD,
DANIEL TEACHEY SR, CHARLES PAGE, MICHAEL SAVAGE, SHERWOOD GRADY, DAVID H.
SWINSON, OWEN STROUD, NICK HALL & HUGH FARRIOR ruled it to be the last will
& testament of BRYAN SOLLIS & ordered it recorded

480. SOUTHERLAND, ROBERT (CR.035.801.10/A-541)
22 Aug 1833 - Oct Term 1835
son WILLIAM B. the whole of my Lands and plantation whereon I now live;
dau. ELIZABETH SEWELL negro Penny; negro Isom in care of my son DAVID to be
hired out yearly to Suport ZILPHA SOUTHERLAND and her Family till her youngest child comes of age; Remaining part of my Estate to Be Sold and Equeally

devided Between DAVID SOUTHERLAND, NANCY MALLARD, WILLIAM B. SOUTHERLAND and
ZILPHA SOUTHERLAND
extrs: DAVID SOUTHERLAND, WILLIAM B. SOUTHERLAND
wit: OWEN BISHOP, HILLORY BISHOP
signed: Robt. Southerland

481. SOUTHERLAND, THOMAS (CR.035.801.10/2-67)
16 Sep 1851 - Oct Term 1851
my interest in negroes Mornay, Jim, Drivder, Mary, Leah, Jack & Mariah
together with my live Stock of Horses, Cattle and hogs and house hold
furniture be equally divided among my brothers and Sisters [not named]
extr: not named
wit: NEEDHAM W. HERRING, J. M. MIDDLETON
                          signed: Thos.   Southerland

482. STALLINGS, JOHN (CR.035.801.10/A-441)
16 Feb 1815 - Apr Term 1815
wife ANN all that part of the land whereon I live that lies on the East
side of Ben's Creek & whereon my dwelling house stands, negroes Bigg Owen,
Patt's Jim, Kater & her children & Nance, five cows & calves, six sows &
piggs, twenty two year old hoggs, my cart and one yoke of Oxen, my horse
called the Bludworth horse, my mare called the Simmons mare, two Feather
beds, bed steads and furniture, two potts, one pail, piggin, churn and Tub,
all my plates, knives and forks & all my cups & saucers, one Chest, one
Table, a set of chairs, my riding chair and Harness, four Bee hives, two
ploughs and geers, two weeding hoes, 2 Axes, one hand saw and fifty dollars
in money and one years provisions laid off to her the year after my decease
by a committee appointed by the court; sons KEDAR & JOSIAH all my lands
except the land that came by wife; sons KEDAR & JOSIAH & dau. ANNE JANE
negroes Burrel, Stephen, Bill, Jesse, Jack, Arthur, Lewis, Aberdeck, Abram,
little Jim, little Owen, Chloe, Luce, Agg, Jane & Susey to be devided when
one of them arrives to full age unless my dau. should mary before Either
of my sons should arrive to age; sisters JANE & ELIZABETH negro Cussa which
is now at my Father's [not named]; executor to purchase of JOHN DICKSON agent
for a land speculator thirty two acres of land and also patten seventy five
Acres which I have given a bond for a title to JACOB FUSSEL; executor to
rent out the place which I myself have rented for the term of five years
belonging to Estate of AARON WILLIAMS decd for the same term of years;
residue of property with the Tarkiln & the Tarkiln on the land at home to
be Sold to pay my Just Debts and the residue divided among my three children
extrs: brother WILLIAM STALLINGS, JOHN BRYAN
wit: JOS. BRICE, THOMAS WILLS
signed: John Stallings

483. STALLINGS, MESHACK (CR.035.801.10/A-450)
4 Jun 1803 - Apr Term 1827
wife WINIFRED the house and plantation on which I now live including several
small tracts of land adjoining and all my other land included, with all my
household goods and chattels, plantation tools, negroes Sam, Pleasant &
Juda, my stock of Horses, cattle and Hogs, a mill with six Acres Joining to
be possessed by her until my son HIRAM comes of age; son SHADRACH 20 shillings;
son HUGH 20 shillings; son HIRAM 585 acres near the mouth of Rockfish and the
Mill and 6 acres when he comes to the age of 21; son WILEY all my other lands

including house and plantation; all my other property equally divided between
my children ALEY, CLARIY, RHODA, WINIFRED, HIRAM & WILEY
extrs: wife WINIFRED,\JOB THIGPEN, JOHN FARRIOR
wit: ROBT. PATE, JOHN BONEY
signed: Meshack Stallings
Codicil:
one acre of land on the South Side of Rockfish to belong to the dowry with
the mill

484. STANFORD, JONATHAN D. (CR.035.801.10/1-52)
10 Jun 1834 - Jul Term 1834
"but temporarily at Fayetteville in the County of Cumberland"
mother MARGRET besides the right to dower to which she is entitled in all my
real estate, an equal share in all my land & property; my lands & property
divided between my brothers & sisters NANCY STEVENS, ELPENICE MOORE & ELEANOR,
MARGARET, COLISTA, SAMUEL, ALEXANDER & THOMAS STANFORD; CATHERINE dau. of
JAMES HOLMES decd. five hundred dollars
extr: brother THOMAS
wit: SIMEON COLTON, COLIN SHAW
signed: J. D. Stanford

485. STANFORD, MARGIT (CR.035.801.10/2-133)
13 Sep 1855 - Apr Term 1858
negroes Pompey, Dave & Tony to be sold, also my yoke of Oxen, Cart & horse
Jupiter and One hundred dollars each to my sons SAML, ALEXR T., and heirs
of THOMAS and my dau. ELPENICE MOORE and fifty dollars to my grand dau.
CALESTA MATHIS and should there be a remainder it to be equally devided
between my daus. ELEANOR & MARGARET; daus. ELEANOR CHESTNUT and MARGARET
MATHIS all of my land so that ELEANOR's part shall comprehend all the Cleard
land; daus. ELEANOR & MARGARET all my Cattle; grandau. COLISTA MATHIS my
mare Sally; all my other property sold and moneys be equally divided between
my daus. ELEANOR CHESTNUT and MARGARET MATHIS
extrs: OZBORN CARR, OWEN R. KENAN
wit: JAMES DICKSON, EVERITT HERRING
signed: Margit Stanford

486. STANFORD, SAML. SENR. (CR.035.801.10/1-38)
10 May 1833 - May Term 1833
wife MARGET slaves Mulatto Yellow Dave, Lunar & her son Toney, Jack, Pompe
& Hannak, two horses at her choice, three ploughs & gear, Cart & oxen, one
half of the House hold & kitchen furniture, the riding chair and harnass,
four Cows and calves, four sows & pigs & eight head of sheep, negro Alley,
negroes Jack & Pomp is to help to raise the young Negroes and support the
family; dau. NANY STEPHENS negroes and property she has already in possession
and negro Jim to be hired out untill she has an appertunity of removing him;
dau. ELPENICE MOOR negroes and property she has already in possession and
negro Caesar to be hired out until she has an appertunity of removing him;
son SAML. land deeded to him and other property he has already in possession,
negro Kenan; son ALEXANDER land on which he now lives & other property he
has in possession, negro Washington; son THOMAS land and other property he
has in possession, negro Bryan; dau. ELEANOR negro Doll and her children,
a bed and Furniture, two Cows and calves; son JONATHAN my plantation on

which I live and negro July & two hundred dollars; dau. MARGARET negroes
Mary, Minerva & Mary's three children Pomp, Sara and Adeline, a bed and
Furniture, two Cows & calves; dau. COLISTA negroes Avy, her son Lot, Nixon
& Polly, a bed and Furniture, two cows and calves; twenty five dollars to
the Missinary Society of Raleigh; twenty dollars to the Bible Society of
Duplin County; five dollars to purchase books for the sunday school of
Grove academy; River plantation to be sold; residue of stock, Horses,
Cows, Sheep and Hoghs, Smith tools, Wagon, cart, oxen, plantation tools,
Household and Kitchen furniture to be sold and an equal distribution be
made among all my heirs
extr: not named
wit: THOS SHEPARD, WM K. FREDERICK
signed: Saml. Stanford Senr.

487. STOAKES, WILLIAM (CR.035.801.10/C-43)
30 Aug 1835 - Nov Term 1835
wife HELON my plantation, farming utensils, Household & Kitching Furniture
and Stock, porperty of every kind; wife HELON negroes Lot, Mike, Shade,
little Lot, Sarah, Mima & Kitty & when she departs this life the land to be
equally divided between my two youngest children JAMES G. & PRISCILLA ANN;
grson WILLIAM KINSEY STOACHES negro Tener; son JOSEPH twenty Dollars; dau.
NANCY WELLS negro Cloe and all her children Ervin, Violet, Isaac, Henry,
Sarah, Salter, Roger, Rose, Jim & Jerry; dau. MARY JAMES one bed and furniture she having received her share by deed of gift already; dau. ELIZABETH
WELLS negroes Chany and her two children & Lewis; son JAMES G. negroes
Jim & Margaret; dau. PRISCILLA ANN one bed and furniture she having received
her share by deed of gift already
extrs: son JAMES G., BONEY WELLS
wit: ANDREW STOAKS
signed: William Stoakes

488. STOKES, ANDREW (CR.035.801.10)
16 Oct 1837 - Apr Term 1838
dau. JAIN negro Abrem, two beds and furniture; dau. ELIZABETH negro Teanah,
two beds and furniture; what property I may possess at the time of my death
Sold and money equally divided betwen my daus. JAIN and ELIZABETH
extr: JOSEPH STOKES
wit: ROBART STOKES, HENRY ✝ STOCKES
signed: Andrew Stokes

489. STROUD, LUTSON JUR (CR.035.801.10/A-429)
22 Aug 1798 - Oct Term 1798
All the property that I possess at this time of all Kinds Be Sold and Remd.
of Money Equally Divided Between my wife HANNAH and Four of my Children
LEWIS, SELAH, WINNEY and ISAAC As ZILPHA and ABEL CROOM STROUD has all Read
had ther part; sons LEWIS and A. CROOM to have one years Schooling a piece;
son ISAAC and dau. WINNEY to have one year and a half Schooling; wife HANNAH
to have the Chance of living on the place whereon I now live until my son
ABEL C. Comes of age But not Clear any more land and if She Dont live on it
it to Be Rented Out and the money for my Son A. C.
extrs: brother ARTHUR, JOHN MAXWELL
wit: THOS. SHELTON, STEPHEN SMITH
signed: Lutson Stroud Jr.

490. SULLIVAN, DAVID (CR.035.801.10/A-451)
25 May 1778 - Jul Court 1778 [original very hard to read]
dau. ANNIE one Cow and Calf and Yearling, one Mair Colt and one Feather bed;
dau. ELIZABETH one Cow & Calf & Year old heiffer and feather bed and one
3 year old Mair Known by the Name of Poney, all the land I bought of my Son
JOHN Known by the name of the pell place; dau. MARY and husband ALEX SANDERS
Six head of Cattle now in their possession the land I bought of DAVID HERRING
and of GEORGE OUTLAW above it only my wife MARY to have her priveledge on the
land during her lifetime then land to be Valued by JOHN WINDERS and CAP. CHAS.
WARD and the Seventh part to remain in my estate and ALEX SANDERS to pay
executors to devide it betwix my daus. ANNIE and ELIZABETH; ELETEAH OUTLAW
and sun JOHN one Young Cow and Calf; son OLIVER one Young Cow and Calf;
son GRANT one Young Cow and Calf; remainder of estate to wife and at her
deceas to sons JOHN, EDWD., WM. and ANES
extrs: sons JOHN & WM.
wit: CHARLES WARD, THOMAS HOOKS, JOHN   KERR [?]
                                          signed: David X Sullivan

491. SULLIVEN, JAMES (CR.035.801.10/2-28)
1 Jan 1848 - Apr Term 1848
wife SALLY all the lands I now possess; son JAMES my shot gun and one
feather bed & furniture; wife SALLY all the other property I may die Siezed
or possessed of Consisting of Horses, Cattle & stock & furniture & farming
tools of all Kinds; in the event of my widows marriage property loaned to
her sold and the proceeds equally divided between my daus. SUSAN, FANNY,
SALLY, KITTY & ZILPHIA; my four single daus. one bed & furniture each
extr: wife SALLY
wit: JAS. G. DICKSON, J. SWINSON
signed: James Sulliven
Codicil: 12 Feb 1848
negroes Penny, Jerry, Rachel, Edney and Ned to my wife Sally and after her
death to be Sold and the proceeds Equally divided among all my children
ELISHA, SAMUEL, HENRY, JAMES, SUSAN, SARAH, KITTY & ZILPHA & FANNY JONES
wit: D. JONES, W. J. KORNEGAY
signed: James Sulliven

492. SWINSON, JOHN SNR (CR.035.801.11/2-122)
2 Feb 1857 - Apr Term 1857
dau. NANCY Fifteen hundred dollars; sons JESSE, ERASMUS, ANDREW and BUCKNER
my Plantation lying on the south Side of Goshen adjoining DR. THOS. HILL &
DANIEL SWINSON on which I now live with this condition that they Shall be
bound in a bond to let my daus. NANCY, MARY SUSAN and SARAH VIRGINIA have a
home in the house and on the Plantation where I now live untill married;
as I have paid one thousand dollars for the land whereon my son DAVID H. now
lives and have given my plantation on which I now live to my four youngest
sons it is my wish that GEORGE S., ROBERT, MARY S. and SARAH V. SWINSON have
one thousand dollars each; all the negroes be equall divided between all my
children; all my Stock, crop, Plantation tools, household and kitchen
furniture be sold and money equally divided between my children
extr: son GEORGE S.
wit: JAS. W. BLOUNT, JAS R. HURST
signed: John Swinson

493. SWINSON, JOHN A. (CR.035.801.11/1-41)
23 Feb 1833 - Aug Term 1833
wife ELIZABETH my plantation lying on the South Side of the North East
River where I formerly lived, negroes Venus, Doll & Hagar, one Horse, Five
Cows & Calves, Two three year old steers, Three Sows & Pigs, Twelve Two year
old Hogs, all my Farming utensils, Household & Kitchen furniture and at her
Death the above mentioned property with my Land lying on the Miry Branch
and negroes Jack, Harry, Cloe, Hannah, Phillis & Tom equally divided between
my daus. NANCY & TREACY ANN; AUSTIN SWINSON my Shotgun; should the Heirs
of HENRY GRADY dcd prosecute my Estate for any more than I have given them
they shall not hold what I have given to them
extrs: JESSE SWINSON JR. and any man whom he will nominate to the Court
            to assist him
wit: D. JONES, B. GARNER
signed: John A. Swinson

494. SWINSON, THEOPHILUS (CR.035.801.11/1-66)
12 Sep 1833 - Apr Term 1835
son JOHN negroes Lulcreek & Tom, one bed & furniture which he has received;
son WM. negroe Jack, one bed & furniture which he has received; grandau.
PATSEY ELIZA negro Lucy; dau. SARAH & her husband DEMPSEY TAYLOR negro
Satirah for her lifetime & then to my children JOHN, WM. and PRUDENCE HEATH;
dau. SARAH one bed & furniture which she has Received; son JOHN negro Rose
for his lifetime and then her first Living child to my grandau. MARY ELIZA
and negro Rose to my grandaus. SUSAN JANE & MARGARET ANN; dau. PRUDENCE
HEATH one bed and furniture which she has received, the cattle that she has
received and the money that I advanced for the Payment of the lands; negro
Betty sold, also all my other Property and two hundred and fifty dollars be
divided between my grandchildren THEOPHILUS HEATH & KITTY HEATH and the
remainder to my children JOHN, WM., SARAH TAYLOR & PRUDENCE HEATH
extrs: sons JOHN & WM.
wit: JAMES DICKSON, OZBORN CARR
                    signed: Theophilus   Swinson

495. TAYLOR, JACOB "Planter" (CR.035.801.11/A-472)
6 Aug 1787 - Jul Term 1788
wife ELIZABETH all my Estate both Real and Personal and after her decease
Seventy Acres adjoining to my dwelling House to Devolve to my youngest Son
JOHN and Seventy five Acres lying in the upper part unto my son JACOB;
all my Personal Estate Equally Divided between my Sons JACOB and JOHN and
my Youngest Dau. JAMIMA
extr: wife ELIZABETH
wit: JACOB MILLARD, ISAAC MILLARD, JOHN PROWSE
signed: Jacob Taylor

496. TAYLOR, KATHRINE (CR.035.801.11/A-465)
18 Feb 1800 - Jul Term 1801
grandsons WILLIAM RHODES and TAYLOR RHODES each a Feather Bed, bedstead
and furniture, two large pewter dishes and four Quart Basons, my Riding
Beast, two Iron pots and a frying pan; grandau. CATHARINE BARFIELD one
large Feather bed, Bedstead and firniture, a Bofat with what it Contains,
a Table and Chest, one small Pewter dish and two large Basons and also all

the remainder of my property
extrs: JOHN RHODES, LEWIS BARFIELD
wit: FRANS. OLIVER, JANE OLIVER
signed: Kathrine Taylor

497. TEACHEY, DANIEL (CR.035.801.11/A-460)
13 Feb 1791 - Oct Term 1794
wife ANNE Quick and Peaseable possession of all that part of my Land to the
East of the Iron Mine Branch Joining DANIEL TEACHEY JUNR and the land that
was formerly JOHN TEACHEY's and known by the name of Tim's Place and at her
Decease to my Son TIMOTHY; wife ANNE negroes Prince, Sophia, Cato, Joe,
Salter, Jack, Nancy & her child Hannah & Cate, all my Stock of Cattle,
Horses, Sheep, Hoggs, Household furniture and plantation Tools; son JACOB
negro Nancy and her child Hannah after Wife's Decease; sons DANIEL & TIMOTHY
after Wife's Decease negroes Prince, Sophia, Cato, Joe, Salter, Jack & Cate,
all my houshold furniture and Stock of Every Kind, all my plantation tools,
young negroes Fortune, Rose, Nancy and Matt; son JACOB Two hundred acres
including the Plantation whereon he now lives on the South Side of the Iron
Mine Branch Joining WIMBERT BONEY and DANIEL TEACHEY, negro Billy; son
DANIEL negroes Pompey and Amy; son TIMOTHY negroes Toney, Hagar & Nancy;
dau. MARY COOK negro Grace; dau. BARBARY GEORGE negro Lucy; son JOHN
Five Shillings Sterling money; dau. CATHRINE BONEY Five Shillings Sterling
money; grandson DANIEL son of JOHN Ten pounds Specie; grandson TEACHEY
COOK Ten pounds Specie; grandson DANIEL GEORGE Ten Pounds Specie
extrs: wife ANNE, sons DANIEL & TIMOTHY
wit: JOSEPH DICKSON, MESHACK STALLINGS, SHADRACH STALLINGS
                              signed: Daniel ⟨mark⟩ Teachey

498. TEACHEY, DANIEL (CR.035.801.11/A-470)
18 Feb 1826 - Apr Term 1826
son JAMES all my possessions of Land Only that my wife MARY have Quiet
possession on the One halfe Includin the plantation wher on I Lived on the
Iron Mine branch During hir Life; dau. ANN W. BONEY negroes Amy with her
Children Clary, Mary & Vergill, Silvey and her children Sarah, Viney, Bob,
Forlin, Mile and her child Margrit, Fortin & Frank; grandson DANIEL son of
WRIGHT BONEY negro Metildy; dau. MARY H. negroes Rose and hir child Tinah,
Morris, Jim, Hagrow, Mary, Toney, Chaine and her Child Lorevy; wife MARY
and son JAMES negroes Joe, Juda, Sarah, John, Ephram, Owen, Cloe, Briant,
Susan, Seale, Bill, Suffer, Sam, Roger, Light, Sotter, Jimmy, Muriah, Lindy
& Jinan Except what may be due JAMES on a Division of my son DANIEL decd.
from a former Will; son JAMES & dau. MARY H. One Bed and Furniture Each;
wife MARY Residue of the household furniture with all the Stock of hogs,
cattle and sheep and JAMES to furnish my wife with one horse & Riding Cheer
from the proceeds of the turpentine on hand and my part of the judgement
obtained against CHARLS HOOKS; son JAMES my Rifle gun
extrs: Brother TIMOTHY, JAMES TEACHEY
wit: WILLIAM MCANNE, BARNET CARR, H. GILMAN
signed: Dl. Teachey

499. TEACHEY, JACOB "Planter" (CR.035.801.11/A-463)
3 Nov 1828 - Feb Term 1829
wife NANCY all and Singular of My worldly Estat; son ISAAC two Hundred

acres Lying on Oaky branch the upper part Joining the Main Road; ALFORD
TEACHY two Hundred acres Lying on Oky branch being part of the Land Left
me by TIMOTHY TEACHEY Dcd.; younger Son DANIEL a Sertin tract of Land
Lying on the East Side of the No. River Known by the Name of Casies Bluff;
ALFORD & ISAAC TEACHY negro Isaac
extrs: DANIEL TEACHEY, WRIGHT BONEY
wit: DAVID HODGESON, DAVID EVANS
signed: Jacob Teachey

500. TEACHEY, TIMOTHY   (CR.035.801.11/A-479)
8 Feb 1826 - Feb Term 1828
MOLSEY TEACHEY Land on which I now Live on little Rockfish Containing six
Hundred acres and after her disease Equally devided Between DANIEL son of
JACOB TEACHEY and the heirs of TIMOTHY TEACHEY decd.; MOLSEY TEACHEY what
Crops that may Be on the premises with all my stock of Cattle, horses, hogs
and sheep, all my plantation tools and household furniture, One Gig; JAMES
TEACHEY and his mother MOLSY negroes Claburn, Wiley, David, Toney, Jack,
Mary, Hagrow, John, Jim, Bill, Charls, Robeson, Isom, Eliza & Hannah;
HENRY & JACOB sons of JACOB TEACHEY decd. Eight Hundred acres Lying one
South side of Oaky Branch; ANN W. BONEY negro Sam, Two Hundred acres lying
on the Shear pocoson; MARY H., dau. of DANIEL TEACHEY decd. negroes Jacob
& Aley; MICHAELL son of JACOB TEACHEY decd negro Jim, fifty Barrells of
Turpintine; heirs of TIMOTHY, HENRY, JACOB & DANIEL TEACHEY [not named]
negroes Cato, Matt, Nance & Cate; sister BARBARA GEORGE three Hundred
dollars Cash; DANIEL son of JOHN TEACHEY One Hundred dollars Cash; JAMES
TEACHEY and his mother MOLSY any money left on hand with what Turpentine
and Tar that may be on hand, all Notes and Accts; JOHN TEACHEY, MARY COOK
& JACOB TEACHEY five shillings sterling
extrs: nephews JAMES TEACHEY & DANIEL TEACHEY
wit: JOHN BONEY, HENRY IRWIN, RICHARD BOWDEN
signed: T. Teachey

501. TEACHY, MARY   (CR.035.801.11)
10 Feb 1857 - Apr Term 1855
"widow of the late DANIEL TEACHY ... in the eighty fifth year of my age"
all the negro slaves which were bequeath to me by the wills of my husband
DANIEL TEACHY and of TIMOTHY TEACHY be devided in to two equal shares one
of which I bequeath to my son in law CORNELIUS McMILLAN and his wife MARY H.
and the remaining share to my grandsons DANIEL T., JAMES W and TIMOTHY W.
BONEY; grandsons DANIEL T., JAMES W. and TIMOTHY W. BONEY one bed, bedstead
and necessary bedding and a half dosen chairs; remainder of my estate,
property and effects both real and personal to my dau. MARY H. McMILLAN
extr: son in law CORNELIUS McMILLAN
wit: R. M. WALKER, WM. A. WRIGHT
signed: Mary Teachey

502. THALLY, ANDREW   (CR.035.801.11)
9 Jun 1815 - Oct Term 1816
wife ELIZABETH all my Notes, bonds and accompts, negro Jane, my house and
plantation, as much of the furniture Sufficient for her use, Fifteen two
year old Hogs, two Sows and pigs, all the Cows and Calves that is called
her own, One Feather bed and furniture, One Horse and Chair and Harness,
with One Half for her Own disposal and the other half at her Death Equally

divided Between MARGARET MARY COLWELL and DAVID THALLY; dau. MARY negro Jane at wife's decease; dau. JANE ARTHUR Five Shillings; son HUGH Five Shillings; son JOHN Five Shillings; dau. ELIZABETH COSTON Five Shillings; Remainder of my property sold and money Equally Divided amongst my first named Children MARGARET MARY COLWELL and DAVID THALLY
extrs: JOHN GILMAN, THOMAS GARRISON
wit: WILLIAM SWINSON, JOHN SWINSON
signed: Andw. Thally

503. THIGPEN, JOHN (CR.035.801.11/A-473)
25 Apr 1818 - Oct Term 1818
son WILEY the land whereon he now lives, One Horse & Saddle, one Bed & furniture, One Cow & Calf, four head of Sheep; son BRYTHAL the land whereon he now lives, one Mair and Saddle, One Bed and furneture, one Cow & Calf, four head of Sheep; dau. LAVINEY BROWN the land where on She Now lives, One Horse and Saddle, One Bed & furniture, One Cow and Calf, four head of Sheep; dau. TRICEY BROWN the land where on She now lives, One Horse and Saddle, One Bed & furniture and One Cow & Calf, four head of Sheep; son JOSEPH Land and Plantation whereon I now live, one Hundred acres lying between SHERROD BROWN and SAMUEL WHALEY, one Horse and Saddle, one Bed & furniture, One Cow & Calf, all my Cider Cask, Two Plows, one Grubing hoe, one ax, a weeding hoe; daus. DICEY, ANNIE, ELSEY & SALLY Each one Bed & furniture, the Guard Pocoson Survey; ballance of Estate Except my Cattle so far as respects my dau. DICEY Equally divided Between my daus. DICEY, ANNIE, ELSEY & SALLY
extrs: sons WILEY & BRYTHAL
wit: NATHAN WALLER, JOSEPH T. RHODES
                    signed: John ✗ Thigpen

504. THOMAS, GREGORY (CR.035.801.11)
5 May 1854 - 20 Mar 1869
dau. JANE COX decd living children [not named] negro George and property heretofore given their Parents as their full share; son JOHN J. ten dollars which with other property heretofore given him is his full share; dau. RACHEL ANN DAVIS an interest in property hereafter to be mentioned; dau. HANNAH ASHTON JUDGE an interest in property hereafter to be mentioned; dau. SARAH GREEN QUINN an interest in property hereafter to be mentioned, negroes Nelly and her children Henry, Bashy & Leah & Sarah with other property heretofore given her by deed; dau. EADY MERENDA MUMFORD an interest in property hereafter to be mentioned, negro Violet and her children Ellick, Jerry & Polly with other property heretofore given as her full share; son CHARLES GREGORY Two hundred dollars with other property heretofore given as his full share; dau. NANCY MARIAH negroes Luke, Jack, Fereby & her child Joseph, & Rosey & her five children Alice, Jane, Mary, Moses and Penia; dau. ELIZABETH C. negroes Dover, Ned, Chelsy, Clary and her child Agnes, Benjamin, Sely, Fanny & child Frank; daus. NANCY MARIAH and ELISABETH C. all the Lands whereon I now live including my dwellings containing eight hundred and twenty acres composed of Lands I in herited, Lands I patented, Lands bought from JOHN JARMAN, the Lands known as the Waller Land on the East side of the Public Road leading from Hallsville by JOHN EDWARDS to Onslow, also all my Stock of every description, Plantation and farming Tools & Implements, Oxen, Carts, Mills, Mortars, Troughs, Poultry, Provisions both for Man and Beast on hand, Grindstone, Looms & appendages, wheels and cards, Houshould & Kitchen furniture

and they to hae responsible for the comfortable support of my negro Old Leah;
executors to sell negro Sam and all the Waller Land except that east of the
Onslow Road and the money divided into five equal parts one each for RACHEL
ANN DAVIS, HANNAH ASHTON JUDGE, SARAH GREEN QUINN, EADY MERENDA MUMFORD and
the children of JANE COX decd.
extr: THOMAS HALL
wit: G. L. SMITH, EDWARD BROW, JERE PEARSALL
signed: Gregory Thomas

505. THOMAS, ISAAC (CR.035.801.11/A-467)
22 Jan 1803 - April Term 1803
wife JEAN all my Horses and plantation tools, Household and Kitchen furneture,
work and Labour of negroes Phillis, March and Dick for Bringing up, Raising
and Euducating my children; wife JEAN all my land and plantation whereon I
now live for her & my children's Support; son WILLIAM negro Bob when he
arrives at age of Twenty one years; son JAMES negro Dennis when he arrives
at age of Twenty one years; dau. NANCY one Sixth part of my Stock of Cattle
and hogs, one feather bed and furniture, a Sixth part of my Household furniture at her marriage or coming Womans age; dau. SILVIA one Sixth part of my
Stock of Cattle and hogs, one feather bed and furniture, a Sixth part of my
Household furniture at her marriage or coming Womans age; dau. MORENDA one
Sixth part of my Stock of Cattle and hogs, one feather bed and furniture,
a Sixth part of my Household furniture at her marriage or coming Womans age;
dau. PENELOPE one Sixth part of my Stock of Cattle and hogs, one feather bed
and furniture, a Sixth part of my Household furniture at her marriage or
coming Womans age; dau. POLLEY one Sixth part of my Stock of Cattle and
hogs, one feather bed and furniture, a Sixth part of my Household furniture
at her marriage or coming Womans age; son LEWIS one Sixth part of my Stock
of Cattle and hogs, one feather bed and furniture, a Sixth part of my Household furniture when he arrives at Twenty one years of age; sons WILLIAM,
JAMES and LEWIS all the Land that I possess
extrs: LEWIS JONES, ROBERT SOUTHERLAND Esq.
wit: BENJN. DULANY, JOSEPH T. RHODES
signed: Isaac Thomas
Codicil
son LEWIS negro Dick after death of my wife; after death of my wife negroes
Phillis and March sold and money Eaqually divided among my daus. NANCY, SILVIA,
MORENDA, PENELOPE and POLLEY
wit: BENJN. DULANY, JOSEPH T. RHODES
signed: Isaac Thomas

506. THOMAS, WILLIAM (CR.035.801.11/A-477)
29 Mar 1781 - Jan Court 1782 [original missing]
grandson ISAAC all land, Houses, Orchard, Horses, Plows and Plantation Tools
belonging to the Plantation Except a little Orchard I gave to my Negro Dover;
grandson ISAAC negro Phillis & her child Peter to my grandson WM when he
shall arrive at twenty one years but Peter to be under the care of my dau.
RACHEL RHODES; increase of negro Phillis to the children of my son WM [not
named] until each shall have one and then residue that may be born to my
grandson ISAAC; Should grandson ISAAC be called to the war then negro Phillies
and what children may be to be under the care of my dau RACHEL RHODES until
he comes back and the plantation to be under the care of his Father WM.;

grandson ISAAC one Long Pair of Iron Doggs fixed in the chimney stove, Pewter
dishes, Six Plates, one Iron Shovel & Tongs, one Box Iron, 2 heaters, three
Pewter Basins, one of 2 quarts one of one quart, one hour Glass, one pair
Billows, 3 Iron Pots, one of Three Gallons, one of 5 Gallons, one of 8 Gallons,
two iron chandlersticks, one Grit iron, one Frying pan, one Bread Griddle,
one Elbow chair, one Table, one case with twelve Bottles, one Safe, five
knives, one pair of Silver Buckles, one Shotgun, all my shirts & the rest of
my wearing appearll Except my Blue Great Coat which is for my son BILLY;
grandson RICHARD when he comes of age twenty one negro Dover Eleven years
old but the work & labor of said negro to my son WILLIAM in Consideration of
his care and clothing him; son BILLY two Hundred acres of uncultivated Land
on Broad Branch and one hundred acres joining the land I live on and my Son
BILLY and all my hogs; son BILLY, RACHEL RHODES & ELIZABETH HULLING all my
sheep and cattle, all my money; son WILLIAM, grandson ISAAC, dau. RACHEL
RHODES & ELIZABETH HOLLINGSWORTH two beds and furniture; negro Phillis the
bed she lyed on and three blankets and all her wearing appearl; grandson
ISAAC my Big Bible, my part of my Garden the same as JAMES HOWELLs of Onslow;
grandson JOSEPH THOMAS RHODES my Mill stones of my grandson ISAAC; son
WILLIAM my share of my Book Entitled Booklet of the New Testament in possession of my son JAMES HOLLINGSWORTH; sons BILLY & WILLIAM and daus. RACHEL
RHODES and ELIZABETH HOLLINGSWORTH big iron pot containing Sixteen gallons
extrs: BENJAMIN RHODS, son WILLIAM
wit: WM. HOUSTON, BENJA. SMITH, JOHN HUMPHREY
signed: Wm. Thomas

507. THOMASON/THOMPSON, WILLIAM nuncupative will (A-456)
11 Jun 1785 - Jul Court 1785
the desire of WILLIAM THOMASON on his death Bed on June 9th, 1785 to Wit
son JOHN the Mainer plantation Containing one hundred acres; son BENJAMIN
he was living on with the land belonging to the sd Survey; grandsons EZEKIEL
CARTER and LAWRENCE THOMAS Two hundred acres on the waters of Suttons; Stock
of Cattle Equeally divided Between his children [not named]
wit: JOHN THOMSON, BARSHABA THOMPSON, WINIFIRD THOMSON
Sworn befor JAS. OUTLAND J. P.

508. THOMSON, DAVID (S.S. Wills/CR.035.801.11)
6 Mar 1773 - 26 Oct 1773
son WILLIAM negroes Jo and Theana, One hundred Acres lying in the fork between
buck hall and the Spring branch; son DAVID negroes Boson and Jack, One hundred and forty four Acres lying on Cow Marsh, my set of black smith's tools,
my Grey mare; son in law ROGER SNELL negro Dinah; son in law JESSE DARDEN
negro Phillis; son JAMES negroes Brister and Peter, my plantation on Buck
hall, all my lands joining thereunto containing One hundred and ninty Acres,
my white horse, One feather bed and furniture, one writing desk; son STEPHEN
plantation where I now dwell and all my lands Joining thereunto containing
four hundred and one acres, negroes Andrew, Tom & Cloe, part of the still,
my feather bed which I now lie on with the furniture belonging thereto, four
cows and calves, sixteen head of other cattle, my large book called Burket
on the new Testament; dau. AMELIA negroes Cate, Moll & Peg, one feather bed
and furniture she taking her choice of the beds; dau. MARTHA negroes Hannah,
Doll and London one feather bed and furniture, four cows and calves, six head

of other cattle; sons WM, DAVID and JAMES the remainder part of my stock of
cattle; sons in law ROGER SNELL and JESSE DARDEN my sheep that is with THOMAS
IVEY and EDWARD BYRD; son WILLIAM all my carpenters and Joiners tools; my
black horse and bay horse, two flukes and one plough, my Iron bound cart with
all the gears, my crosscut and whip saws, all my Stands and Barrels be for
the use of the plantation where I now Live and my Negroes be continued on the
Plantation until the next crop be finished; son WILLIAM one feather bed and
furneture; son DAVID one feather bed and furneture; dau. MARTHA one small
Horse colt
extrs: brother ANDREW, son in law ROGER SNELL
wit: HENRY HOLLINGSWORTH, JOHN THOMSON, THOMAS THOMSON
signed: David Thomson

509. THOMSON, JOHN (A-464)
3 May 1781 - Jul Term 1786
cousin LEWIS MOORE one thousand acres including the Plantation whereon I now
live; ELIZABETH MOORE four hundred and Seventy five acres including plantation whareon RICHD. RUNEALS now lives, a horse Known by the name of Laepon;
Cousin JOSEPH MOORE my Riding mare; Cousin JAMES MOORE my negro Senure;
residue of Property to be Equally divided between my legatees afore mentioned
extrs: HARDY HOLEMS, DAVID DODD
wit: WILLEM PERSONS [?], JAS. THOMPSON, JAMES MOORE
signed: John Thomson

510. TREADWELL, ADONIRAM "of Black River" (CR.035.801.11/A-475)
6 Jan 1779 - Oct Term 1782
Heir of my Deceased son GILIAD [not named] one shilling Lawful Money of
England; sons ADNIRAM and JOHN and daus. PHEBE and BULAH and grandson ENOS
MATHIS Each One Shilling Lawful Money of England; wife MARY all and Singular
my lands, messuages and tenements, all my Goods and Chattels, Real and personal by her freely to be possessed
extr: wife MARY
wit: RD. HERRING, ABNER STEPHENS, ENOCH HERRING
signed: Adoniram Treadwell

511. TURNAG, CADER (CR.035.801.11/A-476)
17 Dec 1829 - Jul Term 1825
Cosin HENNERY BLALOCK One Cow; Cosin MARTHAANN KURNEGAY one heffer; my
Hors, Bridle and Sadle to Be Sold and five Dallers I give to my Sister
PATSEY KORNEGAY, five Dallars to my Cosin POLLEY NARRESS, five Dallers to my
Cosen RUTHY TURNAG, five Dallers to my Sister ANN KORNEGAY; Cosin NANCY
JEAN BLALOCK one Spotted Gilt Sow; Balance of my property I Give to my
Mathe [not named]
extrs: WILLIAM TURNAG, ELIJAH BIZZEL
wit: RICHARD KETHLEY, BRIGHT I. SANDERSON
                              signed: Cader Turnag

512. TUTLE, ANN (CR.035.801.11/A-546)
22 Oct 1842 - Jul Term 1844
grandson JAMES P. DAVIS negroes Frank about fifty four years of age and
Hiram about twenty three years old; dau. HEPZBAH negroes Mary, Harry, Balaam,
Nelson, Jim, Dianah, Reuben, Austin, George & Lydia, one bed and furniture,

one Gig and Harness, two common Chest, all my wearing cloths
extr: not named
wit: HENRY SWINSON, A. O. GRADY
signed: Ann Tutle

513. TUTLE, HEPHZIBAH (CR.035.801.11/2-27)
14 Dec 1844 - Apr Term 1848
JAMES P. DAVIS negro Balaam; JOHN EDWARD DAVIS negro Jim; MARIAH C. DAVIS
& SOPHRONIA E. DAVIS negroes Harry & Lydia & each one chest; SOPHRONIA E.
DAVIS one bed, bed stead & furniture; JOHN E. DAVIS one bed & furniture;
all my nieces ELIZABETH, NANCY, WINIFRED, EMMA, MARIAH & SOPHRONIA DAVIS
the ballance of my chests, Trunks, Bedcloths, Tables & my Wearing apparel;
ballance of my negroes be sold & the proceeds equally divided between my
nephews CALVIN DAVIS, SETH DAVIS & IRA DAVIS & my Nieces ELIZABETH PIPKIN,
NANCY SWINSON, WINIFRED JARMAN & EMMA JACKSON
extr: nephew JAMES P. DAVIS
wit: ALSAS GRADY, A. O. GRADY
signed: Hephzibah Tutle

514. UNDERHILL, WILLIAM (CR.035.801.11/A-457)
25 Nov 1801 - Jan Term 1802
son JOSEPH negro Lusa at the death of my wife SPISA and my Son JERRY have
the first child that Lusa shall bare; dau. PEGGE One Cow and calf; son
WILLIAM money due me from ROBERT MERRETT which is Forty Pounds two Shillings
& the money he Ows me Which is Six pounds; Money due me for my Lands from
JERY BLANDSHARD be laid Out in the purchace of Other Lands and my Wife SPYSA
have a quiet and peasible possession of it her lifetime and then Divided
between my Sons JOSEPH and JERRY; wife SPYSA all the rest of my property
that has not be Named; Son in law WILLIAM JOHSTON five Shillings; dau. SARAH
ASBELL five Shillings; dau. ANNA five Shillings
extrs: wife SPYSA, JOHN GORE, WILLIAM POLLOCK
wit: DAN HICKS, DENNIS CANNON, WILLIAM ꝙ UNDERHILL JUNR
                                   signed: William 𝍢 Underhill

515. WADE, JOSEPH (CR.035.801.11/A-530)
22 Oct 1794 - Oct Term 1795
wife MARY all my Estate real and Personal as long as my wife is able to Keep
House and to have a Childs part when she is not; daus. DICY, DRILLEY and
ELIZABETH Three Cows; after my wife is past Housekeeping my Plantation with
all the stock and Household Furniture be sold and money Divided amongst my
Dau. [not named] & JAMES WADE my Grandson; sons JAMES, JOSEPH and SAMUEL One
Shilling Currency Each
extrs: JOHN BRADLEY, LEVIN WATKINS
wit: JOHN BRADLEY, RICHARD BRADLEY, JESSE ✗ BRANCH
                                   signed: Joseph   Wade
dau. SUSANNAH GREEVES an Equal part with my Other Daughters
wit: JOHN BRADLEY, RICHARD BRADLEY, JESSE   BRANCH
                                   signed: Joseph 🙵 Wade

516. WALLER, JAMES (CR.035.801.11/A-487)
28 Jan 1823 - Apr Term 1823
wife SARAH during her natural lifetime one third part of my land whereon I
now live and all of my Stock of Cattle, one Sow and Pigs, all of my Sheep,
all of my House hold property and Kitchen furniture and Plantation Tools;
dau. ELIZABETH ROGERS the whole of my land and Plantation whereon I now live

during her natural life time and after her death to her Son THOMAS; Balance
of my property sold to pay my Just Debts and to Support my wife
extr: LOFTIN QUIN
wit: JOHN BISHOP JR.
signed: James Waller

517. WARD, JOHN "Planter" (CR.035.801.11/A-534)
3 May 1777 - Oct Court 1777 [original missing from folder]
son SAMPSON one cow and calf, all that I have given him that he has; son
JESSE one cow & calf, one feather bed and Bolster, one dish and bason, two
plates all now in his possession; son JOHN one cow and calf, one feather
bed & one bolster, one Dish, one Bason and Two plates; dau. SARRAH one
cow and calf, one Eastin [?] heifer, Two ewes and lambs, one feather bed &
bolster & furniture and bedstead, one large pot, one chest, one iron box
and heaters, one Linnen wheel, one wollen wheel, one small Trunk, one Dish,
one Bason, two plates, one pewter Tankard, one dozen tea cups and sausers,
two sows and pigs; wife JANE one feather bed and furniture and bedstead,
one chest, one large black horse, saddle, bridle and halter, one plow and
gear, one sorrel horse, saddle, bridle and halter, one plow and geer, one
cart and wheels, one Linen wheel, one pot and frying pan, Two harrow axes,
one broad ax, to weeding hoes, one grubbing hoe, all the rest of my pewter,
all the rest of my cattle, hogs and sheep, all my gees, all the rest of my
Estate; son JESSE part of the plantation whereon I now live Beginning on
Smith Swamp; son JOHN JR. the remainder of my land and plantation
extrs: son JESSE, wife JANE
wit: RICE BLACKMAN, JOEL BLACKMAN, JOHN ✝ WARD JR.
signed: John ⨎ Ward Sr.

518. WARD, JOHN (CR.035.801.11)
1 Nov 1828 - Oct Term 1839
wife FRANCES negros Bradick, Mary, Hannah, Filles, two feather beds, bed
steds & furniture, two horses Maryann & Pat, one Riding Chair & harness,
Six cows & Calvs, six sows & pigs, fifteen head of Sheep, one cart, one
yoke of oxen, six plows, two pairs of geer, all the plantation Where on I
now live on the North west side of the Mill branch with the privalige of
Geting Rail timbor & Fire wood; daus. CHARLOT & SUSAN the whole of my
Negroes, the stock of horses with the exception of the old sorrel horse
cald Ball & the old mair Lusinda which is to be sold, the Stock of cattle
& sheep except one heffer to my grandson DAVID Son of JOHN SWINSON; daus.
CHARLOT & SUSAN the whole of my Lands Containing five hundred and sixty
eight acres & the mill to belong equally to Both; grandau. NANCY dau. of
JOHN SWINSON all the notes and acounts that I now have; daus. CHARLOT &
SUSAN all my stock of hogs
extr: DAVID HOOKS
wit: JE. TURNAGE
signed: John ✝ Ward

519. WARD, LUKE (CR.035.801.11/A-526)
30 May 1796 - Jul Term 1796
wife BRIDGET all my Estate real & personal; son LUKE at his mother's
Death all my Land or Right or Claim of Lands and he shall lend Unto his
sister PENNY a part of said Dweling house and Forty acres of cleard land
During her being Unmarried and if he Dies without heir to be Equally

Divided between my daus. PENNY and ELIZABETH POLLOCK; dau. PENNY negroes
Bob & Hannah; dau. ELIZABETH PALLOCK negroes Nan and Jack; dau. PENNY
one bed and firniture, one chist & Case; Remaining part of my property
be Divided between my six children [not named]
extrs: wife BRIDGET, son LUKE
wit: C. HOOKS, JAS. WRIGHT, THO. WRIGHT
                    signed: Luke ✗ Ward

520. WARD, PRISCILLA (CR.035.801.11/A-515)
17 Mar 1828 - May Term 1828
all my property of every description sold and the Mony arising to be disposed of as follows One Hundred Dollars each to ROBERT JOHN, PRISCILLA &
MARY children of the late ISAAC HUNTER when they arrive at lawful age or
marry; One Hundred & fifty dollars each to ELIZA CATHARINE & SARAH PRISCILLA
children of the late SARAH MOLTON when they arrive at lawful age or marry
and residue of money equally divided between my children ANN HOOKS, JOHN
HUNTER, HOGAN HUNTER, CATHARINE HURST, ELIZABETH TATE and my Grand Children
the children of the late ISAAC HUNTER & the late SARAH MOLTON
extr: JEREMIAH PEARSALL
wit: JERE PEARSALL, JOHN GRIMES, JAKEY ✗ STEPHENS
                    signed: Priscilla 🌀 Ward

521. WATERMAN, WILLIAM "Planter" (CR.035.801.11/A-508)
31 Dec 1819 - Jan Term 1820
wife SARAH negroes Dinah, Primus and Chaney, five cows and calves, Two
featherbeds and furniture, my house and Plantation with the Plantation
tools, household furneture and Shop tools and after her decease to my
children ELEAZAR, ELIZABETH and SUSANAH; wife SARAH my Stock of hogs,
sheep and horses, old jack to be kept and mentaned during his liftime,
negroes bed and Yong Jack and at her death they to be valued and go to make
up the lots of Negroes left to my children; son ELEAZAR negroes Jam, Rose
and Edeth, one feather bed and furniture and one hundred and seventy Six
dollars already receaved by him; dau. ELIZABETH EDWARDS negroes Jane,
Jelord and Ireland, two cows and calves, two feather beds and furniture,
one yoke of oxen, four Sows and pigs, four Ews and lambs, two bee hives;
dau. SUSANAH negroes Eliza, Hannah and Sander, two cows and calves, four
sows and pigs, four Ews and lambs, two feather beds and furniture when
she Marries or coms of age
extrs: SAML. STANFORD, ARON MORGAN, son ELEAZER
wit: SAML. STANFORD, WILLIAM ✝ MEASELS, SIMEON ✝ JONES
signed: William Waterman

522. WATKINS, LEVEN (CR.035.801.11/A-518)
31 Nov 1811 - Oct Term 1812 [original hard to read]
wife SARAH negroes Davie, Sam, Reue & Minny, three feather beds and steeds
and cords and mats with full furniture, three horses, five cows & calves,
five hed of Sheep, five Sowes, and pigs, one huderd & fifty dollers; son JAMES
one hondreand and fifty dollars; son JSSE negrow Roda, one bed, bedsteed
and furneture, two hundreaned dollars; son JOHN one negrow Jow, one
hondeand dollars; son WILLIAM negrow Isaack, one hondrahd dollars; son
MATCHET [?] negrow Abram, one hondeand dollars; son LEVIN negrow woman
and child, one Beed and steed and farnutune, five heed of cattle, five heed

of Sheep, one fifth part of money from sall of all my Land; son PETER
negrow Silve and hir child Rose, one horse or mare, one Bed and Steed,
five heed of cattle, five hed of sheep, one fifth part of money from sall
of all my Land; son BRYAN negrowes Tilis [?], Gould and Cat, one cold named
Ratler, one hondred dollars, one fifth part of money from sell of all my
land; son BECTON negrows Tener & Kindeter, two of Silves childenn, one
fifth part of the mony arising from the sell of my lands; executors to sail
land, wife SARAH to get intrest on money for one year, Rest of my property
to be Sold but my old negrowes Jinne and Heray they both to be set free at
my death and money to be diveded Betwein my Son BECTON, my gradaughters
EDIETH WITFULL, BETTHA WITFIELD and NEEDHAM WITFIELD
extrs: son JOHN, JAMES RADAIN
wit: not named
signed: Levin Watkins

523. WEBB, SAMUEL (CR.035.801.11/A-509)
2 May 1816 - Jul Term 1816
Property of Every Nature and Kind whatsoever to remain in the possession of
my wife HANNAH for the use of her support with her chuldren and In case of
her marrage executor may have an Equal Division of the property between my
wife HANNAH and her Two Children DOLLY and JOHN W.
extr: JOHN GRIER
wit: T. TEACHEY, DAVID CAR
                signed: Samuel ✝ Webb

524. WELLS, BONEY SENR (CR.035.801.11/3-50)
11 Dec 1849 - Jan Term 1862
wife NANCY my Plantation whereon I reside with all woods and buildings
attached, negroes Chloe, Irvin, Henry, Violet, Isaac, Sarah, Andrew,
Pleasant-Ann, Missouri, Julius & Chloe, my stock of cattle, horses & hogs
and Sheep, Crop of all Kinds, working tools, household and kitchen furniture; son JAMES my Plantation whereon I now reside subject to the life
estate of my beloved wife; all personal property bequeathed to my beloved
wife at her death to be distributed between my children STOAKS, JACOB JUN,
BONEY JUN, NANCY WILLIAMS, JAMES, MARY PRISCILLA BONEY, ELLEN SLOAN &
LUCINDA KATHARINE
extrs: sons STOAKS & JAMES
wit: W. R. WARD, TIMOTHY W. BONEY
signed: Boney Wells

525. WELLS, JACOB (CR.035.801.11/A-516)
5 Dec 1806 - Apr Term 1808
son JACOB negroes Joe, Stotter, George & Pheby, six hundred & forty Acres
On Shear pecoson; son WILLIAM negroes Bazel, James, Ryel and Jean, the
land whare he now lives, part of a New Survay; dau. JEAN STALLINGS Twenty
Pounds in Cash; grandau. MARY negro Clo; dau. MARY BONEY negro Lucy, Ten
Pounds In Cash; dau. BARBERY LINTON negro Haner, Plantation whare I now
live and a part of a new Servay the North end of it Joining the plantation
that I have given to her; grandson WELLS LINTON negro Nance; grandau.
SARAH LINTON negro Billy; grandson GEORGE LINTON negro Rachel; grandau.
MARY LINTON negro Lot; grandau. BETSY LINTON fifteen Pounds in Cash;

dau. ANN SLOAN one feather bed, Steed and fineture; all my Stock of Horses, Cattle & hogs and Sheep be sold, also all the House hold firneture and plantation Tools and the Mony a Rising be Equally devided betwixt my daus. ELIZABETH MURPHY, ANN SLOAN & BARBERY LINTON; negro Jack be sold and one half of the Money a Rising to dau. ANN SLOAN and the other half Equally devided betwixt daus. ELIZABETH MURPHY & BARBERY LINTON; grandau. ESTHER MURPHY one fether bed, Sted and firniture; grandson BONEY my Saddle & bridle and my Shoot Gun
extrs: son JACOB, WM. STOAKES, DANIEL TEACHEY
wit: GIBSON SLOAN, JOHN MAXWELL, AUSTIN BEESLEY
                     signed: Jacob Wells

526. WELLS, JACOB SNR. (CR.035.801.11/A-495)
1826 - Oct Term 1826
son BONEY One Feather Bed and Firneture, One Cow and Calfe; WILLIAM WELLS One Feather Bed and Firneture; son JACOB One Feather Bed and Furniture; son DAVID One Feather Bed and Firneture; dau. CATHRAN SOUTHERLAND One Feather-Bed and Firneture, One Cow and Calfe; MARY NEW One Feather Bed and Firneture, One Cow and Calfe; dau. ELIZABETH PIGFORD One Feather Bed, One Cow and Calfe; dau. MARTHEW WILLIAMS One Feather Bed and Firneture, One Cow and Calfe; dau. JEAN A. [JEANET ?] TURNER One Feather Bed, One Cow and Calfe; dau. NANCY WILLSON One Feather Bed and Firneture, One Cow & Calfe; son TEACHEY One Hundred and fourteen acres on the North side of Rockfish Creek at the Mouth of a bottom Run, the mouth of a branch with the North Est prong of the Branch to the head in the piney woods paralell with JERRY SOUTHERLAND, the Crop Now Growing on the said premises Excepted to the Use of my wife ANN one Feather Bed; Two Hundred and Twenty acres Joining Champeans line and One Hundred and Thirty Seven acres Lying between the miery Branch pocoson and JOHN DUFF be sold to pay Debts; wife ANN Have peaceable and Quiet possessean of Two Hundred and Twenty Eight acres in- clooding the plantation where on I Now live during her Life, all the Crop Now growing, all my stock of Cattle and hogs, horses and sheep, plantation tools and after her decease the Lands devided Bettween my sons MIKAEL and JOSEPH; wife ANN negroes Sarah, Seale, Mariah & John during her life and after her decease to my sons MIKAEL and JOSEPH
extrs: sons BONEY, JACOB & DAVID
wit: T. TEACHEY, BENJAMIN BLANTON
signed: Jacob Wells Snr

527. WELLS, WM B. (CR.035.801.11/3-78)
14 Oct 1859 - Jul Term 1863
wife MARGARET M. all my tract of land whereon I now live during the term of her natural life to make a maintainance for herself and her four children [not named]; wife MARGARET M. negroes Brister, Kitty, Cynthia, Isaiah, Jacob, Francis, John Wright and Susan Jane so as to enable her to maintain and school my four children; wife MARGARET M. all my stock, tools, pro- visions, household & Kitchen furniture, moneys and notes; wife MARGARET M. and my children ELIZABETH JANE, JOHN WM, JAMES McDANIEL and MARY CAROLINE remain together for there mutual benefit untill the youngest one becomes of age
extr: JAMES K. WILLIAMS
wit: J. R. EZZELL, MAJOR J. TAYLOR
signed: Wm B. Wells

528. WELTS, ELIZABETH (CR.035.801.12/A-507)
27 Jan 1814 - Jul Court 1817
negro Bella for meritorious Services done me be freed from Slavery and
that my Executor deliver her one cow and calf, one Sow and Pigs, one bed &
bedstead and furniture with my household & Kitchen furniture, my year old
colt; friend NANCY McINTIRE negroes Diana, Jinny, Ben, Sally and Hannah,
my oldest mare; negroes Lucy & Cato may have one cow & calf, one Sow & Pigs
and negro Judith one Cow and calf and Cato to have any colt the mare gifted
to NANCY McINTIRE should have; residue of estate to ANDREW McINTIRE
extr: ANDREW McINTIRE
wit: STEPHEN GRAHAM, JAMES CHAMBERS SENER
                              signed: Elizabeth   Welts

529. WELTZ, JOSEPH (CR.035.801.12/A-484)
no date - April Term 1812
[the name JOSEPH FOLDS appears in the body of the will]
wife ELIZABETH FOLDS all my Land, Negroes, horses, Cattle, Hogs, plantation
tools and hosehold Furniture
extr: not named
wit: LEWIS CHAMBERS, JOHN CHAMBERS, ALEXANDR FERGUSSON
The Signiture of JOSEPH WELTZ's name has been defaced previous to the Will
being proved in Court--
          Test. WM DICKSON CC

530. WESSON, EDWARD (CR.035.801.12/A-522)
3 Feb 1769 - Jul Term 1798
son REUBEN my manner plantation and Land; sons BENJAMIN, ABSOLOM and
REUBEN all my Worldly Goods
extr: son REUBEN
wit: S. D. WARRIN, WM. ROBESON, TRACY WARRIN
                              signed: Edwd   Wesson

531. WESTON, ABELSOM (CR.035.801.12/A-510)
1 Nov 1775 - no probate
nephue RUBEN son of RUBEN WESTON My plantation with Two hundred and fifty
acer there unto belonging; JOHN JONSON to have the sd plantation til the
Tearm of the boys Coming of age and to have it Two years Rent free and to
Clear two acers of Land for Every year he lives on it afterwards; JOHN
JONSTON all the Corn there is on the plantation Now and two hundred weight
of pork or two sows and Pigs and a work beast; nephue BETHENA dau. of
RUBEN WESTON one fether bed and firneyture & c.; brother RUBEN all my
Horses and hogs and bridle and sadle and two beds; nephew SEWRANEY dau.
of RUBEN WESTON one Colt; nephew HAPSEBETH dau. of RUBEN WESTON al my puter
extr: not named
wit: JM   SULIVEN, BENJAMIN SNIPES, PELETIAH   OUTLAW
                              signed: Abelsom   Weston

532. WHALEY, SAMUEL (CR.035.801.12)
___ Feb 1849 - Jan Term 1857
wife ELIZABETH one hundred and forty acres where I now live including my
mansion House and all out houses, all my stock of all discreptions, all my
house hold and kitchen furniture, all my corn, bacon, etc., negroes Edy,

Tom, Uriah, Mary & Emily; son HENRY J. after the death of my wife one
Hundred and forty acres the plantation whereon I now live, an Equall Shear
of all my Stock of Horses, hogs, Cattle, Sheep, Poultry and House hold &
Kitchen furniture; son JOHN THIGPEN Five dolers; dau. ELIZABETH THIGPEN
Five doleers; grandchildren the children of my dau. ELIZABETH THIGPEN
[not named] an Equal Sheor of all my Stock of Horses, hogs, Cattle, sheep,
poultry, Household and Kitchen furniture
extrs: WM. FARIOR, EDWARD ARMSTRONG
wit: J. E. HALL, THOMAS HALL
                    signed: Samuel *D* Whaley

533. WHITEHEAD, CHRISTOPHER B. "of Onslow County" (CR.035.801.12/2-148)
no date - Jan Term 1859
an amount set apart for educating my niece MARGARET dau. of CHAS M OGLESBY
she to have a regular collegiate education at some institution in North
Carolina and then to spend one year at Patapsco Institute near Baltimore;
remainder of my property to the oldest son of CHAS. M. OGLESBY a Sufficient amount being given during his minority for a regular course of
Collegiate Studies at the University of North Carolina; Should either die
before receiving their shares property is to go to CHAS M. OGLESBY
extr: ROBERT BRYAN CARR (of Maxfield)
wit: J. G. SCOTT, J. A. AVIRETT JUNIOR
signed: Christopher B. Whitehead

534. WHITEHEAD, JOHN (CR.035.801.12)
14 May 1838 - no probate
ANN OGELSBEY land where on she now lives Containing Eighty three acres hir
choice of my negroes, my mare Molly, my Buggy & harness, two sows & pigs,
fifty dollars; SARAH ELIZA, JOHN, BURWEL, CHRISTOPHER B. & WILIE OGELSBEY
all the lands I now possess as they come of age, all the negroes I now
possess namely Willis, Arabella, Bill, Cyrus, Moses, Jim, Robbin, Anny,
Mary, Edmund, Willey, Margaret, Susan, Martha & Ben as they come of age;
brothers JACOB, BURWELL & LASARAS & sisters SARAH, ELIZABETH and ZILPHA
five dollars each
extr: JAMES DICKSON
wit: A. MAXWELL, JAMES MAXWELL
signed: John Whitehead

535. WHITFIELD, JOHN (CR.035.801.12/A-523)
31 Jan 1825 - Apr Term 1825
wife NANCY negroes Matilda, Olly & Easter, one bay mare, two cows and calves,
one three year old heifer, her choice in the cattle, one choices bed and
furniture, one chest, wheel and cards, Loom, one table, three cheers, one
pot, dutch Oven, one case of Knives and forks, set of tea cups and saucers,
and plates and a dish, one bridle and Side saddle, all the remaining part
of my household and Kitchen furniture; dau. SALLY MARIER Eighty one acres
and a Quarter lying in the fork of Rooty Branch and Jumping Run, Seventeen
dollars; wife NANCY all the remaining part of my land for and during her
natural life time and after her death divided among my present wifes children
HESTER, ISAAC and one she being pregnant with at this time; wife NANCY All
the rest and residue of my estate of what nature or Kind soever; mother and

father [not named] to take charge of my dau. SALLY MARIA untill she shall
come of age or marry
extr: wife NANCY
wit: HARGET KORNEGY, L. W. KORNEGAY
signed: John Whitfield

536. WHITFIELD, JOSEPH (CR.035.801.12/1-64)
4 Feb 1835 - Apr Term 1835
wife MARY slaves April, Allen, Curtis, Hannah, Primer & Bias, the Ballance
and Remainder of my Parishionable property, my Land lying on the South
Side of Mill Pond; after the Death of my Wife my land, Negroes and all the
Parishable Estate Sold and my Son JOSEPH have one hundred Dollars; Ballance of the Money Be Equally Divided into Eleven Shares with one each
going to my son WILLIAM, dau. ELIZABETH OUTLAW, son BRYAN, son JOSEPH, son
HENRY, dau. HESTER GRADY, dau. SALLY, dau. CHARRITY LOFTIN, dau. RACHEL,
son JOHN's Children and son TIMOTHY's children
extrs: son WM., DANIEL JONES, GILES T. LOFTIN
wit: JAMES SULLIVENT, JAMES OUTLAW JR.
signed: Jos. Whitfield

537. WHITFIELD, JOSEPH (CR.035.801.12/2-68)
20 Feb 1852 - Apr Term 1852
wife PENELOPE all of my property off ever name and natur just as it now
Stands to rase and Keep the Family Together and If She Should Marry all my
property to be Sold and her to have a Childes part and for all my Children
to receive agreable to what they have or have not recieved; son BENJAMIN H.
and JOHN W. if they choose to take off one Hundred acres a pease at the
upper End of my Land It being the Same as I have give my Son N. B.; son
GEORGE F. One Hundred and fifty five Dollars to words paying for his lands
extr: not named
wit: HARDY REAVES, DAVID REAVES
signed: Joseph Whitfield

538. WHITFIELD, SALLY (CR.035.801.12)
21 Oct 1836 - Jan Term 1837
mother [not named] negroes Milly and Silvy with all my other property of
every kind during her Natural life; after the death of my mother negroes
Milly and Silvy sold and the money divided into four Equal Shares with one
share each to my sister ELIZABETH OUTLAWs Children, sister HESTER GRADYs
Children, sister CHARITY LOFTIN's Children & sister RACHEL OUTLAWs Children;
Niece ELIZA OUTLAW My Bed with common furniture; Nephew JOHN OUTLAW My
Colt Fancy; EDITH OUTLAW my Side Saddle; Niece MARY OUTLAW my Trunk;
brothers & sisters WILLIAM, JOHN's Children, JOSEPH, BRYAN, HENRY, TIMOTHY's
Children, ELIZABETH OUTLAW, HESTER GRADY, CHARITY LOFTIN and RACHEL OUTLAW
all that part of property left me by the Last will and Testament of my
Father JOSEPH decd.
extr: LEWIS OUTLAW
wit: D. JONES, C. M. SANDERSON
                    signed: Sally ⚡ Whitfield

539. WHITHEAD, JOHN (CR.035.801.12)
13 Apr 1842 - Oct Term 1842
[this will is the same as that of JOHN WHITEHEAD #534 except that SARAH ELIZA,
JOHN, BURWELL, CHRISTOPHER & WILEY are listed as Whitehead instead of Ogelsbey]
wit: A. MAXWELL, AMOS KILLPATRICK
signed: John Whithead

540. WILKINS, JOHN (CR.035.801.12/A-493)
13 Jul 1792 - Oct Term 1792
wife MARY my Land and plantation where on I now live, one feather bed and
furnetire, one horse, Sadle and bridle, three cows and calves, one three
year old Stear, one Iron pot, one skillet, all the reast of my house hold
furntude, two thirds of my Stock of hogs and crop of corn, all my working
tuls and at her deathe all moveables sold and Equly devided among all my
children; son BENJAMIN forty shillings which I leave in the hand of my
sone WILLIAM; son MICHEL one hundard and fifty acors he now lives on; son
JAMES two hundard acors lying on a branch cald ground nut; dau. LEADEY JONES
one hundard acors it being the place where She now lives, one third part of
my hogs, one mare; dau. MARY TALOR one three year old bull, one chist;
dau. NANE WESTBRUSKS one cow; dau. SARAH TANNOR one two year old heffor,
one Feather bead and furneture; son WILLIAM one young mare, Eighteen
pounds in money, one parr of Iron wedges, one Frow and one hand Saw, to
agars, one drawing Knife, one chiszel, one gouge, one Rasor and hone, one
two year old bull
extr: son WILLIAM
wit: CHRISTOPHER MARTIN, JOHN HUTSON
                    signed: John ⨏ Wilkins

541. WILKINS, ROBERT (CR.035.801.12/2-112)
3 Oct 1856 - Jan Term 1857
wife FANNY all the Interest I now hold in lands and premises which is one
half of the plantation I now live on and one half my son WILLIAM occupies
as reference to a title that I made to my sons STPHEN & WILLIAM will show,
one Mare, Buggy and Harness, one Cow and calf, one Sow and pigs, Seven
Sheep, one Bed and furnature, all the Household and Kitchen furnature;
eldest son JAMES Ten Dollars in addition to previous advancements in Land
and other Property; son WILLIAM Ten Dollars in addition to previous
advancements in Land and other Property; dau. MARY one Cow and Calf, four
head of Sheep, one Bed and furniture; son STPHEN Ten Dollars, One Bed and
furniture, one Shot gun, two pair of Cart wheels, the Ballance of Stock
of Cattle, Hogs and Sheep in addition to the advancement that I have previously made to him in lands; dau. MARGARET one Cow and Calf, four Sheep,
one Bed and furniture; dau. PENICY one Cow and Calf, four Sheep, one Bed
and furniture; dau. ELIZABETH one Cow and Calf, four Sheep, one Bed and
furniture; wife FANNY, son STPHEN, daus. MARY, MARGARET, PENICY and RLIZA-
BETH all my Corn, Pease, Potatoes, Bacon, Pork or Fat Hogs to share and
share alike; daus. MARY, MARGARET, PENICY and ELIZABETH all the money I
have in hand, all the Notes or accounts or Debts, all my present Crop of
Turpentine
extrs: wife FANNY, son STPHEN
wit: BIZZELL JOHNSON, LUTHER R. MATTHIS
                    signed: Robert ⅀ Wilkins

542. WILKINS, WILLIAM (CR.035.801.12/4-108)
6 Oct 1860 - 28 Jul 1876
wife SARAH two hundred and forty two acres upon which we now live for her
natural life; dau. MARY all the tract of land whereon I now live after the
death of her Mother; wife SARAH two beds, bed Steads and furniture, all the
Kitchen furniture, one horse, two Cows and Calves, two Sows and ten or
twelve pigs or Shoats, all the domestic fowl and poultry, twenty barrels of
Corn, twelve hundred pounds of pork or eight hundred pounds of bacon, two
thousand pounds of blade fodder and fifty dollars, negroes Sarah, Hannah
and Isaah; son JAMES negroes Lucy and Isaah after the death of his Mother;
dau. MARIA BROWN negro Hannah after the death of her Mother; dau. MARY
negro Peggy; daus. MARIA & MARY one bed, bed stead and furniture each, two
Cows and calves each; residue of my estate sold and proceeds divided
between my children JAMES, MARIA and MARY
extr: not named
wit: WM. FARRIOR, BENJN. F. HALL
signed: W. Wilkins

543. WILKINSON, BARBARA (CR.035.801.12/A-488)
10 Feb 1827 - Apr Term 1827
son LINCOLN SHUFFIELD negro Maria & her two children Lott & Sam, one bed,
bolster & two pillars, one half of the bed cloths, three of my best chest;
dau. SUSAN HOOKS negro Silvy, one bed, bolster & two pillars, the other
half of the bed clothes; son WILLIAMS DICKSON one bed; grandson THOMAS
ARMSTRONG one bed & furniture which is to be furnished with bolster, pillars,
Sheets, coverlet, etc.; my Kitchen furniture & Stock sold the money equally
divided between LINCOLN SHUFFIELD, SUSAN HOOKS, WILLIAMS DICKSON and the
children of EDWARD ARMSTRONG
extr: DAVID HOOKS
wit: DAVID D. BUNTING, WILLIAM HODGES
                              signed: Barbara X Wilkinson

544. WILKINSON, JOHN JR. (CR.035.801.12)
18 Oct 1836 - Jul Term 1837
wife MARY a part of my plantation whereon I now live Beginning on the main
Road near the Cross Roads on JANE WILKINSONs line to the run of Mill branch
opposite a large ditch in the Edge of McGowens low Grounds to the Head on
the East Side of the branch with Timber Sufficient for Rails and firewood
from all my Lands, negroes Jackson, Horace & Milly and at her decease to
MARY WHITE HOUSTON; wife MARY my Clock during her natural lifetime and
then to WILLIAM J. HOUSTON; wife MARY my Side Board during her natural
lifetime and then to my grandau. MARY ELISA MURRAY; wife MARY two Beds,
Bedsteads and furniture, Six Chairs, Two Tables, one chest, one Trunk,
Fifty Barrels Corn, Fifteen hundred weight of Pork, fifty dollars, one
Hundred dollars for the Support of My old Nego Woman Silva, One Horse, one
Bereaush and Harness, four Cows and Calves, Three Sows and pigs, one ox,
one cart, all the Geese and poultry; son in law SAMUEL HOUSTON a certain
piece of land lying in Possimon Swamp Betwen his lines and the land I Sold
to ABRAM KORNEGAY, negro Peter; dau. ELISABETH ANN HOUSTON negroes Loo,
Patience, Sylva, Nance, Mint, Bill & Horace and negroes Peter and George to
be at her disposal; grandchildren MARY ANNE, HARRIET CAROLINE, SARAH
ELISABETH and JOHN WILKINSON heirs of my dau. HARRIETT SANDLIN all my Lands
on the So Side of Poscimmon, negroes Peter, Ned, Bob, Bill & Alfred as they

arrive at age or marriage; grandson JOHN WILKINSON negro Silvay and Should
he die before he arrives at the age of twenty one his Share to his Brothers
and Sisters Except ROBERT; MARY CATHERINE, THOMAS JAMES, ELIZABETH ANN,
HARRIET PRISCILLA & JULIA HARRISON WILKINSON negroes Nancy and children
Hannah and Martha; grandson ROBERT W. WILKINSON One dollar in addition to
what I have given him by Deed of Gift; dau. MARY JANE MURRAY negroes Jack
and Harry and all my lands lying on the No Side of Possimon and the South
Side of Mill Branch; grandau. HARRIET JANE MURRAY negroe Naomi; grandau.
MARY WHITE HOUSTON negroe Sarah; negroes left to wife MARY be Equally
divided between my grandsons JOHN N. MURRAY, JOHN WILKINSON, JOHN W. HOUSTON
and JOHN W. SANDLIN; Ballance of property Sold and monies Divided into
four Shares Between ELIZABETH ANN HOUSTON, MARY JANE MURRAY, my dec'd dau.
HARRIET SANDLIN's Children and my Dec'd son JAMES WILKINSON's Children
(Except ROBERT); son in law JEREMIAH SANDLIN and dau. in law JANE WILKINSON
One dollar each
extrs: sons in law SAMUEL HOUSTON & HIRAM MURRAY
wit: WILLIAM SWINSON, JAMES B. B. MONK
signed: John Wilkinson Jr.

545. WILKINSON, MARGARET "of Craven County Widdow" (CR.035.801.12/A-532)
27 Aug 1761 - Nov Court 1761
decently buried in the County of Onslow as near to the Bodies of my late
Dear Husband & Child as Conveniently may be; son DAVID SULIVAN land near
Tuckahoe Swamp Devised and Bequeathed to me for work & Labour Done by ROBERT
JERMAIN Late of Craven County now in the Occupation of JOHN JERMAIN Son of
the Late ROBERT, one Bed, one Course bed tick which is at Mr. Whites.
Spining Wheel, bed stead and table at JOHN JERMAINS, forty shillings, four
Barrells of Corn, 7 Yards of Linnen, two pair of Stockings all Left to me
by ROBERT JERMAIN, one Cow & Cow Calf Red and White, one Heifer with her
first Calf, a Bull, a Yearling Heifir White Backed, a Large Brindle Heifer;
grandau. of my Son RICHARD BURNETT at Lynches Creek one Calimanco Gown, one
Country Cloth Gown, one Blue and White Calico Gown, a Black Silk Crape
Petty coat and four Yards of Sky Blue Tammy, apair of Worsted Steockings,
a pair of Home Spun Stockings, a Blue Cloak
extr: WILLIAM HOUSTON
wit: THOS. WORLEY, DOMENI DONAHO, WILLIAM HOUSTON JUR
                                        signed: Margaret   Wilkinson

546. WILLIAMS, AARON (CR.035.801.12)
5 Mar 1808 - Jul Term 1808
wife MARY negroes Jerry and Zilpah, five cows and calves, two feather Beds
and furniture, the house and plantation where I now live; son DAVID negro
Black Bob, my mill and all the Lands Joining the same; son ISAAC NEWTON
WILLIAMS negro yellow Bob, my upper plantation at the Run of Taylor Creek
at the mouth of a small Branch Call'd the Middle Branch to the Edge of a
pond to the Back line by Island Creek Pocoson; sons ZCHEREAH MATHIS WILLIAMS
negro Bruster, all the Land on the North Side of Taylor Creek, 100 acres
lying on Reedy Branch, 30 acres lying on Rockfish Creek abouve the Main
Road; son SAMUEL PINKNEY WILLIAMS negro George, land on the west side of
the Mill Swamp as far as the Run which I had of DAVID WILLIAMS, 35 acres
secur'd in my own name, Eleven acres Secured in my own name, 100 acres on
the west side of Rockfish at Goff's Race paths Joining Devane, Hufham and

Cummins; son ENOCH negro Hannah, my home Plantation at the Mouth of a
Small Branch of Taylor Creek Call'd the Middle Branch with ISAAC NEWTON
WILLIAMS line to the Back line to the Run of the Mill pond; dau. PHEBE
COOPER negroes Pat & Maurace, two Cows and Calves, one Bed & furniture;
dau. MARY MURREY negroes Dines & Jam, one Bed & furniture; dau. ESTHER
negroe Omey, one Bed and furniture; dau. ANN JANE negroe Rhoda, one Bed
and furniture; if my wife Brings the Child She now is Pregnant with and
it should be a son it to have my River Plantation Joining J. KENAN & WM.
PICKET, 200 acres on the south side of Maxwell's Swamp, if it is a dau.
these lands to be for ZACHEREAH M. WILLIAMS & the dau. to have an Equal
Portion with its Sisters
extrs: wife & son DAVID
wit: WILLIAM EZZELL, STEPHEN WILLIAMS, LEWIS ✷ HEDGEMAN
signed: Aaron Williams

547. WILLIAMS, ANTHONY   (S. S. Wills/DRB2)
3 Jul 1751 - 14 Apr 1752
son STEPHEN WILLIS the plantation wher on I now live & three Hundred acres
Joyning to it, negroes Arther & Rachel, one water mill & ninty acres Joyning to it only allowing my wife ye Benifit of Sd. Mill till my Son Come to
ye age of ninten years; son STEPHEN all ye Rest of my lands & one Still
allowing my wife ye Benifit of Sd. Still till my Son comes of age & afterwards to Still her own Lickquor & also allowing my Son BENJAMEN his own
Lickquer that he makes at home; son STEPHEN one new Riphel gun which is
now my Hunting gun & his Choice of all my Breading mairs Except one Bay
mair Called Blaize, five Sows Each Sow having five pigs, two Ews & Lambs,
a Ram, one new feather Beed & firniture ye Bed having thirty weight of new
feathers, one Sizeable Eyron pot & one Eyron frying pan; EDWARD CARTER my
whole wright to two Hundred acres of land which he Hath got a pattent for
in my name; brother JOHN one Hundred & fifty acres Joyning ye plantation
that WILLIAM DRESCOT [PRESCOT ?] now Lives on; son STEPEN one Lott of
Cooppers tools & one whip Saw he allowing his mother ye uce of it and
Likwise Let his Brother BENJAMIN have ye uce of sd. Saw; son BENJAMIN ye
Remainder part of ye tract of Land I now Live on called ye Beaver Dam neck
& ninty three acres Lying on a Small Branch cald The Whit oak & mother &
Brother STEPHEN to Bear an Equal in paying ye quit rents of Sd. Land untill
he comes to ye age of ninteen Ears & Likwise his Brother STEPHEN to Build
him a Sufficient Dwelling of ye Bigness of twenty & Sixteen foot that is
ye holl only to be Done wokman Like, negroes Lucy & Mark, thirty weight of
new feathers, a pair of new Blankets ann Bed tick & Boulsters Tick, a
Sizeable new Iron pt, a new frying pan, one new Deep puter Dish, two new
puter Basons Each Bason to Hold two Quarts, Half a Duzen of new puter plates
& Half a Duzen of new puter Spoons, five Likly young Cows & Calves, one
Likley young mair of ye age of three years & five Sows Each Sow having five
pigs, one Ewe & Lamb & one Ram; dau. MARY wife of MOSES POWEL ye value of
five pounds Sterling Credit in any store in ye county where I have any Deal-
ings; dau. PENELLIPEY ye first young negroe that is Born in ye Stock Either
of ye Girls arlready mentioned or of ye ould wench, five Likly young cows &
calves, one Likly young mair, thirty weight of new feathers, a new Bed tick
& Boulster, one pair of Blankets, Two Likly young Sows & ten pigs & one Ewe
& Lamb, one Sizeable Eyron pot, one frying pan, Two new puter Basons Each
holding two quarts, Six new puter plates & Six new puter Spoons; dau. PHERIBE

one young negroe ye Second that is Born of ye Stock Either of ye ould
wench or of Either of ye young ones Spoken of & to be taken from ye wench
at ye age of Eighteen months, five Likly yong cows & calves & one Likly
young mair & thirty weight of new feathers, a new bed tick & Boulster &
one pair of new Blankets & two Likly young Sows & ten pigs & one Ewe &
Lamb, one Sizeable Eyron pot, one frying pan, Two new puter Basons Each
holding two Quarts, Six new puter plates & Six new puter Spoons; dau. EASTER
the third young negro that is Born in ye Stock Either of ye ould wench or of
Either of ye young ons mentioned & it to be taken of at ye age of Eighteen
months, five Likly young Cows & Calfes, one Likly young mair, thirty weight
of new feathers, a new Bed tick & Boulster & a pair of new Blankets, two
Likly young Sows & pigs Each Sow having five pigs & one Ewe & lamb, one
Sizeable Eyron pot, one frying pan, two new puter Basons Each holding two
Quarts, Six new puter plates & Six new puter spoons; dau. SIVELITY the
fourth & fifth young negroes that is Born in ye Stock not Depriving my Son
STEPEN of a Bove three of ye increace of his wench, five Likly young Cows
& Calves, one Likly young mair & thirty weight of new feathers, a new Bed
tick & Boulster, one pair of new Blankets, two Likly young Sows & ten pigs
& one Ewe & Lamb, one Sizeable Eyron pot, one frying pan, two new puter
Basons Each containing two Quarts, Six new puter plates, Six new puter Spoons;
grandson CADER POWEL the Sixth young negroe that is Born in ye Stock; cousen
ANTHONY BEVELY ye Vellue of five pounds Virginia currancy to be paid to him
when he come of age in Live Stock; wife MARY all the Rest of my Estat Movable
& immovable and after her Decece all the moovables in Ye House Equally Divided
Between my two Sons STEPHEN & BENJAMIN & all ye Live Stock Equally Devided
Between my four youngest Daughters; my father in Law [not named] may have
a Sufficient maintainance in ye family During his pleasure; negro Will to be
Sold & another young fellow Bought with ye money for ye uce of ye plantation
During my wife's Widdow Hood & after to my Son STEPHEN he paying three fourths
of ye value to his four youngest Sisters two thirds to ye youngest & ye Rest
to ye other three; old negro wench Shall Serve my wife as long as She Lives
upon ye plantation & after to Have her Choice Either to Serve her time out
Equally amongst my four youngest Daus. or to be Disposed of in ye Same manner
as ye fellow
extrs: JOB BROOKES, WILLIAM MAIRS
wit: SAMUELL JONES, GEORGE SMITH, JOHN ‡ WILLIAMS
signed: Anthony Williams

548. WILLIAMS, BLANEY (Sampson Bk 1, p. 414)
5 Mar 1833 - May Term 1852
wife MARY JANE my Plantation in Green County lying & being on the Swamp
called Fort Run containing four hundred & forty two acres, my plantation in
Duplin County on Wolf Branch containing two hundred & forty acres, negroes
Pender aged about sixty or seventy, Amos aged about forty five or fifty,
Bob aged about sixty, Abram aged about seventeen, Steven aged about fifteen,
Toney aged about Ten, York aged about four, Anna and all her increase aged
about Thirty, Zilla aged about Seven, Sarah four or five years, Easther aged
about two, Lucy aged about two, Rose aged about twenty, another Rose aged
about thirty, Frank aged about twenty five, Lucy & two children, Harry being
now in the western country carried by WILLIAMS COOPER, Sarah & all her children, Hiram, Joe, Henry, whole rest and residue of my property either real or

personal, stock of every discription, hogs, horses, Cattle, sheep, household & Kitchen furniture, corn, fodder & bacon
extr: wife MARY JANE
wit: J. A. EVES, ISAAC ✗ PHIPS
signed: Blaney Williams

549. WILLIAMS, EDWARD (CR.035.801.12/A-531)
10 May 1825 - Jan Term 1826
mother TEMPERANCE my lands & negroes Jim & fred and after hir death the said
lands & negroes to my sisters ELIZABETH COTTLE, DICEY HOUSTON, CHELLY
HOUSTON & POLLY HOUSTON; EDWARD son of WILLIAM HOUSTON my young filly;
EDWARD son of HENRY HOUSTON forty dollars
extrs: mother TEMPERANCE, GEORGE E. HOUSTON
wit: ABEL MORGAN, SOLOMON BEESLEY
signed: Edward Williams

550. WILLIAMS, ELIZABETH (CR.035.801.12/A-527)
15 Aug 1821 - Oct Term 1821
GEORGE & JACKSON WILLIAMS negroes Caleb, Sale and Toney; sister PATENCE my
Bonit; Father [not named] the Ballance of my Share of the Estate to Ceep
his Lifetime; Father Gairdean for the above Children
extr: not named
wit: LUKE M. HUGGINS, WILLIAM ✗ HUDGGINS
                                    signed: Elizabeth ✗ Williams

551. WILLIAMS, ELIZABETH (CR.035.801.12/4-126)
1 May 1858 - 5 Jan 1878
sisters PHEBE and ZILPHA all the property both Real and personal of which
I may be possessed at the time of my decease it being all my right in the
property bequeathed to me by my father STEPHEN
extrs: sisters PHEBE and ZILPHA
wit: HANSON F. MURPHY, DAVID H. WILLIAMS
                                    signed: Elizabeth ✝ Williams

552. WILLIAMS, FRANCIS (CR.035.801.12/4-7)
3 Jan 1854 - 27 Oct 1868
daus. MARGARET C., SARAH A., PARMELIA & ROSA P. My Dwelling Home where I now
live with Two Hundred acres adjoining, all my Household & Kitchen furniture,
Plantation and farming Tools, Stock of every Kind; son CHARLES FRANCIS all
the ballance of my lands; daus. MARGARET C., SARAH A., PARMELIA and ROSA P.
negroes Treasy, Caroline, George, Joseph, Lucinda, Virginia, Markes, Exerline,
Dilsey, Ransom, Julia, Harriet, Maria, Zilpha, Dick, Crocket & Danil; son
CHARLES F. negroes Moses, Violet and Lucy; dau. MARY I. DRAUGHON negroes
Judith, Shade, Amanda, Margaret, Senia & Friday; dau. EMILY wife of BLACKSMON
COX negroes Mary, Henry and John; negroes Allen, Linda and Squire sold for
payment of debts
extr: son CHARLES FRANCIS
wit: ISAAC B. KELLY, K. BRYAN
signed: Fr. Williams

553. WILLIAMS, GEORGE (CR.035.801.12/A-520)
11 Sep 1816 - Apr Term 1817
wife TABITHA negroes Kit, Jim, Amos & Lettice, one Fetherbed, all the household & kitchen furniture, plantation tools, all the Horses, Cattle & Hogs,
every other kind of Stock; son JACOB & daus. MOURNING SHEPPARD, PATSEY BEST,
MARY HARRIS, & grandau. MARY dau. of HENRY STOAKES negroes left to wife;
grandau. MARY dau. of TEMPERANCE one Featherbed; grandson ROBERT son of
ABSALOM BEST one Featherbed
extrs: GEORGE E. HOUSTON, EDWARD WILLIAMS
wit: JOHN PEARSALL, WILLIAM HARRIS
signed: George Williams

554. WILLIAMS, HOPKINS (3-110)
25 Sep 1856 - Jul Term 1866
committee in laying off my wife's years allowance for her self and family
to consider her dau. & grandau. KITTY E. ROUSE as part of her family; daus.
REBECCA and HULDA one bed, bedstead & furniture each with one cow and calf
and one hundred and fifty dollars each; son JACOB one hundred and fifty
dollars; grandson JAMES BRANTLEY BISHOP one hundred dollars provided he
remains untill he is twenty one; all the perichable property sold and mony
equally divided between all my daus.
extr: not named
wit: JAMES HALL, GEORGE M. WILSON
signed: H. Williams
Oct Term 1867
jury found said paper writing is not and does not contain any part of the
last will and testament of the said HOPKINS WILLIAMS deceased and that the
probate and record of the same be cancelled and ordered that BRYANT KENNEDY
be appointed administrator of the estate

555. WILLIAMS, JAMES (CR.035.801.12/A-536)
25 Mar 1797 - Jul Term 1797
wife EMELE My Late Dwelling house with a Third part of the manner plantation, Two head of my horses, Four Cows & Calfs, Fore head of Dry Cattle,
Sows & Pigs and hogs, one feather Bed, Bedstead and firniture, all my tools;
son JAMES one Dollar Besides what he hath already had; son EZEKIEL one
Dollar Besides what he hath already had; son BURWELL One horse, bridle,
all the Land I now possess, two Cows & Calves, one Feather Bed, Bed Stead
and furniture, one iron pot, three puter plates, half Dozen of Knives and
forks; dau. CHARITY MANER one Dollar with what she has already had; dau.
EMILE one Bed, Bedstead and firniture, One iron pot, three puter plates,
half Dosen of Knives and forks, one Cow and Calf; dau. BETHAH One Cow and
Calf, one iron pot, three puter plates, half Dozen Knives & forks, one
feather Bed, bedstead and furniture; dau. ZILLA One Cow & Calf, one iron
pot, Three puter plates, half a dozen of Knives & forks, a feather bed,
bedsted and furnature; one half of Remainding part of my Estate to son
BURWELL and the other half to Be equally Divided amongst the other Children;
at my wife's Death all the Estate then Remaining one half to go to my son
BURWELL and the other half to Be equally Devided amongst the other Children
extrs: sons JAMES & EZEKEL
wit: THOS. SHELTON, JOHN MAXWELL, REBECKAH SHELTON
signed: James Williams

556. WILLIAMS, JAMES (CR.035.801.12/2-104)
28 Nov 1848 - Oct Term 1856
wife [not named] all the lands I am now in possession of on the East side
of the publick road leading to Grove Swamp and on to the court house including my mansion house, also the lotts on the west side of this road where my
barns and stables are standing, all the property of whatever kind that was
settled upon her upon our marriage, three horses, five cows, twenty head of
sheep, all my geese and chickens, three best ploughs and gear, all my household and Kitchen furneture; dau. ADORA all the property given her by deed
of gift; daus. ADORA and MARTHA ELIZA all the ballance of my property both
real and personal, all the lands I own and negroes Tony, Cherry, Washington,
Rose, Noel, Dick, Mary, Julia, Primus, Sarah, Lemon, Kenion, Tony, Adam,
Squire, Jacob, Aaron, Chancey, John, Henry, Chancy, James, Edward & Parmelia
and should they die without barring a child or children property to go to
my nephews JAMES CICERO son of my Brother ROBERT and JAMES son of my Brother
HARPER; dau. ADORA two beds and the necessary furneture; dau. MARTHA E.
two beds and the necessary furneture
extrs: brother HARPER, nephew JAMES CICERO
wit: WM B. MIDDLETON, LEBBEUS MIDDLETON
signed: Jas. Williams

557. WILLIAMS, JAMES SR. (CR.035.801.12/2-43)
26 Sep 1846 - Apr Term 1849
son JAMES JR. and daus. MARY KENNEDY, ZILPHA SOUTHERLAND, BARBARY BROWN &
CILVY BROWN mony arising from the sale of one hundred acres lying on the
west side of the North East River; negro Peter hired out annually and
monies arising Kept on interest until my son MERRILL dec'd youngest son
[not named] comes of age, then Peter sold and monies arising together with
those from his hire equally divided between my son MERRILL's three sons
THOMAS, GARRESON and MERRILL JAMES; dau. in law PENELOPE N. my plantation
whereon I now live; residue of my estate sold and surplus equally divided
between my son JAMES JR. and daus. ZILPHA SOUTHERLAND, BARBARY BROWN and
CILVY BROWN; son MERRILL and dau. PRISCILLA KENNEDY one dollar each
extrs: WILLIAM FARRIOR, DAVID BROWN
wit: JOHN B. KENNADY, A MAXWELL
signed: James Williams Sr.

558. WILLIAMS, JESSE SR. (CR.035.801.12/2-119)
30 Jan 1853 - Apr Term 1857
wife SARAH one third of the land on which I now reside on the east side of
Muddy Creek, one hundred and fifty dollars, one bed, bedstead and furniture,
two cows & calfs; sons JESSE & THOMAS H. my land lying on the west side of
Muddy Creek; son LUCIAN lands on the east side of Muddy Creek for his life
and then to my daus. MANSEY and SARAH ELIZA wife of JOHN BOSTICK; dau.
MANSEY one bed, bed stead & furniture, one loom & gear; dau. MANIRVA wife
of GIBSON SLOAN one hundred and fifty dollars; dau. THERESEY wife of
MARSHEL SLOAN one hundred dollars; residue of my property including
negro Frank sold and ballance of money divided between my children JESSE,
THOMAS H., MANERSAY and SARAH ELIZA
extr: son JESSE
wit: JOHN J. WHITEHEAD, CHRIS. B. WHITEHEAD
signed: Jesse Williams

559. WILLIAMS, JOHN (CR.035.801.12/A-497)
2 Aug 1758 - Aug Term 1761 [original missing from folder]
wife PRUDENCE the Liberty to Live up and Improve the one half of my Plantation which I now Live upon and one half of my houses and one half of my
house hold Stuff and one half of my Stock both Cattle, horoesses, hogs and
Sheep and on her marage or death to Return unto my Son JAMES; son JOHN all
my Rite to a Plantation which I formily lived at fer Plantation _[?]_ ,
negroes Mary and her Childe Rose, one Ewe and Lamb, one sow and Pigs; dau.
CHARITY PRESCOT one Ewe and Lamb, one Sow and Pigs besides what she has
already had; dau. PERCELLI BARFIELD one Ewe and Lamb, one Sow and Pigs
besides what she has already had; son JAMES all my Plantation which I now
live uppon with all my land being in Duplin County with all my buildings
and fences and orchards, all my house hold Stuff with all my movaeble
Estate; grandson WILLIAM PRESCOT ten _[?]_ out of my Estate
extrs: son JAMES, JOSEPH SUTTON
wit: not named
          signed: John ⊢)y Williams

560. WILLIAMS, JOHN (CR.035.801.12/A-503)
16 Jun 1790 - Jul Term 1790
wife PRESELLA the maner plantation whereon I now Live, negroes Moll, Santee,
Charles, Jack & Jinnea if they prove Ordaly & submittive & if not to Be
hired out & the profits to Raise & School my Children, use of negro Rotch
untill son JOHN is twenty one, three horses, two Cows & Calves, five Steares,
five Sows & pigs, all the Sheep & Geese, fore feather Beds & furniture, all
the plantation tools, Twenty five pounds in money to Give my youngest Son
fore yeares Schooling & my Three youngest Daughters Two Years Schooling
Each; dau. EASTHER QUINN negro Beck; dau. ZILPHA negro Arthur, Eighty
pounds, five Cows and Calves, one feather Bed and furneture; dau. JURASA
negroes Little Dinah & Tony, fifteen pounds money; dau. PRUDANCE negroes
Hannah & Major; dau. SEANEY negroes Frank and Luce; dau. PATIENCE negroes
Cheals and Lonnon; son JACOB Land & plantation where THOMAS QUINN Now
Lives, every part and percil of Land I at this time posses in Onslow County,
all the plantation tools, the Blacksmith tools, negroes Rose, Abraham & Tom,
Six Cows & Calves, One young mare, Saddle & bridle, use of Negroes Cesar,
Bob, Tone, Charles, Jack & Green for six months for to Build a Mill & finish
of Complett also negro Dick; son LEWIS all and Every part & percil of Land
that I possess at this time in Wake County, land I perchased forom LOTT
GREGORY, negroes Jeen, Amey & Ginna, five Cows & Calves, One young horse,
Bridle and Sadle, a Suit of Aparrel to the price of ten pounds; son JESSE
the Manor plantation that I now Live on with all the Land that I at this
time possess in Duplin County with all the plantation tools thereon, negroes
Bob & Nathan, one young hors, Bridle and Saddle, a suit of Apparel to the
amount of ten pounds price; son FOUNTAIN Every part & percell of Land that
I at this time possess in Jones County with all the plantation tools there
unto, negroes Cesar & Big Dinak, one young horse, Saddle & Bridle, a Suit
of apparrel to the amount of ten pounds price; son JOHN the Land that I
Bought of LUTSON STROUD and RICHARD PRESCOAT, negroes Rotch & George, one
young horse, Saddle & Bridle; son in law WILLIAM HEATH negro Catoe; personal estate Sold & Mony Equally Divided Between my Five Sons
extrs: son JACOB, Brother in law ARCHELUS BARNS
wit: WILLIAM HUBBARD, THOS. SHELTON
signed: John Williams

561. WILLIAMS, JOHN (CR.035.801.12/A-513)
22 Jan 1803 - Apr Term 1803
nefew WILLIAM one Hundred pounds owing to me from JOHN NEAL; nefew EDWARD
Seventy Dollars, thirty five Dollars in hand the other half to be raised
out of my bacon; mother ROBETHA my Sorrel mare and after hir Death to my
nefew WILLIAM and mare be put to horse and her first Colt to my nefew
EDWARD; nefew WILLIAM my Small bay mare for the use of my Fathers Negro
Fellow Kit; nefews WILLIAM & EDWARD my Cattle and hogs; executors to
sell my bacon for ready mony and brother JACOB to get ten dollars which
I owe him and residue of money Eaqually divided between my nefews WILLIAM
and EDWARD
extrs: EDWARD PEARSALL, nefew WILLIAM
wit: EDWARD PEARSALL, GEORGE WILLIAMS
                              signed: John ✝ Williams

562. WILLIAMS, JOHN (CR.035.801.12)
25 Aug 1836 - Apr Term 1840
wife ANN negross Nan & Dinah, one half of my land, Stock, Household &
Kitchen firniture, all my plantation tools; son STEPHEN negro Dinah after
wifes death; dau. ELIZABETH FUSSELL negro Nan after wifes death; dau.
MARGRET M. negroes Brister & Cint, two Cows & calves, two feather beds,
bedstids and firniture; son JAMES K. negroes Clarah, Susan and Jacob,
two feather beds, Bedsteads & firniture, all my House hold & Kitchen
firniture, plantation tools and stock of all Kinds; son in law ISAAC N.
WILLIAMS one Cow & calf, one feather bed, Bedstid & firniture, two ewes &
lambs, one table, one Dollar in cash; dau. ANN WILLIAMS children MOLCY A.,
ELIZABETH JANE, MAHALE, CAROLINE M. & DAVID H. negro Hannah to remain with
executors until the youngest Child comes of age then to be sold and mony
equally divided betwin my dau. ANN's children; son STEPHEN negro Pheb;
son BYRD negroes Fred & Jude; dau. ELIZABETH FUSSELL negro Het; dau.
REBECAH JANE negroes Sarah & Henry
extrs: sons STEPHEN & JAMES K.
sit: STEPHEN WILLIAMS, ANN JANE WILLIAMS
signed: John Williams

563. WILLIAMS, MARGARET (CR.035.801.12/3-39)
2 Apr 1857 - Oct Term 1861
nephew CHARLES FRANCIS negroes Caster, Hariet, Eliza, John, George, Henry
& Abram; brother FRANCIS five dollars; brother BRANCH five dollars;
brother HARPER five dollars; brother ROBERT's heirs five dollars; brother
JAMES' heirs five dollars; brother BLANEY five dollars; sister POLLY.
COOPER five dollars; sister SARAH PRIDGION's heirs five dollars; sister
PATIENCE HUNTER's heirs five dollars; sister ROSA COOPER's heirs five
dollars; residire of estate after paying debts and legacies to nephew
CHARLES FRANCIS
extrs: brother FRANCIS, nephew CHARLES FRANCIS
wit: JOHN D. STANFORD, D. M. McINTIRE
                              signed: Margaret ✗ Williams

564. WILLIAMS, PHEBE (CR.035.801.12/4-124)
1 May 1858 - 5 Jan 1878
sisters ELIZABETH and ZILPHA all the property both Real and personel of

which I may be possessed at the time of my decease it being all my right in
the property bequeathed to me by my father STEPHEN WILLIAMS
extrs: sisters ELIZABETH and ZILPHA
wit: HANSON F. MURPHY, DAVID H. WILLIAMS
signed: Phebe ✗ Williams

565. WILLIAMS, REDEN (CR.035.801.12/2-54)
30 Dec 1849 - Apr Term 1850
son BARACHIAS BELL and dau. MARY ELIZER BELL Children of DEBORAH BELL Deceased
all my Land and negros Chany, Lonnon, Boson, Silvey & Edward with my Stock of
all kinds, Household and kitchen furniture (both underage)
extr: DANIEL BOWDEN
wit: D. B. NEWTON, B. BOWDEN
signed: Reden Williams

566. WILLIAMS, RICHARD "of Southampton" (CR.035.801.12/A-490)
__ Nov 1770 - Apr Court 1774
wife LYDIA negro Jacob, one horse, bridle and Saddle, Six head of Cattle,
one Feather bed and furnature, Negro Ancey, four Dishes, four basons, Eight
puter plates, one Dozen of Spoons; cosin JOSHUA DAUGHTRY negro garl after
wifes Disease; cosin JOSHUA DAUGHTRY the plantation on Where on I Now
Live With three hundred acer, a grist mill, one hundred and fifty acres
Whereon WILLIAM WIGGINS now Lives to be sold
extrs: wife LYDIA, JOSHUA DAUGHTRY
wit: WILLIAM WEST, BENNET BIRDSONG, LEUSEY ✝ HEDGPETH
signed: Richard Williams

567. WILLIAMS, ROBERT (A-491)
22 Aug 1810 - Jul Term 1819
wife MARY negroes Cloe & Mauney, the plantation where I now life, my movable
property, all the provisions, my stock for the use and purpose of supporting
my younger children; son FRANCIS negro Don; dau. MARY COOPER negro Tillah
and her children; dau. SARAH PRIDGEN negro Honae and her children; four
youngest sons BLANY, BRANCH, HARPER and JAMES the land I possess in this
County and in Greene County; five youngest sons ROBERT, BLANY, BRANCH,
HARPER and JAMES a negro man a piece out of my Stock of Negroes as they
reach the age of twenty one; daus. now living with me PEGGY, TOBITHA,
PATIENCE and ROSE be made Equal in Negro property with my five sons; sons
and daus. BLANY, BRANCH, HARPER, JAMES, PEGGY, TOBITHA, ROSE and PATIENCE
have a horse and a bed and furniture a piece
extrs: wife MARY, sons FRANCIS and ROBERT
wit: EDWARD PEARSALL, GEORGE BEST
signed: Robert Williams

568. WILLIAMS, STEPHEN (CR.035.801.12/A-486)
23 May 1840 - Apr Term 1841
wife [not named] plantation whereon I live, all my cattle, horses, hogs &
sheep for her lifetime; daus. ELIZABETH, PHEBE and ZILPHA all the land on
the north east side of Rockfish creek as far as the most So run of said creek;
grandson JAMES T. JOHNSON all my lands on the South side of Rockfish creek as
far as the South run of said creek; grandson GEORGE WASHINGTON all my lands
on Taylors Creek; grandson JAMES T. JOHNSON and daus. ELIZABETH, PHEBE
& ZILPHA one half of my stock of cattle and sheep;
daus. BRIDGET and MARY the remaining half of the cattle

and sheep; daus. ELIZABETH, PHEBE and ZILPHA all my stock of horses and hogs; dau. ANN to remain with my grandson JAMES T. JOHNSON or her sisters ELIZABETH, PHEBE & ZILPHA and that they furnish her every comfortable necessary of life but in no wise subject to the benefit of her husband ISAAC WILSON; dau. MARY one feather bed; grandson JAMES T. JOHNSON one feather bed and its necessary furneture; daus. ELIZABETH, PHEBE and ZILPHA the remaining part of my household and Kitchen furniture and farming eatensils, all cash, notes and accounts extrs: son in law STEPHEN WILLIAMS, grandson JAMES T. JOHNSON
wit: STEPHEN WILLIAMS, BRIAN N. WILLIAMS
signed: Stephen Williams

569. WILLIAMS, CAPT. STEPHEN (CR.035.801.12/2-48)
8 Jan 1849 - Jul Term 1849
wife ANNA JANE negroes Isaac, Tom, Mint, Judy, Lucy & Sarah; son SAMUEL A. negro Isaac at wife's death; son BRYAN N. negroes Crog, Brister & Roger; son JOSEPH T. negroes Bill, Jim, Curtice, & Julia; son DAVID H. negroes Holley, Isham, Fennel & Martha; son SAMUEL A. negroes Suffer, Ander, Sollomon, John (Suffer's Son) & Stephin; dau. MARY ANN HUFHAM negro Rachel and all her Children Mariah, Shad, Lucy Jane, Siller, Mariann & Thankful; dau. RACHEL C. WELLS negroes Little Jude, Stoake, Tabitha Jane & Morris; dau. ELIZABETH negroes Nance in the possession of STOAKES WELLS and little Isaac, Rachel Ann and Derry, one Bed and furniture, one Cow and calf; dau. HARRIET ADALINE negroes Suff, Sam, Sarah Eliza and little Mint, one Cow & Calf, a bed and firniture; grandchildren MARY CAROLINE and BRYAN S. HERRING negroes Eliza & Feraby and all there children except Jo wich is Eliza's Child and Jo to Son in law STEPHEN HERRING; son BRYAN N. 750 Acres on the So. side of the Bever dam Swamp which he now lives on; son JOSEPH T. all the Land my Father Bought of my uncle JOSEPH WILLIAMS which is part of the plantation I now live on, a small Survey a joining WM. RIVENBARK JR., a small piece joining ANN DAVIS's land, one Sorrel Horse, one Yoak of Steers, one bed and firniture; son DAVID H. my SAMUEL DAVIS tract, my Campbell Survey, both lying in the fork of Rockfish & Doctors Creek, my PAYTEN POWEL Survey of 120 Acre lying on the So. Et. Side of Rockfish and both sides of long Branch, one young Horse, one yoke of Oxen, one bed and firniture, a Cow & Calf; son SAMUEL A. all the rest of my lands including my House I now live in and my Grist Mill on both sides of Rockfish from the run of Long Branch to STEPHEN HERRINGs, all my tools of every kind, one yoak of Steers, one bed and firniture; dau. MARY ANN HUFHAM and her two daughters [not named] live with my wife & son S. A. as part of the family; wife all my Stock of every kind that I have not Willed, all my Household firniture and Kitchen firniture; negro John Williams sold to pay Debts; wife negro Rose
extrs: sons B. N. & D. H.
wit: JOSEPH J. WARD, ISAIAH ROBINSON, JAMES T. JOHNSON
signed: Stephen Williams

570. WILLIAMS, THOMAS (CR.035.801.12/A-532)
26 Oct 1774 - Jan Term 1775
nuncupative will
ZACHERIAH FAIRCLOTH and SARAH FAIRCLOTH made oath that THOMAS WILLIAMS Desired when he Lay upon his Death Bead but in his proper Senses that CHARLES BUTLER should have all his things
before JOHN WILLIAMS Esqr.

571. WILLIAMS, THOMAS (CR.035.801.12/A-539)
16 Jan 1823 - Apr Term 1823
wife POLLY my Lands and Plantation, all my house hold and Kitchen furniture,
four cows and calvs or yearlings, two Sows and pigs, four head of Sheep,
my black horse Frozen, and at her death sold and the profits Equally Divided
between BRICE WILLIAMS and SALLY BAISDEN; nephew JOSEPH one hundred acres
on the South West Side of Lime Stone branch; BRICE WILLIAMS the Land and
Plantation whereon I now Live on the north east side of Limestone Swamp;
wife POLLY my horse cart during her natural life, all the corn that is now
in by crib and all the pork [torn], two plows, [torn] axes; sisters
CHRISTIAN and PATIENCE one Dollar Each; brothers LEMUEL and NATHAN one
Dollar Each; brother LEWIS ten Dollars
extrs: JASON GREGORY, friend BRICE WILLIAMS
wit: JESSE BASDEN, SALY BASDEN
                    signed: Thomas   Williams

572. WILLIAMS, WILLIAM W. (CR.035.801.12/3-2)
28 Dec 1858 - Apr Term 1859
mother [not named] all of my property both real and personal that I inher-
ited from my father's [not named] estate
extr: not named
wit: ROBERT G. PRIDGEN, S. D. LAFAYETTE PRIDGEN
signed: William W. Williams

573. WILLIAMS, ZILPHA (CR.035.801.12/4-122)
1 May 1858 - 5 Jan 1878
sisters ELIZABETH and PHEBE all the property both Real and personal of
which I may be possessed at the time of my decease it being my right in the
property bequeathed to me by my father STEPHEN WILLIAMS
extrs: sisters ELIZABETH and PHEBE
wit: HANSON F. MURPHY, DAVID H. WILLIAMS
signed: Zilpha Williams

574. WILLIAMSON, SHADRACH (CR.035.801.12/A-514)
2 Oct 1807 - Oct Term 1807
wife MARY all my provisions, my Stock of Cattles and hogs, my houshold
furniture and plantation tools, use of my Land for the purpose of raising
my Children and after the death of my said Wife my little persanal property
equally divided between my children CHARLES, JOHN and SARAH, also my land
containing one hundred acres
extrs: EDWARD PEARSALL, ANDREW STOKES
wit: EDWARD PEARSALL, ANDREW STOAKES
                    signed: Shadrach   Williamson

575. WILLIAMSON, WILLIAM M. (CR.035.801.12/3-119)
11 Jul 1854 - Apr Term 1867
wife FRANCIS all my property consisting of Negroes, stock of all Kinds,
poultry, household and Kitchen furniture; executor to sell enough of my
property to purchase a tract of land for my wife and children [not named]
to live on costing some eight hundred or a thousand dollars; wife FRANCIS
one Mare named Poll, one young hors named Jim, also one buggy & harness
extr: HOLOWAY SIKES
wit: JOS. W. BLOUNT, D. B. NEWTON
signed: W. M. Williamson

188

576. WILLSON, JOHN SEN. (CR.035.801.12/A-528)
11 Jun 1829 ~ Aug Term 1829
wife ELIZABETH all the Lands I possess, the mare that I possess at this
time, Seven head of Sheep, all my stock of hogs and Catle, beads and their
furniture, household and Chichan furniture with all my working tolls, my
gun; son DANIEL too head of Sheep; son ALEXANDER too head of Sheep; son
WILLIAM too head of Sheep; son ISAAC twenty five Cents; dau. ANN BOWEN
twenty five Cents; son JOHN one Dollar; dau. CHATRIN BLONTON twenty five
cents; son THOMAS twenty five cents; after the rasing my family and the
ckooling of my children and death of my wife sons DAVID and MARGIN to
Posess the land now belonging to me and Property given to wife to be
devided Amongst daus. REBECA, ELIZABETH, MARY and SARAH
extrs: wife ELIZABETH, DAVID WELLS
wit: ALLEN CANNON [?], JAMES NEWTON, ALEXANDER WILSON, REBECCA WILSON
signed: John ✝ Willson

577. WORLEY, ANN "Widow" (CR.035.801.12/A-499)
24 May 1794 - Jan Term 1795
grandau. ANN SOWEL one Cow and Calf; grandau. ELIZABETH MILLER one Cow and
Calf; grandau's. Son JACOB LAWHORN Be Schooled to the amount of Six pounds;
son LOFTIS and Two daus. ELIZABETH JONES & WINNEY SMITH negroe Called Pegge,
my stock of all kinds, household firniture, all my working tools, Everything that I possess after all my Just Debts is paid and the Remr. to be
Equally Divided amongst my Son & Daughters; Pegge may take her Choice who
of the Three She will have to live with
extrs: son LOFTIS, THOMAS SHELTON
wit: GEORGE MILLER, JOHN ✝ JONES
signed: Ann ✝ Worley

578. WORSLEY, JOHN (CR.035.801.12/A-483)
30 Aug 1796 - Oct Term 1796
wife ELIZABETH negro Jesse, five Cows & Calves, one Bed and firniture, five
pounds in Gold, one Mare, Saddle & Bridle and at her Death to dau. CHARLOTTE;
dau. CHARLOTTE negroes Hannah, Jo, Prince, Dave & Doniel, five pounds in
Money to Be paid in Gold, one Bay mar with two whele Jut; grandson WILLIAM
all the Land that I possess on the North Side of Panthur Swamp, Fifteen Cows
and Calves, one Hundred Silver Dollars, negro Toney; grandson PITMAN all
the land and primises I Possess on the South side of panthur swamp Whereon
I Now live, one Hundred Silver Dollars, negroe Friday, one Bed & furniture,
Fifteen Cows and Calfes; dau. SARAH WILKINSON Five pounds in money; dau.
MARY CHERRY Five pounds in money; Remanns part of my Estate to Be Sold and
money Equally Divided amongst my dau. SARAH WILKINSON, MARY CHERRY and CHAR-
LOTTE
extrs: Sonesin law ROBART CHERRY & LOFTIS WORLEY
wit: THOS. SHELTON, JONES BOYET
signed: John Worsley

579. WRIGHT, DAVID (CR.035.801.12/A-500)
13 Mar 1827 - Apr Term 1827
in order to enable my wife the better to raise my small children and educate
them without her being obliged to charge them board and clothing I leave her
old negroes Venus & Mack as long as she thinks they will be of service to
her; wife [not named] Lands I now live on except the land I bought of Brother THOS untill my son DAVID becomes of lawful age, negroes Brister, Easter.

Milly, Jim, Jack and Dorcis, my household & kitchen furniture, my new gig, harness and old horse called Mark, two Mules; son THOS. H. negroes & mare which he has already received, the furniture given by me to him, negro Jackson; son JOHN the money he has already received & horse, the negroes he has already recieved, negro Britton, one hundred dollars for his attendance on me while on my sick bed; dau. MARY C. wife of LEWIS B. BUSH the negroes, mare & furniture she has already recd and to her son WILLIAM negro Manuel; dau. REBECCA E. wife of THOMAS C. HOOKS negroes she has in possession, the furniture she has recieved, seventy dollars to by a horse; dau. PATSEY E. negroes Judy, Hannah and Dolly and one hundred dollars to buy her a horse, one bed, bedstead & furniture; son DAVID my lands I bought of my Brother THOS, my young black mare, one bed, bedstead & furniture; son ISAAC the balance of my Land at the death of his mother, one bed, bedstead & furniture, one hundred dollars when he marries or becomes of age; little daus. ELIZA SMITH & KITTY ANN negroes Hary, Mary, Dorcis, Toney, Maria, Gillis, Evaline & Edmund, one bedstead & furniture to each; negroes George, Stephen & Calvin to be sold if necessary to pay debts together with the Judgement of mine against JOHN B. WRIGHT and if not necessary George to dau. PATSEY E., Stephen to son DAVID and Calvin to son ISAAC; negro Sally & child Roderick sold to pay debts
extrs: sons THOS. H. & JNO.
wit: WILLIAM HODGES, WILSON HODGES
signed: D. Wright

580. WRIGHT, ELIZABETH C. (CR.035.801.12)
18 Jan 1840 - Jul Term 1841
children THOMAS H., JOHN, MARY BUSH & REBECCA E. HOOKS five dollars each; dau. MARTHA E. SHINES one Bed & furniture; son DAVID my wagon & harness & a half dozen Silver table spoons, a trunk; dau. ELIZA S. a half Dozen Silver teaspoons, a trunk, my Gig & harness & her Choice of my horses; dau. CATHARINE A. a half Dozen Silver teaspoons, a trunk, her second choice of my horses; children DAVID, ELIZA S. & ISAAC Jointly residue of my property consisting of Corn, Fodder, Cattle, Hogs, horses, household & Kitchen furneture, plantation tools and all other articles not mentioned; son ISAAC negro Calvin and a half dozen Silver teaspoons, a trunk, my mare that is called his, one hundred Dollars left him in his father's will
extr: brother BUCKNER L. HILL
wit: THOS. HILL, JOHN S. HILL
signed: Elizabeth Wright

581. WRIGHT, JAMES "Planter" (CR.035.801.12)
24 Oct 1839 - Apr Term 1840
wife KITTY sum of nineteen hundred and ninety nine dollars; sons ISAAC and WILLIAM in special trust for my grandchildren the sons of JOHN B. deceased viz JOHN BECK, JAMES MUNROE, ISAAC and WILLIAM minors all my real estate in Duplin County; grandsons JOHN & JAMES the sons of BRYAN my real Estate in Cumberland & Bladen on the North west river now in possession of my son BRYAN; negroes including Fanny & her children now in possession of ALEXANDER McALLESTER divided into six equal parts or shares with Rose and her children thrown into the Lot for the use of my son BRYAN and Fanny & her children thrown into the Lot for the use of ANN McALLISTER, one sixth part to my son ISAAC, one sixth to son WILLIAM, one sixth to ISAAC & WILLIAM in special trust for my Son BRYAN and his Children, one sixth to ISAAC & WILLIAM

in special trust for my dau. CHELLY MURPHY & her children, one sixth to
ISAAC & WILLIAM in special trust for my dau. ANN McALLISTER & her children,
one sixth to ISAAC & WILLIAM in special trust for my grandchildren the sons
of my deceased son JOHN B. and none of the slaves given in trust are to be
Sold but if deemed advisable by my sons ISAAC & WILLIAM they may put the
negroes thus divided into the possession of my son BRYAN and sons in Law
JOHN MURPHY & ALEXANDER McALLISTER as they live at a distance; dau. ANN
McALLISTER Three hundred dollars for her sole and seperate use; dau.
CHELLY MURPHY one thousand dollars, one Bed & furniture; dau. ANN McALLISTER
one Bed & furniture; should my son in Law JOHN MURPHY bring any suit against
my Executor then ISAAC & WILLIAM are not only to with hold the onethousand
dollars but apply the proceeds of all the slaves bequeathed to his wife and
children to defray any expense or trouble which may arise therefrom
extrs: sons ISAAC & WILLIAM
wit: JOS. G. DICKSON, D. B. NEWTON, DAVID WRIGHT
signed: James Wright
Codicil: 24 Oct 1839, 11 Nov 1839
negroe John Mirric should be added to the list of Slaves for the use of the
sons of my deceased son JOHN B; sons ISAAC & WILLIAM to use all my real
estate in Duplin County both the lands on which I reside & where AGATHY
WRIGHT resides and all adjoining or detached Tracts to supporting grandsons
the sons of my deceased son doctor JOHN B. and to divide the Same where they
deem it necessary; sons ISAAC & WILLIAM to use all of my real estate in
Cumberland County & Bladen County on the North West River & Wallis's Creek
to supporting my son BRYAN and his sons JOHN & JAMES and to divide the Same
where they deem it necessary
wit: JOHN S. HILL, DANIEL BOWDEN, HENRY BOWDEN
signed: James Wright

582. WRIGHT, JOHN (CR.035.801.12/A-511)
22 Jan 1798 - Apr Term 1800
wife REBECKAH the whole plantation whereon I now live including all my lands
from the Oaks near the plumb Trees upon the Hill by the swapt to my son
DAVIDS to my son THOMAS' line, half of the still, all my negroes, all my
Stock of every Kind whatever including all my horses, Cattle, Hogs and
sheep, all my houshold and kitchen Furneture, my riding Chair; son THOMAS
after the decease of his Mother the part of my Land whereon I now live the
west side of the Avenue to his Corner at the Trees where the old Still
formerly stood including my dwilling houses as far as the upper part of my
cleard land near a piny Slash to near the crooked Causway, one Feather bed
which he recieved when he was married; son DAVID after the decease of his
Mother the part of the plantation which lies on the east side of the Avenue,
Child which my Negroe Grace brought named Polydon; dau. ELIZABETH BECK
negro Patsey; dau. REBECKAH BECK negro Damond; dau. MARY CLARK negro
Virgil; wife REBECKAH negroes Phillis and Grace and after her decease to
my daus. ELIZABETH, REBECKAH and MARY; children JAMES, JOHN, THOMAS, DAVID,
ELIZABETH BECK, REBECKAH BECK, and MARY CLARK after the decease of my wife
negroes Durham and Mack, all my plantation Tools of every kind and all my
Stock of every kind
extrs: son THOMAS, JAMES CLARK
wit: WM. DICKSON, ARCH WRIGHT, ISAAC WRIGHT
signed: John Wright

583. WRIGHT, ROBERT "of Edgecombe County" (CR.035.801.12/A-524)
7 Jan 1798 - 8 Oct 1774 [?]   [also filed in Pitt County]
wife SARAH Ten Breeding Cattle, one breeding Mare, one feather bed, one Iron
pot, one bason, Three Ews and one hundred Acres; FRANCES PATRICK one Shilling;
dau. JANE Six breeding Cattle, one breeding Mare, one bason, One Small Dish,
one Skillet, two Ews, one ram; son ROBERT two hundred and twenty Acres with
the Plantation that LEWIS PATRICK now lives on, Six breeding Cattle, tree two
year old Stears, one Large bason, one pot, two Ews and Lambs, one ram, one
young breding Mare and a gun; grandson WILLIAM PATRICK one Cow and Calf, one
young Mare, one Ew and Lamb; wife Rest of my Estate
extrs: wife SARAH, RICHD. SESSOMS
wit: HENRY TANTONY, JOHN ⨏ CLARK, RICHD. ✦ WELCH
signed: Robert Wright

584. WRIGHT, THOMAS (CR.035.801.12/2-9)
__ Mar 1845 - Jan Term 1847
wife ELIZA all my negroes, all my horses, stock of Cattle, furniture, farming
utensils with the view and for the express purpose of furnishing a home for
my dau. SUSAN C. WHITFIELD; wife ELIZA all my real estate in the counties of
Duplin and Sampson including my dwelling and out houses; negro Charles to
executors in Trust for grandau. ELIZA C. WHITFIELD, one bed and its necessary
firniture; negro Mordecai to executors in Trust for grandau. RACHEL J. WHIT-
FIELD, one bed and its necessary firniture; grandson JOHN HAYWOOD WHITFIELD
Two hundred and Fifty dollars; negroes Edmond and Randleson in trust for dau.
SUSAN C. WHITFIELD and After her death negroes sold and the proceeds divided
into eight shares one share each to go to JOHN, W. B., THOMAS, ALFRED, COUNCIL,
RICHARD WASHINGTON, REBECCA SLOCUMB and one in trust to my executors for dau.
SARAH E. HOOKS and her children; son COUNCIL R. Three hundred dollars;
residue sold and Five hundred dollars retained as an additional support for
my dau. SUSAN C. WHITFIELD; executors to retain money enough from the sales
of my property to fix grave yard and the graves when my wife and my self will
be enterred; residue of proceeds from Sales divided into eight shares with
one share each to JOHN, W. B., THOMAS, ALFRED, COUNCIL, RICHARD WASHINGTON,
REBECCA SLOCUMB and one share to executors in trust for dau. SARAH ELIZA HOOKS
now in Alabama
extrs: sons JOHN and W. B.
wit: KILBEE FAISON, FRAS. H. FAISON
signed: Tho. Wright

585. YOUNG, PETER (CR.035.801.12/A-458)
25 Nov 1799 - Jul Term 1802
wife JEANE one Mair, one halfe of my Stock of Catle and hoggs and Sheep, my
household furniture and plantation tools; son JAMES one hundred Acres
inclooding the plantation whaire on I Now Live, one horse, Saddle and Bridle,
one halfe of the Remaining part of my Stock of Cattle, hogs and seep and
house hold firniture and plantation tools; sons JOHN & WILLIAM and PETER
five shillings Sterling Each; daus. MARGRET BROWNE and ANN BLANTON five
shillings Sterling Each
extr: TIMOTHY TEACHEY
wit: TIMOY TEACHEY, JOHN ✦ WILLIAMS, JOHN BAZIN
                              signed: Peter ⨏ Young

APPENDIX

Duplin County Wills, 1861 - 1900

Albritton, Samuel 9 Feb 1900 - 14 Apr 1902 5-62
Alderman, Joseph 5 Sep 1895 - 3 Jun 1905 CR.035.801.1 / 5-170

Barfield, Isaac 23 Jul 1861 - Oct Term 1862 CR.035.801.1 / 3-61
Bass, Lewis G. 6 Apr 1876 - 6 Aug 1886 CR.035.801.1 / 4-280
Batts, Lewis 27 Mar 1861 - Jan Term 1862 CR.035.801.1 / 3-47
Batts, Nathaniel 23 Nov 1895 - 27 Jun 1896 CR.035.801.1 / 4-478
Beasley, Bass 16 Nov 1880 - 9 Jul 1881 CR.035.801.1 / 4-187
Beasley, Daniel J. 24 Oct 1891 - 10 Dec 1891 CR.035.801.1 / 4-397
Becton, Cora A. 16 May 1885 - 28 Oct 1885 CR.035.801.1 / 4-268
Bell, Walter R. 18 May 1885 - 22 May 1885 CR.035.801.1 / 4-253
Bennett, E. J. 26 Sep 1898 - 28 Nov 1898 CR.035.801.1 / 4-526
Bennett, S. L. 28 Jan 1880 - 15 Jun 1883 CR.035.801.1 / 4-166
Best, Howell 12 Feb 1864 - Apr Term 1864 CR.035.801.1 / 3-89
Blanchard, John H. L. 25 Feb 1864 - 17 Jan 1891 CR.035.801.1 / 4-385
Bland, Daniel 20 Nov 1865 - 10 Jan 1871 CR.035.801.1 / 4-41
Bland, Gabriel 1 Aug 1874 - 5 Dec 1893 CR.035.801.1
Bland, James 25 Sep 1862 - Jan Term 1863 CR.035.801.1 / 3-67
Blanton, Abraham 19 Oct 1870 - 3 May 1874 CR.035.801.1 / 4-90
Blount, Dr. James W. of Kenansville 3 Feb 1887 - 20 Jul 1903 5-90
Boney, Barbara C. 15 Feb 1892 - 24 Jul 1894 CR.035.801.2 / 4-450
Boney, Danl. W. 29 Nov 1894 - 15 Apr 1894 CR.035.801.2 / 4-462
Boney, James Wells 25 Jun 1885 - 8 Sep 1885 CR.035.801.2 / 4-262
Boney, John A. 14 Sep 1864 - 2 Feb 1871 CR.035.801.2 / 4-32
Bourden, Clarissa S. 26 Aug 1892 - 5 Dec 1898 CR.035.801.2 / 4-528
Bowden, Wilson 26 Apr 1892 - 23 Jun 1892 CR.035.801.2 / 4-407
Boyette, Balaam 9 Mar 1891 - 8 Aug 1891 CR.035.801.2 / 4-382
Boyette, Susan A. 25 Jun 1895 - 26 Feb 1897 CR.035.801.2 / 4-499
Bradshaw, Samuel 20 Jan 1877 - 26 Aug 1886 CR.035.801.2 / 4-284
Branch, James G. Sr. 28 Mar 1862 - 13 Jan 1873 CR.035.801.2 / 4-70
Brice, Francis 14 May 1881 - 13 Jun 1881 CR.035.801.2 / 4-196
Brice, Margaret A. 5 Dec 1899 - no probate CR.035.801.2
Brice, William 14 Jul 1897 - 14 Feb 1902 5-54
Brill, Margaret 5 Dec 1899 - 3 Aug 1905 5-173
Britt/Brill, Jacob 3 Jul 1866 - Jul Term 1866 CR.035.801.2 / 3-108
Brock, Lavina J. 23 Jan 1895 - 6 May 1895 CR.035.801.2 / 4-464
Brooks, Peter 2 Feb 1885 - 12 May 1903 5-81
Brooks, William A. 24 Feb 1896 - 26 Feb 1903 5-258
Brown, Adaline E. wife of David 25 Apr 1879 - 4 Aug 1889 CR.035.801.2 /
    4-551
Brown, Isaac no date - 9 Jul 1879 CR.035.801.2 / 4-143
Brown, William S. 7 Apr 1891 - 1 Jun 1891 CR.035.801.2 / 4-376
Bryan, Andrew 11 Jan 1864 - Jan Term 1864 CR.035.801.2 / 3-88
Bryan, John A. 17 Jul 1896 - 31 Aug 1903 5-95
Bryant, Henry T. 28 Feb 1894 - 3 Aug 1897 CR.035.801.2 / 4-506
Burton, Charlotte of Cypress Creek Township 10 Jun 1889 - 12 May 1890
    CR.035.801.2 / 4-357

Carlton, A. W. 13 Sep 1895 - 3 Oct 1898 CR.035.801.3 / 4-520
Carlton, John L. 20 May 1882 - 30 Jun 1884 Cr.035.801.3 / 4-228

APPENDIX (cont.)

Carlton, Sarah E.   20 Mar 1897 - 11 May 1911   5-429
Carlton, Theroyal   30 Apr 1892 - 7 Nov 1898   CR.035.801.3/   4-523
Carr, Jacob Wesley   2 Mar 1898 - 26 Apr 1898   CR.035.801.3/   4-518
Carr, James   1 Apr 1873 - 9 Aug 1882   CR.035.801.3/   4-201
Carr, John   1 Jan 1870 - 1 Sep 1879   CR.035.801.3/   4-149
Carr, Linda   widow of William   6 Apr 1868 - 19 Jan 1885   CR.035.801.3/
     4-241
Carr, Ozborn   8 Mar 1866 - 15 Oct 1869   CR.035.801.3/   4-18
Carroll, L. R.   of Sampson County   written 18 Feb 1885   Witnessed
     25 Jun 1890   probated 7 Dec 1905   CR.035.801.3/   5-186
Carroll, John D.   2 Jun 1871 - 28 Mar 1885   CR.035.801.3/   4-247
Carroll, William C.   14 Jun 1884 - 10 Nov 1884   CR.035.801.3/   4-236
Carter, Senas Job   5-
Cavenaugh, James   10 Dec 1896 - 18 Mar 1899 CR.035.801.3/   4-533
Chambers, John   8 Sep 1873 - 8 Jun 1875   CR.035.801.3/   4-95
Chasten, Joseph   10 Jun 1866 - Jan Term 1867   3-114
Chasten, Mary   16 Dec 1887 - 19 Nov 1888   CR.035.801.3/   4-331
Chasten, Richard   27 Feb 1867 - Jan Term 1868   CR.035.801.3/   3-129
Chesnutt, Eleanor E.   13 Apr 1888 - 5 Oct 1895   CR.035.801.3/   4-469
Chesnutt, Wm. C.   30 Mar 1895 - 24 Jun 1895   CR.035.801.3/   4-467
Chesnutt, William K.   of Sampson County   9 Nov 1887 - 8 Mar 1898
     Sampson Probate 14 Mar 1906   CR.035.801.3/   5-202
Cole, Clerkey   25 Aug 1888 - 11 Feb 1889   CR.035.801.3/   4-336
Cooper, John   25 Oct 1865 - Apr Term 1867   CR.035.801.3/   3-117
Cox, John Andrew   10 Jan 1885 - 20 Feb 1902   Sampson Probate 19 Dec 1901
     5-56
Crow, Theophilus   9 Aug 1865 - Oct Term 1865   CR.035.801.3/   3-101
Currie, A. G.   9 Dec 1899 - 24 Feb 1902   5-59

Dail, Curtis   30 Jul 1864 - Jul Term 1865 & Oct Term 1865   CR.035.801.4/
     3-100
Deal, Abel   1 Apr 1867 - Oct Term 1867   CR.035.801.4/   3-123
DeVane, Milton K.   of Magnolia   22 Mar 1883 - 15 Sep 1888   CR.035.801.4/
     4-323
Dickson, James G.   13 Jun 1867 - Oct Term 1867   CR.035.801.4/   3-122
Dickson, Mary Catherine widow of Robert   13 Mar 1868 - 5 Oct 1871
     CR.035.801.4/   4-50
Dobson, John   24 Apr 1869 - 7 Feb 1871   CR.035.801.4/   4-34
Dobson, P. H.   15 Nov 1888 - 22 Oct 1891   CR.035.801.4/   4-392

Edwards, Elizabeth P.   16 Nov 1878 - 22 Jan 1880   CR.035.801.4/   4-205
Edwards, Fredrick   20 Oct 1862 - Apr Term 1863   CR.035.801.4/   3-75
Edwards, Marry   24 Jun 1875 - 30 Jan 1878   CR.035.801.4/   4-130
English, Stephen   20 Oct 1896 - 15 Nov 1902   5-69
Ezzell, Fannie M.   31 Dec 1891 - 10 Jul 1899   CR.035.801.4/   4-548
Ezzell, John   26 Jul 1884 - 6 Jan 1890   CR.035.801.4/   4-349

Faison, Elias   31 Jul 1865 - 4 Mar 1871   CR.035.801.4/   4-37
Faison, Henry E.   7 Jul 1885 - 2 Jan 1886   CR.035.801.4/   4-270
Faison, Hettie   7 Jun 1893 - 11 Aug 1894   CR.035.801.4/   4-452
Faison, Mary E.   10 May 1876 - 7 Aug 1876   CR.035.801.4/   4-111
Faison, Virginia James   20 Nov 1894 - 3 Nov 1899   CR.035.801.4/   4-558

194

APPENDIX (cont.)

Farrior, Hugh 21 Aug 1884 - 19 Nov 1884 CR.035.801.4/ 4-238
Farrior, Nicholas J. 2 Jul 1896 - 28 Jul 1896 CR.035.801.4/ 4-485
Forehand, William 7 Jul 1883 - 28 Aug 1883 CR.035.801.4/ 4-216
Fountain, Joab 6 Feb 1896 - 1 Feb 1904 5-121
Frederick, Norris 7 Sep 1867 - Jan Term 1868 CR.035.801.4/ 3-131
Fryar, Henry 19 Nov 1895 - 17 Oct 1899 CR.035.801.4/ 4-556

Gardiner, Minnie L. no date - 23 Jun 1891 CR.035.801.5/ 4-380
Garner, Henry 6 Jan 1888 - 12 May 1900 CR.035.801.5/ 4-569
Garvey, Ann 2 Aug 1872 - 7 Sep 1872 CR.035.801.5/ 4-59
Glisson, Daniel 18 Sep 1873 - 1 May 1880 CR.035.801.5/ 4-203
Glisson, Henry J. __ Jun 1885 - 27 Jul 1888 CR.035.801.5/ 4-315
Grady, Alexander H. 10 Feb 1881 - 18 Aug 1881 Cr.035.801.5/ 4-161
Grady, Barbara 9 Oct 1891 - 1 Jun 1893 CR.035.801.5/ 4-428
Grady, John 30 Jun 1897 - 5 Jun 1899 CR.035.801.5/ 4-536
Grady, Patsy 1 Dec 1890 - 2 Jun 1891 CR.035.801.5/ 4-378
Grady, Pennie wife of Dr. James M. 2 Mar 1894 - 31 Jan 1910 5-351
Grady, Thomas 9 Apr 1861 - Jul Term 1865 CR.035.801.5/ 3-99
Grady, Thomas M. 29 Jun 1881 - 8 Aug 1881 CR.035.801.5/ 4-162
Grady, Thomas W. 26 Jun 1886 - 17 Aug 1887 CR.035.801.5/ 4-301
Grady, Winifred 17 May 1882 - 6 Dec 1890 CR.035.801.5/ 4-368
Gresham, Thomas 11 Oct 1879 - 15 Aug 1881 CR.035.801.5/ 4-173
Guy, Sarah E. 1 Apr 1891 - 6 Apr 1891 CR.035.801.5/ 4-374

Hall, Alfred & Lucy C. 5 Aug 1897 - 14 Apr 1899 CR.035.801.5/ 4-540
Hall, James 17 May 1870 - 15 Aug 1870 CR.035.801.5/ 4-21
Hardy, Phineas no date - 24 Feb 1897 4-500
Harper, Daniel 25 Mar 1869 - 11 Oct 1871 CR.035.801.5/ 4-44
Harrell, Jacob no date - 23 Dec 1878 CR.035.801.5/ 4-137
Harrell, Linda E. 30 Jan 1891 - 3 Sep 1891 CR.035.801.5/ 4-394
Harvel, Helen P. 11 Jun 1879 - 7 Nov 1882 CR.035.801.5/ 4-154
Heath, Thelma B. no date - 21 Sep 1876 CR.035.801.5 [Will missing from
     folder]
Heath, Thomas B. 30 Sep 1875 - 21 Sep 1876 CR.035.801.5/ 4-113
Herring, Catharine 28 Jan 1875 - 7 Jan 1878 CR.035.801.5/ 4-128
Herring, Daniel __ 1861 - Jan Term 1865 CR.035.801.5/ 3-95
Herring, Everitt no date - 29 Nov 1892 CR.035.801.5/ 4-417
Herring, Lucinda 6 Oct 1896 - 14 Jul 1899 4-550
Herring, William 17 Sep 1872 - 7 Jan 1873 CR.035.801.5/ 4-67
Hicks, James H. 1 Jun 1874 - 16 Oct 1874 CR.035.801.6/ 4-85
Highsmith, Sarah 30 Jan 1862 - 21 Jul 1862 CR.035.801.6/ 3-57
Hill, Christopher D. 9 Feb 1874 - 27 Aug 1874 CR.035.801.6/ 4-82
Hill, Thomas 25 Feb 1861 - Jan Term 1862 CR.035.801.6/ 3-48
Hill, William E. 20 May 1899 - 30 May 1900 CR.035.801.6/ 4-570
Hobbs, Annie D. __ Sep 1900 - 8 Aug 1901 5-35
Hollingsworth, Henry 15 May 1885 - 18 Jul 1893 CR.035.801.6/ 4-433
Horn, Howell 27 Oct 1877 - 5 Feb 1890 CR.035.801.6/ 4-352
Horn, Thomas 5 May 1870 - 27 Sep 1872 CR.035.801.6/ 4-61
House, Dolly S. 18 Nov 1884 - 20 Feb 1907 5-229
Houston, Calvin I. 10 Jul 1861 - Jul Term 1861 CR.035.801.6/ 3-35
Hurst, Cathorine 18 Jan 1876 - 15 Mar 1877 CR.035.801.6/ 4-118
Hurst, George W. B. 25 Apr 1861 - Apr Term 1866 CR.035.801.6/ 3-106

APPENDIX (cont.)

Hurst, James R. 8 Jul 1872 - Feb Term 1879 & 24 Feb 1879
     CR.035.801.6/ 4-139   4-191
Hussey, Toney 18 Jan 1893 - 1 May 1893 CR.035.801.6/ 4-430

Johnson, Bizzell 3 Mar 1885 - 16 Nov 1895 CR.035.801.6/ 4-472
Johnson, Ira J. 31 Jan 1900 - 6 Jan 1902 5-41
Johnson, Wm. S. 22 Jul 1861 - Apr Term 1863 CR.035.801.6/ 3-71
Jones, Gilbert A. 13 Jun 1887 - 21 Jul 1887 CR.035.801.6/ 4-299
Joyner, Everett Sr. 18 Jul 1877 - 12 Jul 1901 5-37

Karnegay, A. G. 21 Apr 1880 - 10 Nov 1880 CR.035.801.7/ 4-170
Keathley, F. M. 1 Feb 1898 - 22 Feb 1898 CR.035.801.7/ 4-516
Keathley, James M. 20 Apr 1899 - 1 May 1899 CR.035.801.7/ 4-543
Keathley, Mark 19 Sep 1873 - 18 Nov 1873 CR.035.801.7/ 4-75
Kenan, Thomas S. 19 Jan 1891 - 27 Dec 1911 CR.035.801.7/ 5-504
Kenedy, Nancy Jane 31 May 1895 - 25 Mar 1910 5-368
Kennedy, Bryant 17 Oct 1887 - 14 Feb 1888 CR.035.801.7/ 4-312
Kilpatrick, Thomas __ Dec 1900 - 2 May 1904 5-136
Kornegay, Henry C. 4 Feb 1887 - 24 Apr 1894 CR.035.801.7/ 4-444
Kornegay, Harget 18 Apr 1869 - 28 Aug 1875 CR.035.801.7/ 4-99
Kornegay, H. R. 20 Sep 1897 - 7 Feb 1898 CR.035.801.7/ 4-513
Kornegay, Nancy O. 30 Sep 1887 - 5 Nov 1888 CR.035.801.7/ 4-329

Lamb, George W. 29 Jan 1892 - 16 Feb 1897 CR.035.801.7/ 4-493
Lanier, Allen 25 Dec 1866 - 29 Nov 1870 CR.035.801.7/ 4-30
Lanier, Dennis 21 Aug 1871 - 14 Nov 1871 CR.035.801.7/ 4-54
Lanier, Holden 17 Apr 1868 - 13 Sep 1869 CR.035.801.7/ 4-16
Lanier, Hosea G. 20 May 1885 - 6 Jul 1885 CR.035.801.7/ 4-259
Lanier, Rachel 17 Dec 1875 - 5 May 1879 CR.035.801.7/ 4-141
Lanier, Thomas 10 May 1877 - 7 Apr 1884 CR.035.801.7/ 4-223
Lawson, Christopher 20 Mar 1880 - 26 Jul 1881 CR.035.801.7/ 4-157
Loftin, Sarah A. 9 Aug 1884 - 16 Sep 1884 CR.035.801.7/ 4-232

McGowen, J. Q. 10 Aug 1889 - 17 Jul 1890 CR.035.801.7/ 4-361
McMillan, George J. 13 Oct 1894 - 12 Jun 1900 CR.035.801.7/ 5-4

Mallard, Liston Lee 3 Dec 1897 - 6 Dec 1897 CR.035.801.8/ 4-510
Maready, Obed 10 Jun 1884 - 24 Aug 1888 CR.035.801.8/ 4-320
Martin, David Mordecai 9 Jun 1890 - 3 Apr 1899 CR.035.801.8/ 4-538
Mathis, Elizabeth 19 Dec 1896 - 16 Mar 1899 CR.035.801.8/ 4-530
Maxwell, Houston 5 Feb 1864 - Apr Term 1866 CR.035.801.8/ 3-107
Maxwell, John 30 Mar 1886 - 3 May 1886 CR.035.801.8/ 4-277
Maxwell, Margaret E. 14 May 1888 - 17 May 1890 CR.035.801.8/ 4-359
Merritt, Dolly Jane 29 Jul 1892 - 2 Dec 1907 5-237
Middleton, Bazil 27 Jul 1877 - 5 Jan 1886 CR.035.801.8/ 4-273
Middleton, Cato [nuncupative] 23 Aug 1874 - 31 Oct 1874 CR.035.801.8/
     4-87
Middleton, Clarisa 6 Nov 1884 - 27 Dec 1884 CR.035.801.8/ 4-266
Middleton, D. J. 4 Jan 1897 - 7 Jul 1904 5-148
Middleton, James M. 25 Jun 1868 - 30 Jan 1869 CR.035.801.8/ 4-11
Miller, John R. 28 Nov 1900 - 27 Mar 1905 CR.035.801.8/ 5-163
Moody, Marry 30 Apr 1861 - Jul Term 1867 CR.035.801.8/ 3-121
Moore, Dorothy A. 3 Dec 1873 - 24 Dec 1875 CR.035.801.8/ 4-102

APPENDIX (cont.)

Moore, Rachel 11 Aug 1863 - Oct Term 1863 CR.035.801.8/ 3-82
Morris, Reddick 5 Aug 1872 - 9 Dec 1872 CR.035.801.8/ 4-64
Morrisey, D. G. of Warsaw 9 Sep 1899 - 1 Jul 1901 5-32
Murphy, Eliza F. of Magnolia 3 Mar 1899 - ____ 1900 CR.035.801.8/
    5-12
Murphy, Samuel of Magnolia 4 Dec 1885 - 5 Aug 1886 CR.035.801.8/ 4-291
Murphy, Thomas K. 25 Jan 1899 - 12 Jun 1899 CR.035.801.8/ 4-546
Murray, Guilford S. 22 Jul 1885 - 11 Nov 1889 CR.035.801.8/ 4-347
Murray, Hiram 7 Mar 1871 - 10 Apr 1877 CR.035.801.8/ 4-119
Murray, John W. 1 Jan 1887 - 17 Sep 1889 CR.035.801.8/ 4-342
Murray, Jane 14 Apr 1873 - 26 Sep 1874 CR.035.801.8/ 4-84
Murray, Nathan 10 Sep 1862 - Jan Term 1864 CR.035.801.8/ 3-87
Murray, Nathan 9 Mar 1886 - 22 Sep 1886 CR.035.801.8/ 4-289

Newton, Daniel B. 16 Apr 1888 -
Nicholson, D. B. 1 May 1865 - Jul Term 1866 CR.035.801.9/ 3-113

ODaniel, Alonzo 6 Feb 1891 - 1 Jun 1895 Wayne County Probate 21 Mar 1895
    CR.035.801.9/ 4-466
ODaniel, Archelaus 26 Feb 1864 - Jul Term 1864 CR.035.801.9/ 3-90
Oliver, Benjamin 12 Jul 1872 - 20 Sep 1881 CR.035.801.9/ 4-212
Oliver, John of Lenoir County 24 Apr 1863 - Oct Term 1863 CR.035.801.9/
    3-83
Outlaw, Alexander Sr. 11 Nov 1861 - Apr Term 1862 CR.035.801.9/ 3-52
Outlaw, George 31 Jul 1874 - 7 Dec 1878 CR.035.801.9/ 4-134
Outlaw, Harget K. 28 May 1888 - 8 Sep 1890 CR.035.801.9/ 4-366
Outlaw, Noah 5 May 1892 - 22 Dec 1893 CR.035.801.9/ 4-439
Outlaw, Racheal 15 Nov 1875 - 8 Jan 1876 CR.035.801.9/ 4-104
Outlaw, Sally   - Jul Term 1866 CR.035.801.9/ 3-109
Outlaw, William Senr. 27 Jul 1865 - Apr Term 1868 CR.035.801.9/ 3-132

Page, Charles 3 Feb 1876 - 15 Nov 1883 CR.035.801.9/ 4-221
Parker, Buckner no date - 23 Jun 1879 CR.035.801.9/ 4-147
Pass, James C. 22 Aug 1878 - 19 Sep 1883 CR.035.801.9/ 4-168
Pearsall, Ann 4 Apr 1861 - Jan Term 1865 CR.035.801.9/ 3-97
Pearsall, David M. 17 Mar 1876 - 13 Aug 1894 CR.035.801.9/ 4-455
Pearsall, James D. 3 Oct 1863 - Oct Term CR.035.801.9/ 3-84
Pearsall, Jeremiah 5 Nov 1868 - 26 Aug 1871 CR.035.801.9/ 4-47
Pearsall, Joseph 22 Apr 1876 - 2 Feb 1901 CR.035.801.9/ 5-19
Peterson, John W. 19 Apr 1873 - 26 Feb 1874 CR.035.801.9/ 4-79
Phillips, Thomas 6 Jul 1886 - 21 Jun 1889 CR.035.801.9/ 4-338
Pickett, Fredric 16 Dec 1891 - 21 Oct 1893 CR.035.801.9/ 4-436
Pigford, Edward T. 29 Apr 1885 - 20 Sep 1900 CR.035.801.9/ 5-8
Pope, John Thomas 29 Jul 1897 - 21 May 1910 5-377
Potter, Frederick 26 Dec 1864 - 12 Nov 1870 CR.035.801.9/ 4-29
Pridgeon, Robert P. 22 Feb 1868 - 30 Jan 1869 CR.035.801.9/ 4-9

Quinn, Ichabod 18 Mar 1862 - Oct Term 1862 CR.035.801.10/ 3-60

Reaves, Ann Jane 18 Oct 1889 - 14 Apr 1892 CR.035.801.10/ 4-405
Reaves, David 10 Aug 1880 - 9 Oct 1883 CR.035.801.10/ 4-219
Rich, Priscilla 24 May 1890 - 5 Sep 1899 4-554

APPENDIX (cont.)

Robinson, Lucien W. of Wallace 18 Jun 1897 - 15 Jan 1900
    CR.035.801.10/ 4-560
Rouse, David Sr. 18 Jun 1865 - 29 Aug 1870 CR.035.801.10/ 4-24
Rouse, David 9 Feb 1885 - 23 Mar 1885 CR.035.801.10/ 4-244

Sandlin, Nichodemus 12 Jan 1872 - 5 Mar 1877 CR.035.801.10/ 4-116
Sasser, Wiley B. 9 Apr 1890 - 22 Feb 1893 CR.035.801.10/ 4-420
Scheuermann, Henry 8 Aug 1868 - 2 Nov 1868 CR.035.801.10/ 4-1
Shine, Martha 29 Jul 1882 - 28 Dec 1882 CR.035.801.10/ 4-152
Sholar, David 2 Sep 1875 - 7 Mar 1892 CR.035.801.10/ 4-399
Simmons, Daniel H. 11 Jan 1881 - 3 Oct 1888 CR.035.801.10/ 4-326
Sloan, Claborn 29 Aug 1885 - 19 Jun 1897 CR.035.801.10
Sloan, Ellen 3 Jan 1863 - Oct Term 1863 CR.035.801.10/ 3-81
Sloan, Gibson 18 Jan 1867 - 6 Oct 1868 CR.035.801.10/ 4-5
Sloan, Susan 29 Jul 1869 - 27 Nov 1869 CR.035.801.10/ 4-20
Smith, Bryant 29 May 1880 - 11 Nov 1882 CR.035.801.10/ 4-176
Smith, Chauncey no date - 1 Sep 1889 CR.035.801.10/ 4-233
Smith, Jacob no date - 26 Feb 1897 CR.035.801.10/ 4-496
Smith, Jones 5 Oct 1886 - 17 Aug 1887 CR.035.801.10/ 4-305
Southerland, Alexander 7 Feb 1894 - 24 Dec 1896 CR.035.801.10/ 4-489
Southerland, David 12 Feb 1870 - 24 Feb 1879 CR.035.801.10/ 4-208
Southerland, Delilah 7 Jun 1866 - Jul Term 1866 CR.035.801.10/ 3-111
Southerland, James 26 Aug 1886 - 9 May 1887 CR.035.801.10/ 4-297
Southerland, John 3 Dec 1878 - 7 Mar 1881 CR.035.801.10/ 4-156
Southerland, Lucy I. 23 Oct 1900 - 20 Jan 1901 5-28
Stevens, Christopher of Onslow County 2 Jan 1883 - 5 Dec 1891 4-572
Stevens, Olivia Raleigh 16 Jun 1887 - 8 Nov 1887 CR.035.801.10/ 4-310
Stokes, James G. 18 Jul 1879 - 24 Nov 1882 CR.035.801.10/ 4-194
Strickland, Elizabeth 1 Jan 1889 - 20 Nov 1891 CR.035.801.10/ 4-390
Strickland, Hardy 1 Jun 1872 - 20 Jul 1880 CR.035.801.10/ 4-183
Strickland, Major 23 May 1874 - 20 Oct 1887 CR.035.801.10/ 4-308
Stricklind, Jesse 17 Feb 1870 - 17 Jul 1872 CR.035.801.10/ 4-56
Stroud, William 18 Mar 1884 - 13 Mar 1889 4-355
Sullivan, Insil 8 Jan 1890 - 17 Jan 1891 CR.035.801.10/ 4-371
Sullivan, Samuel 15 May 1896 - 10 Jul 1896 CR.035.801.10/ 4-482
Sumner, Edith 6 Nov 1881 - 19 Sep 1896 CR.035.801.11/ 4-487
Swinson, B. F. 26 Apr 1861 - Jan Term 1863 CR.035.801.11/ 3-69
Swinson, Daniel 14 Jun 1864 - Oct Term 1864 CR.035.801.11/ 3-92
Swinson, John 21 Jul 1864 - Jan Term 1866 CR.035.801.11/ 3-104
Swinson, Major 5 Jan 1885 - 16 Mar 1886 CR.035.801.11/ 4-275
Swinson, Polly 7 Jul 1873 - 7 Oct 1873 CR.035.801.11/ 4-77
Swinson, Sharlotte 18 May 1867 - 7 Jun 1875 CR.035.801.11/ 4-92

Taylor, Isham U. 28 Feb 1894 - 16 Jul 1894 CR.035.801.11/ 4-448
Taylor, J. Wells 1 Oct 1889 - 7 Feb 1910 5-359
Taylor, Major J. ___ ___ 1862 - Oct Term 1865 CR.035.801.11/ 3-102
Teachey, Arnold 20 Dec 1879 - 9 Feb 1893 CR.035.801.11
Teachey, Wiley 27 Nov 1884 - 6 Apr 1887 CR.035.801.11/ 4-294
Thigpen, Allen 3 Nov 1884 - 9 Jun 1885 CR.035.801.11/ 4-255
Thomas, Gregory 5 May 1864 - 20 Mar 1869 3-13
Turner, David W. Sr. 8 Mar 1893 - 20 Feb 1894 CR.035.801.11/ 4-441
Turner, James H. 3 Aug 1887 - 10 Sep 1892 CR.035.801.11/ 4-412
Turner, Solomon 8 Jun 1867 - Oct Term 1871 CR.035.801.11/ 4-52

APPENDIX (cont.)

Usher, William 23 Aug 1866 - Oct Term 1867 3-129

Vann, John Robert 20 Aug 1883 - 1 Sep 1884 CR.035.801.11/ 4-234

Wallace, John R. 11 May 1864 - 27 Feb 1873 CR.035.801.11/ 4-73
Wallace, Robert 8 Jul 1890 - 13 Mar 1893 CR.035.801.11/ 4-422
Wallace, Thomas 26 Feb 1878 - 27 Sep 1892 CR.035.801.11/ 4-414
Ward, Alfred 26 Aug 1867 - 7 Nov 1868 CR.035.801.11/ 4-3
Ward, Nancy 27 Oct 1883 - 9 Jul 1888 CR.035.801.11/ 4-317
Ward, William R. 24 Jun 1885 - 31 Aug 1892 CR.035.801.11/ 4-409
Waters, Nathan M. 18 Jun 1879 - 27 Nov 1880 CR.035.801.11/ 4-157
Wells, Boney 6 Jan 1888 - 25 Aug 1890 CR.035.801.11/ 4-363
Wells, James 16 Dec 1898 - 6 Jun 1903 5-85
Wells, Stoakes 1 Mar 1887 - 17 Jan 1889 CR.035.801.11/ 4-333
West, Noah 14 Dec 1878 - 2 Dec 1895 CR.035.801.11/ 4-475
Westbrook, Jesse E. 6 Feb 1883 - 15 May 1884 CR.035.801.12/ 4-225
Whaley, Kincey 3 Nov 1861 - Jul Term 1862 CR.035.801.12/ 3-56
Whitfield, Charlotte E. 13 Sep 1880 - 19 Oct 1880 CR.035.801.12/ 4-164
Whitfield, John T. 17 Dec 1875 - 17 Feb 1876 CR.035.801.12/ 4-106
Williams, Elizabeth A. 7 May 1892 - 21 Jan 1902 5-47
Williams, James B. of Rockfish Township 15 Jan 1900 - 3 Apr 1911 5-422
Williams, Martha 22 Jan 1870 - 11 Jun 1875 CR.035.801.12 / 4-97
Williams, Parmelia C. no date - 8 Aug 1887 4-303
Williams, Thomas H. 20 Jul 1861 - Oct Term 1864 CR.035.801.12/ 3-91
Williams, W. H. now in *The City of Goldsboro County of Wayne* 24 Nov 1885 -
     16 Oct 1889 CR.035.801.12/ 4-344
Wilson, Anna 10 May 1878 - 19 Aug 1878 CR.035.801.12/ 4-132
Winders, D. J. 1 May 1861 - Oct Term 1862 CR.035.801.12/ 3-60
Winders, Dollie 23 Mar 1895 - 14 Sep 1900 CR.035.801.12/ 5-15
Winders, Edward 19 Dec 1890 - 30 Mar 1893 CR.035.801.12/ 4-425
Winders, Pearcey of Wolfscrape Township 30 Jul 1894 - 7 Dec 1894
     CR.035.801.12/ 4-457
Winders, W. H. 15 Feb 1881 - 12 Feb 1900 & 13 Apr 1903 CR.035.801.12/
     4-564/ 5-72
Wright, Isaac 4 Oct 1861 - Oct Term 1861 CR.035.801.12/ 3-42
Wright, Randelson 9 Mar 1891 - 9 Sep 1891 CR.035.801.12/ 4-388
Wright, William 6 Aug 1881 - 4 Oct 1881 CR.035.801.12/ 4-178

Young, David S. 9 Apr 1894 - 12 Mar 1895 CR.035.801.12/ 4-459

BLUNT, Mary 456; William 456
BOEN, Elisebeth 127
BONEY, Ann W. 498,500; Barbara 47; Cathrine 497; Daniel 47,380,498; Daniel T. 51,501; Dorothy 49; Eliza 49; Elizabeth 390; Gabriel 49; Jacubb 52; James W. 47, 51,334,501; Jno 50; Jno. Q. Q. 389; John 48,51, 138,483,500; John A. 380; John William 49; Linda 51; Matilda 417; Mary 48,50,91,525; Mary Jane 92; Mary Priscilla 524; Poley 109; Susan L. 49; Timothy 47; Timothy W. 51,501,524; Wells 48,50; William 47,48, 50; William D. 47; William Senr 49; Wimbert, Wimberk 47,497; Wright 48,50,51,498,499; Wright, Col. 417
BONHAM, Nathaniel 389; Thankful 389
BONNEY, Jacob 52; John 52; Wimbert 335
BOON, Henrey 64
BORDEN, Betty 234; Charlotte 17; Joseph 234; Levi 18,136,229; Wm B. 153
BORDIN, Levi 291
BOSTIC, Emily 53; John 53; John Miller 53; John Sr 53
BOSTICK, Elizabeth 438; Jacob 233; John 558; Polly 308; Sarah Eliza 558
BOT, Eaphriam 59
BOURDEN, B. 227; Bryan 463; Charity 182; Elizabeth 151; H. 287; Mary 182; Nancy 237,239; Nicholas 34,360; Samuel 431; Sarah E. 479; Sarah Elizabeth 479; Seny A. 479; Wilson 405
BOURDENS, Halsted 92
BOWDAIN, Samuel A. 165
BOWDAN, S. R. 375
BOWDEN, Ann A. 479; B. 565; B. C. 202; Benjamin 455; Daniel 155,202, 211,565,581; Halsted 234; Henry 581; John C. 234; Lamuel 442; Nicholas 260; R. C. 211; Readen 301; Richard 500; William W. 479
BOWDLEN, D. 212
BOWEN, Ann 576; Cliften 299; Dann 296
BOWIN, Fedrick 100
BOWZER, Emanuel 54; Mary 54,55; Susanah 55
BOYET, Anne 56; Arther 56,59; Jesse 133; John 59; Moses 56; Samuel 59; Sarah 283; William B. 59
BOYETT, Alfred 196; Ancram A. 87; Martha 57; Moses 56; William 26
BOYETTE, Anna 265; Jonas 233
BOYKIN, Edey 58; Jon 58; Joseph 58; Mary 58; Sarah 58; Smeddick 58; Thomas 271; William 58, 121

BOYT, Hardy 59; Phereby 59; Samuel 59
BRABHAM, Stephen 174
BRADEY, Nancy 162
BRADLEY, Charles 166; John 103,515; Jonathan 251; Richard 444,515
BRADSHAW, Daniel 382
BRANCH, Archebil 60; Archilaus 61,205,434; Archilaus Bright 61; Arthur 60,62; Benjamin 60; Bryant 60; Easter 205; Edelph 62; Hepsebeth 60; James G. 61, 307,434; Jesse 62,515; Martha 455; Matthew 62; Reuben 60; William 62
BRAY, Joseph 84,132
BRIANT, Jacob 467; Margaret 80
BRICE, Amanda 64; Ann Jean 437; Eliza 64; Eliza Ann 377; Frances 64; Francis 65,327; George, Geo. 63,318; John 63,64,65; John L. 64; Joseph, Jos. 64,65, 482; Martha 64,65; Martha Ann 63; Mary 63, 437; Massey 437; Rachel 64; Rachel A. 64; William, Wm. 64,65,389; William B. 64
BRICKELL, Th. H. 252
BRIGHT, William 66
BRINSON, Elizabeth 109
BRITTON, Caterine 67; Edmond 67; Elizebeth 67; John 67; Thomas 67
BROCAS, Richd. 388,456
BROCK, D. 120; David 364; Elizabeth 69; Hannah 442; Jesse 281,412; John 52,68,437; John A. 69; Leavin 455; Lewis 69,464; Mary 120,364, 442; Polly 464; Sarah 442; Sary 206; Seley 68; Steppen 215; Tabitha 455
BROCKSON, Noancey 348
BROOKES, Job 547
BROOKS, Joseph 118
BROW, Edward 504; John 282; John Jr. 8
BROWN, Abigale 74; Alsa 70,71; Artheor 179; Arthur 72; Barbary 557; Benjamin 71,74; Betsey 30; Brantley 71; Cathran 71; Cilvy 557; Council 73; Daniel 74; David 71,557; Dolly 70; Edward, Edwd. 72,242; Elisabeth 73; Eliza 70; Elizabeth 351,353; Felex 75; Fredreck 75; Henry 74,356; Henry 74, 356; Howel 75,76; Isaac 71; Jacob 74; Jacob Senr 74; James 30,73; Jesse 74,260; John 74, 75,285; Killey 71; Laviney 503; Lidea 75; Maria 542; Mary 75,149; Mirrim 174; Mourning 72; Nancy 76; Needom 73; Patience 77; Polly 402; Prudence 72; Robert H. 70; Sally 77; Sarah 73; Sary 75; Sherrod 72,503; Stephen 74; Susanah 72; Tricey 503;

BROWN con't
William, Wm. 73,289
BROWNE, Margret 585
BROWNS, Wm. 73
BRYAN, Ann 138,368; Austin 244; Jacob 80; John 330, 371,482; K. 552; Kedar 79,264,367,368; Margarette Jane 78; Needham 78; Rigdon 79,368; Timothy 376
BRYANT, Anne 80; Auston 244; Cathrin Jane 80; David 80; Easter 80; Elizabeth 80; Jacob 80, 467; Mary 80,467; Nancy 80; Susannah 80; William 80
BRYEN, James 478
BUCKMAN, Brunette 81; Charle G. 81; George L. 81; Guy E. 81
BULL, Esbel 330; William 330
BULLS, Mary 213
BUNTING, David D. 237,543
BURCH, Ann 82; Araminty 82; Benjamin 82; Charles 82; Christopher 82; John 82; Joseph 82; Richard 82
BURKE, Mrs. 274
BURNETT, Richard 545
BURNIM, Feribay 428; John Futerel 428; Marsilley 428; Nancy 428; William 428
BURNS, Sarah 446; Susanna 183
BURRILL, William 340
BURTON, Basil 423; Cyrene 126; John 384; Stratten 126; Thomas 423
BUSH, Lewis B. 579; Mary 580; Mary C. 579
BUSHEE, Consider 426
BUSSY, Mary 213
BUTLER, Charles 570; Robrt 199; William 72,199; William Senr 454
BUXTON, Rachel 3
BYRD, Beththiah 83; Cathrine 83; Edward 83,508; Elizabeth 209; James 214; John 83; March 404; Michael 83,153; Nancy 213; Polley A. 209; Robert 107,111,164; Selah 83; William 78,476

CALVIN, Catherene 257
CAMBLE, Jon 241
CAMMISON, Sarah 148
CANADAY, Demzey 85
CANADY, Archibald 84; David 84; Jean 84; Joseph 84; Maryann 74; Patrick 85
CANEDAY, John 477
CANIDO, James 391
CANNADY, Abia 85; Abigail 85; Alixander 85; Elisabeth 85; Joshua 85; Patrick 85; Sarrah 85
CANNE, William 52
CANNON, Allen 576; David 86; Dennis 19,514; Henry 86,374; Mary 86
CANNONE, Edward 293
CAR, David 523; William 93
CARE, John W. 49,50
CAREY, Elizabeth 99

DAIL con't
Elezabeth 124,125; Fred-
erick 281; Isaac 124;
Melinda 179; Mornening
125; Polley 125; Salley
125
DANIEL, Clarky 61; Clary
A. 61; John 286; O. O.
206; Robert 306; Sally
209; William 209
DARDEN, Charles 126; Jesse
508; Mariann 126; Mary
126; Patience 126
DAUGHTRY, Joshua 566
DAUPHIN, Darling 413;
James 413
DAVIS, Ann 127,569; Calvin
130,281,513; Catharine
130; David 127; Eliza-
beth 513; Emma 130,513;
Francis 131; Ira 130,
513; James P. 130,512,
513; Jane 129; John, Jno.
128,426; John E. 513;
John Edward 513; John
Edward T. 130; Lewis 131;
Lucy 475; Malchier 129;
Maria C. 130; Mariah C.
513; Mehalay 127; Nancy
130,513; Rachel 129,426;
Rachel Ann 504; Rebecca-
ann 127; Richard 236;
Samuel, Sm. 129,130,182,
187,200,569; Sary Jane
127; Sephronia E. 130,
513; Seth 130,513; Simon
131; Windol Senr 129;
Winifred 130,513;
Zachariah 129
DAWSON, Isaac 191
DEBRUHL, Mary 300
DEEMS, Charles F. 234
DEMPSEY, George F. 233
DE ROSSET, Armond 97
DICKSON, Alexander, Alexr.
132,134,135,185,254,261;
Alfred 133; Ann 141;
Anne 134; Anne Jane 134;
Anney 133; Barbara 138;
Benadick 133,137; Bryant
133; Calvin J. 39; Cat-
harine 79,136,337;
Catharine A. 141; Cor-
nelia Ann 141; David C.
135; Dorathy 134,138;
Edward 138,241,254,453,
468; Elisabeth 134; Eliza
136,141; Elizabeth Jane
133,135; Ellinor 134,
141; Florida 141; India-
na 141; James 10,51,92,
101,133,134,135,140,141,
159,241,320,327,345,372,
380,417,433,468,472,485,
494,534; James D. 135;
James G., Jas. G. 40,162,
185,186,265,491,581;
James Senr. 465; Jane
128,368; John 79,93,132,
137,138,141,159,430,451,
482; Jones 132; Joseph
84,89,132,133,134,135,
138,141,327,329,354,355,
360,367,368,376,421,497;
Lewis 111,136,141; Mar-
gared 468; Margaret 134,
468; Maria 141; Mary
134; Mildred 141; Moltin
367; Morris 137; Patsey
136,141; Robert, Robt.
79,91,102,113,132,134,
135,138,139,140,329,
346,430,433; Robert
Sloan 468; Samuel 137;

DICKSON con't
Sarah 137; Susan 140;
Susan Ann 135; Susana
345; Susannah 133,134;
Sindey 134; W. 164;
William, Wm. 133,134,
138,141,164,183,247,250,
274,376,529,582; William,
Col. 141,184,392; Willi-
am, Dr. 451; William
David 468; Williams 139,
468,543; Zilpha 326;
Zilphia 142
DILWORTH, John MCanne 147
DOB, James 12
DOBSON, Elizabeth 129,143;
Hanner 144; James 27,
143,144; John 143; Lewis
144; Patience 27; Peory
143
DOD, David 58; Elizabeth
58
DODD, David 20,509
DONAHO, Domeni 545
DOPSON, Hanner 145
DOWD, Emanuel 146; James
146; John 146; Sarah 146;
Weliby 146
DOWNIE, Alexander 147
DRAKE, Willm. 85
DRAUGHON, Mary I. 552
DRESCOT, William 547
DREW, George 137; Lucy 137
DUACKS, Elizabith 148;
Henry 148; Magdelane 148;
Nance 148; Presley 148;
Rhoade 148; Robert 148;
Selah 148; William 148;
William Jur 148
DUDLEY, Ambrose 119; Levi
420
DUFF, John 526
DULANY, Benjn 505
DUMPSEY, Alsa 143
DUNCAN, Edmond 149,150;
George 149,150; Grace
149; Isaac 150; Sucke
150; William 149,150
DUNKAN, Anne 151; Edmond
151; George 151; Isaac
151; Jacob 151,152; John
Charles 151; Joseph 151;
Lewis 151; Sarah 151;
Stephen 151,152; William,
Wm. 33,151; William Junr
151
DUNKIN, Cullin 152; Fanney
152; Frances 111; Jacob
152; James 152; Luke
152; Susanna 152
DUNMARK, James 33
DUNN, Elisabeth 153;
Francis 153; James 153;
John 259; Robert 153;
Samuel 23,153; William
153,165

EDMUNDSON, James 62; Polly
62; Richard 62; Sally
62; Smithy 62; William
62
EDWARDS, Anne 154; Dolly
101; Elizabeth 521;
Fanne 154; Felix 154;
James 154; John 504;
Matthew 154; Sene 154;
Susanah 154
ELICE, Joseph 155; Major
155; Wiley 155
ELIOT, Elizabeth 156; John
229; John Jnr 106; Mary
106; William 156; Zaca-
riah 156

ELIS, Wll. 155
ELKINS, Elizabeth 344
ELLIS, Evan 259
ELLISON, Ackiss 157; Ann
157; Charlottie 157;
Jesse 157; Jordan 157;
William 157
EMANUEL, Ephraim 121
ENGLISH, Mary 127
ERVIN, Milly C. 25; William
25
ESOM, Benjamin 16; Gibson
16
EVANS, Ann William 453;
Benjamin 159; Betsey 158;
Bryant 287; David 38,158,
159,499; Elizabeth 159;
Elizabeth Ann 332; James
159,327,346; Kizey Jane
287; Rebeca 158; Rebekah
159; Rice 416; Samuel 332,
466; William Burton 159
EVENS, Benjamin 266
EVERETT, David 234
EVERIT, Sarah 199
EVES, J. A. 548
EZELL, Bengamin 160; Denis
161; Dolly 161; Fedrick
160; George 160; Henry
160; John R. 161; Joshua
R. 162; Lucy 161; Mikel
160; Nancy 43,160,162;
Patrick 161,162; Reubin
160,161; Salathail 161;
Sarah 160,161; William
160
EZZEL, Fanny 371; Raiburn
371
EZZELL, J. R. 527; Joshua
R. 180A; Salathel 342;
Sarah A. 212; William 546

FAIRCLOTH, Sarah 570;
Zacheriah 570
FAISON, Diana 164; Elias
106,136,141,153,163,164,
165,166; Elias K. 163;
Elizabeth A. 400; Fanney
164; Frances 165; Francis
166; Fras. H. 584; Helen
C. 389; Henry 164,165,
166; Isham, Isom 106,164,
165,166; Julian P. 389;
Killbee 584; Margaret
163; Martha 166; Mary E.
163; Nancy 164; N. C. 163;
Patsey 106,164,166; Polly
164; Sarah 165; Thomas
S. 104; William W. 400
FARIOR, John 53,108,118,
167,381,439; Martha 168;
Nancy 167; Sarah 168; Wm.
118,532
FAROR, John 443
FARRIAR, William 349
FARRIER, Hugh 168; John 77;
Martha 168
FARRIOR, David 169; Edward
169; Edward W. 169; Eliz-
abeth 169; E. W. 70; Fany
256; Hugh 479; James 167;
John 7,169,170,174,314,
483; John Junr 167; Mar-
gret 170; Martha 169;
Nicholas 256; N.J. 53;
Sarah Catharine 218;
William, Wm. 15,53,70,
169,170,436,542
FENNEL, Jemima 344; Pene-
lope 171
FENNELL, Geo. 339; Penelope
63; Pennelopa 171
FERGUSSON, Alexandr 529

FFORIS, Abraham 295
FINDLEY, Thomas 89
FLORRENS, Samuel 234
FLOWERS, Jesse 479
FOLDS, Elizabeth 529;
Joseph 172,529
FORD, John 16
FORLAW, David W. 173;
Elizabeth 173; Elizabeth
J. 173; John 173; Nancy
173; Priscilla W. 173;
Robert 173; Thomas 173
FORT, Abner 225; Thomas
225
FOSTER, Mary Ann 116
FOUNTAIN, Joab 72,174;
Jacob 174; John 174;
Mary 174,244; Sarah 174;
Tammey 174
FRAIZER, George 16
FRAZAR, George 105; Sarah
20
FREDERECK, Norris 81
FREDERICK, Betsey James
175; Caroline 166; Cat-
harine 24; Edith 209;
Felix 31,46,176,213;
Hanner Jane 26; Jacky
176; James 159,175,176;
Katharine 176; Mariah
166; Martha Faison 166;
Nancy 106,175; Norice
176; Noris 26; Patrick
176; Patsey Eliza 25;
Peter Coffee 175; Thomas
Kenan 176; William 175,
176,327; William K., Wm.
K. 175,197,251,351,486;
William Kenan 175
FREDERICKS, Peter 354
FREDRICK, Felix 156,176;
William 31
FURLOW, John 87
FUSEL, Benjamin 177; Eliz-
abeth 177; John 177
FUSSEL, Benjamin 44; Jacob
266,482
FUSSELL, Benjamin 178,201,
236; Elizabeth 178,562;
Jacob 236; John 176;
John E. 332; Nancy 47;
Stephen 178
FUTCH, Mary 54

GARNER, B. 493; Bassil 179;
Esther 434; Henry 179;
Nathan 303; Nathan Senr
179; Penelope 303,305;
Rachel 179; Simeon 179
GARRASON, Adonijah 449;
Ephraim 449
GARRESON, Thomas 349
GARRISON, David 180; Elin
244; Ephram 180,346;
Jenny 180; Polly 180,
395; Thomas 159,179,502
GAVIN, Ally 19; Charity
180A; Charles 181;
Edward C., Edwd. C. 40,
87,180A; John 181; Lewis
181; Patience 181; Samuel
181; Samuel James 180A
GEORGE, Barbary 497,500;
Daniel 47,497
GIBBENS, George 352
GIBBS, Ba 182; Bershaba
182; Charity 183; Char-
les 183,463; John 32,
183; John Senr 183;
Sarah 183; Thomas 182
GIBS, John 86
GIBSON, Daniel 376; Fran-
cis 376

GILBERT, Abraham 330
GILLESBE, James 198
GILLESPIE, Catharine 185;
Clermont M.P. 185; D.
459; David 184,185;
James 98,184,185,254,
327,329,441,451; Jane
184,185,186; Jo. 185;
John W. 389; John W.S.
185,186; Joseph 141,184,
185,346,347,354; Joseph
George W. 185; Lucy 184;
Mary A. 417; Mary Ann
417; Mary W. 417; Mild-
ard Ann 184; Oliver 417;
S.G.R. 186; Shadrach G.
389; Shadrach G.R. 185,
186; Shadrach Gaius Rowe
185; Susanna 141; Willi-
am D. 185
GILLISPIE, James 204
GILLMAN, John 147
GILMAN, H. 498; John 319,
335,447,502
GILMON, John 223
GILMOORE, Nancy 209
GILSTRAP, Ann 87; Lewis 54
GLISSON, Abraham 187,188;
Bryan 187,230; Bryan H.
187; Celey 145; Charity
230; Daniel 230,405;
Dav. 164; Fredk 188;
Gufford 188; Henry 230;
Hettie 230; Isaac 188;
Jacob 187; John Junr
188; John Senr 188; Lew-
is 188; Mary 187,361;
Michal 188; Millard 228;
Pearsis 230; Rachel 188;
Sally 187,230; Sally
Jane 187; Stephen H.
187; Susannah 187; Zil-
phea Ann 187
GODDEN, William 12
GOFF, Elizabeth 189; John
189; Sabra 344; Thos.
189; Tomzan 344; William
189
GOODMAN, Elizabeth 33;
Mary 191; Willm 445
GORE, Elizabeth 190; Fran-
ces 190; Isaac 190; John
190,514; John Senr 190;
Jonathan 56,190; Nelly
190; Rebecah 190; Sarah
19; William 190
GOUFF, Elizabeth 220;
John 220
GOUGH, John 253
GRADDY, Aleander Jr. 192;
Alexander 191; Alexander
Snr 192; Ann 191; Chari-
ty 408; Fradrick 191;
Henry 408; James 191;
John 191; Lewis 191;
Mary 191; Timothy 408;
William 191,406,462
GRADY, A.A. 394; Abner 193;
A.I. 194; Alexander Sr.,
Alexr Sr. 192,193;
Alexr. 409; Alexr Jr.
193,394; Alsas 513; An
11; Anna 192; A.O. 69,
192,193,194,387,407,475,
512,513; Atlas I. 194;
Barbara 29; B.F. 194;
B.W. 194; Eliza 195;
Elizabeth 194,308; Eli-
zha 402; Elizza Ann 193;
Fred 193; Goodman 193;
H. 194; Hack W. 193;
Harriett 194; Henery
193; Henry 69,194,409,
493; Henry G. 195;

GRADY con't
Hester 536,538; James M.
193; James Sr. 193; Kee-
nan 193; Louisa 179; Mary
193; Nancy 193; Outlaw
193; Patience 409; Putney
193; Rebekah 29; Repsey
193; Sherwood 195,479;
S.M. 194; Susicy 125;
Theodosia 195; Thomas M.
307; Timothy 409; T.M.
362; Whitfield 308;
William W. 195
GRAHAM, Chauncey W. 196,
197; Chauncey Williams
197; C.W. 25; G.W. 142;
J. 263; Mary Eliza 196,
197; Nancy 197; S. 222,
416; Sally 196; Sarah R.
197; Stephen 24,132,139,
196,197,459,528
GRAINGER, Caleb 456
GRANADY, John 300
GRANT, Berriah 97; Eli 322;
Hezekiah 253; Sarah 422
GRAY, Elizabeth 198; Ellen
198; James 198; John 198;
Nathan 341; Thomas, Tho.
105,198,462; William, Wm.
97,198,341
GREEN, Ann 200; Elizabeth
200; James 199,201; John
200,448,459; Lott 201;
Martha 201; Phebe 200;
Rebeckah 201; Samuel 201;
Sarah 200,201; Sary 127;
Susanna 291; Timothy 200
GREENE, Timothy 200
GREER, John 398; Mary 90
GREEVES, Susannah 515
GREGORY, Jason 571; Lott
67,560
GREY, John 202; Lewis 202;
Morris 202; Owen 202;
Rebecar 202
GRIER, John 523
GRIFFIN, John 164
GRIMES, Catharine 176;
Charles 204,267; Ellender
204; Hugh 203; James 204,
205,283; Jane 176; Jesse
203,205; John 204,416,
520; Joseph 203,204,416;
Mary 276A; Salley 143;
Sampson, Samson 203,204,
205; Thomas 204; William
205
GRIMSLEY, Elishe Gore 206;
Elisha Gorge 206; James
206; John 206; Margret
206; Polly 206; Sarah
206; Shearad 232
GRISWOLD, Ann 234; Benjamin
234
GROVES, John K. 342; Robt.
271
GUFFORD, Andrew 207; Elen-
dor 207; Hanner 207; J.
207; James 60,207; Rachel
188; Stephen 207
GULLEY, Caty 208; Henry
208; James 208; Jesse
228; William 208,209
GULLY, Henry 209; James
209; Jesse 209; John 209;
Nancy 34; Patsey 209;
William 209; William Jr.
209
GURGANUS, Benjamon 210;
Betsey 210; Cooper 210;
Elizabeth 210; Eurias
210; John 210; Jonathan
210; Mary 210; Nancy 210;
Sarah 210; Uriah 210

GUY, Alfred 212; David
Thomas 212; Elizabeth
214; Hannah 30; James
211,213; Jesse 214; John
211,212,213,271; Lemmuel
213,271; Lewis 211; Lim-
uel 212; Mary 212; Morris
30,211; Owen 211; Polly
111; Rebecca 212; Rebe-
car 211; Samuel 213;
Sarah 131,213; Stephen
212; Theophilus 214;
Theops 392; Thomas 214;
William 213,214,374;
Zilpha 212; Zilpha
Stephen 212

HAGANS, Offerias 199
HAGINS, Rachal 199
HAIRGROVE, Aaron 222; Edith
222; Henry 222; John 222;
Lamuel 222; Margaret 222
HALL, Abraham 367; Albert
G. 389; Alford 217; Benjn
F. 542; Blanchy 215; Cat-
harine 218; Catharine P.
216; Catharine Priscilla
218; David 220; Drucy 99;
Drury 215,219; Edward P.
221; Edwd. 92; E.J. 218;
Elinor 220; Elizabeth
220,221; George 216;
George M. 218; Herring
217; Isaac N. 221; James
99,215,221,367,416,554;
James E. 218; James
Edward 216; Jane 292;
J.E. 216,532; Jemima 220;
John W. 436; Lewis 217,
221; Lucresa 220; Marga-
ret 92; Margaret L. 216,
320; Mary 217,219,220;
Nancy 215; Nansay 220;
Nicholas, Nich. 218,221,
479; Penelope 215; Polly
7; Rachal 220; Sarah 219;
Sival 220; Solomon 215;
Susan 328; Susana 215;
Thomas 218,220,504,532;
Thomas P. 221; William,
Wm. 102,221,367; W. T.
218
HALLINGSWORTH, Elizabeth
506
HALSO, Arthur W. 364; John
76,309
HANCHEY, Marten 223; Moses
232; Sarah 223; Wm. 223
HANCOCK, Stephen 381
HANFORD, Saml. 326
HANSLEY, W. H. 250
HARDEN, Thomas 199
HARDISON, Hammond 409
HARDISTY, Kezia 267
HARGROVE, John 222
HARPER, James 281,282;
Simpson Jr. 373
HARREL, Butha 145; James
447; Seney 255
HARRELL, Alethea 230;
Jas. 339
HARRING, Charity 191
HARRIS, Amos 55,267; John
330; Mary 267,553;
William 151,462,553;
Zachariah 149
HARRISON, Edward Junior 259
HARROD, Sarah 260
HART, Richard 474
HARVELL, Ruth 224; William,
Wm. 224,339
HARVILL, Gabrel 224; James
224; Ruth 224; William
224

HASSELL, Dempsey 48
HATCH, Harriet 234; Joseph
R. 234; Julia 234,307;
Lemuel D. 234; Martha
234; R. C. 234; Rhodes
Clarissa 234; Richard
234
HAUL, Lazarus 121
HAWES, Pene 389
HAWKINS, Gidon 174
HAY, John 456
HEARICK, Elizabeth 225;
Jesse 225; Mary 225;
Nancy 225; Richard 225;
Sarah 225; Thency 225
HEATH, Alexander 226;
Betsey Ann 337; Clarris-
sey W. 171; Dorathy 226;
James 226; John 185;
John Henry 171; Kitty
494; Lenora A. 171; Pru-
dence 494; Theophilus
494; Thomas 337,338;
Thomas B. 370,479;
William 185,337
HEATHE, Jcob 337
HEDGEMAN, Lewis 546
HEDGPETH, Leusey 566
HENRY, Hannah 116; Mary E.
45
HERICK, Mary 225
HERREL, Henry 244; Jacob
244; Kedar 244
HERRING, Abraham 476,477;
Alexander, Alxr 62,227,
228,230,463; Ally 229;
Bright 357; Bright
Middleton 354; Bryan S.
569; Bryan W. 228;
Charity 286,401; Daniel
61; David 490; Drury 229;
Elenor 354,357; Elisha
62,141,228,230; Enoch
510; Everitt 485; Fanny
43; Frederick 229; Lewis
144,227; Lewis Stephen
227; Luke 187; Maria
228; Mary 237,239; Mary
A. 306; Mary Caroline
569; Mary Elizabeth 306;
Nancy 228,357; Needham
W. 481; N.W. 51; Patience
223; Patsey 228; Phebe
390; Polly 228,229;
Rachel 229; Rd. 225,510;
Rebaca 477; Rebecca 227;
Samuel, Saml 229,230;
Sarah 230; Stephen 66,
230,357,459,569; Stephen
B. 230,237; Stephen
Bright 230; Susan 228;
Sylvia 229; Thomas 162;
William 229; Willis 230
HICKS, Albert 106; Albert
R. 166; Dan 290,514;
Isham F. 166; James 166;
James H., Jas. H. 153,
165,362,414; Malcy Jane
64; Martha Faison 166;
Martha W. 166; Molsey J.
65; Service 290; Thank-
ful 231; Thomas 232;
William 166
HICKSON, Eleanor 410;
Joseph Rd. 410
HIGHSMITH, Elizabeth 42;
Jacob 42; John 233,251;
Sara 393; Sarah 233
HIGHTOWER, W. C. 45
HILL, Anna M. 234; Betsey
223; Buckner L. 234,580;
Calhoun 234; Catharine
38; C.D. 234,235A,239;
Christopher D. 235A;

HILL con't
Edward 235; Felix 38;
Felix K. 235; Frances
234; Henry 48; James 235;
James K. 57,239,304; Jane
38,237; Jeen 235; John
38,235,324; Jno W. 400;
John L. 324; John S. 155,
176,580,581; Sarah 17,
235; Sarah A. 257; Thomas,
Thos. 61,234,235,492,580;
Thomas B. 234; Thos. Jr.
283; W.E. 235A; William
E. 235A; William K. 235;
William L. 235A
HILLS, William L. 139
HINES, Daniel 324; Iry D.
324; James 180A; Joel
209; Lotty 324; Margaret
Ann 180A; Nelly 190;
Patience 209; Rebekkah
22; Wm. 180A
HIX, Thankful 231
HOBBS, Sarah 351
HOBS, Sarah 353
HOCKINGS, Ann 236; John 236;
Lattesa 236; Mary 236
HODGE, Wilson 227
HODGES, Benjamin 237; Eliz-
abeth 237; Frances 237;
Franklin 238; H. 62,238;
Henry 324; Henry Hollo-
well 238; Hollowell 237,
238,239; Holoway 324;
Isaac 238; Lemuel 238;
Sarah 238; Susan 237;
William 237,239,543,579;
William F. 238; William
Thomas 238; Wilson 237,
289,579
HODGESON, Aron 240; David
499
HODGISON, Ann 240; Aron
240; John 240; Joseph 240;
Lewis 240
HODGS, Wm. 436
HODGSEN, Aaron 119
HOGG, John 38; Robert 38
HOLDEN, Alexander 430
HOLDON, Alexander 241;
Jeremiah 241; Jno 89;
John 241
HOLEMS, Hardy 509
HOLLAND, Millae 56
HOLLENSWORTH, Elizer 324;
Sally 234; Zebeedee 324
HOLLEY, James 242; John
242; Sarah 242; Tamar 242
HOLLINGSWORTH, Celia 243;
Elizabeth 243,506; Henry
1,95,162,181,220,243,244,
508; Jacob 243,244; James
506; Lydia 243; Sarah
243; William, Wm. 244,
267; William Wright 253
HOLMES, Catharine 244;
Frederick 245; Gabriel
261,456; Gorge 245; Hance
245; Hardy 245; James
484; John 245; Kea 245;
Sarah 292; William 245
HOMES, Doratha 246; Edward
246; Gabriel 246; John
246; Mary 246
HOOKS, Ann 520; C. 519;
Charles 139,159,247,248,
323,498; Curtis 247;
David 136,139,141,153,
227,247,248,518,543;
David, Col. 141; Dickson
136,139; Hillary 247,248;
Rebecca E. 579,580;
Robert Dickson 139; Sam-
uel Dunn 153; Sarah Eliza
584;

HOOKS con't
Sivil 153; Susan 543;
Susana 247,248; Thomas,
Thos. 234,247,248,490;
Thomas C. 579; Whitmel
248; William 247,248
HORICK, Jessey 36
HORN, Thomas 8
HORRICK, Jessey 36
HORROCK, Jessey 36
HOUSTON, Alfred 249; Aman-
da 234; Calvin J. 249;
Catharine 175; Chelly
549; Dicey 549; Edward,
Edwd. 386,549; Edward A.
457; Edward W. 249; Elis-
abeth Ann 544; E.W. 249;
Ezabel 250; Ezabella 250;
George 386; George E.
553; George E. Jr. 249;
George E. Senr. 249;
Henry 549; Henry Clay
249; Henry W. 249; H.W.
249; James 249,250; John
175; John W. 544; Mary
Ann 294; Polly 549; Ro-
bart J. 250; Samuel 544;
Tabitha 249; Temperance
W. 249; Mary White 544;
William, Wm. 259,293,
363,506,545,549; William
J. 544; William Jur 545;
W.J. 356,380; Wm. A. 247,
280
HOWARD, Betsey 92; James
468; John 92; Mary 468
HOWELL, James 506
HUBBARD, William 560
HUDGGINS, William 550
HUDGINS, Abnor 132
HUFHAM, Cloarisa Caroline
251; George 251; George
W. 39,42,63,166,251;
Harriet 251; Helen M.
251; James 251; James M.
251; John, Jno. 24,63,
127,251,377; Johnathan
251; Margaret A. 251;
Mary Ann 569; Nancy 251
HUGGINS, Luke 417; Luke M.
550; Mary E. 45; Single-
ton 418
HULETTE, Mary 112
HULLING, Elizabeth 506
HUMPHREY, John 506
HUNTER, Anney 254; Celea
53; Edward 253,254;
Hardey 254; Hogan 159,
257,520; Hosea 53; Howel
253; Isaac 252,293,520;
Jobe 253; John, Jno. 132,
159,395,444,520; John
Edward 253; Mary 254,520;
Mary Eliza 252; Ned 253;
Nicholas 253,254,439;
Patience 252,563; Pris-
cilla 520; Priscilla
Ann 252; Right 439;
Robert John 252,520;
William, Wm. 253,254,
439; Wm. Jackson 439;
Wright 253
HURST, Andrew 252,304;
Andrew J. 257; Catharine
520; Charles 324; David
S. 304; Frankey B. 255;
George William 256;
Henry B. 256; James B.
255,428; James R., Jas.
R. 257,492; John 324;
John B. 255; John J. 257;
Joseph B. 255,428; Mar-
garet 304; Mary 304;
Mary E. 304;

HURST con't
Narcissa S. 257; Robert
K. 304; Samuel B. 255;
William B. 255,256;
William Be. 255; William
H. 257; Zilph B. 446;
Zylphia B. 256
HUSSE, John E. 154
HUTCHINS, Susan 239
HUTSON, John 540

INGRAM, Abner 258; Eliza-
beth 258; Ferebah 258;
John 258; John, Esqr.
214; Samuel 258
IRELAND, Eliza 45; Samuel
R. 45
IRWIN, Henry 500
ISHAM, Charles 259; James
259; Jane 259; Margaret
259
IVEY, Elizabeth 260; John
260; Leah 260; Lemuel
260; Thomas 508

JACKSON, Emma 513; Patsey
194
JAMES, Ann 261; Barbara 8;
Betsey 175; Cathrine R.
261; Charity 435; Char-
les 262; Dorethy 261;
Elias 262; Elizabeth
261,262; Gabriel H. 132,
261,262; Gabriel Holmes
261; Isaac 8,100; James
261; John 368; John J.
109,435; Joseph 262;
Margot 262; Martha 84;
Mary 261,263,487; Miriam
390; Rachel 262; Rebecca
261,263; Sarah 381;
Sivel 189; Thomas 368;
Thomas E. 261; William
115
JANACUM, Elisha 271
JARMAN, H.J. 372; J.H. 387;
John 504; Winifred 513;
Wm. 215
JEANES, David 52
JENKINS, Mary 412
JERMAIN, John 545; Robert
545
JERMAN, Jephzibah Adelia
130; James H. 130
JERNIGAN, Calvin 265; D.
214; Dicy 265; Jane 264;
Jesse 20; Neomy 20;
Sarah 16; Thomas 56,264;
Watson 265; Zilpah 183
JIRNIGAN, Sarah 16
JOHN, David 266; John 266;
Margret 266; Mary 266;
Susannah 266; Thomas 266
JOHNSON, Abraham 301; Al-
fred 163; Amos 267,309,
427; Benjamin 268,270;
Betsey Jean 269; Bizzell
178,541; Enock 339;
Ephraim 42; Henry 416;
Hepsey Ann 269; Isaac
269; James 34,339; James
T. 568,569; Jane 270;
Joel 224; John 268,269;
Jonathan 382; Joseph
261; Kitty Ann 269;
Lany 269; Louiza 269;
Margaret Ann 427; Mar-
garet Susan 268; Martha
Ellen 268; Mary 268;
Milla 427; Needham 269;
Nercissa 269; Perego
344; Ruben 152;

JOHNSON con't
Sally 269; Sapphier 267;
Sarah Eliza 268; Sloan
270; Susannah 42; Thomas
270,367; William 267,
268,458
JOHNSTON, Benjamin 271,291;
Elizabeth 272; Ezabel
273; Frances 271; Hannah
272; Hepsy Ann 269; Is-
sabell 276,358; James 34,
151,273,276,358; James
Robert 271; Jane 271,273,
276; John 269,272,274,
275,276,367,455; John
Ambert 271; John Jur 272;
Joseph 276; Louiza 269;
Mary 458; Nercissa 269;
Rachel 271; Robert 273,
276,358; Sarah 250,269,
273,276,358; Susannah 276;
Sythe 271; Thomas 134,
198,367,368; William 261,
271,273,276; Wm T. 423
JOHSTON, William 514
JOINER, Benjamin David 155;
Jane 155
JONES, Ann 279; Anthony
283; Augustine 251; Beysey
Jane 57; Catthern 279;
Clarissa 479; C. Y. F.
276A; D. 179,281,276A,
361,491,493,538; Daniel
277,536; David 128,145,
265; David Snor 177; E.
276A; Edward 283,357;
Elizabeth 279,280,577;
Elijah 276A,277; Elisha
277; Emma 283; Esther
276A; Fanny 491; Francis
B. 284; Frederick 283;
Griffin 57,145; Haywood
283; Jesse 278; Joel 277,
276A; John 279,280,471,
577; John J. 315; Jonas
283; Leadey 540; Lewis
195,280,505; Marget 369;
Martha 281,282; Marshall
283; Mary Ann 279; Mat-
thew 277; Nancy 276A,283,
284,305; Patte 279;
Pheraba 479; Polly 228;
Richd. 425; Robert 282;
Ruth 6; Samuell 547;
Saml C. 383; Sarah 283;
Sare 279; Simeon 521;
Solomon 283; Stephen 284;
Tamer 369; Thomas 279;
William 137,228,279;
William A. 195; Zilpha
277
JONSON, John 531
JONSTON, John 531
JUDGE, Hannah Ashton 504
JULIAN, Andrew 275; Ann W.
275; Charles W. 275;
Murdock 275
JUSTICE, Jaky 234

KANEGAY, Abram 285; Anna
285; Henry 285
KEATHLEY, John 286; Jonot-
han 286; Mark 286; Nancy
286; Richard 206,286
KEATHLY, Jonathan 286
KEATON, Elizabeth 2; Polley
2
KEETHLY, Mark 409
KELLY, Catharine 459; Isaac
B. 372,459,552; John J.
30
KENADA, Nancy 289
KENADAY, David 287; Eliza 287;

207

MILLS, Ann 232,364; Betty 232; Bomler 232; Cattron 240; Elizabeth 365; Frederick 231; Hicks 232; Hix 231; James 231,232; J. C. 231; Leonard 232; Lorena 232; Mary 231; Rebecca 231,232; Sarah 232; Shadrack 231; Thankful 231,232
MITCHEL, Dolly 448; James 448
MOAN, Dorethy Ann 345
MOBLEY, Ollen 366; Martha 366
MOLTEN, Abraham 367,368, 374; Cathrine 368; Elizabeth 367,368; John 367,368; Mary 368; Michael 367,368; Patience 367; Sarah 367,368; Tamer 369
MOLTON, Abraham 264; Abraham Ser 264; Eliza Catharine 520; John 264; Sarah 520; Sarah Priscilla 520; Thomas 416, 463
MONK, Bruster 371; Elizabeth Ann 370,372; Jacob 371; James B. B. 544; James Brewster 372; J.B.B. 171,186; Jno W. 370; John 371; John Wilkinson 372; J. W. 372; Sarah 371
MOODY, James 474; James Sr 373
MOON, Cassander 345; David 345; Dorethy A. 345
MOOR, Annis 374; Backey 374; Betsey 374; Elpenice 486; James 374; John 374; Mary 374; Maurice 374; Morris 392; Orson 374; Sarah 374; Sucky 374; William 374
MOORE, Alfred 380; Ann Victoria 380; Charity 380; Charles H. 375; Charles Henry 356,375; David C. 375; D. C. 338, 375; Eliza 380; Elizabeth 375,509; Elpenice 484,485; George 380; Huldah 380; James 246, 380,509; John 288; Joseph 509; Levi 375; Lewis 456,509; Mathew 375; Mary Elen 375; Rachel 375; Rebekah 262; Sarah E. 375; Thomas 375; Thomas M. 375; William 185
MORE, D. C. 185
MOREAU, A. 326
MORGAN, A. 263,337,353; Aaron 338,352,452; Abel 549; Aron 184,521; Dorcas 390; Elizabeth 184; James W. 452; James Washington 184
MORIS, George 292; Sarah 292
MORISEY, D. G. 375; Thomas Jr 268
MORREY, G. 31
MORRICEY, George 290
MORRICY, Jane 290
MORRIS, Ascion 70; John 11; Lucretia 404; Peter 91; Rebecca 404; Thomas 266
MORRISS, Peter 138

MORRISSY, Elizabeth 290
MUMFORD, Charlotte 184; Eady Merenda 504; Joseph 184; Mille 274
MURDOCK, David 272
MURDOUCK, David 416,453
MURFFY, Timothy 189
MURPHEY, Barbary 376; David 377; Elisabeth 376; Henry 377; Jemima 377; Mary 377; Mary Jane 377; Phebe 377; Timmothy 376; Timothy 376,377; Timothy W. 377; William, Wm. 346,376,377
MURPHY, Chelly 531; Cornelius T. 389; C. Tate 78; Daniel 147; Elizabeth 525; Esther 525; Hanson F. 50,216, 380,389,551,564,573; Henry 65; John 581; Patrick 342; Pressellah 449; Timothy 241; William 78
MURRAY, Aaron W. 379; Anne 314; Arther 381; Asa 397; Barbary 379; Cathorun 383; Daniel 100, 223,379,382; Daniel H. 379; David 379; Dicey Ann 10; Eliza 379; Harriet Jane 544; Hiram 379,380,382,544; Hosea 380,382; James 379,381, 382,383,419; James Esquer 299; James Jr. 460; James W. 379; John N. 544; Jonathan 380; Joshua 397; J. W. 328; Margaret 101; Mary C. 379; Mary Elisa 544; Mary Jane 544; Murdock Williams 334; N. 460; Nathan 379; Nicanor 382; Robert Franklin 334; Rhoda 380,382; Thomas 379; William 334
MURREY, Arthur 267; Mary 546; Sarah 267
MURRY, Arthur 384; Nathan 384; Sarah 384
MURY, Betholemy 385
MYHAND, James 58

NARRESS, Polley 511
NEAL, John 249,386,561
NEATHERCUT, Betsey 387; Eliza 387; G. F. 387; George F. 387; John H. 387; Kitty 387; Loftin 387; Marshal Money 387; Nanay 387; Temmy 387
NEMAN, Sarah 199
NETHERCUT, John 443; William Brian 443
NEW, Bet 388; George 388; John 388; Margaret 388; Mary 388; Nancy 230; Peggy 388; Tab 388; William 388; Winny 388
NEWKIRK, A. 73; Benja. H. 389; Benjamin R. 389; Bryan B. 389; Bryan Senr 389; Elizabeth Ann 365; Francinia 389; George B. 389; H. 171; Harriet Adelaide Wayne 389; Jacob F. 389; James L. 389; John A. 389; Joseph 389,438; Kitty Carline 365; Mary 251,365; Rachal 365,437;

NEWKIRK con't Rebecah 365; T. 171; Timothy 65,185,389; Timothy Jr 389
NEWTON, Abraham 393; Abram 233; Ann 390; Daniel 391; Daniel B. 45,46,391; D.B. 176,565,575,581; Eliza 391; Elizahela 393; Elizabeth 114,393; Elvy 392; Enoch 390; Esher 390; Esther 390; Isaac 390,392; James 4,316, 391,392,393,576; Jemima 390; John 392; Julious 56,391; Kitty 391; Lucretia 42; Major 391,392; Majr 46,391; Mary 391, 392; Mary Ann 324,391; Mary Elirzar 56,391; Patrick 392; Sarah 3,393; Susannah 392; William 42,156,176,324,391,392, 393; William W. 391
NICHOLSON, David B. 417; James L., Rev. 417; James L. J. 417; Lucy J. 417; Zilpha 417
NIGHT, Mary 160
NITHERCUT, Elizabeth 394; George F. 394; John H. 394; Marshal M. 394; Nancy 394
NIXON, Danl 354; James 354; Sarah 354,357; Susan 468; Susanah 468; William 468; Wm H. 468
NOBLES, Nancy 20
NORMAN, Patcy 395; Richard 395
NORMENT, Betsy Jane 396; Catherine 396; Sally 396; Sarah 291; Thomas 396
NORRES, Isom 397,419; James 397; Jesse 419; Jessy 397; Joseph 397; Lewis 397; Mary 397,419; Molsey 397; Reuben 397
NORRIS, Elizabeth 47; Eunicy 398; Isom 398; Lewis 397; Mary 305; Reuben 398; Riel 398

OATES, Artisha 399; Claiborne J. 45; Curtis C. 81; David 400; Eleanor 45; Elizabeth 399; James 399,400; Jesse 399; Jethro 399,400; John 165, 399; Lewis 400; Michael 399; Ortesha 399; Susannah 399,400
OATS, Anna M 400; Jethro 400
ODANIEL (ODaniel), Alexdr 188,401; Ann 401; Charity 401; O. 188,401,402,473; Owen 401,402,470; William 401
ODON (ODon), Wm. 9
OGELSBEY, Ann 534; Burwel 534; Christopher B. 534; John 534; Sarah Eliza 534; Wilie 534
OGLESBY, Charles M. 169, 533; Margaret 533
OLIVER, Ann 418; Ann Jane 135,140; Anne 403; Benjamin, Benjn. 135,140, 403,404,405,417; Fereby 409; Fran R. 151; Francis 151,260,403,405,462; Frans. 403,431,442,496;

OLIVER con't
Isaac 403; J. 27; James
403,404; James A. 404;
Jane 496; John 403,404,
405; Lucretia 403; Mary
404; Rebekah 403; Sarah
403,404,405
OLLINS, James 432
ORME, Robart 300
OUTLAND, Jas. 507
OUTLAW, Alexander, Alexr,
Alxd 406,408,409; Anna
406; Bryan R. 407; Edith
409,538; Edward Sr. 407;
Edward 406,408,409; Edwd.
2,343,407; Elesabuth
191; Eleteah 490; Eliza
538; Elizabeth 343,406,
407,408,409,536,538;
George 407,490; James,
Jas. 406,407,408,409,
507; James Jr. 536; James
M. 407; James Monroe 407;
James Sr. 407; John 409,
490,538,408; J. W. 193;
Lewis 2,409,538,408;
Mary 406,409,538; Olive
409; Patience 406,409;
Peletiah 531; Rachel 538;
Sally 409; William, Wm.
406,408,409; William Jr.
407,479
OWENS, Ann 271

PACEY, Sally 103
PADGET, Benjamin 253;
Elizabeth 154
PATGETT, Cray 315
PAGE, Charles 339,429,479;
Elizabeth 339,429; Mary
339; Susan 111
PARISH, Ann 410; Charles
410; Edward 410; Henry
410; Jeremiah 410;
Judith 410; Nanny 410;
Sarah 410; Thomas 410;
William 410
PARKER, Brambly 392; Daniel
32,277; Elizabeth 411;
Hardy 54,55; Hezekiah
422; Jerusha 412; Jo-
nathan 344; John 411;
Joseph 388; Jos. R. 234;
Mary 41,411; Pete 32;
Peter 277,411; Peyton
R. 342; Rachel 411;
Sarah 260,411; Susana
412; William 412
PARRADIS, Sabrina 126
PARRADISE, Nancy 126;
Sabrina 126
PATE, Robt. 483
PATRICK, Frances 583; Lewis
583; William 583
PAXTON, James 318
PEACOCK, Jesse 367
PEARCE, Alexander 413;
Cythe 413; Hugh 413;
Mary 413; Sampson 413;
Snoden 413; Wilea 413;
Wm. Alexander Jr. 413
PEARCELL, Edward 254;
Jeremiah 417
PEARSAL, James 87; Jere-
miah 87
PEARSALL, Ann 140,141,214,
416,417,418,414; Benja-
min 275; Edward, Edwd.
28,134,204,273,275,276,
414,415,416,417,418,
451,453,561,567,574;
Edward John 275; Edward
o. 414,479; Elisabeth 416;

PEARSALL con't
Fereby 404,416,418;
Hugh 415,416,418; J.
249; Ja. D. 417; James
101,261,275,416,417,451;
James D. 415; Jas. 249,
328; Jemima H. 29; Jere.
29,61,101,357,362,504,
520; Jeremiah 27,173,
261,275,357,414,415,
416,418,423,520; Jo. D.
418; Jo Dickson 416;
John, Jno. 275,553; John
D. 414; John H. 415;
Joseph 101,417; Joseph
D. 417,418; Jre. 27;
Kitty 357; Lucy J. 418;
Lucy Jane 416; Margaret
204,345,415; Mary 414;
Susan 414; Susan A. 414,
415; Thom U. 414; W. D.
51,404; William Dickson
416; William F. 415;
William J. 414; Wm. D.
233
PEARSELL, Edwd. 184;
James 401
PECK, Anne Eliza 165
PENNEY, Edward 236
PENNINGTON, Noel 388;
Temperance 247
PEPIN, Amy 114
PERCE, Sarah 419
PERSEL, James 341
PERSONS, Willem 509
PETERS/PETTERS, Ann 420;
Christian 420; Damaris
420; Elias 420; Eliza-
beth 420; James 420;
Jesse 420; John 420;
Rebeaca 420; Samuel 420
PETERSON, John W. 178
PHILLIP, Polly 30; Thomas
30
PHILLIPS, Benjamin 421;
Dorothy 421; Frances
421; Hannah 137; John
421; Mary 421; Thomas
59,352,421
PHIPS, Isaac 548; Sarah
213; Thomas 156
PICKET, Celia 422; Ester
381; Frances 126;
Francis 147; Fredrick
253; William, Wm 267,
546
PICKETT, Andrew J. 423;
Ann Jane 423; Asenah
422; Darkis 422; Dawson
422; Dennis 15; Dicy
422; F. 109,384; Frances
141; Frank 422; Frede-
rick 423; Hester 423;
Hugh 322; James 423;
Larkins 422; Mary J.
423; Mary Julia 423;
Olive 423; William Dick-
son 141; William R. 141,
423; William Senr 423;
Wm. 384
PICKETTE, John S. 439;
Mary 439; Mary Jane 439;
Wm Dossen 439
PIERCE, Buckner 243; John
58; Margaret D. 235A;
Wentworth W. 234
PIERSALL, Jeremiah 404
PIGFORD, Alfred 424; Ann
424; Elizabeth 424,526;
Enoch 424; James B.
180A; James L. 233;
Jean 424; Jurusha 424;
Martha 424; Right 424;
Sarah 424; Sollomon 424;

PIGFORD con't
Susan Matilda 180A; Timo-
thy 424; William 424
PILCHER, Edward 210
PIPKIN, Catharine 151;
Elizabeth 130,513
PITMAN, Elizebeth 126;
William, Wm. 266,478
PLATT, Joshua 55
POLLOCK, Elizabeth 519;
Susan Ann 135; William
514
POPE, Constance 425; James
425; Jesse 425; Obediah
425; Robt. 425; Seley
425; Thomas, Thos 425;
Thos the Elder 425;
Thos the Younger 425;
William 58,425
PORTER, Elizabeth 454;
Henry 19; Sarah 361
POTTER, Andrew J. 45; Beady
426; Dalham 426; Daniel
426; Danl Jr. 426; Eliz-
abeth 426; Major 426;
Wm. 426
POWEL, Britian 4; Cader 547;
Elisha 251; Ester 240;
Hardy 41; Mary 547; Moses
547; Payten 569; Rachel
41,42; Thomas 32
POWELL, Amelia 429; Brit-
tain 427; Elisha 316,
427,429; Elizabeth 427;
Ferabay 428; George 430;
Isaac 427,429; Jacob 427,
429; John 427,466,467;
Joseph 438; Martha 427;
Mary 393,429; Mary Mag-
delon 430; Nancy 437;
Patrick 430; Reston 164;
Susey 466; Williby 339
POWERS, Francinia 389;
John D., Jno D. 216,389;
John R. 270
PRESCOAT, Richard 560
PRESCOT, Charity 559;
William 559
PRICE, Catharine E. 292;
Elizabeth 291; Mutildy
303; Nancy 277
PRIDGEN, Jesse C. 238;
Robert G. 572; Sarah 567;
S. D. Lafayette 572
PRIDGION, Sarah 563
PROWSE, Elizabeth 431; John
431,495; Thomas 431
PUMPHREY, Ann 432; Jesse
432; John 432; Nancy 432;
Sallah 432; Silvenus 432

QUIN, Loftin 516; Mary 367;
Thomas 67; Virginea 267
QUINN, Catherine 433; David
433; Easter 433; Easther
560; Elizabeth B. 25;
Jesse 434; Jesse B. 25,
434; Martha 434; Mary
353; Sarah Green 504;
Thomas 560; Watson F. 434

RADIN, James 522
RAINER, Marshall 435; Step-
hen 435
RALLEY, Sarah 160
REARDON, James 137,213,
235,392
REASONS, George 361; Nancy
361; Rachel 65
REAVES, Anna 149; Catron
149; David 537; Hardy 537;
Jesse 151

REAVIS, Harriet 179
REED, Andrew 386; Eliza-
beth 386
REGISTER, Anna Jane 297;
David 297
REID, D. 142
RHOADS, Joseph 37
RHODES, Ann 436; Benjamin
363,437,440; Charles E.
234; Henry 417; Jacob
437; Jacob R. 438;
James 234,237; James T.
219,437,438; James Tho-
mas 438; John 438,496;
John F. 436,437,438;
John Felix 438; Joseph
438; Joseph T., Jos. T.
7,45,74,131,219,243,400,
436,437,438,440,503,505;
Joseph Thomas 437,438,
440,506; Josephus Thomas
438; J. T. 219,231,243;
Kate 234; Martha 417;
Mary 439; Rachel 437,
440,506; Sarah 440;
Solomon 440; Taylor 496;
William 237,415,496
RHODS, Benjamin 506
RICHERSON, Wm. 461
RIGBEY, Owen 273; William
132
RIGBY, Owen 358; William
Junr 421; William Senr
354,421
RINCHEY, Adem 441; Searah
441; Seragh 441
RIVEINGBERG, Ann 1
RIVENBARK, Ann 127; David
F. 43; Frederick 264;
Sally 62; Wm Jr. 569;
Wm W. 200
RIVININGBARK, John 177
ROACH, Charlottey 150;
Sarah 149,150
ROBERSON, Wm 21
ROBERTS, John 151
ROBESON, Wm. 530
ROBINSON, Ann 135; Isaiah
569; John 276,367
ROCHELLE, Amos 8
ROGERS, Annalina 445; Asa
442; David 442; Elisha
446; Eliazar 445; Eliza-
beth 442,445,516; Isaiah
442; Joel 442; John 442,
446; Mark 444; Mary 443,
445; Nancy 444; Nansey
33; Nicholas 19; Patrick
241; Rachel 87; Sarah
22,442; Stephen 444,446;
Tamzarine 183; Thomas
516; William 185,442,
445; Zachariah 445
ROGGERS, Mary 443
ROGILES, Charles 446;
Elisha 446; Mark 446;
Tammey 446
ROLINGS, Robart 5
ROUSE, Alexander S. 407;
David 447; David Jr.
112; Elizabeth 449;
George 159,447; Henry
90,448; Kitty E. 554;
Martain 449; Nathan 447;
Phillip 180,449; Re-
becca 448; Rhoda 447;
Ruban 447; Solomon 17,
229
ROUTLEDGE, A. 478; Anne
450; Catharine 451;
Cathrine 453; Doriethe
Pearsall 452; Edward
Pearsall 452; Elizabeth
453; Ellinor 453;

ROUTLEDGE con't
Ezekiel Morgan 452;
Margaret Eleanor 452;
Marian 452; Mary 453;
Mildred 452; Nicolas
452; Nicholas R. 450;
Thomas, Thos. 91,261,
451,452,453; Thomas Jr.
452; Thomas Sr. 451;
William 453
ROWSE, Lewis 229
RUNEALS, Richd. 509
RUNNELS, Amos 72; Mary
454; Robert 454; Shad-
rach 454; Willis 454
RYALL, Ann Owens 271;
Lewis 271; Wright 72
RYLAND, Benonly 271;
Polly 271

SALMON, Anna Jane 178;
Kilby 178; Mary 455;
William 455
SAMPSON, James 456; John
72
SANDERS, Alex 490; Caty
34; Mary 490; Morgan
Smith 300
SANDERSON, Bright I. 511;
C. M. 538; Isaac 294;
Sylvia 294
SANDIFUR, Jos. 16
SANDLIN, Catharine 70;
Harriet Caroline 544;
Harriett 544; Henry 73;
Jeremiah 544; John W.
544; John Wilkinson 544;
Mary Ann 544; N. 169;
Sarah Elisabeth 544
SANLIN, Samuel 131
SASSER, Joel 151
SATCHWELL, S. S. 380
SAVAGE, Michail 479
SCARBROUGHT, Nathan 267
SCOT, Mary 369
SCOTT, Ader 457; Ashea
457; Jerusha 457; J. G.
533; Jonathan 457; Jo-
seph 457; Mary 457;
Nehemiah 457; Peggy
457; Rachael 8
SCREWS, Joseph 431; Mary
442; Nancy 462
SEAVEY, Ann Julia 389;
J. B. 389
SELLARS, William Senr 377
SELLERS, John 87
SESSOMS, Richd. 583
SEWELL, Elizabeth 480
SHAFIELD, Amos 347
SHARPLES, W. 38
SHAW, Colen 17,166,484;
Elias 166; Fanny 106;
Rachel 17
SHEAR, Roweana 22
SHEFFIELD, Edith 458;
James 458; John 458;
William 458
SHELTON, Rebeckah 555;
Thomas, Thos. 280,471,
489,555,560,577,578
SHEPARD, Barbary 449;
Charlotte 459; Eliza
101; Georgeetta 459;
Mary 101; Mary Jane 459;
Sarah Ellis 459; Thomas
E. 459; Thomas Jr 459
Thos 486; Thos E. 104
SHEPPARD, Mourning 553;
Thomas 261
SHEROD, Honry 360
SHINE, Martha E. 234
SHINES, John 436;

SHINES con't
Martha 436; Martha E.
580
SHITTON, Thomas 274
SHOLAR, Ann 422; David 366;
Elizabeth 422; Ephraim
460; Hannah 366; Isham
460; James H. 366; James
Rily 366; Levy 460; Pene-
lopey 422; Solomon J. L.
366; Tishy E. 366;
William 366,383
SHOLARS, James 461; Mary
461; Moses 461; Solomon
461; Wriley 461
SHUFFIELD, Arthur 462;
Bryan 462; Catharine 382,
462; Elizabeth 462;
Ephraim 462; Isham, Isom
138,462; John 462; Lin-
coln 138,543; Louisa
462; Marry 138; Polly
462; Tabitha 462; West
98,462; William 462;
Wright 462
SIGERIST, John 420
SIGGRIST, John 72
SIKES, Frederick 463; Holo-
way 575; Kedar 237;
Willis 463
SIMMONS, Axy, 179; Calvin
361; D. H. 475; Eliza
Ann 194; S. H. 193
SIMMS, Catharine 357; Sarah
Ann 357
SINGLETON, Mary 262
SLOAN, Ann 525; Ann Eliza
345; Cassandria 465;
David 48,80,112,140,464,
465,466,468; David D.
389; David Snr 466; Dick-
son 345,347,371,465;
Eleanor 465; Ellen 524;
Gibson 19,345,464,465,
525,558; John 464,467;
Manerva 465; Margrate
464; Marshel 558; Nancy
466; Robert 321,468;
Susan 48,50; Susanna 464;
Theresey 558; William 467
SLOANE, Robert 89
SLOCOMB, Elijah 410; Lavinia
247; Mary Ann 16; Polly
247
SLOCOMBE, Mary Ann 16
SLOCUMB, Ezekill 247; John
Chas 469; Joseph 469;
Lavinia 247; Levina 248;
Mildred 469; Polley 247,
248; Samuel 469
SMITH, Abijah 475; Andrew
Jackson 470; Ann 234;
Benja 506; Bryan 471,473;
Bryan Senr 473; Buckner
234; Catharine 472; Cha-
rity 260; Charlotte 308;
Clarrissa 475; Colonel
37; Daniel E. 234; David
471; Edna 283; Edward
234,473; Elijah 470;
Eliza 234,470; Elizabeth
473; Frederick 471;
George 12,307,348,432,
471,473,547; George Juner
348,471; G. L. 504;
Henry 472; Ivy 475; James
473; James L. 69; Jesse
471; John 234,294,317,
318,331,473,474; Jonas
473; Jones 471,473; Lewis
114; Louisa 234; Lydia
361; Martin F. 475; Mary
473; Mary Blenda 180A;
Mary E. Shine 234;

SMITH con't
Nancy 470,471,473; Penny
Suzan 470; Roger <u>474</u>;
Samuel 234; Sarah <u>2</u>,474;
Sarah Ann 234; Sarah
McRee 331; Stephen 489;
Susannah 219; Susey
Jane 473; William 72;
William H. 180A; Winni-
ford 282; Winney 577;
Wright 282; Z 402; Z Jury
402; Zaccheus Sr <u>475</u>;
Zacheus 475; Zacheus Jr.
475
SMYTH, Stephen 350
SNELL, Ann 477; Elizabeth
476; James <u>476</u>,477;
Partheny 477; Roger 399,
476,<u>477</u>,508
SNIPES, Benjamin 531
SNOW, Elisabeth 478; Mar-
gret 478; William <u>478</u>
SOAKES, James G. 50
SOLLIS, Benajah 479; Bryan
415; Bryant <u>479</u>; Luther
B. 479; Nancy 479
SOUTHERLAND, Alexr. 13;
Alsa 142,256,356; Bowde
212; Caroline 459; Cat-
hren 526; Chauncy 142;
Daniel 389; Danl. Junr
74; David 71,133,142,
143,289,365,459,480;
David J. 459; Davie 349;
Dilley 389; Edward 169;
Eliza 169; Gorg 137;
James 356; Jerry 526;
Jesse B. 169,233; John
137,235; John D. 294;
John David 169; Lucy 92;
Martha Eliza 65; Mary
169; Needham 179; Phill
333; Rilley 289; Robert,
Robt. 13,67,154,333,388,
<u>480</u>,505; Roubert 231;
Sarah 169; Soloman 77;
Thomas <u>481</u>; W. 13;
William <u>98</u>; William B.,
Wm B. 365,480; Zilpha
480,557
SOUTHERLIN, Boney 389;
Isham 359,446; Robert
Jun 232
SOWEL, Ann 577
SPARKS, William S. 80
SPEARMAN, Edward 236
SPEARS, Jane 271; John 271
SPENCE, Isaac 431; Timothy
431
SPRINGS, Sarah 385
SPRUNT, Ellen 218; James
M. 218
STALINGS, Ethalindy 382
STALLINGS, Aley 483; Ann
482; Ann Jane 482;
Clariy 483; Elizabeth
482; Hiram 99,483; Hugh
483; Jane 482; Jean 525;
John <u>482</u>; Josiah 389,
482; Kedar 389,482; Me-
shack <u>483</u>,497; Rhoda
483; Shadrach 385,483,
497; Susan 377; Wiley
78,377,483; William 64,
482; Winifred 483
STANDLEY, Faraba 213
STANFORD, Alexander 486;
Alexr T. 485; Ann 292;
Colista 486; Eleanor
484,485,486; J. D. <u>484</u>;
John D. 563; Jonathan
486; Jonathan D. 484;
Margaret 484,486; Margit
<u>485</u>,486; Margret 484,485;

STANFORD con't
Samuel, Saml 111,484,
485,486,521; Saml Senr
<u>486</u>; Sarah 345; Thomas
484,485,486
STANLEY, Amos 129; James
129; Nancy 328; Sarah
Graham 196; Susannah 129
STEPHENS, Abner 510; Bet-
sey 234; Hardy 72; Jakey
234,520; Jemima 72;
John Isham 263; Mary
Eliza 263; Nany 486;
Susannah 42; Thomas B.
234
STEVENS, Nancy 484
STEVINS, Lydda 399
STEWART, James 230; Mary
343
STILES, John 366
STOACHES, William Kinsey
487
STOAKES, Andrew 574; Cat-
harine A. 50; Helon 487;
Henry 553; James G. 171,
317,389,487; John Willi-
am 389; Joseph 487;
Mary 328,553; Priscilla
Ann 487; William, Wm.
189,<u>487</u>,525; Wm Jur 122
STOAKS, Andrew 487
STOCKES, Henry 488
STOKES, Andrew 488,574;
Elizabeth 488; Jain 488;
Joseph 488; Marinda G
25; Robert 30,488
STON, Robart 464
STREETS, Mary 47
STRICKLIN, Elizabeth 173;
Ephraim 173; Hardy 171
STRICTLING, Elizabeth 180
STROUD, A. C. 489; Abel
C. 489; Abel Croom 489;
A. Croom 489; Arthur
489; Hannah 489; Isaac
489; Lewis 489; Lutson
560; Lutson Jur <u>489</u>;
Nancy 205; Owen <u>479</u>;
Selah 489; Winney 489;
Zilpha 489
SULIVAN, David 545;
Sally 277
SULIVEN, John, Jno 203,531
SULLIVAN, Anes 490; Annie
490; David <u>490</u>; Edwd.
490; Elizabeth 490;
Grant 490; H. 117; John
490; Mary 490; Oliver
490; Wm. 490
SULLIVEN, Elisha 491;
Fanny 491; Henry 491;
James <u>491</u>; Kitty 491;
Sally <u>491</u>; Samuel 491;
Susan 491; Zilphia 491
SULLIVENS, Samuel 205
SULLIVENT, James 536
SUMMERLING, Charity 188;
Mary 188
SUTTON, Elisabeth 160,262;
Joseph 559
SWINSON, Andrew 492; Aus-
tin 493; Buckner 492;
Daniel 492; David 518;
David H. 479,492; Eliza-
beth 493; Erasmus 492;
George S. 492; Henry
512; J. 277,491; J. A.
408; J. E. 130; Jesse
479,492; Jesse Jur 281,
493; J. H. 238; Jno A.
409; John 140,472,494,
502,518; John A. <u>493</u>;
John Snr <u>492</u>; Levi 34,
283; Margaret 197;

SWINSON con't
Margaret Ann 494; Martha
Elizabeth 281; Mary
Eliza 494; Mary S. 492;
Mary Susan 492; Nancy
492,493,513,518; Patsey
Eliza 494; Robert 492;
Sally 34; Sarah 494;
Sarah V. 492; Sarah Vir-
ginia 492; Susan Jane
494; Theophilus 475,<u>494</u>;
William, Wm. 197,226,
458,494,502,544; Winifrid
281

TAILOR, Jacob 317
TALER, Cathren 11, Kathe-
rine 82; LeBeth 11
TALOR, Isaac 176; Mary 540
TANNOR, Sarah 540
TANTONY, Henry 583
TATE, Elizabeth 520
TATOM, Clary Maria 393;
Elazabeth 393; Saraann
393
TATUM, Laban 225
TAYLAR, M. J. 389
TAYLOR, Anny 176; Catherine
129; Dempsey 494; Dems
411; Elizabeth 495;
Jacob 370,495; Jamima
495; John <u>495</u>; Kathrine
<u>496</u>; Major J. 527; Sarah
<u>494</u>; Wm. 66,86,445
TEACHEY, Alford 499; Anne
497; Catharine A. 48;
Daniel <u>497</u>,<u>498</u>,499,500,
525; Daniel Junr 497;
Daniel Senr. 115,479;
Henry 500; Isaac 499;
Jacob 497,<u>499</u>,500; James
263,498,500; John 497;
Mary 261,498,<u>501</u>; Mary
H. 498,500; Michaell 500;
Molsy 500; Nancy 499;
Rody 6; T. 424,523,526;
Timothy 54,497,498,499,
<u>500</u>,585; Timoy 55,585
TEACHY, Danell 6; Daniel
501; Mary 501; Timothy
501; Timoy 6
TECHEY, Timmothy 123
TENNESSE, Martha 306
THALLY, Andrew, Andw 113,
123,134,465,<u>502</u>; David
502; Elisabeth 6,502;
Hugh 502; John 123,502;
Mary 502
THIGPEN, Annie 503; Brythal
503; Darkis 422; Dicey
503; Drew 53; Elizabeth
532; Elsey 503; Job 174,
309,381,483; Jobe 381;
John <u>503</u>,532; Joseph 503;
Molsey 53; Wiley 503
THOMAS, Billy 506; Charles
Gregory 504; Elizabeth
C. 504; Gregory <u>504</u>;
Isaac <u>505</u>,506; James 505;
Jean 505; Jonathan 214,
367; John J. 504; Law-
rence 507; Lewis 505;
Morenda 505; Nancy 505;
Nancy Mariah 504; Pene-
lope 505; Polley 505;
Richard 506; Sally 367;
Silvia 505; William, Wm.
233,505,<u>506</u>
THOMASON, Benjamin 507;
John 507; William <u>507</u>
THOMPSON, Barshaba 507;
Elizabeth 182; Jas. 509;
Lawrence 182; William 507

211

WILLIAMS con't
Elizabeth Ann 162; Elizabeth Jane 562; Emele 555; Enoch 546; Esther 546; Ezekiel 555; Fountain 560; Francis 356, 552,563,567; Frederick 224; Garreson 557; George 194,550,553,561; George Washington 568; George W., Geo W. 178,297; H. 99; Harper 30,175,249, 556,563,567; Harriet Adline 569; Hopkins 554; Huldah 554; Isaac N. 562; Isaac Newton 546; Jackson 550; Jacob 194,408, 409,553,554,560,561; James 312,555,556,559, 563,567; James Cicero 556; James Jr. 557; James Jr. 557; James K. 162,527,562; James Sr. 557; Jennet 472; Jesse 439,358,560; Jesse Sr. 558; John 67,194,262, 299,439,547,559,560,561, 562,570,585; Johnathan W. 169; Joseph 262,296, 299,361,367,569,571; Joseph T. 569; Jurasa 560; Kenan 361; Lemuel 571; L. F. 110; Lott 439; Lucien 558; Lydia 566; Mahale 562; Manersay 558; Mansey 558; Margaret 563; Margaret C. 552; Margaret M. 562; Martha 219; Martha Eliza 556; Matthew 526; Mary 129,219, 390,409,438,439,546,547, 553,567,568; Mary Jane 101,548; Mc. 305; Merrill 557; Merrill James 557; Molcy A. 562; Nancy 60,178,361,524; Nathan 258,420,571; Nathaneal 242; Outlaw 194; Parmelia 552; Patience 550, 560,567,571; Peggy 567; Pennelipey 547; Penelope N. 557; Phebe 551,564, 568,573; Pheriba 547; Polly 571; Prescella 560; Prudence 559,560; Rebecca 554; Rebecah Jane 562; Reden 564; Richard 327,566; Robbin 417; Robert, Robt. 28, 303,556,563,567; Robertha 561; Rosa P. 552; Rose 567; Rt. 252; Samuel A. 569; Samuel Pinkney 546; Sarah 116,154,558; Sarah A. 552; Seaney 560; Sivelity 547; Stephen 178,201,296,546,547, 551,562,564,568,573; Stephen Capt. 569; Stephen Willis 547; Tabitha 553,567; Temperance 249, 549,553; Thomas 557, 570,571; Thomas H. 558; William 331,561; William W. 572; Wright 250; Zachereah M. 546; Zchereah Mathis 546; Zella 555; Zilpha 551,560,564, 568,573
WILLIAMSON, Charles 574; Francis 575; John 574; Mary 574; Sarah 574; Shadrach 574; William M. 575; Willis 361

WILLIS, Jonathan 3
WILLKINS, Sally 289
WILLS (see WELLS also)
Jacob 185; Thomas 482; Wm 122
WILLSON, Alexander 576; Ann 405; Daniel 576; David 576; Elizabeth 576; Isaac 576; John 576; John Sen. 576; Joseph 119; Margin 576; Mary 576; Nancy 526; Rebeca 576; Sarah 576; William 576
WILSON, Amanda K. 65; Amonda 389; Ann 568; George M. 554; Isaac 568; James 371; Jemima 390; John 65,389; John T. 297; Joseph Franklin 65; Mary 209,217; Thomas 209; Willis 26
WINDERS, Almirer 324; Catharine 324; Charles 257; Henry 257,324; James 324; John 66,324, 490; Stephen B. 276A; William 324
WINDORS, Edward 2; Nancy 2
WINGATE, Joshua McCanne 147
WITFIELD, Bettha 522; Needham 522
WITFULL, Edieth 522
WITHERSPOON, Catherine 234
WOLF, L. P. 234; Richard 110
WOOD, Mark 126
WOODARD, David 470; Isaac 22; Rachal 33
WOODDARD, Rachel 33
WOOLF, Gilbron 155
WOOTEN, Oliver 404; Peter 360; Sally 403; Sarah 404
WORLEY, Ann 577; Loftis 280,577,578; Ned 363; Sally 402
WORREL, Mary 33; Patte 33
WORSLEY, Charlotte 578; Elizabeth 578; John 578; Pitman 578; William 578
WRIGHT, Agathy 581; Alfred 584; Arch 582; Betsey 234; Bryan 581; Buckner L. H. 234; Catharine A. 580; Charity 16; Council R. 584; D. 34,62,111, 141; David 23,62,141, 227,234,396,579,580,581, 582; Edward 275; Eliza 584; Eliza S. 580; Eliza Smith 579; Elizabeth 17; Elizabeth C. 580; Gordon 234; Isaac 234,579,580,581,582; James, Jas. 17,278,323, 396,519,581,582; James Munroe 581; Jane 583; Je 323; John 86,579,580, 581,582,584; John B. 579,581; John Beck 581; Kitty 581; Kitty Ann 579; Patsey E. 579; Priscilla 234; Rebecca Slocumb 584; Rebeckah 582; Richard Washington 584; Robert 583; Sarah 583; Tho. 519; Thomas, Thos. 17,32,323,396,579, 582,584; Thomas H., Thos. H. 234,275,452, 579,580; W. B. 256,584;

WRIGHT con't
William, Wm. 234,240,581; Wm A. 501

YARBROUGH, James 295; John 83,476; John Sen 295
YOUNG, James 585; Jeane 585; John 585; Peter 177, 585; William 585

213

GILLESPIE con't
Catharine 186; Charles
185; Charlotte 185;
Chloe 185; Christopher
185; Clary 185; Daniel
184,185; Daniel Jr 185;
Derry 185; Dick 185;
Edy 185; Flora 185;
Frances 184; George 185;
Harry 185; Harvey 184;
Howard 417; Jack 184;
Jim 185; Joe 185; Joh-
anna 184; Judy 184;
Junius 185; Laura 186;
Lavinia 186; Leonora
184; Lewis 185; Litle
Toney 184; Livinia 389;
Lot 184; Lucy 185,186;
Mariah 184; Martha 186;
Mary 186,417; Mary Ann
185; Matilda 185; Moiley
184; Nance 184; Old
Bristol 185; Old Toney
184; Penny 417; Pensory
184; Rachel 417; Sally
185; Satora 184; Sam
185; Sarah 185; Satio
184; Sophia 185; Spencer
185; Stuttering Nelly
185; Susy 185; Tamerlane
185; Toby 184; Tom 184,
185; Turrisman 417;
Warwick 184,185; Yam 185
GILMOORE, Clarissa 209
GLISSON, Jack 230; Jenny
230
GOFF, Amey 344; Clo 344
GORE, Samo 19
GRADY, Boron 194; Boson
409; Dinah 194; Frank
194; Jenny 409; Julia
194; Larry 194; Luce 194;
Mary 194; Pender 194;
Rose 194,409; Sal 194;
Sary 194
GRAHAM, Albert 196; Amanda
196; Betsey 196; Betty
196; Charity 196; Doll
196; Emy 196; Hannah 197;
Jack 196; Jeanette 196;
Julia 196; Louisa 196;
Lucinda 196; Metilda
196; Rachail 196,197;
Simon 196; Tom 196;
Washington 196
GRAY, Pleasant 198
GREER, Jack 90
GREY, Betsey 202; Dick 202;
Henry 202; Juliana 202
GRIMES, Adam 204; Benard
204; George 276A; Hanah
204; Hester 276A; Jacob
204
GRISWOLD, Council 234;
Easter 234
GULLEY, Sile 208
GULLY, Allis 209; Ally
209; Anna 209; Asha 209;
Bristeo 209; Candos 209;
Clarissa 209; Hinton
209; July 209
GURGANUS, Mingo 210
GUY, Andrew 214; Betsey
211; Candace 214; Clara
214; Clarissa 214;
Cortiz 214; Cudjo 214;
Cupid 214; Derry 214;
Dick 211; Dinah 111;
Grace 214; Henry 211;
Juliann 211; Lucy 211;
Margaret 212; Milie 214;
Nancy 214; Phillis 214;
Rachel 214; Rebecca 214;
Rose 214; Sam 214;

GUY con't
Sary 212; Virgil 214;
Willis 214

HAIRGROVE, Daniel 222;
Dinah 222; Lucy 222
HALL, Aberdeen 217;
Baalam 292; Bess 221;
Betsy 221; Caroline 218;
Dilly 218; Everette 217;
Frank 218; Hannah 219;
Harriett 218; Jim 218;
Judy 217; Katharine 389;
Linda 218; Lucy 217;
Martha 218; Mary 217,
218; Molsey 217; Moss
217; Ollen 217; Peter
367; Rebecca 217; Samuel
217; Sarah 218; Susan
218; Wright 218
HARPER, David 282
HARDISTY, Jack 267; Plea-
sant 267; Zilpha 267
HARGROVE, Daniel 222;
Dinah 222; Lucy 222
HARRELL, Ned 230
HARRIS, Toney 267
HARROD, Harry 260
HATCH, Abby 234; Cassy
234; Charles 234; Curtis
234; Edward 234; Frank
234; George 234; Isham
234; Joe 234; Kit 234;
Laura 234; Louisa 234;
Lucinda 234; Martha 234;
Old Hannah 234; Orange
234; Peggy 234; Phillis
234; Rachel 234; Roxy
234; Syvil 234; Tony 234
HEATH, Catoe 560
HERRING, Agga 230; Alex-
ander 228; Alfred 228;
Beck 228; Bet 227,230;
Betey 477; Bitty 354;
Bob 227,230; Cass 237;
Cassey 228; Cate 227,
230; Cesar 230; Chloe
354; Clara 228; Clarry
237; Curtis 228; Daniel
228; Dauy 230; Dennis
228; Edy 227; Elias
228; Eliza 228,569;
Feraby 569; Fillis 230;
George 228; Haley 228;
Harry 228; Henry 228;
Jack 230; Jane 228;
Jenny 230; Jim 228,230;
Jo 228,569; John 228;
Leah 227; Little Alfred
228; Little Sarah 354;
Lizett 227; Lovett Lewis
228; Lucy 228; Marinda
228; Mary 228; Nathan
228; Ned 227,230; Need-
ham 228; Nicy 228; Orris
228; Phillis 228; Rachel
228; Rose 228; Rouse
228; Sarah 357; Sary
228; Sena 228; Serena
228; Sharper 227; Sinda
228; Solomon 228; Squire
230; Susanah 228; Sylvia
228; Theophilus 228;
Tom 228; Violet 354;
Washington 228; Weldon
227; Winny 228
HICKS, Chelly 166; Harriet
166; Mingo 232; Pleasant
232; Rose 232; Sanders
232; S. Kenders 232
HIGHSMITH, Daniel 42;
Lucy 233

HILL, Abby 234; Adam 235A;
Aleck 234; Allen 234;
Alvin 234; Amelia 234;
Amy 235A; Anthony 234;
Becky 234; Becky Ann 234;
Betsey 234; Big Squire
234; Billy 234; Binah
234; Bo 234; Bryant 234;
Calvin 234; Cassy 234;
Catharine 234; Charles
234; Chelly 234; Clarissa
234; Council 234; Cullen
234; Curtis 234; Daniel
234; David 234; Easter
234; Edney 234; Edward
234; Eli 234; Elvy 234;
Emanuel 234; Emily 234;
Fanny 234; Farise 235A;
Flora 234; Frank 234;
George 234; Green 234;
Grandison 234; Hannah
234; Henry 234; Hepsey
234; Hester 234; Isham
234; Ivy 234; Jacob 234;
Jackson 234; Jeoffrey
234; Jim 234; Joe 234;
John 234; Jonas 234;
Julia 234; Kit 234;
Laura 234; Leah 234;
Liaz 324; Litha 234;
Louis 234; Louisa 234;
Lucinda 234; Lucy 234;
Mandy 235A; Margaret 234;
Martha 234; Mary Ann 234;
Mary Eliza 234; Mary Jane
234; Milly 234; Mingo
234; Nancy 234; Narcissa
234; Ned 234; Needham
234; Old Becky 234; Old
Daniel 234; Old Hannah
234; Old Hester 234; Old
Mary 234; Old Milly 234;
Old Peter 234; Orange
234; Owen 234; Patsey
234; Peggy 234; Peter
234; Phillis 234; Rachel
234; Rhodes 234; Robert
234; Roxy 234; Sam 274;
Sarah 234; Sena 234; Sina
234; Solomon 234; Stanley
234; Stephen 234; Sylva
234; Syvil 234; Tempe
234; Thena 234; Tony 234;
Washington 234; Will 234;
William 234; York 234
HINES, Hinton 209
HODGES, Abbe 237; Alfred
239; Alick 238; Allen
237; Alvin 239; Black
Jack 237; Cass 237; Chloe
237; Clarry 237; Daniel
237,238; Dinah 237; Est-
her 237; Hannah 238;
Harry 237; Isham 237;
Jack Ireland 237; Jerry
238; Joe 237; Lena 237;
Lencey 237; Lewis 237;
Lina 238; Lizzy 238;
Lucy 237; Maria 238;
Milley 237; Nance 238;
Peter 237,238; Rachel
237,238; Ransin 239; Rose
237; Sam 237; Sidney 238;
Silas 238; Squire 238;
Teaner 239; Travis 238;
Violet 237; Winny 238
HOLDON, Dover 241
HOLLENSWORTH, Ben 324;
Betty 324
HOLLINGSWORTH, Roze 243
HOMES, Charles 246; Hall
246; Joan 246; Nann 246;
Sarah 246
HOOKS, Ann 153; Bett 247;

HOOKS con't
Betty 247; Bob 247;
Candace 247; Cato 153;
Chloe 153; Clary 153;
Daniel 247; Hariot 247;
Jack 247; Jim 247; Lam
247; Leah 247; Lucy 247;
Manuel 247; Mary Ann
247; Millay 247; Rachell
153; Sam 247; Silvy 543;
Spicey 247; Vina 247;
Violet 153
HOUSTON, Amanda 249; An-
drew 247; Betsey 249;
Bill 249,544; Bob 249;
Buck 249; Caroline 249;
Dave 249; Denny 249;
Dick 249; Emanuel 249;
Hannah 249; Hary 249;
Hester 249; Horace 544;
Huldy 249; Isaac 249;
Jack 249; Jackson 234,
544; Jerry 249; Jilica
249; Jim 249; Jimmy 249;
Joe 249; John 249; Kit
249; Lewis 249; Litha
234; Loo 544; Louis 234;
Manday 249; Margaret
234; Mariah 249; Martha
249;· Matilda 249; Mike
249; Milly 544; Mindis
249; Mint 544; Mustipher
249; Myma 249; Nance
544; Ned 249; Patience
544; Peggy 249; Peter
544; Penny 249; Plinty
249; Rachael 249; Rhodes
249; Rose 249; Sam 249;
Sarah 249,544; Silva
249; Sylva 544; Tom 249;
Wright 249
HOWARD, Ady 468; Alfred
468; Anthony 468; Bryan
468; Clarricy 468; Dan-
iel 468; Jin 468; John
468; Mariah 468; York
468
HUFHAM, Andrew 251; Betsey
251; Bill 251; Caithy
Ann 251; Cleery 251;
Comfort 251; Esther 251;
Faney (?) 251; Gene 251;
George 251; Gracie 251;
Hannack 251; Harriet
251; Jack 251; Jesse
251; Jim 251; Peter 251;
Rachel 251; Sparks 251;
Susann 251; Tim 251;
Violet 251
HUNTER, Cezar 255; Jack
255; Lucy 255; William
254; Winny 252
HURST, Ann 256; Black Edy
256; Brister 257; Esther
256; Frank 256; Irvin
256; Jeffrey 256; Lucy
Senr 257; Peter 256;
Rhody 256; Yellow Edy
256

INGRAM, Abram 258; Alse
258; Dyce 258; Elias 258
IRELAND, Jack 45,237;
Nelly 45
ISHAM, Jupiter 259; Roger
259
IVEY, Anthony 260; Cush
260; Demsy 260; Harry
260; Jane 260; Lucy 260;
Phillis 260

JAMES, Chole 263; Joe 263;
Milly 263; Sall 261
JERMAN, Ama 130; Joe 130;
Tenor 130
JERNIGAN, Cate 16; Mingo
264; Patience 264; Rose
20; Tiller 264
JOHNSON, Bess 267; Chloe
267; Hannah 267; Jack
267; Jim 267; John 42;
Pleasant 267; Rachel
267; Tamer 267; Toney
267; Tonna 267; Venus
267; Zilpha 267
JOHNSTON, Bett 271; Char-
les 271; Lier 271;
Nitten 271; Moses 271
JONES, Abram 57; Alice 57;
Allen 277; Bet 277; Bet-
sey 276A; Bob 283;
Caezar 57; Caroline 57;
Cate 278; David 282;
Dolly 57; Edea 277;
Esther 277; George 276A;
Haley 228; Hannah 276A,
277; Harry 276A,277;
Hester 276A,277; Isham
276A,277; Jack 277; Jane
228; Lovett Lewis 228;
Lucy 277; Marenda 277;
Moses 277; Ned 277;
Penney 277; Rachel 57,
276A,277; Sena 228;
Stephen 277; Tener 284;
Toney 57
JUSTICE, Old Hester 234;
Old Peter 234; Patsey
234; Sena 234

KAVE, Frank 53
KEATHLEY, Jan 286
KELLY, Big Ben 459; Jenny
Ann 459; Liberty 459
KENADA, Jinne 289
KENAN, Aleck 291; Amanda
196; Anthony 293; Baalam
292; Betsey 196; Billy
292; Caesar 293; Charity
290; Derry 293; Easter
291; Edmond 292; Esther
292; Floir 293; Floris
293; George 292; Hagar
291; Hannah 293; Hector
38; Henry 291; Ira 293;
Ireland 291; Isaac 291;
Jack 196; Metilda 196;
Moll 293; Moses 291,292;
Polly 291,292; Sedy 290;
Simon 196; Thena 291;
Tom 293; Washington 196
KENEDAY, Aamey 289; Abel
289; Bryant 289; Cloo
289; Drendor 289; Ham-
mons 289; James 289;
Jinne 289; John 289;
Lucy 289; Mary 289;
Mornin 289; Ories 289;
Sam 289; Teanor 289;
Tim 289; Toney 289
KENNADY, Fanny 294; Jack
294
KETHLEY, Rows 60; Sall 60
KING, Bes 477; Cloe 295;
Grace 399; Ned 295;
Need 477; Robin 295;
Simon 399
KORNEGY, Luce 194; Mary
194; Rose 194
KORNEGAY, Aaron 302; Adam
305; Agnes 305; Alex-
ander 302; Alfred 302;
Allen 308; Anthony 300;
Austin 302; Ben 300;

KORNEGAY con't
Bob 301; Boston 300;
Cassey 305; Cato 301;
Caty 302; Celah 302;
Charles 301,302,305;
Clary 302; Dave 308;
Dilse 308; Ede 308;
Elsey 302; Esther 301;
Friday 302; Gim 305;
Ginne 302; Gorge 305;
Green 305; Guff 301;
Hannah 300; Hanner 308;
Harriot 302; Hary 302;
Henry 302; Honer 301;
Jack 300,301; Jenny 301;
Jim 301; Joe 308; Little
Tom 301; London 304; Lucy
305; March 302; Matilda
302; Matthew 301; Mike
302; Milley 303; Moses
302; Nead 303; Neady 305;
Ned 302; Old Easter 302;
Olly 302; Pege 308; Pegg
300; Peter 300,308; Pom-
pey 300; Pope 300; Prep
300; Prince 308; Rachel
300,305,308; Sally 305;
Sam 308; Sarah 308; Sene
305; Silocy 301; Stark
308; Tom 300; Toney 300,
301; Tuffey 305; Violet
301; Will 300,301; Wiley
302; Willis 308; York 300

LANCASTER, Bill 468
LANGSTON, Milley 343
LANIER, Derry 141; Henry
311; Jackson 141; Jane
15; Jim 311; Rias 15;
Sidney 141; Tame 311
LARKINS, Adaline 417; Cash
417; Hannah 417; Jerry
417; Steuart 417; Swan
417
LAWS, Rose 111
LEE, Edmund 42
LENYEAR, Joe 87
LEWIS, Emily 234; Joe 389
LINTON, Billy 525; Haner
525; Lot 525; Nance 525;
Rachel 525

McCULLY, Albert 116
McCURDY, Balaam 324; Ben
324; Betty 324; Citty
324; Clarry 324; Hager
324; Liaz 324; Moses 324
McGEE, Dick 325; Esther
326; Frank 325; Guy 326;
Kate 326; Violet 325
McGOWEN, Big Sam 416; Bil
416; Bob 416; Candace
247; Dick 327; Jim 247;
Little Sam 416; Nancy
327; Roze 327; Sal 416;
Seal 416; Silvey 416;
Vina 247; Will 327
McINTIRE, Bella 329; Ben
528; Cate 329; Cato 329;
Cesar 329; Daniel 329;
Derry 329; Diana 528;
Hannah 528; Ireland 329;
Jinny 528; Little Cato
329; Luce 329; Sall 329;
Sally 528; Sam 329;
Warwick 329
McMILLAN, Dick 325; Frank
325; Violet 325

MALLARD, Ada 334; Alfred
334; Amanda 334; Betsey 334

MALLARD con't
Calvin 334; Chaney 334;
Charity 334; Clarra 334;
Daniel 334; Eliza 334;
Hillory 334; Hulda 334;
Isham 334; Jack 336;
Jerry 334; Jo 334; Lenon
334; Letty 338; Manson
334; Mary 334; Ming 90;
Nance 74; Netter 334;
Patrick 334; Prince 338;
Robert 334; Sarah 334;
Shade 334; Susan 334
MANNING, Lyddy 7
MARTEN, Rachel 214; Sam
214; Tener 284
MASHBURN, Amos 339; Dick
339; Dilsy 339; Edith
339; Esther 339; George
339; Hannah 339; Little
Dick 339; Peggy 339
MATCHET, Fillas 340; Fridy
340; Hanna 340; Jain
340; Moll 340; Old Iscac
340; Young Iseac 340
MATHEWS, Ann 342; Cassu
343; Charles 342; Char-
lot 343; Columbus 342;
Dave 342; Ede 343; George
342; Hanah 343; Henry
342; Jim 343; Joe 342;
Macolm 342; Milley 343;
Olive 342; Penny 342;
Rile 342; Rile Senr 342;
Rose 343; Sam 342; Stan-
norb 342; Stays 342
MATTHEWS, Lucy 233
MATTHIS, Amey 344; Bill
389; Briston 344; Clarry
344; Clo 344; Duplin
344; Esseck 344; Hager
344; Hannah 344; Isaac
344; Jan 344; Mansfield
389; Miles 344; Nancy
389; Peter 344; Reddick
344; Sam 344; Sarah 389;
Teen 344; Toomer 344
MAXWELL, Allen 352; Balaam
347; Becke 346,347; Bid-
dy 346; Big Worrick 347;
Bill 140,345; Billy 346;
Bob 352; Cade 347; Cain
345; Caroline 135; Catoe
352; Charles 347; Chloe
347; Claryan 352; Cloe
346; Daniel 352; Dave
347; Dick 346,352; Dill-
away 352; Drinder 135;
Eliza 352; Eliza Ane
345; Hagan 140; Hannah
346; Harry 345,347,352;
Jack 346,352; John 135;
Kelly 345; Kent 352;
Kitty 345; Larry 347;
Laura 345; Luke 345;
Margret 352; Mary 345;
Milley 135; Morris 352;
Nettis 140; Owen 135;
Peggy 135; Phereba 345;
Phillis 352; Quack 347;
Rachel 345; Rose 352;
Sall 352; Sam 135;
Sylvia 347
MCANNE (MCanne), Hagar
321; Lewis 320; Limrick
321; Mary 320; Mary Ann
320; Ned 320,321; Nell
321; Philis 321; Sam
320,321
MERCER, Evaline 69
METTS, Betty 196; Dall
196; George 196; Henry
196
MIDDLETON, Abel 356;

MIDDLETON con't
Abram 356; Ailsy 356;
Albert 353,356; Alex
353; Alice 356; Allen
356; Alonzo 356; Amanda
356; Amelia 356; Amy
354; Anthony 353; Asha
356; Austin 417; Balam
353; Billy 354; Bitty
354; Caesar 353; Cale-
donia 356; Cass 356;
Catharine 356; Caty 352;
Cesar 352; Charles 353;
Chelsea 354; Chilsey
353; Chloe 354,417;
Christiana 356; Civil
356; Claray 354; Claris-
sa 356; Clary 352; Cler-
ry 356; Clew 356; Daniel
353,356; Dick 353,356;
Dilsey 353; Dolly 356;
Dophiny 356; Edy 354;
Elias 352; Eliza 353,
357; Ester 352; Esther
353,356; Fan 353; Fanny
417; Finetta 356; George
353,356; Hagar 353;
Hannah 352,353; Hardy
356; Hariot 354,356;
Hasseltine 356; Henry
356; Hesse 354; Huldah
356; Isaac 356; Jack
354; Jane 356; Jasper
356; Jenny 353,356;
Joanna 356; Joe 353;
John 356; Jude 354; Julia
356; Julio 356; June
353,356; Kate 353,356;
Kenan 356; Lestina 356;
Lewis 353,356,417;
Liberty 355; Lisha 356;
Little Sarah 354; Little
Worrick 352; Lot 351,
353,354; Lotte 356;
Lucy 356; Luisa 356;
Lunga 356; Maggy 351;
Mariah 356; Marshall
356; Mary 356; Melissa
356; Merinda 356; Mil-
berry 417; Miley 354;
Mingo 356; Mog 353;
Nancy 354; Ned 354,356;
Nick 356; Ochre 354;
Pegg 353,354; Peggy 356;
Phoeba 356; Pompey 354;
Primus 356; Quash 354;
Rachael 352; Rane 356;
Rilly 356; Rose 356;
Sam 354; Sampson 353,
356; Sanders 356;
Sarah 354,356,357; Susan
356; Tener 353; Tone
353; Toney 354,356;
Venas 352; Violet 354;
Warrick 354; William
356; Winifred 356
MILLARD, Alforde 360;
Caty 361; Henry 359;
Jordan 360; Manuwell
360; Moses 361; Nice
360; Phillis 361; Step-
hen 360; Tildy 359;
Tome 360
MILLER, Ames 362; Ben 362;
Big Clary 362; Daniel
362; Denny 249; Frank
362; George 362; Hannah
249; Harriet 362; Herma
362; Jane 362; Jimmy
249; John 362; Kit 249;
Linda 362; Lom 166;
Luce 362; Malvina 362;
Mariah 249; Mary 362;
Miles 362; Old Sarah 362;

MILLER con't
Rhody 166; Sip 362
MILLS, Clove 232; Mingo
232; Philip 232; Philis
232; Pleasants 232; Rose
232; Sanders 232,365
MIRRIS, John 581
MOAN, Bill 345; Laura 345
MOLTEN, Arry 367; Ben 367,
368; Caesar 367,368;
Chloe 367; Harry 367;
Ishmael 367; Jack 367;
Jupiter 367; Old Celah
368; Pen 367; Peter 367;
Pompey 367; Rachel 367;
Sall 367
MOODY, Jane 373; Knowel
373; Solomon 373
MOON, Eliza Ane 345
MOOR, Ceasar 374,486; Dor-
cas 374; Davy 374; Doll
374; Nan 374; Tom 374;
Venus 374
MOORE, Aanness 380; Aaron
375; Aly 380; Annie 380;
Bernette 380; Bob 380;
Bunyon 380; Candis 380;
Caroline 380; Catharine
356; Charlotte 375;
Clarissa 380; Durry 375;
Elizabeth 380; Elon 380;
George 380; Grace 380;
Hannah 380; Harriet 380;
Hasseltine 356; Henry
356; Howard 380; Isaac
380; Jere 380; Jerry 380;
John W. 380; Julia 380;
Kenan 380; Kitty 380;
Laura 380; Leah 380;
Lindy 380; Little Amy
380; Little Anniss 380;
Little John 380; Little
Mahala 380; Little Norman
380; Little Tempy 380;
Lucy 380; Maggie 380;
Mahala 380; Mariah 380;
Marshall 356; Martha 375;
Mary 375,380; Matilda
380; Nancy 380; Nelson
380; Norman 380; Old Amy
380; Patrick 380; Peter
380; Phillis 380; Polk
380; Quince 380; Quincey
380; Rose 375; Sarah 356;
Senure 509; Shepard 380;
Silvia 380; Susannah
380; Sylva 380; Tempy
380; Washington 380;
Westley 380; Williams
380; Wingate 380
MORGAN, Big Sam 184; Cate
184; Johanna 184; Lenora
184; Moilcy 184; Toby
184
MORIS, Moses 292
MUMFORD, Ellick 504; Jerry
504; Polly 504; Violet
504
MURPHEY, Arthur 376; Black
Jupiter 376; Blainey 376;
Cato 376; Celah 376;
Charls 377; Chloe 376;
Grace 376; Hannah 376;
Jack 376; Jean 376; Jerry
376; London 376; Lucy
376; Sam 377; Stephen
376; Teiner 377; Tener
377; Yellow Jupiter 376
MURPHY, Helen 389; Sophia
389; Yellow Jupiter 376
MURRAY, Adeline 380; Aly
380; Amanda 334; Anness
380; Bernette 380; Betsy
334; Bob 380; Bunyon 380;

MURRAY con't
Calvin 334; Candis 380;
Carolina 380; Chaney 334;
Clarissa 380; Cornelia
380; Dick 10; Eliza 10,
334; Elizabeth 380; Elon
380; Esther 380; Etna
380; George 380; Grace
380; Hillory 334,380;
Hannah 380; Harriet 380;
Harry 544; Howard 380;
Hulda 334; Isaac 380;
Jack 544; James 380;
Jenny Lind 380; Jere
380; Jerry 334; Jessee
380; Jo 334; John 380;
John W. 380; Joseph 10;
Julia 380; July 10;
Kenan 380; Kitty 380;
Leah 380; Lindy 380;
Little Amy 380; Little
Chaney 380; Little John
380; Little Mahala 380;
Little Norman 380; Little
Tempy 380; Lucy 380;
Maggie 380; Mahala 380;
Mariah 101,380; Marlin
380; Mary 380; Matilda
380; Murdock 380; Nancy
380; Naomi 544; Nelson
380; Netter 334; Noah
380; Norman 380; Old Amy
380; Old Chaney 380;
Patrick 380; Peter 380;
Phillis 380; Polk 380;
Quince 380; Rachel 101;
  Robert 334; Sam 380,
381; Sarah 10; Shepard
381; Silva 381; Sophia
380; Susan 334; Susannah
380; Sutton 381; Tempy
380; Thursay 380; Tom
383; Washington 380;
Westley 380; Williams
380; Wingate 380
MURREY, Bess 267; Dines
546; Jam 546; Tamer 267
MURRY, Bes 384; Frank 384;
Peter 384; Sam 384
NEW, Allen 230
NEWKIRK, Abram 389; Ade-
laide 389; Aga 389;
Alvira 389; Aly 389;
Amanda 389; Beatty 389;
Becca 389; Bill 389;
Bryant 389; Candace 389;
Calvin Fennell 389; Car-
oline 389; Crosby 389;
Edmund 389; Elisabeth
389; Eliza 389; Essex
389; Eveline 389; Fran-
cinia 389; Hannack 251;
Harriet 389; Helen 389;
Henry 389; Insane Jane
389; Isaac 389; Isabel
389; Isaiah 389; Ivey
389; Jack 251; Jere 389;
Jim 389; Jim O. 389;
Joe Crocket 389; Joe
Lewis 389; John 389;
Jordan 389; Katharine
389; Levi 389; Lewis
389; Livinia 389; Lucy
389; Mansfield 389;
Milton 389; Mima 389;
Mingo 389; Molsay 389;
Nancy 389; Pearsall 389;
Pence 389; Rachel 389;
Sam 389; Sanders 365;
Sarah 389; Sophia 389;
Spencer 389; Stephen
389; Sylvester 389;
Tom 389; Usher 389;
Victoria 389

NEWTON, Balaam 324; Doll
392; Dorcas 392; Grace
390; Moses 392; Pat 392;
Peter 392; Phillis 45;
Prince 42; Tom 392

NICHOLSON, Alfred 417;
Elizabeth 417; Gurly
417; Jackson 417; Jinny
417; John 417; Laura
417; Matilda 417; Rose
417; Silva 417
NIXON, Chelsea 354; Claray
354; Dick 468; Garret
468; Hannah 468; Henry
468; Isham 468; Jack
354; John 468; Miley
354; Ned 468; Pheriby
468; Sarah 354,468
NOEL, Andrew 386
NORMENT, Ben 396; Bob 396;
Cork 396; Ireland 291;
Josh 396; Mary 396;
Mingo 396; Nane 396;
Nepton 396; Peg 396;
Phyllis 396; Sall 396;
Silva 396; Tom 396;
Young Derry 396

OATES, Ben 399; Grace 399;
Jena 399; Milley 400;
Simon 399
ODANIEL (ODaniel), Bill
402; Claben 401; Dilsey
402; Fib 401; Jackson
402; James 401; Jane
401; Jim 402; Mike 402;
Squier 402; Toney 402
OGELSBEY, Anny 534; Ara-
bella 534; Ben 534; Bill
534; Cyrus 534; Edmund
534; Jim 534; Margaret
534; Martha 534; Mary
534; Moses 534; Robbin
534; Susan 534; Willey
534; Willis 534
OLIVER, Anthony 403,404;
Clarrissey 135; Glasco
404; Hardy 403; Hister
404; Juda 403; Lewis
403; Lucy 403,404;
Matilda 135; Miley 403;
Rachel 135; Rachel 135;
Rose 403; Tenir 135;
Violet 404; Willis 403
OUTLAW, Abbe 409; Allen
407; Andrew 407; Balaam
407; Ben 407; Boson 409;
Daniel 407; Etha 407;
Flora 406; Hannah 407;
Henry 407; Isham 407;
Jack 406; Jenny 409;
Kate 407; Lewis 409;
Lewis jr 407; Mariah
407; Phillis 407; Rose
407,409; Simon Sr. 407;
Suckey 407; Sylva 407;
Tom 407; Toney 406

PAGE, Esther 339; Lucy
111; Peggy 339
PEARSALL, Adaline 417;
Alexander 417; Alfred
414,417; Allen 417;
Andrew 414; Anny 415;
Arthur 416,417; Austin
417; Barbara 417; Beck
414; Belford 416; Ben
416; Betty 416; Big Sam
416; Bill 416,417; Bob
416,417; Buck 415,416;

PEARSALL con't
Caleb 416; Calvin 417;
Candace 214,414,417;
Caroline 417; Cash 417;
Cate 416; Charles 416;
Charlotte 416; Chloe 417;
Clara 214,414; Clarissa
214; Clary 417; Daniel
416,417; Dick 417; Eady
416; Elizabeth 417;
Fanny 417; Flora 416;
Frank 414; Garry 414;
Grace 417; Gurly 417;
Hagar 416,417; Hannah
417; Harry 417; Haywood
417; Henry 416; Howard
417; Isabel 414; Jacob
416; Jack 416; Jackson
417; Jerry 414,417; Jinny
417; Joanna 417; John
417; Julia 417; Kitty
414; Laura 417; Leah 417;
Lewis 417; Liberty 417;
Little Sam 416; Luke
345,415; Martha 414,417;
Mary 345,415,417; Matilda
417; Milberry 417; Milo
417; Muro 416; Nancy 416;
Old Clow 416; Old Daniel
416; Old Phillis 416;
Penny 416,417; Polly 415,
417; Rachel 414,417; Re-
becca 214; Rose 416,417;
Sal 416; Sam 414; Sarah
417; Seal 416; Sidia 416;
Silva 417; Silvey 416;
Simon 416; Sophia 414,
417; Stuart 417; Swan
417; Turrisman 417; Vir-
gil 417; Warsaw 415,416;
Young Clow 416; Young
Daniel 416; Young Phillis
416
PECK, China 165; Dublin
165; Levi 165; Young
Nance 165
PHILLIPS, Chelsea 421;
Doll 421; George 421;
Isom 421; Jenny 421;
Nimrod 421; Teener 421
PICKETT, Ben 423; Candice
422; Dick 422; Isaac 423;
Jerry 423; London 422;
Mahala 423; Martha 422,
423; Martin 141; Mary
422; Matilda 423; Sarah
423; Sook 422
PICKETTE, Jim 439; Misier
439; Sarah 439
PIERCE, Adam 235A; Amy 235A;
Fanny 234; Farise 235A;
Mandy 235A; Peter 234;
Will 234
PIGFORD, Peter 424
PIPKIN, Dinah 151
PLEASANT, Henry 25
POLLOCK, Jack 519; Julia
Ann 135; Nan 519
POWEL, Mariah 42; Phebe 32
POWELL, Brittain 427; Re-
dick 427; Richard 427
POWERS, Calvin Fennell 389;
Elizabeth 389
PRICE, Marenda 277; Ned
277
PRIDGEN, Honae 567
PUMPHREY, Deno 432; Mary
432; Pharoh 432

QUINN, Bashy 504; Beck 560;
Chloe 267; George 433;
Grant 434; Henry 504;
Jim 434; Leah 504;

QUINN con't
Levi 434; Liza 434;
Marenda 25; Nelly 504;
Sarah 434,504; Tom 434;
Tonna 267

RHODES, Aleck 438; Anthony
234,438; Arthur 438;
Beck 438; Betsey 234;
Bill 436; Bob 417; Bos-
ton 436; Caroline 417;
Caster 438; Charlotte
437; Chelay 438; Chel-
ly 438; Daniel 437,438;
Dave 439; Easter 436;
Fanny 234; Franck 437;
George 437,438; Gerewy
438; Hagar 417; Hannah
438,439; Harriet 436,
438; Henry 234; Heziah
438; Jack 438; Jim 234,
439; Jinsey 438; Jo 438;
Joanna 417; Jupiter
438; Killis 438; Lewis
438; Luui 438; Milo 417;
Mingo 437; Misier 439;
Nancy 234; Ned 438;
Pearce 438; Peggey 438;
Peter 437,438; Phebe 438;
Philus 438; Pompey 438;
Rebecca 436; Rhodes 234;
Rose 436; Roze 437,438;
Sam 438; Sarah 234,436,
439; Squire 438,439;
Stephen 234; Zilpha 438
ROUSE, Andrew 407; Balaam
407; Ben 407; Hannah
407; Kate 407; Mariah
407; Rose 407; Simon Sr
407; Suckey 407; Sylva
407
ROUTLEDGE, Boson 451;
Candice 451; Cate 450;
Clarissa 452; Diana 451;
Fanny 451; Isaac 450,
451; Jack 451; John 452;
Jupiter 450; Lony 450;
Old Pompey 451; Peter
451; Phebee 450; Priour
450; Rachel 451; Sam
451; Sarah 450; Seley
450; Tom 451; Young
Pompey 451

SAMPSON, Aaron 456; Arthur
456; Beckey 456; Ben
456; Betsy 456; Billy
456; Candice 456; Chloe
456; Darcy 456; Hannah
456; Harriot 456; Joe
456; Johnny 456; Juland
456; Moll 456; Molly
456; Old Toney 456;
Peggy 456; Polly 456;
Statira 456; Tommy 456
SANDLIN, Alfred 544; Bill
544; Bob 544; Mary 70;
Ned 544; Peter 544;
Thussey 70
SCOTT, Jim 457; Jimmy 457;
Jinne 457; Will 457
SEAVEY, Adelaide 389;
Caroline 389
SEWELL, Penny 480
SHAW, Isaih 166
SHEPARD, Augustus 459;
Big Ben 459; Boston 459;
Eveline 101; Isham 459;
Jenny Ann 459; Jinny
101; Joe 459; Julia 459;
Liberty 459; Little Ben
459; Louis 459;

SHEPARD con't
Louisa 459; Mary 459;
Old Mary 459; Peter 459;
Randolp 459
SHUFFIELD, Lott 543; Maria
543; Sam 543
SIKES, Fred 463
SIMMONS, Nelly 179; Pen-
der 194
SIMMS, Eliza 357
SLOAN, Abram 468; Ady 468;
Aleck 468; Alfred 468;
Anthony 468; Back 464;
Bill 468; Bill Lancaster
468; Bryan 468; Caesar
468; Chaney 465; Charles
468; Clarricy 468;
Daniel 465,468; Davi
465; Dick 468; Edmond
465; Eliza 48; Emily
50; Ephraim 468; Frank
464; Garret 468; Hannah
468; Henry 468; Isaac
465; Isham 468; Israel
468; Jim 468; Jin 468;
Joe Jr. 468; John 468;
Jordan 389; Juda 50;
Liney 468; Luce 468;
Lum 464; Manirva 468;
Mariah 468; Mary 468;
Mingo 464; Muriah 468;
Nance 468; Ned 468;
Pheriby 468; Primus 468;
Rhoda 468; Rosella 468;
Sall 468; Sam 48,468;
Sarah 28,468; Silvia
465,468; Temperance 468;
Tom 468; Tome 464;
Willis 468; Winson 468;
York 468
SLOCUMB, Jenny 16; Maneul
247; Sam 247
SMITH, Abram 471; Allen
475; Arch 475; Asa 69;
Bill 473; Billy 234;
Bob 234; Calvin 234;
Catherine 234; Chana
471; Charry 471; Cullen
234; Daniel 234; Ervin
475; Fanny 234; Ginney
473; Hannah 234,473,475;
Hanner 473; Henry 234;
Jacob 234; Joe 475;
Jonas 234; Leah 234;
Linday 475; Luce 471;
Lucy 234; Milly 234;
Morris 475; Needham 234;
Old Milly 234; Priscilla
475; Roda 475; Sarah 473;
Stanley 234; Tener 473;
Thena 234; Venus 471;
Worrick 473
SNELL, Andrew 477; Ben
476,477; Bes 477; Betey
477; Dinah 508; Green
477; Harry 477; Lonon
477; Lue 476,477; Nat
477; Need 477; Sezer
477
SOLLIS, Bob 479; Boston
479; Mary 479; Moses
479; Needham 479; Sarah
479
SOLMON (Salmon), Sarah 178
SOUTHERLAND, Aaron 142;
Abram 142; Anthony 142;
Augustus 459; Charles
142; Denis 142; Dilce
169; Drendor 289; Driv-
der 481; Eastir 142;
Hammons 289; Isham 459,
480; Jack 481; James
289; Jim 142,481; Joe
Crockett 389; Leah 481;

SOUTHERLAND con't
Louisa 459; Lucy 142;
Margaret 169; Mariah 481;
Mary 289,481; Matilda
142; Mornay 481; Mornin
289; Penny 480; Phebe
169; Rachel 142; Sam 142;
Sarah 142; Seer 169;
Teanor 289; Wright 142
SOUTHERLIN, Essex 389
SPRUNT, Caroline 218; Linda
218; Wright 218
STALLINGS, Aberdeck 482;
Abram 389,482; Agg 482;
Arthur 482; Bigg Owen
482; Bill 482; Burrel
482; Chloe 482; Cussa
482; Edmund 389; Henry
389; Jack 482; Jane 482;
Jesse 482; Jim 482; Juda
483; Kater 482; Lewis 482;
Little Jim 482; Little
Owen 482; Luce 482;
Nance 482; Pleasant 483;
Sam 389,483; Spencer
389; Stephen 482; Susey
482
STANFORD, Adeline 486;
Alley 486; Avy 486; Bryan
486; Caesar 486; Dave
485; Doll 486; Hannak
486; Jack 486; Jim 486;
July 486; Kelly 345;
Kenan 486; Lot 486; Lunar
486; Mary 486; Minerva
486; Nixon 486; Phereba
345; Polly 486; Pomp 486;
Pompe 486; Pompey 485;
Rachel 345; Sara 486;
Tony 485,486; Washington
486; Yellow Dave 486
STANLEY, Jeannette 196
STEPHENS, Allen 234; Amelia
234; Betsey 234; Bryant
234; Cassy 234; Cathe-
rine 234; David 234;
Eli 234; Emanuel 234;
Flora 234; George 234;
Grandison 234; Henry 234;
Hepsey 234; Hester 234;
Ivy 234; Jeoffrey 234;
Jim 486; Julia 234; Mar-
garet 234; Martha 234;
Mary Jane 234; Mingo 234;
Narcissa 234; Old Daniel
234; Old Hester 234; Old
Mary 234; Old Peter 234;
Owen 234; Patsey 234;
Phillis 234; Robert 234;
Sena 234; Sina 234;
Solomon 234; Sylva 234;
Tempe 234; William 234;
York 234
STEVINS, Ben 399; Jena 399
STEWART, Hanah 343
STOACHES, Tener 487
STOAKES, Aly 50; Chany 487;
Cloe 487; Ervin 487;
Henry 487; Isaac 487;
Isaiah 389; Jerry 487;
Jim 487; Kitty 487; Lewis
487; Little Lot 487; Lot
487; Margaret 487; Mike
487; Mima 487; Patsey
50; Pene 50; Roger 487;
Rose 487; Salter 487;
Sarah 487; Shade 487;
Tener 487; Tom 50;
Violet 487
STOKES, Abrem 488; Hannah
22; Little Calvin 25;
Peter 25; Spicy Jane 25;
Teanah 488
SULIVAN, Hannah 277; Penney
277

220

SULLIVEN, Edney 491;
Jerry 491; Ned 491;
Penny 491; Rachel 491
SWINSON, Cloe 493; Doll
493; Hagar 493; Hannah
493; Harry 493; Jack
493,494; Lucy 494;
Luleruk 494; Phillis
493; Satarah 494; Tom
493,494; Venus 493

TAYLOR, Satarah 494
TEACHEY, Aley 500; Amy
497,498; Bill 497,498,
500; Bob 498; Briant
498; Cassia 48; Cate
497,500; Cato 497,500;
Chaine 498; Charls 500;
Claburn 500; Clary 498;
Cloe 498; David 500;
Eliza 500; Ephram 498;
Forlin 498; Fortin 498;
Fortune 497; Frank 498;
Grace 497; Hagar 497;
Hagrow 498,500; Hannah
497,500; Isaac 499;
Isom 500; Jacob 500;
Jack 497,500; Jim 498,
500; Jimmy 498; Jinan
498; Joe 497,498; John
498,500; Juda 498;
Light 498; Lindy 498;
Lorevy 498; Lucy 497;
Many 498; Margret 498;
Maria 48; Mary 498,500;
Matt 497; Metildy
498; Mile 498; Morris
498; Muriah 498; Nance
500; Nancy 497; Owen
498; Pompey 497; Prince
497; Robeson 500; Roger
498; Rose 497,498; Sal-
ter 497,498; Sam 498,
500; Sarah 498; Seale
498; Silvey 498; Sophia
497; Suffer 498; Susan
498; Tinah 498; Toney
497,498,500; Viney 498;
Virgill 498; Wiley 500;
Wright 48
THALLY, Jane 502
THOMAS, Agnes 504; Alice
504; Bashy 504; Benjamin
504; Bob 504; Chelsy
504; Clary 504; Dennis
505; Dick 505; Dover
504,506; Ellick 504;
Fanny 504; Fereby 504;
George 504; Henry 504;
Jack 504; Jane 504;
Jerry 504; Joseph 504;
Leah 504; Luke 504; March
505; Mary 504; Moses
504; Ned 504; Nelly 504;
Old Leah 504; Pinea 504;
Peter 506; Phillis 505,
506; Rosey 504; Sarah
504; Sely 504; Violet
504
THOMSON, Andrew 508; Boson
508; Brister 508; Cate
508; Cloe 508; Dinah
508; Doll 508; Hannah
508; Jack 508; Jo 508;
London 508; Moll 508;
Peg 508; Peter 508;
Phillis 508; Senure 509;
Theana 508; Tom 508
TORRANS, Dick 40; Rosena
40
TURRANCE, Sedy 290
TUTLE, Austin 512; Balaam
512; Dianah 512;

TUTLE con't
Frank 512; George 512;
Harry 512; Hiram 512;
Jim 512; Lydia 512; Mary
512; Nelson 512; Reuben
512

UNDERHILL, Lusa 514

VANN, Joe Lewis 389;
Molsay 389

WALLER, Hannah 267
WARD, Bob 519; Bradick
518; Filles 518; Hannah
518,519; Jack 519; Mary
518; Nan 519
WATERMAN, Bed 521; Chaney
521; Dinah 521; Edeth
521; Eliza 521; Hannah
521; Ireland 521; Jam
521; Jane 521; Jelord
521; Old Jack 521; Pri-
mus 521; Rose 521; San-
der 521; Yong Jack 521
WATKINS, Abram 522; Cat
522; Daniel 247; David
522; Gould 522; Hariot
247; Heray 522; Isaack
522; Jack 247; Jinne
522; Jow 522; Kindeter
522; Leah 247; Mary Ann
247; Milly 247; Minny
522; Reue 522; Roda 522;
Sam 522; Silve 522;
Spicey 247; Tener 522;
Tilio 522
WELLS, Andrew 524; Bazel
525; Billy 525; Brister
527; Caroline 389; Chany
487; Chloe 524; Cloe
487,525; Cynthia 527;
Ervin 487; Francis 527;
George 525; Haner 525;
Henry 487,524; Isaac
487,524; Isaiah 527;
Irvin 524; Jacob 527;
Jack 525; James 525;
Jean 525; Jerry 487;
Jim 487; Jinney 87; Joe
525; John 526; John
Wright 527; Julius 524;
Kitty 527; Lewis 487;
Lot 525; Lucy 525; Mari-
ah 526; Missouri 524;
Nance 525; Pheby 525;
Pleasant Ann 524; Ra-
chel 525; Roger 487;
Rose 487; Ryel 525; Sal-
ter 487; Sarah 487,524,
526; Seale 526; Stotter
525; Susan Jane 527;
Violet 487,524
WELTS, Bella 528; Ben 528;
Cato 528; Diana 528;
Hannah 528; Jinny 528;
Judith 528; Lucy 528;
Sally 528
WEYMS, Edney 234; Greene
234; Mary Eliza 234
WHALEY, Edy 532; Emily
532; Mary 532; Tom 532;
Uriah 532
WHITE, Dinah 194; Julian
194; Luce 194
WHITEHEAD, Anny 534; Ara-
bella 534; Ben 534;
Bill 534; Cyrus 534;
Edmund 534; Jim 534;
Margaret 534; Martha
534; Mary 534; Moses 534;

WHITEHEAD con't
Robbin 534; Susan 534;
Willey 534; Willis 534
WHITFIELD, Abbe 409; Allen
536; April 536; Bias
536; Charles 584; Curtis
536; Easter 535; Edmond
584; Hannah 536; Matilda
535; Milly 538; Mordecai
584; Olly 535; Primer
536; Randleson 584; Sab-
rina 16; Sam 16; Silvy
538
WILKERSON, Jackson 175
WILKINS, Hannah 542; Isaah
542; Lucy 542; Peggy 542;
Sarah 542
WILKINSON, Alfred 544; Bill
544; Bob 544; George 544;
Hannah 544; Harry 544;
Horace 544; Jack 544;
Jackson 544; Loo 544;
Lott 543; Maria 543;
Martha 544; Milly 543;
Mint 544; Nance 544;
Nancy 544; Naomi 544;
Ned 544; Patience 544;
Peter 544; Sam 543;
Sarah 544; Silva 544;
Silvy 543; Sylva 544
WILLIAMS, Abraham 560;
Abram 548,562; Aleck 438;
Allen 552; Amanda 389;
552; Amey 560; Amos 548,
553; Ancey 566; Ander
569; Anna 548; Anthony
438; Arther 547,560;
Beck 560; Big Dinah 560;
Bill 569; Black Bob 546;
Bob 548,560; Boson 565;
Brister 561,569; Bruster
546; Caleb 550; Caroline
552; Caster 562; Catoe
560; Cesar 560; Chany
565; Charles 560; Cheals
560; Chelay 438; Cint
561; Clarah 561; Cloe
567; Crag 569; Crocket
552; Crosby 389; Curtice
569; Danil 552; Dave 439;
Derry 569; Dick 552,560;
Dilsey 552; Dinah 178,
561; Dines 546; Don 567;
Easther 548; Edgar 101;
Edward 565; Eliza 562,
569; Exerline 552; Fen-
nel 569; Feraby 569;
Frank 548,558,560; Fred
549,561; Friday 552;
George 162,546,552,560,
562; Ginna 560; Green
560; Hannah 71,439,546,
560,561; Hariot 438,562;
Harriet 552; Harry 548;
Henry 548,552,561,562;
Het 561; Hiram 548;
Holley 569; Honae 567;
Isaac 162,569; Isham
569; Jacob 561,566;
Jack 438,560; Jam 546;
Jeen 560; Jerry 546;
Jim 389,549,553,569;
Jinnea 560; Jo 438,569;
Joe 548; John 101,552,
562,569; Joseph 552;
Jude 561; Judith 552;
Judy 569; Julia 552,569;
Kate 101; Kit 553; Let-
tice 553; Lewis 409,438;
Linda 552; Little Dinah
560; Little Isaac 569;
Little Jude 569; Little
Mint 569; Lonnon 560,
565; Luce 560; Lucinda 552;

WILLIAMS con't
  Lucy 547,548,552,569;
  Lucy Jane 569; Major
  560; Margaret 552; Ma-
  riah 552,569; Mariann
  569; Mark 547; Markes
  552; Martha 569; Mauney
  567; Maurace 546; Mary
  162,552,559; Mima 389;
  Mint 569; Moll 560;
  Morris 569; Moses 552;
  Nan 561; Nance 569;
  Nathan 560; Ned 438;
  Omey 546; Pat 546; Peter
  557; Pender 548; Pheb
  561; Philus 438; Pompey
  438; Rachel 547,569;
  Rachel Ann 569; Ransom
  552; Rhoda 546; Roger
  569; Rose 162,548,559,
  560; Rotch 560; Sale
  550; Sally 101; Sam 569;
  Santee 560; Sarah 548,
  561,569; Sarah Eliza
  569; Sary 162; Senia
  552; Shad 569; Shade
  552; Siller 569; Silvey
  565; Sollomon 569; Stephen 569; Steven 548;
  Stoake 569; Squire 438,
  439,552; Suff 569;
  Suffer 569; Susan 561;
  Tabitha Jane 569; Thankful 569; Tillah 567; Tom
  560,569; Tone 560; Toney
  548,550,560; Treasey
  352; Usher 389; Violet
  552; Virginia 552; Will
  547; Yellow Bob 546;
  York 548; Zilla 548;
  Zilpah 546; Zilpha 552
WILLKINS, John 289; Lucy
  289; Tim 289
WILSON, Ally 209; Ireland
  65; Isabel 389
WINDERS, Citty 324; Hager
  324; Moses 324
WITHERSPOON, Aleck 234;
  Becky 234; Washington
  234
WORLEY, Pegge 577
WORSLEY, Daniel 578; Dave
  578; Friday 578; Hannah
  578; Jesse 578; Jo 578;
  Prince 578; Toney 578
WRIGHT, Alvin 234; Binah
  234; Brister 579; Brit-
  ton 579; Calvin 580;
  Charles 584; Chelly 234;
  Clarissa 234; Damond
  582; Dorcis 579; Durham
  582; Easter 234,579;
  Edmond 584; Elvy 234;
  Fanny 581; George 234;
  Grace 582; Henry 234;
  Jack 579; Jackson 579;
  Jim 579; John 527;
  Julie 234; Louisa 234;
  Louisana 17; Mack 579,
  582; Manuel 579; Milly
  579; Mordecai 584; Ned
  234; Old Becky 234; Pat-
  sey 582; Phillis 582;
  Polydon 582; Randleson
  584; Rose 581; Sam 234;
  Sarah 234; Venus 579;
  Virgil 582

Maple Swamp 194,417
Mare Branch 354
Marsh Branch 72,199,352
Marsh Branch Plantation
 185
Marsh Land 371
Marsh Swamp 199
Matchet's Branch 130
Mathews Branch 130
Maxfield 533
Maxfile Swamp 90
Maxwell Creek 468
Maxwell Swamp 90,131,337,
 441,546
Melus Tract 15
Messor Land 473
Michael Field 185
Middle Branch 546
Miery Branch Pocoson 526
Mill Branch 179,339,397,
 412,479,518,544
Miller Road 308
Millers Creek 19
Miry Branch 2,92,206,327,
 409,493
Mississippi 234,389
Mobly Tract 366
Molton Lands 417
Mores Creek 126
Mount Pleasant 194
Mudd Creek 438
Muddy Creek 224,356,422,
 438,558
Mulbery Branch 322
Murphy footway 346
Murray Place 438
Murrays Branch 87
Murrows Branch 88

Nahonja Swamp 30
N. E. Pecoson 151
Neuse River 234
Newbern Road 459
New Ground Field 48
New Hanover County 38,126,
 321,327,354,368,376,382,
 423,424,468,475
New Hanover Precinct 97
New River 210
NoEast 151,409
No. Et. Rivor 123,151
No. River 499
Northeast 300
North East, The 2,179
North East River 15,64,169,
 197,493,557
Northwest River 581
Norwest 107

Oaky Branch 499,500
Oates Plantation 165
Oky Branch 499
Old Place 322
Onslow (Onelaw?) County
 397
Onslow County 118,161,141,
 210,215,354,471,504,506,
 533,545,560
Onslow Road 504

Panter Mill 473
Panter Swamp 473
Panther Branch 164
Panther Swamp 12,107,578
Parish of St Gabriel 88
Parting Branch 392
Paster Branch 392
Pastor Branch 322
Patapsco Institute 533
Pearce's Place 261
Pell Place 490

Percosin Old Field 332
Perrys Branch 384
Persimmon 87,141
Persimmon Swamp 141,451
Persimon Branch 16,327
Piney Woods Field 162
Pitt County 583
Pierce's 15
Poley Branch 234
Poley Bridge 322,343
Poly Bridge Branch 110,
 111,308,366,479
Poplar Branch 153,164
Posimmon Swamp 544
Powel Place 80
Powells Field 346
Powells Swamp 339
Powel's Branch, Va. 41
Priests Branch 21
Prise Place 206
Province of Pencelvany 119

Quinn Lands 417

Rabeys Branch 410
Raccoon Branch 40
Ralays Brach 410
Ready Branch 426
Red House Tract 87
Reedy Branch 4,72,153,
 164,426,546
Reedy Meadow 322
Reedy Meadow Land 322
Robeson County 18
Rockfish 64,376,483,546,
 569
Rockfish Creek 546
Rock Fish Creek 48,526,
 568
Rocky Mash 242
Roling Path 289
Rooty Branch 535

Salmon Place 206
Sals Pocoson 213
Sampson County 17,162,163,
 165,180A,342,357,389,584
Sampson Hall 456
Samson County 33
Sander Branch 471
Sandy Run 426
Sante Georgs Necke, Penn.
 119
Sarecta 218,475
Schoolhouse, The 374
Schoolhouse Spring Branch
 319
Second Botom 213
Serecta 218
Shear Pecoson 525
Sheen Pocoson 500
Sholer's 15
Six Runs Swamp 476
Sleepy Creek Land 234
Smith Swamp 517
Snake Branch 185
Southampton 566
South Carolina 517
Speculating Lands 169
Spring Branch 300,353,374,
 508
Spring Hall 38
St. Gabriel 198
Stewards Creek 87,350
Stewarts Creek 180A,367
Stockinghead 376
Stocking Head Swamp 197
Streets Branch 47
Strickland Depot 135
Stricklandsville 104
Stuerts Creep 352

Sullivan Lands 61
Suttons 507
Suttons Branch 130
Swan Land 126

Tarekiln Branch 159
Taylor Creek 546
Taylors Creek 568
Tennessee 134,141,416,451,
 465
Thomas County, Geo. 65
Thunder Swamp 300
Thunder Swamp Pesocon 151
Timber Landing 212
Tim's Place 497
Tom Field 371
Towerhill Plantation 130
Town Creek 45
Trip Place 206
Tuckahoe Swamp 545
Turbevill Land 374
Turkey Pen Branch 164
Turkey Swamp 202,211,212,
 213
Tuscaloosa County, Ala. 304

University of North Carolina
 533
Urethego March 90
Urethego Meadow 90

Virginia 41

Wake County 560
Waller Land 504
Wallers Mill 437
Wallis's Creek 581
Ward Land 237
Wards Road 249,417
Warsaw 81
Watering Hole Branch 366
Wayne County 234
Wayne Plantation 234
Weats Ford 223
Wells Place 389
Welsh Tract 38
Western Country 548
Western Waters 355
White Oak Branch 33
White Oak Plantation 423
Whiteoak Swamp 235A
White Oake 33
White Oake Branch 12
Whit Oak 547
Wildcat Pond 19
Williams Land 417
Wilmington 38,58,234,367,
 453,461
Wilmington & Manchester
 Rail Road 234
Wilmington & Raleigh Rail
 Road 135
Wilmington & Weldon Rail
 Road 234
Witt Sand Road 249
Wolf Branch 85,548
Wolf Pond 384
Woolf Branch 60

Yellow Creek 465

www.ingramcontent.com/pod-product-compliance
Lightning Source LLC
Chambersburg PA
CBHW021901020426
42334CB00013B/433